The Translator's Handbook

The Translator's Handbook

Eighth Revised Edition

Morry Sofer

Schreiber Publishing
Rockville, Maryland

The Translator's Handbook
8th Revised Edition
Morry Sofer

Published by:
Schreiber Publishing, Inc
www.schreiberlanguage.com
PO Box 4093 • Rockville, MD 20849 • 800-296-1961

First Edition, 1996
Second Edition, 1998
Third Edition, 1999
Fourth Edition, 2002
Fifth Edition, 2004
Sixth Edition, 2006
Seventh Edition, 2009
Eighth Edition, 2013

Library of Congress Cataloguing-in-Publication Data

Sofer, Morry
    The translator's handbook / Morry Sofer. — 8th rev. ed.
    p.cm.
Includes bibliographical references and index.
ISBN 978-088400341-0
1. Translating and interpreting—Handbooks, manuals, etc. I. Title.
    P306.S59 2013
    418.02—dc22

                                                    2013944280

Printed in the United States of America

ACKNOWLEDGEMENTS

The first seven editions of this book attest to its continued popularity among translators everywhere. Translators-to-be as well as well established and highly regarded translators all over the world have used and praised this book. To all of them my heartfelt thanks. Without them, there would be no eighth revised edition.

I have not attempted to cite in the text all the authorities and sources consulted in the preparation of this handbook because of space limitations. Literally hundreds of people have been consulted, and all of them deserve my sincere thanks. A particular word of thanks to all those who sent us comments on the previous editions, helping us update and improve each subsequent edition.

Each edition of this work is built upon its predecessor. I would like to thank the staff of Schreiber Translations, Inc. for all the help in previous editions, especially Irina Knizhnik, who advised me on Russian, Japanese, and Chinese dictionaries; Margaret Flynn, who helped edit the second revised edition; and particularly Marla Schulman,. Also, my heartfelt thanks to Dan Poynter, the "patron saint" of independent publishers, without whose wise and practical words this book and this publisher would still be in the realm of dreams. For the seventh edition, Walter Stankewick offered his advice on the new sections on localization, translation memory, and machine translation. Caroline Murphy helped me update the dictionary section.

This new edition owes much to the work of Nicole Battisti, who edited and researched and updated. And thanks to Nouf Al-Khaja of Dubai, UAE, and Mike Kayser for their expert advice.

Finally, a word of thanks to the hundreds of colleagues, past and present, from whom I learned everything I know about translation, one of the most fascinating activities I have ever had the privilege to pursue.

WARNING — DISCLAIMER

This book is designed to provide information in regard to the subject matter covered. It is sold with the understanding that the publisher and author are not engaged in rendering legal, accounting or other professional services. If legal or other expert assistance is required, the services of a competent professional should be sought.

It is not the purpose of this handbook to reprint all the information that is otherwise available to the author and/or publisher, but to complement, amplify and supplement other texts. You are urged to read all the available material, learn as much as possible about translation, and tailor the information to your individual needs. For more information, see the many references in the appendices.

Translation is not a get-rich-quick scheme. Anyone who decides to pursue translation, either as a freelancer or as a full-time career, must be prepared to invest a great deal of time and effort with a view to making it a long-term, preferably a lifelong pursuit. Not everyone who knows more than one language is *ipso facto* a potential translator. But many are, and they stand to benefit from it.

Every effort has been made to make this handbook as complete and as accurate as possible. However, there *may be* mistakes both typographical and in content. Therefore, this text should be used only as a general guide and not as the ultimate source of translation and/or interpretation information. Furthermore, this handbook contains information on translation current only up to the printing date.

The purpose of this handbook is to inform and to help. The author and Schreiber Publishing shall have neither liability nor responsibility to any person or entity with respect to any loss or damage caused, or alleged to be caused, directly or indirectly by the information contained in this book.

If you do not wish to be bound by the above, you may return this book to the publisher for a full refund.

CONTENTS

INTRODUCTION

When you stop and think about it, everything in life is translation. We translate our feelings into actions. When we put anything into words, we translate our thoughts. Every physical action is a translation from one state to another. Translating from one language into another is only the most obvious form of an activity which is perhaps the most common of all human activities. This may be the reason people usually take translation for granted, as something that does not require any special effort, and at the same time, why translation is so challenging and full of possibilities.

There is nothing easy or simple about translation, even as there is nothing easy or simple about any human activity. It only looks easy because you are used to doing it. Anyone who is good at a certain activity can make it appear easy, even though, when we pause to think, we realize there is nothing easy about it.

Translation in the formal sense deals with human language, the most common yet the most complex and hallowed of human functions. Language is what makes us who we are. Language can work miracles. Language can kill, and language can heal. Transmitting meaning from one language to another brings people together, helps them share each other's culture, benefit from each other's experience, and makes them aware of how much they all have in common.

To pursue a translation career means to become a servant of language, a master well worth serving. But more importantly, it means serving your people and other people, bringing them closer together, working towards better understanding among people and nations everywhere. Linguistic isolation breeds xenophobia, prejudice, fear. Translating means building bridges across all the chasms of ignorance and isolationism that surround us.

So, if your work is not always appreciated, take heart. Notoriety is reserved for evil, while the recognition of good is almost always slow in coming. Over the ages, translators brought the world closer together, moved it from paganism to monotheism, from the Dark Ages to the Renaissance, from the rule of despots to the time of enlightenment and individual freedom, a process which is still going on, and will continue for a long time to come. This handbook is an attempt to better define translation, and to help its practitioners improve and prosper.

The author is offering this book to his colleagues as a token of appreciation for all the great work they have done and will continue to do in the service of their people and all people.

HOW TO GET THE MOST OUT OF THIS HANDBOOK

This handbook has many uses. Some parts of it can be read by both experienced and beginning translators to learn about certain aspects of translation, and other parts are informational in nature and will be of use when you look for a certain dictionary, a certain source of translation work, etc. It is intended to serve as a sourcebook for all translators in all languages, both in the United States and abroad.

We urge all translators to read Chapter 2, **Historical Overview of Translation**. Little has been written about the history of translation, and for those of us who practice translation it is important to have a historical perspective on our craft.

Beginners are encouraged to read Chapters 3 and 4, **Requisites for Professional Translators** and **Translator's Self-Evaluation**. These chapters should help the beginner get a better idea as to (a) whether or not to pursue translation in the first place, and (b) where one stands in one's development as a translator.

Having read those chapters, the beginner may want to continue with Chapter 6, **Translation Techniques**. Chapter 7, **Translation, Computers, and the Internet** is "must" reading for the beginner, and recommended for the advanced. Since it deals with digital technology, an area which is changing constantly, it is of equal importance to all of us, since we are all constant learners when it comes to this subject.

The rest of the chapters depend on individual needs. Certainly all of them are important for the beginner, as they deal with the key issues of translation work, and the advanced can use them selectively. It is our intention to keep them up-to-date, since things change so fast these days in all of these areas.

The second half of the book consists of appendices. These are meant to be used as a reference guide on resources for translators, such as dictionaries and dictionary sources, software in all languages and where to find it, publications for translators, and more.

Appendix 4 is of particular importance to freelance translators. Here we have provided information on hundreds of translation companies and other sources of translation work in the United States, with descriptions of the specific needs of many of them. They are arranged alphabetically, followed by a listing by state and city, to help you find companies in your part of the country. This vital list has been completely updated since our previous edition.

Appendix 5 should be of interest to the beginner who is looking for translator training, and for the advanced who may wish to expand his or her horizons in a new area of translation.

Finally, we draw your attention to the **Glossary**, which is an extensive source of information on key translation terms, computer terms of interest to translators, and the terminology of the Internet.

1. THE USES OF THIS HANDBOOK

The world of translation is forever growing and fast changing. Since this handbook first appeared thirteen years ago, more has changed in the translation field than at any other time in the past. About every two or three years, a new edition has appeared, reflecting the many changes in the field.

Actually, this book has its origins in a smaller book, which appeared almost twelve years ago, titled *Guide for Translators*. For years Morry Sofer had felt the need for such a book, and since he couldn't find it anywhere, decided to write it himself. The initial success of the *Guide* made it clear that a much expanded book was needed, and the idea of a handbook was born.

While the *Guide* remains largely valid and useful, and contains a great deal of material that will continue to be useful in the future, the *Handbook* attempts to cover as much of the field as possible, and it is the full intention of the publisher to continue to update it regularly, so that it can serve as an up-to-date sourcebook for translators, especially for freelancers, who depend on timely information to maximize their effectiveness in this fast-changing field.

The Nature of Translation

Many people assume that any literate person who knows more than one language can translate. Nothing is farther from the truth. Translation is a talent few people possess, although many think they do. Without an innate aptitude for translation, one can go through the motions of replacing words with their equivalents in another language, but the results are likely to fall short of the intent and flavor of the original. Even the finest translation is never a full and true reflection of its source, simply because no two languages in the world, not even the most closely related, are identical in their way of using words and nuances. The best one can

1

hope for is a rendition close enough to the original not to alter any of its meaning, full enough not to omit any detail, no matter how seemingly insignificant, and elegant enough to provide at least some of the stylistic character of the original text.

Precisely because there is no such thing as a perfect translation of an original source, translation is always a challenge that requires skill, training and experience. The purpose of this handbook is to help those who know at least two languages and have an aptitude for translating take the necessary steps to sharpen their skills through training and practice, and hopefully, go on to start acquiring the experience necessary to become truly productive and effective translators.

This handbook is the result of the author's 40 years of translation experience as a literary translator with several book translations to his credit, later on as a technical translator for U.S. Government agencies, and, since 1983, as the founder and president of a translation service which engages hundreds of translators in over 90 different languages and dialects throughout the United States and abroad. For this edition, we have also had the support and advice of professionals in the translation field from around the world.

During the last 30 years, we have witnessed a dramatic change in the role of translators in this country and around the world. Opportunities for translators are growing as never before. This is due to the fact that the "global village" idea is becoming a fact of life with every passing day, thanks to the disappearance of the Iron Curtain, multinational alliances like the European Union, the growing global role of the United Nations, the globalization of business, and the miracle of modern communications. Such tools as the fax and email enable translators to receive text that was sent, say, from Washington to Athens, translate it, and send it back to Washington at an affordable cost and without wasting any valuable time in transit.

The continuous improvements in the computer technology have tripled and quadrupled the output of the professional translator, and have made the task of translating much easier. It is quite clear that mobile devices will play an even greater role in the translation field in years to come, making translation more affordable and widely used. (A word of caution: Those who maintain that use of technology will soon replace human translators altogether are not familiar with all the facts. The general consensus among the experts today is that computer and mobile technology will continue to enhance translation, but only as an aid to, rather than a replacement for, human translation.)

For Whom is this Handbook Intended?

This handbook is designed to be used by anyone who has any interest in translation. This includes the professional as well as the occasional translator, the freelancer and the career translator, the oral interpreter engaged in escort, consecutive, simultaneous or conference inter-pretation and, last but not least, the translation student.

It is designed both as a learning and a reference tool. By reading its text thoroughly, you are certain to acquire a familiarity with the translation field, both theoretical and practical. By using the appendices, you will be able to find your way through the complex world of translation equipment, dictionaries, and sources of translation assignments. Combined with the publisher's Website (*www. SchreiberLanguage.com*), it will enable you to be in constant touch with this fast-changing and dynamic field.

There are thousands of students in American colleges and universities who major in foreign languages. Many of them wonder what to do with their degree once they graduate. Many consider the possibilities of translation, only to find out there is little opportunity to break into this field, since there seems to be a gap between the formal education stage and the professional stage of working as a trained or accredited translator. They too can benefit from this handbook, which is designed to bridge this gap by offering information that, combined with a training program geared to help improve the aspiring translator's skills, will provide the necessary preparation for a professional translation career. This handbook will point anyone interested in translation in the right direction. The rest is up to you. Once you begin to pursue your own translation career, you will start formulating your own guidelines, develop your own techniques, and be ever on the lookout for new words, new knowledge, new linguistic sources, and a better understanding of how to communicate words and ideas, which, after all, is what translation is all about.

From ancient Egypt to the Renaissance to today's world, translators have played a key role in moving the world from one stage of civilization to the next.

2. HISTORICAL OVERVIEW OF TRANSLATION

The purpose of this chapter is threefold: First, to give you a bird's-eye view of the history of translation since the beginning of time; second, to show you how universal translation is encompassing every corner of the earth; and third, to make you realize how important translation is to human progress.

In the history of the Judeo-Christian-Islamic world, there are three key periods which have determined and defined those three civilizations, and all three periods are characterized by a high level of activity in the field of translation.

The first is the beginning of the Christian era, at which time many languages, most important among them Hebrew, Aramaic, Greek and Latin, interacted to create the new Christian civilization and the transformed Judaic civilization. The second begins with the birth of Islam in the seventh century, and culminates in the twelfth and thirteenth centuries, notably in the city of Toledo, Spain, where Christian, Muslim and Jewish scholars and translators from all parts of Europe and the Middle East undertook the enormous task of translating the Greek and Arabic classics into the new languages of Europe, and, in effect, laid the foundation of those new languages and cultures, providing the bridge to the Renaissance and the Modern World. The third key period is today. All the major civilizations of the world are at present in a state of flux. The world as a whole is being transformed as never before in recorded history, and at the same time languages are being transformed, and translation has taken on a new significance unlike anything since the end of the Middle Ages.

Translation is one of the oldest occupations in the world. Among the discoveries by Italian archeologists during the 1970's excavation of the ancient town of Ebla, in the Middle East, was an early dictionary. It is dated to over 5,000 years ago. It is chiseled in clay tablets, using a writing method known as cuneiform. There, on the face of the tablet,

5

are two parallel columns of words, in two different ancient tongues, related to taxation (tax-collecting is also one of the oldest occupations).

Before there was writing there was speaking. Neighboring tribes and nations have always spoken different dialects and even totally different languages. And yet they had to talk to each other in order to engage in trade, or to threaten each other, and, after the folly of fighting was over, to talk peace. To do this, they needed oral interpreters, those linguistically gifted individuals who had managed to master one or more tongues other than their own. From the beginning of time, those interpreters were considered an important asset for the community, or for the leader of the tribe or nation. They played a vital role in both trade and in the affairs of state. Quite often, these multilingual individuals became confidants of the ruler, and enjoyed special privileges.

There was, however, a downside to the life of the interpreter. Since the interpreter was often at the center of important events, taking part in crucial negotiations and decisions, if things went wrong, if a deal failed, or, worse yet, a battle was lost, the interpreter was often used as a scapegoat. Examples of this unfortunate turn of events abound throughout the history of interpretation as well as translation. Writing, has been around for at least 10,000 years, probably longer. In ancient Egypt, the court scribe was one of the most important officers of the Pharaoh's court. He was a highly cultivated person, and most likely knew more than one language. In the Old Testament there is no clear distinction between the scribe and the interpreter or translator. When the Assyrians lay siege to Jerusalem, a Hebrew scribe served as an interpreter between the Hebrew-speaking Judeans and their Aramean-speaking enemies.

Translators, humble servants of knowledge, often nameless, seldom acknowledged, more erred against than erring, forever looking for the right word.

Where would we be without them? How would we in the West enjoy the Rubaiyat without Fitzgerald? How would Europe know the Bible without St. Jerome? How would nations interact, how would they enrich each other's culture and language without their translators and interpreters?

—Anonymous

Human beings have long been fascinated, intrigued and even intimidated by the great variety of languages and dialects in the world. This phenomenon is reflected in the legends and oral traditions of nearly every culture. The biblical story of the tower of Babel is a case in point. Originally, according to this story, everyone spoke the same language. Then people became so presumptuous that they began to build a tower reaching into heaven. Subsequently, the tower was destroyed and the mortals were punished by being made to speak many different languages. In the late nineteenth century, a new language called Esperanto was created by Ludwig Zamenhoff, intended to be the international language. It has enjoyed a certain measure of success, but only among small circles of scholars. In our time, however, the language that comes closest to being an international language is English. Be that as it may, the other languages of the world will not be disappearing any time soon. Clearly, in an ideal world there will be no need for translators, or, for that matter, for physicians, lawyers, as well as hundreds of other occupations. But in the real world we need all of them.

Translating the Bible

The history of translation, not unlike the history of culture itself, begins with religion and eventually enters the secular culture. Language has always been a critical element of religion. To every culture, its language has always been sacred. It was the means of maintaining and transmitting traditions, and of communicating with the higher powers. Therefore, the issue of translating one's sacred writings and prayers into another language was always a very critical decision, which was never taken lightly. It took the Catholic Church many centuries before it decided in the 1960s to allow celebrating Mass in the vernacular, rather than in Latin. However, even now traditionalists abound. Jews and Muslims, still consider praying in languages other than Hebrew and Arabic, respectively, questionable to varying degrees.

The Judeo-Christian-Muslim world derives its culture from a common source, namely, a set of books originally written in Hebrew, known to Christians as the Old Testament, to Muslims as the Holy Books, and to Jews as the Tanakh (an acronym for Torah, Prophets and Writings). The Hebrew Bible was created over a period of some one thousand years, roughly 1300-300 B.C. By the time it was completed, its originators had begun to disperse around the Middle East, and spoke several languages other than Hebrew, including Aramaic and Greek. The original Hebrew text became canonized, hence sacred, but for practical purposes it had to be recited and written in the Aramaic so that masses of believers in places like Babylonia, Syria and even Palestine could understand it. Thus, several Aramaic translations of the Scriptures emerged, known as Targums.

While Jewish life and learning flourished in and around Babylonia, with Aramaic as its main language, a major Jewish community prospered in Alexandria, Egypt. Here the dominant culture was Greek, and the main language spoken by the Jews was Greek. This gave rise to the first great translation of the Hebrew Bible, known as the Septuagint, Latin for "Seventy," the number of scholars that, by tradition, translated the Bible from the Hebrew. Created to serve the needs of the Jewish community of Alexandria, the Septuagint was to play a crucial role in the development of Christianity. It was, in effect, the conduit through which Hebrew beliefs and civilization reached the pagan world about to become Christian and, despite its imperfections, it continued to exert influence on the development of such diverse Christian cultural and linguistic groups as the Ethiopic and Coptic in Africa, the Slavonic in Eastern Europe, and on the rest of Europe through the Latin versions of the Catholic Church.

No translator in history achieved greater honor and acclaim than St. Jerome (347-419), the patron saint of translators in the Catholic Church. Jerome translated both the Greek and Hebrew versions of the Bible into Latin, and produced the Vulgate, the standard Bible of the Church for the next thousand years. Throughout his life in Europe and in the Middle East, translation was his great passion, and despite adversity, he managed to leave the Church a vast corpus of translations and commentaries which were pivotal for the development of Christian civilization.

From a linguistic standpoint, an even more remarkable story related to the development of language and culture is the story of the two brothers, St. Cyril and St. Methodius. The two are credited with introducing Christianity to the Slavic world in the ninth century. To do so, they actually had to devise a new alphabet, based on Greek characters, which eventually became the Cyrillic alphabet, used today in Russia and other Slavic countries. They translated the Holy Scriptures into the language later known as Old Church Slavonic, and in effect laid the foundation for the Slavic cultures.

The ninth century also saw the beginning of Bible translation into English under Alfred the Great, into French under Charlemagne, founder of the Holy Roman Empire, and into German through the efforts of von Weissenburg and others. Here again, biblical translation is closely linked to the development of national cultures during this pivotal period in European history.

However, the great impetus for Bible translation in Europe came immediately after the Reformation in the sixteenth century. The main force behind it was Martin Luther, who not only broke away from Rome and helped establish Protestantism, but also paid close attention to the principles of translation, and to the establishment of the German language as a functional language, ready to pick up where Latin had left off. Indeed, some of Luther's basic translation principles, such as paying close attention to the transmission of meaning to the target language, and the emphasis on clarity and simplicity of translation, have remained valid to this day.

The impact of Luther's translation of the Bible was soon felt in other parts of Europe. Translations of Scriptures were soon to follow in Danish, Norwegian, Swedish and Icelandic, as well as in Slavic languages such as Slovene, Serbian (and Croatian, which is basically the same language), and Czech. The Kralice Bible in the Czech language (1579-1593) is considered the greatest example of classical Czech. All these translations made a seminal contribution to the development of the national cultures of these peoples.

The history of biblical translation in England is particularly fascinating. While it has its beginning with Alfred the Great in the ninth century (as was mentioned before)—the same Alfred who actually rescued the English language from foreign invaders such as the Danes, and ensured its future—it is once again in the sixteenth century that biblical translation in England reached the level of high drama. In the spirit of the time, affected by both the Reformation and the invention of the printing press, the scholar William Tyndall who was at home in both Greek and Hebrew (and a few other languages), translated both the Old and the New Testaments into English, with a view to replacing the Latin, which he considered less adequate for conveying the Bible to his people than their native tongue. Tyndall, who like Luther (whom he met in Germany) put an emphasis on clarity, also emphasized good functional English, which he helped fashion. Politically, however, he was out of favor with the "powers that be" (an expression coined by Tyndall) in England, and had to flee to Belgium where Charles V's agents reached him and managed to have him strangled and burned at the stake.

Human rulers can kill people, but they cannot destroy ideas. Despite the concerted effort in England to eliminate Tyndall's work, including the efforts of Henry VIII, who broke off with Rome and reintroduced the English Bible, which was largely Tyndall's work, without giving the martyred scholar any credit, it survived all the vicissitudes of the sixteenth century. In fact, when what became the Authorized Version of the Bible in England, namely, the King James Version was published in 1611, the product of some 54 scholars, it was largely Tyndall's translation. This version marks a cultural as well as a religious turning point in English history. Together with the work of Shakespeare, it stands at the apex of English culture. Ironically, the authorship of both the Bard's plays and the King James Scriptures has been disputed, distorted, claimed and reclaimed for the past four centuries.

The history of Bible translations is similarly intertwined with the development of national languages and cultures throughout the rest of Europe and many other parts of the world. The Bible is the most translated book in the world, having been translated into over 2000 languages and dialects. Every year new translations of the Bible appear all over the world. The American writer Ernest Hemingway said that he learned to write by reading the Bible. My suggestion to aspiring translators—as well as to seasoned ones—is to keep reading the Bible, not only because of its timeless message, but because of its genius for clarity, brevity, and simplicity, the attributes of all superior translations.

Translation in the East—Islam, Hinduism, Buddhism

In Islam, the *Qur'an* is considered untranslatable. This is why millions of Indonesian Muslims, for example, study it or use it for worship in the original Arabic, rather than in Indonesian. There are, in effect, hundreds of translations of the *Qur'an*, but officially they are considered "explanations," rather than "authorized versions," as would be the case with the Bible in a country like England. Arabic to the Muslim, like Hebrew to the Jew, is the language of revelation. Having said this, however, it is interesting to note that during the centuries of classical Islam, from roughly the seventh to the thirteenth century, translators played a critical role in making Islam the standard-bearer of civilization as Medieval Europe was sinking into ignorance and backwardness.

Soon after the spread of Islam throughout the Middle East, North Africa and Spain, the new Muslim empire undertook ambitious programs of translating the classics, notably Greek philosophy, astronomy and medicine, giving rise to such prominent translators as Hunayn ibn Ishaq (809-875), one of the early great translators of Baghdad, where translation flourished for the next four centuries (until the Mongolian conquest). In retrospect, by translating and preserving the works of Aristotle, Plato and other Greek philosophers, poets and scientists, Islamic scholars served as a bridge between antiquity and the modern world. Our scientific world has its roots in ancient Greece and Rome, but many of its branches have grown on the trunk of Islamic culture, which, in addition to transmitting the knowledge of the ancients through translation, added a great deal to it in areas such as mathematics and medicine.

Linguistically, the subcontinent of India is one of the most varied parts of the world, with more than 1500 languages and dialects, with 16 official languages, the most prominent being Hindi and English. The leading religion is Hinduism, but there are also millions of Muslims, Christians, Buddhists, Sikhs, Jains and Parsis. Needless to say, in such a linguistic kaleidoscope, translation is a thriving industry, moving in many different directions. The most translated work of Hinduism is arguably the *Bhagavad Gita*, originally written in Sanskrit. This religious work has been translated down to our time as a means of promoting the teachings of Hinduism. Some of the more recent notable translations are by Tilak (early twentieth century) into Marathi, and by Mahatma Gandhi (early-mid twentieth century) into Gujarati.

Unlike Hinduism, with Sanskrit as its sacred language, Buddhism is more universal and ecumenical, and has spread its teachings throughout Asia in several languages. The sacred scriptures of Buddhism were translated from Sanskrit into Chinese by the Buddhist monk and pilgrim to India Hsuan-tsang (602-664), one of the great enterprising translators of all time. Upon his return to China, he translated a large body of Buddhist sacred literature, which he had brought back with him after a long journey through mountains and deserts. One of his students in China was the Japanese monk Dosho. While Hsuan-tsang's version of Buddhism proved too esoteric for the Chinese, his disciple Dosho had more luck with it in Japan. After he returned to his native land, Dosho established the Hosso school, which became the most influential of all the Buddhist schools in Japan.

Translators Opening the Door to the Modern World

The most glorious period in the history of translation is represented by the so-called School of Translators of Toledo, which flourished in that beautiful Spanish city during the twelfth and thirteenth centuries. Toledo in those years was the crossroads of the cultures of the world, both spatially and temporally. On one side was the Islamic Empire, now nearing the end of its centuries of political and cultural preeminence. On the other side was Christian Europe, striving to emerge from the Middle Ages. And in the middle were the Jews of Spain, experiencing a Golden Age in their own Judaic and Hebraic culture, unlike anything anywhere since biblical and Talmudic times. Best of all, all three religions, usually at odds with one another, enjoyed a prolonged time of peaceful interaction which often accounts for great intellectual achievements.

In Toledo, the cultures of antiquity, preserved in the Arabic language in thousands of volumes, were translated first into Latin and later into the new languages of Europe. This undertaking has been compared to the discovery of the New World. In fact, the great discoveries of Columbus and others might never have occurred without the transmission of knowledge and science that took place in Toledo in those years. The modern world as we know it today might not exist. What is truly remarkable about the Toledo school is that it attracted translators from all parts of Europe, the most prominent being the Italian Gerard of Cremona, the Englishman Adelard of Bath, and Herman the German. But most critical of all was the part played by the Spanish Jewish translators of that time, who had the advantage of being equally at home in Muslim and Christian cultures, not to mention their own Judaic culture. The most prominent among them was the ibn Tibbon family, a dynasty of translators. The founder, Yehudah ibn Tibbon, has been called "patriarch of translators." His monument stands to this day in Granada, Spain. His grandson, Moses, translated Arabicworks, helping disseminate Greek and Arab culture throughout Europe. The ibn Tibbon dynasty remains to this day the exemplary translators of Judaism, not only because of their great cultural achievements, but because they formulated a theory of translation, based on the knowledge of the source and target languages as well as the knowledge of the subject matter, which has remained valid to this day.

Translation in the New World

The story of translation in the New World is, for the most part, not a happy one. During the age of the Great Discoveries, great explorers such as Columbus, Pizarro, Cortés and others came into contact with new, hitherto unknown cultures and languages, those of the natives of the New World and other parts of the globe. Here again interpreters became the bridge between the white man and the other races. Cortés, the conqueror of Mexico, might have failed in his ruthless mission had it not been for a local native woman who served as his interpreter. The same was true of many other conquerors and discoverers. The great civilization of the ancient Maya of Central America was made known to us through the translation into Spanish of such Mayan classics as the *Popol Vu*.

The conquest of new worlds by the nations of Europe did not, however, result in an attitude of respect on the part of the conquerors towards the conquered, whereby the languages of the latter might have been studied by the former, and their oral or written traditions translated into such languages as Spanish, English, French and so on. Instead, the colonizers looked upon their new subjects as heathens whose language and culture were worthless, and imposed their own language, culture and religion on those who survived the many massacres inflicted upon them by their enlightened conquerors. It would not be until many years later that valuable cultural assets, such as Indian dialects of North America, African languages, and many other oral and written traditions, would be treated with respect, studied, and translated, as is finally beginning to happen in our time, in some cases after the originators of those cultures have all but disappeared.

Nor, for that matter, is the history of translation in the United States particularly uplifting. The European colonists who settled this continent had little need for translation, and soon developed an insular attitude still reflected to this day in the political attitudes of American isolationists. No one has satirized this attitude better than Mark Twain in the celebrated exchange between Huck Finn and Jim, in which the runaway slave wonders why the French can't speak "like the rest of us." One of the great anomalies of American life is the fact that while no other country in history has had a more culturally varied population coexisting as effectively as the population of the United States, translation has a long way to go to become as well-established here as it is in other parts of the world.

The Twentieth Century

Translation in the present century has seen some good times and some bad times. Translation has fared the worst under totalitarian regimes operating under such banners as Fascism, Communism, and Nazism. The history of Communist Soviet Union, Fascist Italy, and Nazi Germany is rich with the suppression and persecution of translators. A more recent totalitarian regime, namely, that of Iran, has engaged in active terrorism against translators, in this case against the translators of the Indian-born British author Salman Rushdie, one of whom was murdered by Iranian agents, and the other wounded.

When the Republic of Ireland was formed in 1922, a major translation program was launched which sought to revive the use and study of the Irish language, or Gaelic. Since the English language and culture had already been deeply entrenched in Ireland, to this day the dominant language remains English. But the example of Ireland is being emulated at present throughout the world.

Another national language that was reintroduced programmatically to both daily life and literature is Hebrew, the same biblical Hebrew we have encountered at the dawn of civilization, now transformed by many old and new cultural influences. Modern Hebrew is one of the great linguistic success stories of all time. Not only has it become the spoken language of several million people who arrived in the new state from over 100 different countries, but, using American English as its working model, it is constantly adding current expressions as well as technical and scientific terminology which has enabled the new society to use Hebrew in all fields of contemporary science and technology.

As the twentieth century came to a close, two linguistic phenomena became clearly dominant. The first is the growing incursion of American English into nearly all the languages of the world, mostly because of American pop culture and high tech. This is bound to have a lasting effect on languages in general in the twenty-first century. The second phenomenon is the reemergence of national languages throughout the world. Until a few years ago, the Soviet Union, encompassing many nations and cultures, conducted all its affairs in one language: Russian. With the breakup of the USSR, there are now dozens of languages all the way from the Baltic Sea to the Far East that are no longer suppressed are have become more common again it official as well as daily usage. In Africa many languages are emerging as well, but there the trends are still hard to define. What is clear at this time is that linguistic diversity as well as a growing influence of one international language, namely, English, should characterize the first few decades of the 21st century.

What all of this means for translators is that we be in the middle of a new golden age for translation, not unlike the one in Spain at the end of the Middle Ages. There is a new cultural openness in today's world, brought about by several factors, the most notable being the end of the Cold War between the West and the former Communist Bloc, the incredible progress in global communications, including such technologies as satellite communications, computers, e-mail, text messaging and the mobile technology, and the fast-growing international trade throughout the entire world, as well as the new international awareness of many languages and cultures that for centuries were subjugated and suppressed. The world today, rather than being dominated by a few colonialist languages such as French, English or Spanish, is finally reaching a stage of linguistic and cultural—albeit not quite yet social and economic—equality, whereby literally hundreds of languages and dialects are beginning to play a part in the global tapestry of human interaction. As a result, hundreds of new dictionaries are being published all over the world, language courses are being offered everywhere in an unprecedented number of languages, and the demand for competent translators is growing at a steady rate.

As once happened during ancient and pre-modern history, the role of the translator has once again become critical in shaping history and helping civilization make the transition into the next age.

How History is "Translated" by the Young

From the neighborhoods of Chicago comes an unidentified document that purports to be a history of the world "pasted together...from genuine student bloopers collected by teachers throughout the U.S., from 8th grade through college level." Excerpts follow:

Ancient Egypt was inhabited by mummies, and they all wrote in hydraulics. They lived in the Sarah Dessert and traveled by Camelot.

David was a Hebrew king skilled in playing the liar. He fought with the Finkelsteins, a race of people who lived in biblical times. Solomon, one of his sons, had 300 wives and 700 porcupines.

The Greeks were a highly sculptured people, and without them we wouldn't have history. They invented three kinds of columns, corinthian, ironic, and dorc, and built the Apocalypse. They also had myths, which is a female moth.

Queen Elizabeth was the Virgin Queen. When she exposed herself to her troops, they all yelled "hurrah." Then her navy went out and defeated the Spanish Armadillo.

During the Renaissance America began. Columbus was a great navigator who discovered America while cursing about the Atlantic. His ships were called the Nina, the Pinta, and the Santa Fe.... Sir Francis Drake circumcised the world with a 100-foot clipper.

Meanwhile in Europe, Voltaire invented electricity and also wrote a book called "Candy." Gravity was invented by Isaac Newton. It is chiefly noticeable in the fall, when apples are falling off the trees.

Johann Bach wrote a great many musical compositions and had a large number of children. In between, he practiced on the old spinster, which he kept up in his attic.

3. REQUISITES FOR PROFESSIONAL TRANSLATORS

Any person who knows more than one language has the ability to explain a word or a sentence in what translators call "the source language" (the language you translate from) by using an equivalent word or sentence in what they call "the target language" (the language you translate into). This, in effect, is the beginning of translation. But it is only the beginning. It does not automatically turn a person into an accomplished translator. Along with the knowledge of the source and the target language, a translator must have an aptitude for translation. Some people are endowed with a talent for translation. It is not an acquired skill, like riding a bicycle. It is rather a talent, like playing the violin. Some people have it and some don't. It is not necessarily an indication of a lower or higher IQ. Nor is it an indication of how linguistically gifted one is. It is an inborn skill that enables a person to change a text from one language into another quickly and accurately, or, if you will, think in more than one language at the same time. If you possess this skill, then it behooves you to develop it and make use of it, because there is never an overabundance of good translators, and it is almost axiomatic that the good ones can always find either full-time or part-time work.

The **first** requisite for the working translator is a thorough knowledge of both the source and the target languages. There is no point in billing oneself as a translator if one is not fully familiar with both languages, or does not possess a vocabulary in both equal to that of a speaker of those languages who has a university education or its equivalent.

The **second** requisite is thorough "at-homeness" in both cultures. A language is a living phenomenon. It does not exist apart from the culture where it is spoken and written. It communicates not only the names of objects and different kinds of action, but also feelings, attitudes, beliefs, and so on. To be fully familiar with a language, one must also be familiar with the culture in which the language is used, indeed, with the people who use it, their ways, manners, beliefs and all that goes into making a culture.

Third, one must keep up with the growth and change of the language, and be up-to-date in all of its nuances and neologisms. Languages are in a constant state of flux, and words change meaning from year to year. A pejorative term can become laudatory, and a neutral term can become loaded with meaning. Forty years ago the English word "gay" simply meant "joyous." Now it is used to define an entire segment of society. We once spoke of the "almighty dollar." Now as we travel around the globe, we may find out the dollar is not necessarily everyone's preferred currency.

Fourth, a distinction must be made between the languages one translates from and into. Generally speaking, one translates from another language into one's own native language. This is because one is usually intimately familiar with one's own language, while even years of study and experience do not necessarily enable one to be completely at home with an acquired language. The exceptions to this rule are usually those people who have lived in more than one culture, and have spoken more than one language on a regular basis. Those may be able to translate in both directions. There are also rare gifted individuals who have mastered another language to such a degree that they can go both ways. They are indeed extremely rare. Given all of this, one should allow for the fact that while the ability of the accomplished translator to write and speak in the target language (i.e., one's native tongue) may be flawless, that person may not necessarily be able to write excellent prose or give great speeches in the source language (i.e., the language from which one translates). Then again, it is not necessary to be able to write and speak well in the language one translates from, while it is to be expected that a good translator is also a good writer and speaker in his or her native language.

Fifth, a professional translator has to be able to translate in more than one area of knowledge. Most professional translators are called upon to translate in a variety of fields. It is not uncommon for a translator to cover as many as twenty or thirty fields of knowledge in one year, including such areas as political subjects, economics, law, medicine, communications and so on. Obviously, it would be hard to find a translator who is an economist, a lawyer, a medical doctor, and an engineer all wrapped into one. In fact, such a person probably does not exist.

One does not have to be a lawyer to translate legal documents. Many a professional translator has been able to gain enough knowledge and acquire a vocabulary in a variety of technical fields to be able to produce perfectly accurate and well-written translations in those fields. This is not nearly as difficult as it may seem, since most technical fields utilize a well-defined number of terms which keep repeating themselves, and as one keeps translating the same subject, they become more and more familiar to the translator. One must, however, have a natural curiosity about many different areas of human knowledge and activity, and an interest in increasing one's vocabulary in a variety of related as well as unrelated fields.

Sixth, an effective translator must have a facility for writing or speaking (depending on whether the method used is writing, speaking, or dictation), and the ability to articulate quickly and accurately, either orally or in writing. Like a reporter, a translator must be able to transmit ideas in real time, and in good understandable language. Translation is a form of writing and speech-making, and a translator is, in a sense, a writer and an orator.

Seventh, a professional translator must develop a good speed of translation. There are two reasons for this: First, most clients wait until the last minute to assign a translation job. As a result, they turn to a translator or a translation service with what is perhaps the most typical question in this business: "How soon can you have this job ready for me?" The professional translator has to be prepared to accept that long job with the short turnaround time, or there will be no repeat business from that particular client or from most other clients, for that matter. Secondly, translation is generally paid by the word. The more words one can translate per hour, the more income one will generate. Translating 50 words per hour is inadequate can land a translator in the poorhouse. Serious translation starts at 250 words per hour, and can reach as high as 1000 words per hour with good word processing software, and close to 3000 words per hour using dictation (the author actually knows such a translator). High volume translators are the ones who will be the most successful.

Eighth, a translator must develop research skills, and be able to acquire reference sources which are essential for producing high quality translation. Without such sources even the best of translators cannot hope to be able to handle a large variety of subjects in many unrelated fields. Dedicated translators are the ones who are always on the lookout for new reference sources, and over time develop a data bank which can be used in their work.

Ninth, today's translator cannot be a stranger to latest developments in technology. The Internet, hardware like mobile devices, apps and other technologies change at a breathtaking rate, and we much keep up. Translation has become completely dependent on electronic tools. Gone are the days of handwriting, the typewriter, and all the other "prehistoric" means of communication. The more one becomes involved in translation, the more one finds oneself caught up in the latest high-tech developments.

Tenth, a translator who wishes to be busy on a fairly regular basis doing translation work must carefully consider the fact that certain languages are in high demand, say, in Washington or in Los Angeles, while others are not. Thus, for example, there is high demand for Japanese, German, Spanish, French, Chinese, Arabic, Russian and Italian in both Washington and Los Angeles, but not nearly as much for Bulgarian, Farsi, Czech, or Afrikaans. If your language falls within the second group, it is extremely advisable to also have language expertise in one of the languages of the first group, or to seriously consider whether your particular language has enough of a demand to warrant a major investment of time and effort on your part. One should always check and see what kind of a potential one's language specialty has in a given geographic area.

The above ten points are the essential criteria for developing a translation career. There are many other considerations, but none as important as these. If you feel that you can meet all of the above criteria, then you should continue reading this handbook and putting it to good use.

The Well-Rounded Translator

The main division in the translation field is between literary and technical translation. Literary translation, which covers such areas as fiction, poetry, drama, and the humanities in general, is often done by writers of the same genre who actually author works of the same kind in the target language, or at least by translators with the required literary aptitude. For practical reasons, this handbook will not cover literary translation, but will instead focus on the other major area of translation, namely, technical translation. High quality literary translation has always been the domain of the few, and is hardly lucrative (don't even think of doing literary translation if your motive is money), while technical translation is done by a much greater number of practitioners, and is an ever-growing and expanding field with excellent earning opportunities. This chapter discusses the characteristics of the well-rounded technical translator.

The term "technical" is extremely broad. In the translation business it covers much more than technical subjects in the narrow sense of the word. In fact, there is an overlap between literary and technical translation when it comes to such areas as social sciences, political subjects, and many others.

One way of defining technical translation is by asking the question, does the subject being translated require a specialized vocabulary, or is the language non-specialized? If the text being translated includes specialized terms in a given field, then the translation is technical.

The more areas (and languages) a translator can cover, the greater the opportunity for developing a successful translation career. Furthermore, as one becomes proficient in several areas, it becomes easier to add more. Besides, many technical areas are interrelated, and proficiency in one increases proficiency in another. In addition, every area breaks down into many subareas, each with its own vocabulary and its own linguistic idiosyncrasies. Thus, for example, translating in Arabic does not make one an expert in all spoken Arabic dialects, yet a knowledge of several of those dialects is very beneficial for the professional Arabic translator.

How does one become a well-rounded translator? The answer can be summed up in one word—experience. The key to effective translation is practice. Since human knowledge grows day by day, and since language keeps growing and changing, the well-rounded translator must keep in touch with knowledge and language on a regular basis. The worst thing that can happen to a translator is to be out of touch with the source language for more than a couple of years. What the rusty translator may find out is that new words, new concepts and new ways of using those words and applying those concepts have come into being during that period of "hibernation," and one's old expertise is no longer reliable.

Translation, therefore, is a commitment one makes not for a limited period of time, but rather long-term. It is to be assumed that anyone who becomes a translator is the kind of person who loves words and loves the challenge of using words effectively and correctly. Such a person will not become an occasional translator, but will make translation a lifelong practice.

Good and Bad Translation Habits

The accomplished translator can develop good as well as bad habits. Starting with the bad, we have already pointed out one—losing touch with the source language for long periods of time. Another bad habit is taking illegitimate shortcuts while translating. There are several types of such shortcuts. The most typical is failing to look up a word, even if one is really not sure how to translate. Being ninety percent sure of a word's meaning is not good enough in professional translation. If one is not sure of a word's meaning, even after all available means have been exhausted, then one must put in a translator's note to that effect, or make it known in some other way that there is a problem with translating that particular word. Anything less would be deceptive.

Another illegitimate shortcut is summarizing a paragraph instead of providing a *full* translation. There is such a thing as summary trans-lation of a paragraph or a document. If a summary is called for, then this is precisely what the translator is expected to provide. But the most common form of translation is what's known in the business as a verbatim translation, which is a full and complete rendition of the source text. When verbatim translation is ordered, anything less than a full translation is not acceptable. Unfortunately, some translators tend to overlook this from time to time, especially when they undertake more work than they can accomplish by a given deadline, and decide to summarize rather than miss that deadline.

Perhaps the worst habit for a translator is to decide at a certain point in time that his or her knowledge of either the source or the target language is so good that it cannot possibly stand any improvement. The moment one stops growing linguistically, one is no longer on the cutting edge of one's profession. The good translator is a perennial language student, always eager and willing to learn more and to keep up with the latest.

As for good habits, the most important, perhaps, are the ones we obtain by reversing the above-mentioned bad habits. But there are many more. One excellent habit is to read professional literature in the field one will be called upon to translate in with reasonable frequency. One good example is *Scientific American*, which can help anyone who translates subjects of science and technology to learn the style or styles used in scientific writing. People who work in the field of translating business documents should definitely read business periodicals, not the least of which is *The Wall Street Journal*. One does not have to be a scientist to translate scientific articles, or have a business degree to translate business documents, but a general understanding of the subject goes a long way towards providing an accurate translation of the subject.

Another excellent habit is to translate not only for profit but also for enjoyment and experience. Most people, unfortunately, are not so taken with their daily work that they would want to continue doing it after hours for fun or practice. But an accomplished translator is someone who will on occasion translate simply for the sake of sharpening his or her skill, or accept a very small fee because of personal commitment to the subject matter, or because of a personal interest. This writer, for example, enjoys translating poetry because of the challenge of doing

---

Stories Translators Tell

Two new immigrants from the Far East meet on the street in Miami.
"I heard your nephew, who moved to Miami last year, is becoming Americanized very quickly."
"How so?"
"He speaks fluent Spanish." •

José goes back to South America after a short stay in the States.
"The gringos are very nice people," he tells his friends. "I went to Yankee Stadium. There were no seats left, so they told me to stand by the flagpole. Suddenly everyone got up, turned to me, and sang in chorus: "José, can you see?""

what is perhaps the most difficult type of translation, and, quite simply, because of the enjoyment of poetry.

Yet another good habit is always to be on the lookout for dictionaries. Many dictionaries are hard to find and are available in few places. This writer in all his travels across the United States and abroad always stops in bookstores to look for dictionaries. One can also order dictionaries from bookstores and from publishers, but then one has to know what to order and from whom (see Appendix 2).

The last good habit I would like to mention is the practice of compiling word lists and building a reference library. Dictionaries do not have all the words and terms a translator needs, nor do they contain all the information which specialized references may have. There are aids for translators put out by certain organizations, and there is professional literature in every field. In recent years there has been a growing awareness of the need for terminology management (see Chapter 9), and with the constant advances in computer technology databases have been proliferating, making the work of the translator much easier than ever before. Good references are worth their weight in gold when they are needed for a specific translation, and over time the experienced translator develops an extensive library of glossaries which become essential for any translation assignment.

Reading poetry in translation is like kissing a woman through a handkerchief.

—Haim Nachman Bialik

Kissing a woman through a handkerchief is actually not so bad.

—Yehudah Amichai

4. TRANSLATOR'S SELF-EVALUATION

The following criteria were developed some years ago by a U.S. Government agency for determining the skill level of a potential translator whom that agency might have liked to hire. You may want to read this chapter carefully to try to make an honest determination as to where on this scale you find yourself at this time. If you are below Level 2+, you need to keep practicing. If you are at Level 3 or higher, you can start doing some professional translating. After Level 4, you are ready for some serious translating, and at Level 5 you can start making a living as a translator.

Regardlesss of level, all translators should have a realistic understanding of their skills, abilities and work habits to avoid making idealistic promises to clients. A good translator knows when to politely decline a project that is beyond his or her abilities or time and refer the client to a translator with the required skill set.

Translator Skill Levels

Level 0

No functional ability to translate the language. Consistently misunderstanding or cannot comprehend at all.

Level 0+

Can translate all or some place names (i.e., street or city designations), corporate names, numbers and isolated words and phrases, often translating these inaccurately.

In rendering translations, writes using only memorized material and set expressions. Spelling and representation of symbols (letters, syllables, characters) are frequently incorrect.

Level 1

Sufficient skill to translate the simplest connected written material in a form equivalent to usual printing or typescript. Can translate either representations of familiar formulaic verbal exchanges or simple language containing only the highest-frequency grammatical patterns and vocabulary items, including cognates when appropriate. Translated texts include simple narratives of routine behavior; concrete descriptions of persons, places and things; and explanations of geography and government such as those simplified for tourists. Mistranslations common.

In rendering translations, writes in simple sentences (or clauses), making continual errors in spelling, grammar and punctuation, but translation can be read and understood by a native reader used to dealing with foreigners attempting to translate his/her language.

Level 1+

Sufficient skill to translate simple discourse for informative social purposes in printed form. Can translate material such as announcements or public events, popular advertising notes containing biographical information or narration of events and straightforward newspaper headlines. Has some difficulty with the cohesive factors in discourse, such as matching pronouns with referents.

In rendering translations, writing shows good control of elementary vocabulary and some control of basic syntactic patterns, but major errors still occur when expressing more complex thoughts. Dictionary usage may still yield incorrect vocabulary of forms, although can use a dictionary to advantage to translate simple ideas. Translations, though faulty, are comprehensible to native readers used to dealing with foreigners.

Level 2

Sufficient skill to translate simple authentic written material in a form equivalent to usual printing. Can translate uncomplicated, but authentic prose on familiar subjects that are normally present in a predictable sequence, which aids the translator in his/her work. Texts may include description and narration in context, such as news items describing frequently occurring events, simple biographical information, social notices, formatted business letters and simple technical material written for the general reader. The prose is predominantly in familiar sentence patterns. Some mistranslations.

In rendering translations, has written vocabulary sufficient to perform simple translations with some circumlocutions. Still makes common errors in spelling and punctuation, but shows some control of the most common formats and punctuation conventions. Good control of morphology of language (in inflected languages) and of the most frequently used syntactic structures. Elementary constructions are usually handled quite accurately, and translations are understandable to a native reader not used to reading the translations of foreigners.

Level 2+

Sufficient skill to translate most factual material in nontechnical prose as well as some discussions on concrete topics related to special professional interests. Has begun to make sensible guesses about unfamiliar words by using linguistic context and prior knowledge. May react personally to material, but does not yet detect subjective attitudes, values or judgments in the material to be translated.

In rendering translations, often shows surprising fluency and ease of expression, but under time constraints and pressure language may be inaccurate and/or incomprehensible. Generally strong in either grammar or vocabulary, but not in both. Weaknesses or unevenness in one of the foregoing or in spelling results in occasional mistranslations. Areas of weakness range from simple constructions, such as plurals, articles, prepositions and negatives, to more complex structures, word order and relative clauses. Normally controls general vocabulary, with some misuse of everyday vocabulary still evident. Shows a limited ability to use circumlocutions. Uses dictionary to advantage to supply unknown words. Translations are understandable to native readers not used to dealing with foreigner's attempts to translate the language, though style is obviously foreign.

Level 3

Able to translate authentic prose on unfamiliar subjects. Translating ability is not dependent on subject matter knowledge. Texts will include news stories similar to wire service reports, routine correspondence, general reports and technical material in his/her professional field, all of which include hypothesis, argumentation and supported opinions. Such texts typically include grammatical patterns and vocabulary ordinarily encountered in professional reading. Mistranslations rare. Almost always able to correctly translate material, relate ideas and make inferences. Rarely has to pause over or reread general vocabulary. However, may experience some difficulty with unusually complex structures and low-frequency idioms.

In preparing translations, control of structure, spelling, and general vocabulary is adequate to convey his/her message accurately, but style may be obviously foreign. Errors virtually never interfere with comprehension and rarely disturb the native reader. Punctuation generally controlled. Employs a full range of structures. Control of grammar good, with only sporadic errors in basic structures, occasional errors in the most complex frequent structures and somewhat more frequent errors in low-frequency complex structures. Consistent control of compound and complex sentences. Relationship of ideas presented in original material is consistently clear.

Level 3+

Increased ability to translate a variety of styles and forms of language pertinent to professional needs. Rarely mistranslates such texts or rarely experiences difficulty relating ideas or making inferences. Ability to comprehend many sociolinguistic and cultural references. However, may miss some nuances and subtleties. Increased ability to translate unusually complex structures and low-frequency idioms; however, accuracy is not complete.

In rendering translations, able to write the language in a few prose styles pertinent to professional/educational needs. Not always able to tailor language to suit original material. Weaknesses may lie in poor control of low-frequency, complex structures, vocabulary or the ability to express subtleties and nuances.

Level 4

Able to translate fluently and accurately all styles and forms of the language pertinent to professional needs. Can translate more difficult prose and follow unpredictable turns of thought readily in any area directed to the general reader and all materials in his/her own special field, including official and professional documents and correspondence. Able to translate precise and extensive vocabulary, including nuances and subtleties, and recognize all professionally relevant vocabulary known to the educated nonprofessional native, although may have some difficulty with slang. Can translate reasonably legible handwriting without difficulty. Understands almost all sociolinguistic and cultural references.

In rendering translations, able to write the language precisely and accurately in a variety of prose styles pertinent to professional/ educational needs. Errors of grammar are rare, including those in low-frequency complex structures. Consistently able to tailor language to suit material and able to express subtleties and nuances.

Level 4+

Increased ability to translate extremely difficult or abstract prose. Increased ability to translate a variety of vocabulary, idioms, colloquialisms and slang. Strong sensitivity to sociolinguistic and cultural references. Increased ability to translate less than fully legible handwriting. Accuracy is close to that of an educated translator, but still not equivalent.

In rendering translations, able to write the language precisely and accurately, in a wide variety of prose styles pertinent to professional/ educational needs.

Level 5

Can translate extremely difficult and abstract prose (i.e., legal, technical), as well as highly colloquial writings and the literary forms of the language. Translates a wide variety of vocabulary and idioms, colloquialisms, slang and pertinent cultural references. With varying degrees of difficulty, can translate all kinds of handwritten documents. Able to understand how natives think as they produce a text. Accuracy is equivalent to that of a well-educated translator.

In rendering translations, has writing proficiency equal to that of a well-educated native. Without nonnative errors of structure, spelling, style or vocabulary, can translate both formal and informal correspondence, official reports and documents and professional/educational articles, including writing for special purposes which might include legal, technical, educational, literary and colloquial writing.

In March of 2009 Secretary of State Hillary Clinton met with Russian Foreign Minister Sergei Lavrov in Geneva. Clinton presented Lavrov with a "reset" button, meant to symbolize a desire to improve relations between their two countries. She added that her staff had "worked hard" to ensure the accuracy of the translation. Unfortunately, as the minister pointed out, "peregruzka," the word on the button means "overloaded" or "overcharged," not "reset."

The correct word is "Perezagruzka., meaning "reset" or "resetting." Perhaps more accurately, it means "rebooting". It is a computer term. The root of each word is the same—"gruz" which means "load". The Russian prefix "pere" can indicate either a repeat action (as in "reset") or an "overdoing" of something (as in "overload.") Although "peregruzka" can mean "transferring of a load" that would not make any sense here. The American translators needed to go to the word for "booting" which is "zagruzka" and then apply the prefix "pere" for the meaning of "rebooting."

Some years ago, when President Carter went to Poland, he said to an audience, "I love you." His American-Polish interpreter translated it as "I lust after you," which elicited loud laughter from the audience. The reason for the mistranslation: The hapless linguist had been away from his native land for over 20 years, during which time some basic Polish expressions had changed.

Generic Language Problems

Human language is an extremely complicated means of communication. This may well be the reason why misunderstanding among individuals and groups of people are so common, and why the human species continues to experience so much conflict with so many tragic consequences. We the members of this species tend to oversimplify the complex phenomena that surround us, and one of the things we greatly oversimplify is what human language is all about. First, we make the erroneous assumption that when we use a basic word like "water," it means exactly the same thing to anyone who speaks English. Nothing is farther from the truth. To a chemist, water is H_2O, or a chemical substance. To a city-dweller it is a substance usually mixed with chlorine, while a to a seashore-dweller the word "water" always raises the question of fresh water and sea water. This is the first source of translation problems. Translation is more than the replacement of one word in the source language with another word in the target language. It is a decision-making process involving a judgment regarding every single word translated, and the best way to translate it.

Second, we tend to oversimplify the relationships among different languages. This is particularly true of Americans, who, unlike Europeans and others, live in a vast country that basically speaks one language. When an American travels around the world, he/she expects every word spoken in a foreign language to mean exactly what it means in American English. The word in Latin American Spanish for "now" is "ahora." When an American tourist in certain parts south of the border is told, "I'll bring it to you now," he/she takes it to mean "right away." "Ahora," however, does not mean "right away." In the local idiom "now" is not measured in "seconds" or a few minutes, but rather anywhere from a few minutes to several hours. The word for "right away" is "ahorita," or, for more emphasis, "ahoritita." And even then there are no guarantees. Let us add in passing that even in the U.S. "right away" is not what it used to be. Perhaps respect for words and keeping one's word is not what it used to be. But this is another matter.

As the twenty-first century begins to unfold, languages around the world are becoming more complicated by the day. Not because human beings wish them to be more complicated. Quite the contrary. As we mentioned before, the common human attitude is to simplify. But because the world is becoming more complicated, and because things are changing so fast these days, the need for new words and for new and different meanings for old ones is becoming overwhelming. Moreover, the unprecedented close interaction among different languages around the world, particularly between American English and all the other languages, is altering the character of languages everywhere, with literally thousands of American words being adopted by other languages, creating a whole new challenge for the contemporary translator not only of language pairs involving English, but also of other language pairs, such as, for example, German-French, trying to decide when and how to use those American words in the context of a language such as German or French.

Add to this the fact that the written word is, after all, a record of the spoken word. It is a set of combined symbols, namely, letters and characters, or, in some languages, ideograms, put together to produce syllables and words and phrases, which invariably fail to convey most of the nuances of the spoken word. When you say a simple word like "really," you can inflect, modulate, resonate in countless ways, which causes the word to convey almost any meaning you wish, from question to affirmation, from sorrow to derision. Writing is incapable of doing this. When an actor looks at a written script of a play, he/she must decide how to pronounce, or rather how to act out the words. When a translator looks at a text in a source language, he/she must decide whether the

---

Levels of Translation

Keep in mind that not all translation is done on the same level. Be sure to find out before you start a translation assignment whether it needs to be merely a rough draft, or a fully correct translation for in-house use, or actually ready for publication.

author is serious, or whether there is subtle or not-so-subtle humor or some other attitude in what the author says. A misjudgment can result in a bad translation.

Another generic problem with the written word is the fact that a writer always has a specific audience in mind when he/she writes a piece, be it general or technical. That audience, to begin with, speaks the same language as the author. Moreover, the audience consists of a specific segment or segments of the population that speaks that language. The author often assumes that his target audience shares a certain body of knowledge with him/her, and therefore does not always spell out everything, but rather alludes or refers to it by implication. Here the knowledge of the language alone will not stand the translator in good stead. He/she also must share that writer's cultural background, and understand the subtleties of the source language text. When an American suspense novel writer has his/her character say, "Let's rock and roll," it does not necessarily refer to dancing, but rather to engaging in some aggressive action.

An even better example of this problem is the use of acronyms. Some acronyms, such as UN, USA, are universally known. But many acronyms are very subject-specific and can easily throw off the best translator.

These, then, are some of the generic problems facing the translator. There are many more. Our intention in bringing these problems to your attention is not to discourage you from pursuing this craft. Rather it is to help you understand what you are up against as a translator, and to be better prepared to face these problems as they occur.

The following sections discuss specific languages and their translation problems vis-à-vis English.

Schreiber Publishing Helps Alleviate Translation Problems

The publisher of this handbook, Schreiber Publishing of Rockville, Maryland, is the only publisher in the U.S. and one of the few in the world dedicated to helping translators with practical translation problems. The form at the back of this book lists such aids as Schreiber's Translator Self-Training series, and technical dictionaries designed especially for translators (*see also* Appendix 1: Dictionaries).

Spanish

Arguably, Spanish is the most translated language in the United States today. In some parts of the country, such as southern Florida, southern California, and parts of New York City, Spanish is no less dominant a language than English. The Hispanic population in the U.S. has been growing steadily in recent years, and American business now has a major stake in reaching this major market segment, as well as its countries of origin, notably, Latin America.

While generically Spanish is one of the easiest languages to translate into English, in practice, Spanish-English technical translation is much more problematic than, say, German-English, or French-English, or even Japanese-English.

This may come as a great surprise to many. But as can be attested to by anyone who has been working with a large variety of technical materials in which Spanish is either the source or the target language, quite often there is hardly a safe way to translate a given text from or into Spanish in a way that would satisfy one's client or one's target audience.

The main reason for this is that there is really no single version of Spanish. There are major differences between the Spanish of Mexico, Central America, northern South America, and southern South America, not to mention such places as Puerto Rico, and, of course, the motherland, Spain. Since we have large populations in the U.S. today hailing from all these parts of the Hispanic world, there is no way of translating a given text in a way that would fully satisfy all of these people.

And this is only the beginning. There is also the problem of the new hybrids of Spanish spawned here in the United States. Thus, we have Chicano Spanish in places like Texas, New Mexico, and California. We have Cuban-American Spanish in Miami, and Puerto Rican-American Spanish in New York. We even have such "exotic" mutations as Salvadoran Spanish in Washington, a new dialect combining American English and Central American Spanish spoken by a community with a distinctive cultural character.

Let's consider a commonplace item such as eyeglasses. A New York manufacturer of eyeglasses wants to promote its product in the Hispanic communities in the U.S. One community refers to eyeglasses as *anteojos*, a second community calls them *gafas*, a third, *espejuelos,* and a fourth, *lentes*. In the promotion mailing, which Spanish word should be used? No one word will fit all. Well, one answer is to customize the translation, namely, provide several versions, based on geography, and use each of the synonyms for its appropriate target audience. This will require market research at considerable expense. Moreover, many common everyday items are referred to by Hispanics living in the U.S. by the English, rather than Spanish, name. A can of spray, for instance, becomes "espray." An electric drill, is, quite simply, a "drill." Any attempt to be a purist and provide the real Spanish word for spray or drill will result in a drop in sales.

An added problem is the fact that while English and Spanish are, in many respects, such similar languages, in many technical areas there is a wide gap between the two. Since the Hispanic world is not as industrialized as the English-speaking world, and since the high tech/digital/information revolution of our time is being played out and defined mainly in American English, the problems of technical translation from and into Spanish, rather than diminish, continue to grow.

There is no easy solution in sight. The worst one can do is to pretend these problems do not exist. Or, for that matter, to make a case for some kind of a standard, universal Spanish that can satisfy everyone's needs, when, in effect, no such Spanish exists, certainly not when it comes to technical translation. One has to come to terms with these problems, and do the best one can in any given situation.

Spanish translators constitute the largest of any group of translators in the United States. They range from very basic communicators of the written and spoken word to some highly trained and skillful technical and literary translators. As in any other language, it is important for the Spanish technical translator to specialize in a particular technical area or areas, such as law, medicine, communications, and so on. In addition, it is very important to gain familiarity with the main varieties of Spanish alluded to in this chapter. In this day and age of global communications, almost anything we do transcends the boundaries of our immediate community, and so it is important to know how Spanish is used in other parts of the U.S. and the world. There are now specialized dictionaries for regional Spanish (and more keep coming out), which are a great help in this respect. (See Appendix 1).

In conclusion, Spanish translation is definitely a career worth pursuing in the United States, provided one approaches it cautiously and with a sense of realism and long-term commitment.

German

German is one of the world's leading languages in all technical subjects and in all areas of human knowledge. In addition, the German-speaking world generates an enormous amount of technical literature which is routinely translated into English. Conversely, a great deal of English-language literature in many fields is translated every year into German. All of which translates into one simple fact: if you can translate German, you are in the right profession.

While it is important in any language pair to have excellent familiarity with the subject matter one translates in, in German it is especially important. This is because German tends to say certain things—even those of a straightforward technical nature— in a less than straightforward way. Unless one is very familiar with the subject at hand, there is a clear and present danger of missing the point and making a fool of oneself. Therefore, it is not recommended for the beginner to plunge into complex subjects when translating German. A period of apprenticeship and some real hands-on experience are required to produce truly accurate German translations.

German lexicography is quite advanced, which means that good dictionaries are available to the German, particularly the German-English (either way) translator. One should have access to the major, latest-edition linguistic sources in one's area(s) of expertise, keeping in mind, of course, that some tend to be expensive.

There are usually good career opportunities for German translators in the United States, and plenty of freelancing opportunities. One has to be alert and make many contacts—with companies, law firms, government agencies, translation services, and so on. The more the better.

This writer feels quite confident that the opportunities for German translators in the U.S. will continue to grow at a good pace. This is due to the fact that those areas where there has been the greatest rate of growth—computers, telecommunications, international trade, life sciences, the automotive industry, scientific research, and so on—are areas in which Germany is either a producer or a major consumer, and the exchange of ideas and information between the two cultures is extremely vital. As all the aforementioned areas become more specialized and more advanced, the need for highly competent and accomplished translators in the two languages becomes more critical. As in any other language, there is never an overabundance of good German translators, and those who apply themselves and make a commitment to pursue a career of German translation seriously, with long-term objectives, stand to benefit from it.

French

French is a very popular language among language students in the United States, as it is around the world. For many years, French has been recognized as one of the world's leading languages, playing a dominant role in all fields of human endeavor, notably in the arts, sciences and technology, and has dominated such major areas as diplomatic relations among nations. With the decline of France as a world power after the two World Wars, however, French no longer enjoys the preeminence it once did, as American English has taken over many of its previous domains. Nonetheless, French continues to enjoy the status of being one of the languages most often translated, and both professional and freelance translators have been known to make a decent living practicing French translation.

There seem to be four primary geographical sources of French documents which require English translation. Those are: France, Francophone Canada, Haiti (where the line blurs between Creole and French), and the French-speaking parts of Africa.

France has made many gains in recent years in many areas, including high tech and international trade, in fact, too many areas to be enumerated in this limited space. The upshot of all of this is that French documents in a great many subjects require translation, and it behooves the practitioners of French translation to remain *au courant* in all matters pertaining to French technical terminology, neologisms, and so on.

Unlike many other languages, including such major languages as German and Japanese, French has been resisting the incursion of American English in such areas as computers, telecommunications, and advertisement. It is very important, therefore, when translating from English into French, to keep this in mind.

Another area that requires special attention is the difference between European and Canadian French. The influence of the English language is much greater in the case of Canada than France. This is due to two reasons: The main language of Canada itself is English, and Canada's only land neighbor is the United States. As a result, the infamous

English word "tax" can appear in Canada as either "impôt" or "tax," while in France it is more likely to be "impôt." The good news is that the Canadian government has developed many good French-English technical dictionaries and glossaries that are now available on a very impressive CD-ROM disk (see Appendix 1).

Matters become more complex when it comes to African or Haitian French, particularly the latter. It is highly recommended that one have personal experience in these varieties of the language, to make sure that local dialect, idioms, special expressions, are not missed.

Secondary sources of French would be such places as the French part of Switzerland, some Caribbean islands, and other places around the world where French is spoken. These, however, rarely come into play in the American translation marketplace.

There are excellent sources of French dictionaries and other technical references that make the job of French into/from English translation manageable. It is expected that more and more French language sources will be available on electronic media, and now is a good time to look into this kind of resources and consider adding them to your arsenal.

Russian

For some seventy years—1917 to the nineties—the relationship between the Soviet Union and the West was basically adversarial. In addition, Soviet society was culturally repressed, and there was hardly any free cultural and scientific exchange of ideas and knowledge between the Communist Bloc and the West. As a result, the West concentrated more on monitoring the Soviet empire and arming itself against it than on any peaceful pursuits, all of which was closely reflected in the kind of Russian-English translation work that took place during those years.

All of this changed radically around 1992. As the Cold War ended, Russia divested itself of its empire and started a new era as a nascent democracy seeking to do the things all democracies do—focusing on economic, legal and cultural issues rather than on the arms race. All of a sudden, those translators who had spent years translating from Russian into English found themselves tackling new fields—finance, insurance, and legal issues, to mention only a few. This radical change is the main source of the problems we encounter today in translating Russian into or from English. We translators are dealing with areas of human endeavor for which the Russian language did not develop sufficient terminology during the twentieth century, presenting a challenge for the Russians themselves and for anyone who translates from or into Russian.

The Russians, fortunately, have not been sitting on their hands for the past ten years. They are hard at work publishing new Russian-English and English-Russian dictionaries for business, law, computers, telecommunications and many other long neglected areas (see Appendix 1). The Russian language, always resourceful and resilient, is adjusting itself to the new realities. While Russia as a society is undergoing political unrest and a prolonged economic crisis, a great deal of interaction between Russia and the West (one of the best examples is the Russian-American joint space program) is taking place, which forces the two sides to participate in the transformation of the Russian language from a tool of Communist propaganda to a free-market economy language.

What persists through all these great changes are the inherent difficulties of the Russian language, by no means an easy language for English speakers to master. Unlike English, which has a rather uncomplicated and relaxed grammar, Russian grammar is fairly complex, especially with respect to the case endings for nouns and adjectives. The verbal system is also a stumbling block and if one does not come to a lucid understanding of the perfective and imperfective, the juggling of prefixes and numerous other subtleties, it is impossible to provide an accurate translation. Additionally, the list of irregular verbs and nouns is virtually endless. The case system in Russian also allows for more flexibility in terms of word order and it is imperative that the translator is aware of all of the possibilities in this regard. Changing the word order changes the focus of the sentence. Quite often a given word order would not be possible in English, but is quite common in Russian. Conversely, Russian natives who translate English into Russian are not always thoroughly familiar with all the nuances of the vast vocabulary of American English and particularly with colloquial American expressions, and they too often fail to convey the exact meaning of American texts.

In today's Russian-English translation environment our advice to translators in these languages is threefold: first, through extensive reading and verbal interaction keep in close touch with current developments in Russian and American English. A solid foundation in literature, both classical and contemporary, will fine-tune your sense of the precise meaning of each word and serve you well, regardless of the area of translation. Secondly, know the major reference works which are available in your area of expertise. Purchase as many as you can, or check their availability on line. Thirdly, master the finer points of Russian grammar, the verbal system, idioms and word order. Native Russian speakers must delve deeper into the complexities of both technical and colloquial American English. A truly accomplished translator is constantly reminded that this undertaking is not an eight-hour-a-day job, but a way of life.

Japanese

Japanese is one of the leading languages in today's world in science, technology, industry, and business. A great deal of technical, scientific and business documentation is generated in Japanese and translated in the United States. At the same time, similar English-language documentation is regularly being translated into Japanese. There are no exact statistics on this subject, but it is safe to assume that along with Spanish, German, French and Russian, Japanese is one of the top five most frequently translated languages in the United States.

A growing number of American college students choose Japanese for their foreign language requirement, or even major in this language. From all indications, given the popularity of the Japanese language and the continued economic importance of Japan, Japanese should continue to play a significant role on the international scene in the new century.

This means that developing one's skills as a Japanese translator is time well spent. The U.S. and Japan continue to interact in all areas of commerce, science and technology. Documentation and literature flow between the two countries in a steady stream. As the global village becomes more of a reality with every passing day, the interaction between Japanese and English intensifies, and requires an ever-growing volume of translation in real time.

Having said this, it comes as a surprise that Japanese-English lexicography is not well developed. There is a great shortage of subject-specific Japanese-English technical dictionaries, which makes it difficult to acquire working glossaries in certain areas. The few good

Japanese-English dictionaries available are very expensive, beyond the reach of many freelancers. This is a problem that cries out for a solution.

Another important consideration is the cultural differences between Japan and the West. There are two basic styles of writing in Japanese— polite, personal writing, and a more formal, precise, informative writing. For scientific texts, the second style is always used. For general topics one must choose between the two, and then stick to it.

The Japanese lexicon is extremely rich. This wealth of vocabulary can be divided into three main categories: (1) Words of Chinese origin, normally written in Kanji; (2) native Japanese words, written in Kanji or Kana; (3) Western loan words, normally written in Katakana unless they have been in Japan so long that their foreign origin has been forgotten (e.g., tobacco, often written as *tabako*). An understanding of these distinctions is helpful because it assists you in looking up new vocabulary.

Another aspect of Japanese text that requires special attention on the part of the translator is sentence and paragraph structure. The internal organization of a written text can be quite different in Japanese and English. One oriental writer has described English as "linear," with individual sentences moving a central idea forward one step at a time. Japanese writers who have not been influenced by Western notions of writing, however, sometimes adopt a "spiral" approach, repeating what has already been said as they gradually converge on their target. This can result in an extended paragraph with only one period and countless commas. The task of the translator is then to grasp what the target is, organize the paragraph into segments of suitable length, eliminate redundant portions, and render what is left into English.

Finally, Japanese and English do not operate in quite the same way. In Japanese, the verb comes at the end, while in English it is normally in the middle of the sentence. In fact, in translating Japanese into English, you have to jump back and forth to pick up the subject and the verb, and reorganize the whole thing. Most notorious is the disregard Japanese has for the plural form, for definite and indefinite articles, and for verb tenses, all of which are often ignored, and have to be figured out from the context.

Despite these difficulties, more than a few Westerners have already succeeded in pursuing an effective career as translators of this particular language pair, and the study of Japanese in the West is increasing.

Chinese

More than 1.2 billion people speak various dialects of Chinese in the People's Republic of China. Another six million speak Cantonese in Hong Kong. An additional 21 million or so Chinese live on Taiwan. And there are countless Chinese communities spread throughout Southeast Asia and the rest of the world. Despite differences in accent and dialect, the written language has historically been the unifying element of the widely dispersed Chinese community.

The written language, however, has split into two. Prior to World War Two, the Chinese characters in use throughout the Chinese-speaking world were essentially the same. In the 1950s, with the avowed goal of shortening the road to literacy, the Communist government began issuing simplified characters. Chinese communities outside mainland China, however, with the exception of Singapore, have for the most part continued to use traditional characters. For instance, in the United States, the vast majority of Chinese newspapers are still published in traditional characters—including the overseas edition of the 人民日报.

In addition, there are regional differences in terminology that go beyond the distinction between simplified and traditional characters. For instance, much of China refers to a bicycle as 自行车. A term often heard in Taiwan is 脚踏车 , while people whose primary dialect is Taiwanese/ Fukinese will be familiar with the terms 孔明车 and 铁马. Speakers of Cantonese often employ the term 单车..The fact that this list is by no means exhaustive provides some insight into the tremendous breadth of vocabulary in Chinese even for simple, everyday objects.

This diversity is reflected in a generation of modern technological vocabulary as well. A computer, even in a scientific text, may be referred to as a 计算机 or a 電腦 . A hard disk is sometimes referred to as an 硬盘 and sometimes as an 硬碟 . Software is known as 软件 and 软體. The list goes on and on.

The bottom line is that, to be competitive, a Chinese-English translator needs to be able to read both simplified and traditional characters fluently, and have a sensitivity for the rapid, sometimes overlapping coining of new words in the Chinese language.

In recent years a growing number of major American companies, as well as other companies from around the world, have been setting up operations in China. The need for technical translations from and into Chinese has been growing accordingly, and many experts maintain that

China will be playing a major global role in the next century. All of this means that the need for Chinese-language translators and interpreters will continue to grow, and if anyone is looking for a language to pursue as a career, Chinese certainly is a good choice.

Italian

The volume of Italian translation in the English-speaking world is not nearly as great as, say, German or French. Nevertheless, Italian is one of the world's major languages, and there is hardly a field of human endeavor where Italian influence has not been felt. This is true of everything from fine arts to science and technology, from fashion to high tech, and other fields too numerous to mention. Whether or not one should pursue a full-time career as an Italian translator in the English-speaking world is hard to say. Certainly there is always a need for Italian freelancers, if only on a part-time basis, and there are indeed people who have successfully pursued full-time careers as Italian translators in countries like England and the U.S. But clearly their numbers are not legion. As a general rule, if one happens to know Italian and has a flair for translation, it is certainly worthwhile to sharpen one's translation skills. If, on the other hand, one chooses to major in Italian in an American college or university with a view to making Italian translation a career, one should first examine the range of opportunities.

We would be remiss not to mention at this point that Italians have always excelled in the field of translation. Italian lexicography is excellent, and the practitioner of Italian-English translation has the advantage of outstanding general and technical dictionaries and references (see Appendix 1). The kinship between the Italian language and the rest of Western culture, and the distinction of this language as arguably the most beautiful of European languages, make the task of Italian translation a unique challenge and a delight.

Portuguese

Portuguese is a language spoken by close to 200 million people around the world. The great majority of these people live in Brazil, while only some 10 million live in Portugal itself. Most of the documents translated from Portuguese into English or vice versa originate in Brazil. Brazilian Portuguese differs from European Portuguese in several respects, including several sound changes and some differences in verb conjugation and syntax. Example: object pronouns occur before the verb in Brazilian Portuguese, but after the verb in European Portuguese. Brazilian Portuguese seems to be developing at a faster rate than its progenitor, and the gap between the two continues to widen. This impacts on the work of the translator, who has to be aware of the differences between the two.

Portuguese-English lexicography is not nearly as advanced as that of other major Romance languages, which hampers the work of the translator in this language pair. Nor is Portuguese technical terminology as well developed in many areas as, say, French. This too makes it difficult at times to do technical translation into or from Portuguese. Nevertheless, Portuguese is a major language representing a major culture and a large segment of the world's population, and it is to be expected that its lexicography and technical vocabulary will continue to develop in the years ahead.

The volume of Portuguese translation in the English-speaking world is not nearly as great as, say, German or Spanish. Nevertheless, the need for Portuguese translation is by no means insignificant. Certainly there is a need for Portuguese freelancers, if only on a part-time basis, and there are indeed people who have successfully pursued full-time careers as Portuguese translators in places like England and the U.S. But clearly their numbers are not legion. As a general rule, if one happens to know Portuguese and has a flair for translation, it is certainly worthwhile to sharpen one's translation skills in this language. If, on the other hand, one chooses to major in Portuguese in an American college or university with a view to making Portuguese translation a career, one should first examine the range of opportunities.

Arabic

Arabic is one of the world's major languages. It is the official language of 18 countries in North Africa and the Middle East, and the mother tongue of at least 165 million people. It is also the language of the *Qur'an*, which makes it the second language for millions of Indians, Iranians, Indonesians and other inhabitants of largely Muslim nations, and the holy tongue of all of the above. Historically, it has been one of the major repositories and catalysts of world culture.

The conscientious Arabic translator is aware of the generic difficulties in working with two languages as different from each other as English and Arabic. First, there are vast cultural differences between a Western language such as English and a Semitic language like Arabic. One cannot translate these languages without paying attention to these cultural differences. In a way, translating between two disparate cultures like these often necessitates explication in addition to direct rendition of words and phrases.

The difference between the alphabets of English and Arabic create other translation issues. Some characters used and sounds pronounced in one language do not exist in the other. Thus, Arabic characters create the problem of correct spelling of personal, place and other proper names, compounded by the absence of some basic consonants in Arabic, such as P or V. This writer once came across the name "Davy Crockett" spelled in Arabic, which sounded like "Daffy Crookit." It took several minutes to figure out who this historical personality was.

As with other languages, translators working with Arabic must be aware of the nuances of the language to correctly address the reader's expectations of style and structure. For example, texts in Arabic tend to use semantic repetition, which is the occurrence of synonymous words in one sentence, and also often repeat the same word or phrase throughout the text. While this is a fault in English, translators must recognize it as part of the language's style. Arabic also uses different grammatical rules and structures than English, such as using verb-subject-object word order rather than the English subject-verb-object word order. A skilled translator must be able to recognize and imitate these linguistic nuances to produce an accurate translation.

In addition, Arabic is in the process of developing technical terminologies for new areas such as computers and telecommunications, and the precise term is not always readily available. Many words commonly used in Arabic may actually be adopted from other languages, the same way that English borrows words from French, Greek, or Latin. Add to this the fact that there are several spoken Arabic dialects that are not always mutually intelligible, such as Syrian and Egyptian, and the fact that even the official written Arabic has different terms and usages in different Arab countries. What all this means is that very often the Arabic translator needs to engage in some additional research to produce a truly accurate translation of Arabic into or from English. When all is said and done, however, meeting the challenge of translating Arabic accurately and elegantly can be a source of great satisfaction.

The volume of Arabic translation in the English-speaking world is not nearly as great as, say, that of German or Spanish. Nevertheless, there is always a need for accomplished Arabic translators. Whether or not one should pursue a full-time career as an Arabic translator in the English-speaking world is hard to say. Certainly there is always a need for Arabic freelancers, if only on a part-time basis, and there are indeed people who have been successfully pursuing full-time careers as Arabic translators in countries such as England and the U.S. As a general rule, if one happens to know Arabic and has a flair for translation, it is certainly worthwhile to sharpen one's translation skills. If, on the other hand, one chooses to major in Arabic in an American college or university with a view to making Arabic translation a career, one should first examine the range of opportunities.

Hebrew

Of all the languages discussed in this chapter, Hebrew is the only one that is not spoken by a particularly large population. Roughly six million people in Israel speak Hebrew, and less than a million in the rest of the world. But the importance of Hebrew on the world scene should not be measured quantitatively, but rather qualitatively. The Hebrew language represents one of the world's major cultures and civilizations, at the center of which one finds the Hebrew Scriptures, and at its most recent stages of development a fast growing and developing contemporary language vigorously engaged in all facets of culture, science and technology.

Hebrew as a modern language owes much of its existence to Eliezer Ben-Yehuda, who beginning in the 1880's, worked tirelessly to introduce new words into the ancient language and advocated the speaking of Hebrew everywhere. When the new state of Israel was born and Hebrew was still struggling to take its place among the languages of the world, the celebrated writer Arthur Koestler compared the attempt to modernize Hebrew as "attaching parts from a Cadillac to a Canaanite chariot." One thing Koestler suggested at the time was to give up the Hebrew script and use Latin characters instead, as was done by Atatürk in Turkey earlier in the century. Instead, much to many people's amazement, Ben Yehuda's vision became reality and Hebrew did become a "full service" modern language even though it did not give up its traditional Hebrew alphabet. It is safe to say that it is easier today to translate Hebrew into and from English than it was sixty-five years ago, because literally thousands of basic words and technical terms which did not exist in Hebrew back then have now become part of the everyday language and the technical vocabulary.

This is not to say that translating Hebrew into or from English is easy. Hebrew is not a European, but rather a Semitic language. Its cousins are Arabic, Aramaic, and other languages of the Middle East. Like Arabic, it operates in a linguistic and cultural world different from the West, notwithstanding the great involvement of present-day Israel with Western civilization. One cannot translate a text directly from or into Hebrew without explicating certain words, terms and phrases, or finding suitable equivalents. As happens today with other languages, very often in doing a technical translation from English into Hebrew, one is forced to keep a certain English term in the Hebrew so as not to lose the meaning. These are some of the challenges facing the practitioner in this particular language pair.

Most Israelis are quite at home with English, and much of Israeli business is conducted in English, which reduces the need for Hebrew-English translation, a phenomenon similar to India, where English is the second official language after Hindi. Pursuing a full-time career as a Hebrew translator in the English-speaking world may not be the most sensible choice of career. But certainly if one is equally at home in Hebrew and English and has a flair for translation, it makes good sense to pursue translation in this language pair as a sideline.

Some final thoughts: This chapter has covered the most salient languages of "technically active" language groups, namely Germanic, Romance, Slavic, Sino-Japanese, and Semitic. There are additional translation problems specific to other languages within each of these groups, which hopefully will be treated in future editions. Also, there are other important languages in Europe, Asia, and Africa which were not discussed here: Turkish, Greek, Korean, Hindi, Farsi, Swahili and Amharic come to mind. It should come as no surprise to anyone if in a future handbook, some of these languages will be discussed.

Today, as always, if a talented translator does not get any assignments, it is the fault of the translator.

6. TRANSLATION TECHNIQUES

The first five chapters of this books were devoted to the background, requisites, and problems of translation in general and certain languages in particular. In other words, the more theoretical aspects of translation. The rest of this handbook is devoted to the "nuts and bolts" of the translation craft and business, the techniques, equipment, tools, and so on. The last part of the book consists of appendices which provide extensive information on dictionaries and where to find them, current sources of translation work, translation study programs, accreditation for translators, and publications of interest to translators. The present chapter discusses the best ways to handle translation assignments.

Preliminary Considerations

You are given a text to translate. Before you commit yourself to doing any work on it, you must ask yourself a few preliminary questions. They are:

1. Is the text legible?
2. Am I familiar enough with the subject to tackle it?
3. Do I have the linguistic resources (dictionaries, human contacts) to decipher unfamiliar words?
4. Is the text complete, or are there any missing parts?
5. Can I do it within the requested timeframe?
6. Do I have a good reason for doing it (doing it as a learning experience, or because you enjoy it, or to help a friend, or because you are properly compensated for doing it)?

Once you have answered all the above questions to your own satisfaction, you are ready to proceed with the translation.

Questions to be asked before undertaking a translation assignment:

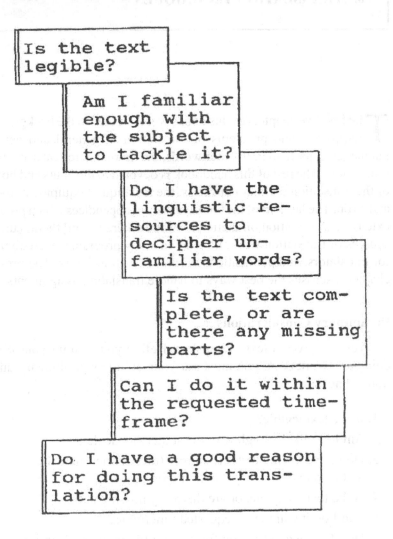

Is the text
legible?

Am I familiar
enough with
the subject
to tackle it?

Do I have the
linguistic re-
sources to
decipher un-
familiar words?

Is the text com-
plete, or are
there any missing
parts?

Can I do it within
the requested time-
frame?

Do I have a good reason
for doing this trans-
lation?

Effective Approaches

There is no single effective approach to translation, and over time translators develop personal techniques that enhance the quality and the speed of their translation. No one set of rules applies equally to everyone, but there are certain methods and means of translation which can help almost any translator achieve greater accuracy and output. The following is a review of some of the key techniques that are becoming almost universal among professional translators.

The first and foremost question a translator must deal with today is what kind of equipment to use in the process of translating. In the days of the pen and the typewriter this question was much less crucial. Today, however, translation has become almost totally dependent on computers, for several good reasons: (a) Word processing allows far greater flexibility in producing text than any other contemporary means. The output of most translators has been tripled and quadrupled through the use of computers; (b) Computers allow text to be stored on a disk and reprinted or modified later on, a function which is invaluable in the translation field; (c) Clients nowadays are getting used to asking for translation on disk, since it allows them to edit, reprint, modify and enhance the physical appearance of a document; (d) If more than one translator is involved in a given translation project, the text from the various translators can be entered by an editor on one disk and equalized or manipulated as necessary, without having to redo any particular portion thereof.

In addition, it is becoming more common every day to use electronic means such as a modem, fax or e-mail to transmit and receive text. These tools are no longer a luxury. Their cost has been coming down, and more and more translators are acquiring them. Many people today are saying they cannot imagine how translators were ever able to manage without them. The answer is very simple: manage we did, but it took us ten days to two weeks to do what we can now receive, translate and deliver in two or three days.

The next question when approaching a translation assignment is: Am I qualified to do this particular translation? Only an honest answer will do. If one is not sure, then chances are one should not tackle that particular task. One must feel confident about a particular assignment if the results are to be satisfactory. The exception to this rule is a case where a client cannot find anyone else to do that particular job, and for some good reason is either willing to take a chance or to receive less than a complete and fully accurate rendition. In such a case it should be made clear between translator and client that the translation is not legally binding.

Once the commitment is made to proceed with the job, the translator will spend some time going over the entire document—even if it is book-length—and do a realistic assessment of the following points:

1. How long will it take to translate the document?
2. What reference tools are needed to get it done?
3. What kind of preliminary steps are needed prior to the actual work of translating?
4. What special problems are related to the document, such as legibility of blurred or poorly copied text or difficult handwriting?
5. Does the document contain text in a language or languages other than the main source language, and, if so, can the translator handle that language?

Regarding the question of time, one can do a quick estimate of the length of the document by averaging words per line, times lines per page, times number of pages. An experienced translator has a pretty good idea of the number of words per hour he or she can translate. This is an essential feature of undertaking a professional translation job, since most clients have tight deadlines and tend to give repeat business to those translators known for keeping to their deadlines.

A freelancer labors 16 hours a day to avoid having to work for someone else 8 hours a day.

Document assessment prior to doing a translation:

```
How long will
it take to
translate the
document?
```

```
What reference
tools are needed
to get it done?
```

```
What preliminary
steps are needed
prior to the
actual work of
translating?
```

```
What special prob-
lems are related to
the document, such
as legibility or
blurred or poorly
copied text or dif-
ficult handwriting?
```

```
Does the document con-
tain text in a language
other than the main source
language, and, if so, can
the translator handle this
language?
```

As for reference tools, if, for example, one is given a document about telecommunications, one should make use of one's own resources in that field and/or borrow from other sources whatever one needs to accomplish the task.

Preliminary steps prior to actual translation can include a consultation with an expert in a specialized technical field regarding a difficult term, phrase, paragraph or concept which the translator does not feel comfortable with. Having access to such experts is one of the translator's most cherished assets. It can make all the difference in the world between a correct and effective translation and one that misses the main point of the entire text. Another preliminary step is a trip to the local, regional or even specialized library to do some research on the subject.

The problem of legibility should be identified before one begins the task, not after. Sometimes the problem may start in the middle of the document and be so severe as to render the translation of the first part useless. In that case, the translator may have wasted a great deal of time. Sometimes the problem is minor, and does not affect the overall outcome of the translation. In other cases, the client may decide to proceed with the translation and simply put the designation [illegible] (between brackets rather than parentheses) wherever a word or part of the text cannot be deciphered.

Unbeknownst to client and translator, when a translation job is first assigned, there may be portions of text inside the source document in a language other than the main language of the document. This can happen in commercial, scientific and scholarly documents. It even happens in Tolstoy's novel War and Peace, when the author starts using French instead of Russian. This too should be detected prior to commencing the translation work, and a decision has to be made as to: (a) Does that text need to be translated? (b) Can the translator handle it? (c) Is it necessary to assign it to another translator?

Once all this preliminary work has been done, one is ready to proceed with the actual translation work.

Depending on the particular text, one should either start translating at this point, or, in the case of a text containing highly specialized terminology which may send the translator on frequent trips to the dictionary, one should first go through the document and make a list of as many unknown or uncertain terms as possible, and then spend some time looking them up and making a word list. This technique saves a

Some Common Misconceptions about Translation and Translators

1. Anyone with two years of high school language (or anyone who lived in another country for three years during early childhood) can translate.

2. There's no difference between translation, transcription, and transliteration.

3. A good translator doesn't need any reference literature.

4. Translators will soon be replaced by computers.

5. Translators don't need to know how to spell, since they can use the spell checker on their computer.

6. A good translator gets it right the first time, without any editing or proofreading.

7. Good translators are a dime a dozen.

8. If you can type in a foreign language then you are an accomplished translator.

9. Translators can translate both ways just as easily.

10. A 100-page technical manual that took four months and three persons to write can be translated into another language by one translator in two days.

great deal of time, since once a list is completed it is much easier to sail through the text, and the time spent initially on making the list is very short compared to the time wasted on repeated interruptions to look up words. Moreover, by first mastering the more difficult terminology of the text, one gains a much better understanding of the subject and is certain to produce a better translation. From the very start, make it a habit to compile word lists and glossaries of subject-specific terminologies, and keep it in a computer database program for future reference. In time, these lists will become your most valuable translation tool.

One should also follow good work habits. Some translators, particularly those engaged in freelance work, tend to overdo it, especially during their "busy season," when they can generate a large income during a relatively short period of time. They will go for twelve or more hours a day, and before they know it they will start complaining of stiffness in the neck and shoulders, blurred vision, and fatigue. One should not translate more than eight hours a day. Six is ideal. Eight is tolerable, provided one takes a few short ten to fifteen minute breaks. Ten is pushing it. Over ten is definitely hazardous to your health.

Before you get ready to submit your translation, go over it again using the following checklist:

Omissions. Did you fail to translate any particular word or phrase, or even paragraph?

Format. Does your format follow the original (breaking into paragraphs, for instance)?

Mistranslations. Did you mistranslate any particular word?

Unknown words. Were there words you were not able to translate which you would like to explore further?

Meaning. Did you miss the meaning of any phrase or sentence?

Spelling. Did you misspell any word which the spell-check function on your computer did not catch?

Grammar. Did you make any grammatical mistakes?

Punctuation. Did you mispunctuate or miss any punctuation marks?

Clarity. Did you fail to clearly convey the meaning of any particular part of the text?

Consistency. Did you call something by one name and then by another without any good reason?

"Sound-alike" words. Did you mistranslate a word because it looks or sounds like the word in your target language but in reality has a different meaning?

Style. Are you satisfied with the way your translation reflects the style of the original text (for example, the original is written in a clear, direct style, while the translation sounds more complex and indirect?)

This checklist is by no means exhaustive, but it does cover the main areas a translator must pay attention to.

As was already explained, your personal computer is your best friend when it comes to translating, editing, and producing a final copy. One can learn a few basic commands, say, in WordPerfect or Microsoft Word, and start using the computer. But there is much more to software than entering, deleting and inserting text. The better acquainted with software you become, the more it will help you with translation. Learn how to do columns and tables, how to use special technical and scientific symbols, do graphic functions, use the spell-check and the thesaurus, create data bases for glossaries and for your own administrative records, and you will tackle a great variety of technical text in many fields at a speed that will amaze you. Remember: speed in translation is the most important thing next to language proficiency. Without it you will not be profitable, and you will be overrun by the competition. With an established record of fast accurate translation you can write your own ticket.

After a few years of using the computer you may want to consider dictation. Personally, I prefer a mix of PC and dictation. When I have an unusually long job and not enough time to do it in, I may revert to dictation. Otherwise, I prefer word-processing. One could argue that by dictating one gets more done and earns more, but there are other things to consider, such as the cost of transcription, the need to edit transcription, and the better control one has over writing than speaking. Some of us are natural speakers; others are writers.

One continues to develop translation techniques over time. One of the most wonderful things about translation, in my opinion, is the fact that your mind is never idle, never in a rut, but rather always being challenged by new tasks, new subjects, new knowledge, and the need to keep up with new developments in language, with different fields of human knowledge, and with the events of the world. As a translator in the Washington area since the late seventies, I have found myself in the middle of world events, beginning with the peace treaty between Egypt and Israel in 1979, when I met Begin, Sadat and Carter, and, more recently, in my daily dealings with events in post-Cold War Eastern Europe, with a strife-torn Middle East, the famine in Somalia, the new North American Free Trade Agreement (NAFTA) between the United States, Canada and Mexico, and the growing involvement of the U.S. space program with the space programs of other nations. Very few people cover as broad an area as a translator. Every day we in the translation business find new challenges, and have to solve new problems. As a result, we are always developing new techniques and finding new answers.

ドₗₐを矢印方向に瞬間的に通過させるのみでバ
ーコード1aを読取れる赤外線フォトセンサー等
…からなる読取手段3が設けられている。また、に
は中央部には段数表示手段である液晶ディスプレ
65　イ（LCD）4が設けられている。

　前記ディスプレイ4の左側P1には、攻撃キー
（バトルキー）5aとパワーアップキー6a、右
側P2には攻撃キー5bとパワーアップキー6b
がそれぞれ設けられている。

70　また、ディスプレイ4の下辺（手前）側には攻
撃側か守備側かの指示や攻撃表示などを示す亘球

明らかに，大きく異なる結果が生じる可能性がある。
GATTの交渉は，農業を含む交渉のすべての分野で成功
するかもしれない。世界貿易は1990年代央から年に7%以
上拡大することもあり得る（これは近年よりも遅い拡大で
あるが，まだ1960年代の年平均9%より低い）。工業園にお
ける多角的繊維協定による規制の廃止及び農業補助金の引
下げは，途上国にとって大きな利益となり得る。あるいは，
成長促進の勢いは，西半球，欧州及び太平洋における域内
貿易の一層急速な拡大から生じるかもしれない。外国投資
によって設立される会社の多くが貿易志向であるので，最
近このような投資が加速していることは後年，貿易の一層
の拡大をもたらすかもしれない。

　しかし，もし1992年プロジェクトが欧州における保護主
義の拡大をもたらし，他の地域が報復すれば，世界生産の
拡大は低下するかもしれない。貿易戦争から生じる損失は，
自由化を前提とする見通しと比較した場合，世界生産の

***Top**, an example of poor-quality Japanese text to be translated
into English; **bottom**, good quality Japanese text.*

HEBREW		ARABIC				GREEK		RUSSIAN	
א aleph	' '	ا	ا		alif	'	A α alpha a	А а	a
ב beth	b, bb	ب	ب	ﺒ	ﺐ bā	b	B β beta b	Б б	b
ג gimel	g, gh	ت	ﺘ	ﺛ	ﺚ tā	t	В в	v
ד daleth	d, dh	ث	ﺜ	ﺛ	ﺚ thā	th	Γ γ gamma g, n	Г г	g
ה he	h	ج	ﺟ	ﺠ	ﺞ jīm	j	Δ δ delta d	Д д	d
ו waw	w	ح	ﺣ	ﺤ	ﺢ hā	ḥ	E ε epsilon e	Е е	e
ז zayin	z	خ	ﺧ	ﺨ	ﺦ khā	kh	Z ζ zeta z	Ж ж	zh
ח heth	ḥ	د	ﺪ		dāl	d	H η eta ē	З з	z
ט teth	ṭ	ذ	ﺬ		dhāl	dh	Θ θ theta th	И и ĭ i, ī
י yodh	y	ر	ﺮ		rā	r	I ι iota i	К к	k
כ ך kaph	k, kh	ز	ﺰ		zāy	z	К κ kappa k	Л л	l
ל lamedh	l	س	ﺳ	ﺴ	ﺲ sīn	s	Λ λ lambda l	М м	m
מ ם mem	m	ش	ﺷ	ﺸ	ﺶ shīn	sh	М μ mu m	Н н	n
נ ן nun	n	ص	ﺻ	ﺼ	ﺺ ṣād	ṣ	N ν nu n	О о	o
ס samekh	s	ض	ﺿ	ﻀ	ﺾ ḍād	ḍ	Ξ ξ xi x	П п	p
ע ayin	'	ط	ﻃ	ﻄ	ﻂ ṭā	ṭ	O ο omicron o	Р р	r
פ ף pe	p, ph	ظ	ﻇ	ﻈ	ﻆ ẓā	ẓ	Π π pi p	С с	s
צ ץ sadhe	ṣ	ع	ﻋ	ﻌ	ﻊ 'ayn	'	Ρ ρ rho r, rh	Т т	t
ק qoph	q	غ	ﻏ	ﻐ	ﻎ ghayn	gh	Σ σ ς sigma s	У у	u
ר resh	r	ف	ﻓ	ﻔ	ﻒ fā	f	Τ τ tau t	Ф ф	f
ש sin	s	ق	ﻗ	ﻘ	ﻖ qāf	q	Υ υ upsilon y, u	Х х	kh
ש shin	sh	ك	ﻛ	ﻜ	ﻚ kāf	k	Φ φ phi ph	Ц ц	ts
ת taw	t, th	ل	ﻟ	ﻠ	ﻞ lām	l	X χ chi ch	Ч ч	ch
		م	ﻣ	ﻤ	ﻢ mīm	m	Ψ ψ psi ps	Ш ш	sh
		ن	ﻧ	ﻨ	ﻦ nūn	n	Ω ω omega ō	Щ щ	shch
		ه	ﻫ	ﻬ	ﻪ hā	h'		Ъ ъ	"
		و	ﻮ		wāw	w		Ы ы	y
		ي	ﻳ	ﻴ	ﻲ yā	y		Ь ь	'
								Э э	e
								Ю ю	yu
								Я я	ya

Whatever language you translate in, it is good to have an alphabet chart on hand in case you run into non-Roman letters.

7. TRANSLATION, COMPUTERS, AND THE INTERNET

Digital technology as it relates to translation and to almost anything else in today's world is in a constant state of change. In the nearly three years since this handbook was last revised, computers have become even more dominant in the translation craft. Most work is now being transmitted by e-mail attachment rather than by fax, which is beginning to disappear. The Internet has become a routine tool for translators—from work search to word search. And a growing number of translators has become involved in the translation of such computer-based material as websites, a process now generally referred to as localization. All this has resulted in this newly revised and expanded chapter that looks at all the above developments and how they benefit or fail to benefit translators.

Once you have read this chapter you will be glad to find out that one thing has not changed, which should come as no surprise: translation continues to be a human, rather than a machine function. Computers are no closer now to replacing human translation than they were three years ago, or at any other time in the past. Notwithstanding the great benefits translators are deriving from the digital revolution, computers continue to be the tools, rather than the decision-makers of the translation process.

Computers and Related Equipment

As was mentioned before, not too long ago a translator would use a pen or a typewriter to translate. In 1980, for example, the ultimate text-producing tool in the world was the IBM Selectric electric typewriter, which we thought we would proudly bequeath to our children and grandchildren. All of this changed forever with the birth of the word processor, and more specifically, the PC, or Personal Computer, which is getting better every year, as if it were a magical tool with boundless possibilities. Certainly the PC has changed the lives of translators, increasing their productivity and profitability three- and fourfold, and enabling them to receive and transmit work, look for answers to linguistic questions, communicate around the world, and take advantage of computer-assisted tools (see below) that in certain cases can save a great deal of time and effort.

Bare Minimum Hardware and the Wish List

The electronic age offers a great deal more than the word-processor. There is the fax, modem, optical scanner, e-mail, various types of translation software such as translation memory, and last but not least, the Internet. No doubt, it all seems quite overwhelming. Which is the best tool? How much should I spend? How much do I need?

Perhaps the best way to start is by asking two questions: What is the bare minimum a translator needs to get started, and, if money were no object, what would be my wish list of electronic equipment?

The first thing you need to get is a good, current personal computer. This is a must. The question is whether to get a desktop PC, or a portable laptop or notebook? The desktop PC is bigger and heavier; it has a larger, easier-to-read screen, and an easier-to-use keyboard. The notebook, on the other hand, only weighs a few pounds, can fit in your briefcase, can be used anywhere (it has a rechargeable battery that gives you several hours of use), and, like a toothbrush, becomes a truly personal item.

To me as a translator and as a writer, the notebook is the best of all

A poster from Switzerland

The German text reads:
"Computers help us solve problems—problems we didn't have before!"

possible worlds. On the other hand, many translators prefer a desktop PC for all sorts of reasons, not all of which are known to me. Since I have access to both, it's hard for me to judge. My suggestion to you is to check around, try both, and make your own decision. But again, a translator without a computer in this day and age is like a painter without brushes. One more thing: The standard computer for translators is the PC, or Personal Computer. The Mac, favored by graphics people, is not nearly as widely used in our field, so we will concentrate here on the former.

Whether you use a PC or a laptop, be sure to have sufficient data storage space on your hard drive, as well as an external storage device that can be plugged into your computer and be used to download files as backups. Over time, you will be saving a large number of documents and other data such as terminology that will help you with future assignments, and you will need the storage space. Another method of saving data is by using CDs, for which you will need a CD burner on your computer.

If you use a laptop, be sure to get a wireless Internet connection for your computer. This will enable you to use your computer in many more places than your desk, where your computer is stationary. As of this writing, the dominant PCs as well as laptops on the market are Hewlett Packard, Dell, and Toshiba, so when you shop for one be sure to check these particular brands.

As for printers, I would recommend the HP (Hewlett Packard) family of printers. Some of the larger models are true work horses, and are ideal for printing long documents. For shorter documents, and for all-around versatility that includes black-and-white and color printing, photo printing, copying, scanning and faxing, the HP All-in-One series, such as the 2400, is ideal. It saves you the need to buy a separate scanner or fax, and does multitasking.

As a translator, you will be making extensive use of your e-mail service. you will send and receive documents by e-mail attachment, and you will communicate with your clients and translation providers by e-mail.

> When purchasing a computer and/or peripherals, first decide exactly what configuration you are looking for. Then look around at retail outlets, mail-order catalogues, and Internet sources. Get the best deal you can get when you are ready to make a purchase.

What Kinds of Software?

The English-language word processing software most commonly used in translation as of this writing is Microsoft Word. As a translator, you also need word processing capability in your other language/s of expertise. MS Word provides capablilities in a variety of foreign languages, covering most European and many non-European languages (see Appendix 3). If, for example, you translate frequently from English into German, you may want to consider purchasing the MS Word version produced in Germany. However, you should be able to make do with the German capabilities of the U.S. MS Word. There are also many other non-English word-processing programs that are MS Word-compatible and very versatile. If you work in an alphabet other than Roman, such as Chinese or Hebrew, and have to deal with non-Roman accents and other symbols, you may want to consider getting software made specifically for those languages.

Some translators use the SDL Trados software for foreign language text. This is primarily a Translation Memory software (see page 86) used by advanced translators for large projects.

If your translation work has graphic components, such as illustrations, photos etc., or includes book-sized projects, you may need graphics and desktop software such as PageMaker or InDesign, Quark for desktop publishing, and PhotoShop for graphics.

Machine Translation vs. Human Translation

Machine Translation, or MT, is the term used to describe translation performed by a computer software program, as an alternative to human translation (HT), performed by a human translator. Machine Translation belongs in the area of artificial intelligence. Artificial intelligence is the branch of computer science that deals with using computers to simulate human thinking. Its purpose is to create programs that can solve problems *creatively,* rather than merely respond to commands. In other words, to operate just like the human brain.

In the late 1950s programmers in organizations such as the U.S. Air Force believed that computers would soon be programmed to accept human language input and translate it into English or into any other language. During the ensuing 50 years, many millions of dollars were spent by the Air Force and by other entities in the hope of enabling computers to replace human translation. So far, the results have been quite limited, for two main reasons: (a) while computers have a seemingly unlimited capacity for processing data, they are far from being able to think creatively like human beings; and (b) human language is not merely a collection of signs and symbols that can be easily programmed, manipulated, and computerized. This is true of human language used not only in poetry and philosophy, but also in technical subjects, in which language expresses thought processes far more complicated than merely "one plus one equals two."

Many people today continue to maintain that computers will soon replace translators. Most of those people are not translation experts. In fact, hardly any of them are. Some point to the fact that computers have already replaced typists and secretaries and reduced the work force of many companies. All this reminds me of a remark by George Bernard Shaw, according to which a monkey could write *Hamlet* if it managed to hit all the right keys on the typewriter. Very few translators can lay claim to creating literary works on the order of *Hamlet*, but lumping translators with typists and office support staff is missing the whole point of translation. As long as language continues to communicate more than the immediate literal meaning of words, as long as there are shades of meaning that keep changing all the time, as long as people have to make value judgments about the meaning and intent of a text, one will continue to need human translators to get the job done.

Example of Machine Translation from Russian into English

Raw machine translation: A contemporary airport is the involved complex of engineer constructions and techniques, for arrangement of which the territory, measured sometimes is required by thousands of hectares (for example the Moscow Airport Domodedovo, Kennedy's New York airport).

Text edited by humans: The modern airport is an elaborate complex of engineering structures and technical devices requiring a large territory, which, in some places, measures thousands of hectares (for instance, Domodedovo Airport in Moscow or Kennedy Airport in New York).

In recent years several companies in the U.S. and around the world have produced software designed to translate from one language into another. This software varies from a very basic word finder for the tourist, to complex programs for translating technical and scientific data. Some of the latter range in price from as low as $250 to as high as $250,000, and have been sold to governments and international organizations. One important lesson, however, has been learned by both the makers of those programs and their consumers. Machine translation does not replace human translation. At best, the former can achieve around 60 percent accuracy, when the goal is as close to 100 percent as possible. Consequently, the expectations regarding MT have been modified, and it is now recognized that to achieve full accuracy such translations must be post-edited by a human translator.

All of the above notwithstanding, Machine Translation does have its uses. Certain limited language environments do allow for machine translation. One example is the Canadian weather bureau, which transmits weather reports in both English and French. The number of words involved in the daily weather report is very limited, and can be easily programmed into a computer for translation from one language into another. Another example is official forms which contain simple basic questions. An organization such as NATO can have forms put out in ten different languages and set up a program to automatically translate each form into those languages. A third example is the Caterpillar company in Illinois that sells its agricultural machinery around the world and maintains operation manuals in various languages. This company has invested millions in its in-house translation software which allows it to update and modify its technical literature in a cost-effective way. In all of the above examples the software was customized for one particular work environment where repetition is the common denominator.

Another use of machine translation is for processing a large body of a foreign language text to find out what the gist of it is, rather than to achieve a fully accurate translation, in order to decide whether or not to select parts of it for accurate (viz., human) translation. This process is only partially reliable.

Translators for the most part are not fond of post-editing machine translation. Often the pay is not adequate, and the work can be harder and more time consuming than translating directly from the original.

This certainly applies to freelancers, but also to in-house translators who are on a salary. At the present time the ones who benefit the most from machine translation are not those who buy such services, but rather the companies who develop and manufacture the software and the translators who work on those machine translation projects either as developers of the programs or editors of the machine-translated text. In other words, machine translation has not made translation cheaper for the average consumer of translation services, and therefore does not pose a real threat to translators.

Translation Memory

One computer tool commonly used today in the area of computer-assisted-translation (CAT) is called translation memory. Here sentences and other parts of translated texts are stored and can be used again when the same or similar translation is required. This tool is best applied to major projects, such as automotive operation manuals that are updated or modified on a regular basis, whereby most of the text remains the same while certain sentences and/or paragraphs are changed.

While this tool has its practical uses, it has been hyped beyond its actual application and has been promoted as a universal aid for translators in nearly all types of translation. Here one should be careful not to invest in this kind of software unless one has a clear ongoing use for it. This applies both to individual translators and to translation companies, since in both cases only a small percentage of the work done is of the above-described kind.

Furthermore, as in the case of machine translation and localization (see below), here too the tools are far from able to accomplish their stated goals, and are still being improved upon. Translation memory is certainly not human memory, and while it does work part of the time, human memory remains irreplaceable.

Localization

Localization is defined as:

the process of creating or adapting a product to a specific

locale, i.e., to the language, cultural context, conventions and market requirements of a specific target market. With a properly localized product a user can interact with this product using his or her own language and cultural conventions. It also means that all user-visible text strings and all user documentation (printed and electronic) use the language and cultural conventions of the user. Finally, the properly localized product meets all regulatory and other requirements of the user's country or region.

Clearly, this definition takes us out of the strict realm of translation into the domain of computer programming and international business. It alludes primarily to the localization of websites (as well as software) in other languages and cultures. Two other terms often used in conjunction with localization are internationalization and globalization. The first refers to the preparation of computer text to be used in localization in such a way that it meets the requirements of the target language and culture. Globalization generally refers to both processes together, namely, internationalization and localization.

With the fast proliferation of websites and the rapid growth of many kinds of computer software, a growing number of translation companies have ventured into the field of localization, and more than a few computer hardware-and software-producing companies (including giants like IBM and Microsoft) have turned to the field of translation as a function of localization.

Thus, localization has been presenting translators with new opportunities and some difficult questions. On the one hand, there is a huge volume of text these days in website and software development that necessitates multilingual translation. On the other hand, for a translator to become involved in localization a specialized knowledge of computers is usually required, since website and software localization requires not only language translation but also adaptation of computer commands to the requirements of the target language. Hence, a translator may want to carefully consider how far he or she may wish to become involved

---

The Internet has opened up opportunities for translators unlike anything before in human history.

in technical computer work that requires skills and training beyond the scope of actual translation work.

It should be mentioned that localization in the sense of translating a text and adapting it to another culture existed long before the computer age. Thus, for example, an American advertisement company in the pre-computer era that planned an international ad campaign for a company such as Coca Cola, had to study the cultures of other countries and customize the ads not only in terms of the target language, but also the cultural conventions, preferences, taboos etc. of the target country. Furthermore, the act of translating itself is in a sense a form of localization, since language does not exist separately from its culture.

Website and software localization has been around now for several years. It relies heavily not only on human translation but also on machine and machine-assisted translation tools, such as translation software and translation memory. Given the limitations of these tools, the often unrealistic expectations of the marketplace and the eagerness to process a large volume of material in record time, localization has been experiencing many problems, and the goals its pursuers have set for themselves are yet to be realized. One should keep all of this in mind before getting involved in this area of translation.

The Uses of the Internet for Translators

The translation field has become increasingly "wired," witnessing a proliferation of sites relating to professional activities, job-hunting, commercial products, and online reference materials for translators. It is not an exaggeration to say that translators do themselves (and potentially their clients) quite a disservice by ignoring the virtual translation community.

This section will introduce you to a selection of highly-regarded and well-maintained sites of use to translators. It assumes basic Web literacy. Of course, the Internet's ever-changing nature guarantees that certain websites will decline or disappear, while new ones will emerge by the time this book becomes available. So please be aware that you will probably have to do some updating of the following information on your own.

Where We Are on the Web

First, let us invite you to Schreiber Publishing's website. Our address: **www.SchreiberLanguage.com**. Its objective is to provide reference literature, training materials, and useful information for translators.

The Almighty Google

One of the latest verbs in English is "to Google." The incredible reach of Google is such that we can no longer live without it—just typing a topic into a search bar will give you almost everything there is to know about that subject. Additionally, Google's Translate function (**www.translate.google.com**) can translate text of your choosing as well as webpages. As in all machine translation, the rate of accuracy here is much less than 100%, but at least it helps you orient yourself through text and terminology.

Professional Activities

Translators wishing to learn about the state of their profession will benefit from a visit to the American Translators Association's site, **www.atanet.org**. I discuss the ATA in greater detail in the chapter on Translators' Organizations; its website includes information on the Association's formal activities such as conferences, publications and certification procedures. Even if you are not an ATA member, the site is useful because it can guide you to other translation-related sites.

Another major website of interest to translators is the site of the inter-national umbrella organization of the world's translator associations, the International Federation of Translators, found on **www.fit-ift. org**.

Aquarius, at **www.aquarius.net,** claims to be "the world's language network." This commercial website lists translation agencies seeking translators and interpreters who, in turn, can post resumes to make their services known. It also links to other translation sites.

Computers will never replace translators, but translators who use computers will replace translators who don't.

—Timothy R. Hunt

More recent websites of this kind are **www.ProZ.com**, which bills itself as "the world's leading enabling and sourcing platform for language professionals," **planettranslation.com** useful for both translators and translation service buyers, also provides tips and terminology, and **TranslatorsCafe.com**, which provides useful fuctions for translators looking for work and resources.

Networking with Other Translators

Translators these days often communicate with one another on the Internet, sharing knowledge, passing on information, checking terminology, or just griping about not being paid on time. It all started with what used to be called "chat rooms," which morphed into various kinds of translations forums located in the U.S. and around the world.

One kind of a forum for translators is the newsgroup: subscribers post messages and receive answers (say, to a specialized translation query). A newsgroup for translators is **http://www.faqs.org/faqs/language/translation-faq/**.

Reference Materials

The Translator's Home Companion at **www.lai.com/companion. html** provides a great deal of useful information for translators.

The Human Languages Page at **www.june29.com/IDP** provides links to other translation-related sites, including some listed here, and to dictionaries.

Online Dictionary Services

Inter Active Terminology for Europe at **http://iate.europa.eu/** is a very useful service, IATE handles many European languages such as Spanish, Portuguese, French, German, Italian, English, Danish and Dutch. Includes many specialized dictionaries in non-technical, legal and technical areas.

Online Dictionaries at **www.yourdictionary.com** covers a far greater range of languages than the above site. It provides links to dictionaries and translations in many specializations.

Glossaries

There are many mediocre glossaries out there in cyberspace, so use caution with this type of online resource. One of the better ones is **http://www.termisti.refer.org/termisti.htm.**

U.S. Government agencies provide some very useful glossaries. For example:

www.epa.gov/glossary (for environmental terminology).

Finding Cultural Information

A quick way to access cultural and historical information on other countries is via The Electronic Embassy at **www.embassy.org.** This service provides links to embassy and/or United Nations home pages of many nations. Most countries' pages include links to cultural resources such as online newspapers, libraries, and so on. You may have to do some digging to find the information you're after, but if it exists online, you will probably find it by starting here. Also the foreign ministries of various countries are a good source for all sorts of information related to that particular country.

Shopping for Dictionaries

A prime source for dictionaries is: **www.schoenhofs.com.**

Major virtual bookstores also have good selections of dictionaries (see box). Examples:
www.barnesandnoble.com
www.amazon.com

You may also wish to consult these websites of major dictionary publishers:

Elsevier at **www.elsevier.com**
Routledge at **www.routledge.com**
McGraw-Hill at **www.mcgraw-hill.com**
Schreiber Publishing at **www.SchreiberLanguage.com**

Freelancers can find out about the payment practices of translation agencies. For the most part, they are free, but you have to join to be able to use them:

www.paymentpractices.net
www.tcrlist.com/

For freelancers in the process of determining their own rates, **www. ProZ.com** offers a Translator Rate Calculator for calculating rates based on work speed and skill, desired income, and related expenses. The site offers many other helpful resources for the freelance translator.

The Power of Language

Once, in the "good old days," the Russian Czar decided to grant clemency to one of his unfortunate subjects who had been sentenced to death. He ordered his communications expert to send a telegram to the prison in Siberia, stating: "Clemency, period, no execution."

The careless clerk at the telegraph office did not proofread the telegram. It came out as: "Clemency no, period, execution."

Dictionaries

No translator, no matter how accomplished or well versed in both the source and the target languages, can do without dictionaries and reference literature. If either language or knowledge were static, remaining the same over a long period of time, then one could conceivably reach a level of expertise where references become marginal. The fact remains that this is not the case, certainly not in our day and age, when both language and knowledge are changing almost daily. If, for instance, you specialize in translating medical subjects, and you stop doing it for a few months, you may find out that there are new names of drugs, medical concepts and procedures which did not exist at the time you stopped translating. Therefore, you need current reference sources that will enable you to handle current medical subjects.

By the same token, the best of dictionaries and reference sources become dated the day they are published, and will never answer all your questions. This handbook—for that matter—will have to be revised almost every year if it is to keep up with all the information it seeks to provide (for updated information, visit our website at: www. SchreiberLanguage.com).

What all this means to you as a translator is that even if you possess the best of linguistic and technical references, as indeed you should, you may want to get in the habit of compiling your own glossaries and

In this work, when it shall be found that much is omitted, let it not be forgotten that much likewise is performed.

—Samuel Johnson, upon completion of his dictionary in 1755

databases in subjects you frequently translate, to keep yourself up to date, and always be on the lookout for new reference sources.

When you start out in this business, you soon discover that the acquisition of good dictionaries and reference literature is quite an expensive proposition. The best general and technical dictionaries in such major languages as Spanish, German, French and Japanese range in price from $100 to over $300 each. Good technical reference books in specialized subjects are not much cheaper. As a beginner, you may not be independently wealthy, and you may get an assignment which would require a couple of expensive dictionaries, but the money you earn from this assignment will not cover the cost. What are you to do?

What I did when I started out some years ago as a freelance translator of Spanish and Hebrew was to go to my regional public library, where they had some of the reference sources I needed. It was not as convenient as having my own, but it worked. Then, as I started earning more money from translation, I gradually acquired the dictionaries I needed. I must confess, sometimes I overindulged myself and bought dictionaries which weren't so good, and which I should have checked out more carefully. But my general policy has been to stay within my budget, and the times when I was able to acquire some of my best and most expensive reference sources were when I got an assignment in one of my languages of expertise big enough to justify the expense.

As of this writing, there is a growing trend in the publishing world to produce dictionaries and references on electronic media, such as computer disk, CD-ROM, and so on. Does this mean we should stop buying dictionaries? I think not. Books are not going to disappear in the next few years, if ever. Typically, a professional translator engaged in a highly technical translation job will be surrounded by dictionaries and reference sources and will be looking up things in as many as ten or twelve different books at the same time. To do all of this on computer would necessitate a ten or twelve-part split screen, with a great deal of keypunching or mouse-clicking, which may be more time consuming than simply having the good old books spread around you. Some day all of this may be overtaken by technology, but for the time being let's stick with books.

For recommendations of good dictionaries and reference sources, See Appendix 1. For major dictionary outlets, see Appendix 2.

Reference Literature

Besides dictionaries, a working translator needs reference books for the subjects being translated. First, there are general references covering general knowledge, data and language. Then there are specific reference works geared towards a given field, such as medicine. This includes medical dictionaries, encyclopedias, handbooks, journals and various compilations of medical data, in both the source and the target language. The third major source of information today is the Internet. Use it extensively.

Terminology Management

Dictionaries and electronic equipment are not sufficient to produce high quality translations. With language changing almost daily, you have no choice but to compile your own glossaries in specific subject areas. Indeed, every new job will add words to your lists. This has always been the case, and today it is more so than ever before. The more extensive a glossary you develop as you go along, and the more accessible you make it, the better your translations will be, and the easier your life will become as a translator.

In the "old days" we simply jotted words on pieces of paper and kept them inside the dictionary, either in the front or in the back. When we translated a specialized item, such as farming equipment or coal mining, we would write down the difficult and unknown terms, do some research, and write down the English equivalents of the foreign terms (or vice versa). Each time we did another piece of translation on the same subject we would refer to that list and get good use out of it.

Now, however, we have become much more sophisticated. We do what is known in professional linguistic circles as "terminology management." To manage all of our glossaries and specialized terminology we rely on two key elements—smart terminology organization, and smart use of the computer.

Types of Terminology

Terminology falls into different categories. The most obvious category is the **main subject area.** Each field of human knowledge and activity has its own terminology. This is particularly true of such areas as law, medicine, computers, engineering and so on. Very often, the same word used in each of those fields takes on a different meaning (a "host" used in a medical sense is different from any other sense). In organizing your glossaries, it is best to start out by putting them into clearly defined categories. You need to identify the categories you will be working in, and put them in alphabetical order, starting with an area such as Agriculture, and ending with Zoology. There are many ways of organizing information on computer, and you can choose one depending on the extent of your terminology management needs. The simplest way is to use your word-processing program, which can automatically alphabetize your entries. At the other end of the scale are programs especially designed for translation management, such as the IBM TranslationManager, a program that costs around $2,000 and is mostly used in very large translation projects handled by teams of translators. Whichever program you use, the idea is to have the information organized in such a way that it is very accessible and easy to use. You should store it on your working drive, create a backup, and also keep a hard copy.

Within each subject there are **subject subspecialties**. Thus, for example, there is real estate law, criminal law, computer law and so on. If you do a great deal of legal translation, you need to segregate your glossaries and keep them according to these sub-specialties. The same holds true in chemistry, medicine, and a great many other areas.

Another major area of terminology is **organizational language.** This refers to major corporations, not-for-profit organizations, and government agencies, all of whom develop their own terminology, which becomes extremely critical in doing translation work. Here you need to organize your glossaries according to clients, with the above categories organized within these client categories. If, for instance, you do a great deal of work for IBM, you need to follow their usage very closely, and be consistent each time you do a translation job for them. What has become very common for large organizations is to produce their own glossaries, word lists, lists of acronyms, and so on. More often than not they will give you those valuable tools at the beginning of their relationship with you. But sometimes they forget, and an experienced translator will always ask for them up front. Very often they only have them in hard copy, and you can either urge them to convert those items into electronic files, so that you can use them on your computer, or else do it yourself (here an optical scanner comes in very handy). Quite naturally, you will be able to keep expanding those official lists.

The other aspect of organizational language is **preferential usage** and **corporate style**. This is not a matter of right or wrong terminology, but of the choice of words and the style of writing of a particular organization. The U.S. Government, for instance, publishes a style manual which reflects the standard usage of the federal government, from punctuation to the use of ambiguous words. The best way to master a specific corporate style is to read a few documents generated by that organization prior to embarking on a translation assignment.

Another major area of terminology management, which every translator is familiar with, is **acronyms** and **initialisms**. More than ever before, documents today are saturated with acronyms and abbreviations. Some are universally known, and are used daily in the media, since any educated person knows them (UN, NATO, UNESCO etc.). Some are known to any translator working in a specific area (a translator of computer literature is bound to know the meaning of CD-ROM, RAM etc.) A great many, however, are either too esoteric, or only used by one particular organization, or are too recent to be widely known. Compiling lists of acronyms and abbreviations and organizing them in a systematic and accessible manner is one of the most important functions of technical translation in today's world. One important aspect of your list of acronyms is the indication whether it is to be left untranslated (for an objective reason or because of an organizational preference), or whether it is to be translated or transliterated.

Creating New Terminology

It is not common for translators to create new terminology. This work is done by specialists in either academia, private industry or government, and by the language academies of various countries. But there are occasions when a translator finds him/herself breaking new ground, and there is no choice but to create new terms. This writer was involved in one such case over a year ago, when his translation agency was given an assignment by the U.S. government to translate a book from Japanese about protecting highways against snow storms. The Japanese government had embarked a few years ago on a major study which combined civil engineering and meteorology, studying the properties of snow in relation to the condition of highways, bridges and tunnels under severe snow conditions. As a result, the Japanese broke new ground in the study of snow, which required new Japanese terminology describing the nature and behavior of snow under certain conditions. In translating this 500-page study into English, it became clear that there were no equivalent words in English for all the newly coined Japanese words. As a result, the translators, one of whom had a degree in civil engineering, and the other a background in meteorology, had to coin new words. This was explained to the contact person at the U.S. government agency which had requested the translation, who instructed the translators to go ahead with the work. Usually one of two things happens in a case like this. Either the new terms are effective, and will become official, or else someone may improve upon them and provide better terms.

To sum up, terminology management is probably the most critical aspect of technical translation. It often makes the difference between a good translator and an excellent one. The better you manage terminology, and the more extensive your up-to-date terminology sources are, the higher your chance is to be looked upon as a truly reliable translator in a given field.

Some Uncomplimentary Statements about Translators

It is difficult in following lines laid down by others not sometimes to diverge from them, and it is hard to preserve in a translation the charm of expressions.

—St. Jerome

Traduttori, traditori. (Translators are traitors.)
—A traditional Italian adage

Some hold translations not unlike to be the wrong side of a Turkey tapestry.

—James Howell

Les traductions augmentent les fautes d'un ouvrage et en gâtent les beautés. (Translations increase the faults of a work and spoil its beauties.)
—Voltaire

Nor ought a genius less than his that writ attempt translation.
—Sir John Denham

9. KEY TRANSLATION AREAS

Some translators spend a lifetime translating basically only one subject. This is true of a translator with a major corporation like Ford, who only translates automotive subjects, or with a government agency like the National Institutes of Health (NIH), who only translates medical subjects. I say "basically," because in reality there is no such thing as a purely automotive or medical translation. Every technical subject is "tainted" by other subjects, notably legal, financial, and so on. But still, the translators in the aforementioned examples do concentrate on one major area.

But as was mentioned before, the typical freelancer has to know a variety of subjects if he or she wishes to make a living translating. The question to ask oneself is, which subjects? Not all subjects were created equal when it comes to translation. Some are translated constantly, and others infrequently. The practical thing to do is ask yourself, which are the most commonly translated subjects? And, do I have enough expertise in at least two or three of those subjects, so that I can give myself a good start in this business?

There are no absolute answers to these questions, since subjects vary from place to place. In a place like the area between San Jose, California and Seattle, Washington, computer-related subjects are very prominent, while in Detroit automotive subjects are prevalent, and so on. But there is a fairly general consensus on certain areas which are more common than others. Here is a working list which is by no means exhaustive, but certainly representative:

- Advertising
- Aerospace
- Automotive
- Business/Finance

- Chemistry
- Civil engineering
- Computers
- Electrical/Electronic engineering
- Environment
- Law
- Medicine
- Military subjects/Martial Arts
- Nautical subjects
- Patents
- Social Sciences
- Telecommunications

The above are very inclusive areas. They break into many sub-areas, and often are mixed together. But let's take a quick look at each one of them, and try to gain a general idea as to what is required to work in those areas.

Advertising

This is a very specialized field. To borrow a term from software translation, to translate advertising copy really means to "localize." One has to go beyond a straight translation of text. Advertisement is in effect an effort to impress people with a few words, and get them to buy something which they may or may not buy otherwise. The key to advertising is the "target audience." The moment one translates any advertising text, it is clearly targeting a different audience, which speaks a different language. Most likely, it will differ from the original audience in more aspects than just speaking another language. There will be cultural, political, and even religious or economic differences. All of this has to be factored in when doing this type of translation. By the same token that it takes a special type of creativity to write advertising copy in the first place, it takes a similar creativity to render that copy in another language. Clearly, translating advertising text requires experience, and it is not something a beginner should jump into.

Pop-a-Message

This is a fun game for several players. Write a message. Cut the message apart so that every word is on a different piece of paper. Then, put each piece of paper inside a balloon. Blow up the balloon and tie it. Give each balloon to a different person. Next, have each person pop her balloon and read her word. Have everyone work together to figure out what the message is. You can play this game with envelopes instead of balloons.

Reviente Un Mensaje

Este es un juego divertido para varios jugadores. Escriba un mensaje. Corte el mensaje para que cada palabra esté en un pedacito separado de papel. Luego, ponga cada pedazo de papel dentro de un globo. Infle el globo y amárrelo. De a cada persona un globo, y luego haga que cada uno reviente el globo y lea la palabra. Haga que todos se unan para descifrar juntos el mensaje. Usted puede jugar este juego usando sobres de cartas en vez de globos.

animal

Sometimes a translation requires some creativity, as in this case of colloquial American English translated into Spanish. Here one seeks to retain the "bounce" of the original text.

Aerospace

Here a distinction should be made between aeronautics and space subjects, which are often thrown together these days under the heading of aerospace. Aeronautics is an older subject than space sciences. Both are highly technical, with the difference being that space subjects are in the process of developing, and therefore present a higher degree of linguistic difficulty than aeronautics. As space exploration continues to develop, entirely new sciences are being created, such as space medicine, space engineering, and so on. One cannot enter this field of translation cold, but rather must go through a process of apprenticeship, unless one already has a background in either aeronautics or space studies or both. On the other hand, the terminologies and nomenclature in these areas are accessible, and with good terminology management one can learn how to operate in these areas fairly quickly.

Automotive

This is a relatively easy technical field for a translator to work in, provided one has good sources of terminology and contact with the technical people involved in the subject. In all major languages there are very good dictionaries for automotive subjects, mechanical and electric engineering, and all other subjects related to cars. The important

---

Automotive Terminology in Spanish
or
How a Car's Trunk Changes Names Throughout the Hispanic World

Spain. Maletero

Chile. Maleta

Argentina. Baúl

Paraguay. Valijera

Bolivia. Maletera

Costa Rica. Joroba

Mexico. Cajuela

thing here is to pay close attention to the actual usage of car-related terminology in the geographical area where the translation is to be used, so that the end-users of your product can use it safely and efficiently in their work.

Business/Finance

This is a highly specialized area of translation. It is not recommended to get involved in translation of financial subjects, such as banking, insurance, stock market, real estate etc., without a background in those subjects. Here the question is not only knowing the terminology, as in the case of automotive subjects, but also understanding the subject one is translating. It is common in financial subjects to have a great deal implied in the text, rather than spelled out. People who write on these subjects generally assume that their readers have a good understanding of the topic, and so they allude to a great many things without bothering to explain them. You will hardly ever see the term "Gross National Product" spelled out in a financial text. It is known as GNP, and the average reader of this kind of material is expected to know what it means. In American English in particular, there is a very rich jargon of financial terms, which must be closely adhered to if one is to provide a translation that makes sense to, say, a stock broker or a financial planner. For that matter, all major languages have their own specific terms, phrases and concepts which flow out of the economic and financial reality of their societies, regions etc., which are not easy to master. Here good dictionaries are only useful up to a point, but are certainly not sufficient for coming up with all the answers. In sum, this is an area one should not walk into too hastily, but be prepared to approach carefully and selectively. (See Appendix 1 for Schreiber's business dictionaries in Arabic, Chinese, French, German, Italian, Japanese, Korean, Portuguese, Russian and Spanish.)

Chemistry

Many of us had chemistry in high school and/or college. But if you talk to a chemist these days, you'll find out that there is no longer one subject known as chemistry, or one kind of chemist. More perhaps than any other science, chemistry has become a multitude of sciences, each with its own specialized nomenclature, terminology, units, abbreviations, jargon, typographical organization and databases. To cite a few examples: Polymers and copolymers, space-related chemistry, geochemistry, petrochemistry, stereochemistry, not to mention such areas as pharmacology, where chemistry reaches into the field of medicine.

Unlike financial subjects, however, things here are laid out quite explicitly, and with good terminology management one can become an effective translator of chemical subjects in a relatively short time. Since chemical subjects are one of the largest sources of translation in the world, those who are interested in this field are well advised to invest in the resources necessary for doing this kind of work, which consist of electronic databases available from government, academic and private organizations, good specialized dictionaries in specific areas of chemistry, and publications which help translators keep in touch with the field. For translators of Arabic, for instance, it certainly pays to specialize in petrochemistry; for translators of German, in nearly any area of chemistry, and so on. Once you have identified the possibilities available to you in this field, you can begin to work on improving your capabilities in it, and you should be getting steady work.

Civil Engineering

This field can be approached in one of two ways. If you already have a background in civil engineering, you are ahead of the game. If you don't, you can ally yourself with a civil engineer who would go over your translation and make technical corrections. The field of civil engineering offers some large translation projects, which can be quite lucrative, and since few translators in any given language happen to be civil engineers themselves, it is quite common for a technical translator to ally him or herself with a civil engineer to ensure the quality of the final product. As in all branches of engineering, here too, terminology can be easily managed once you have the right resources and know how to organize them.

Computers

Computers are arguably the fastest growing field in the translation profession. For a translator, familiarity with computers does not only mean having the right tools to maximize productivity, but also having access to subject matter which provides a large volume of translation work. Computer literature during the past ten years has grown phenomenally. It includes how-to books, manuals for computers, printers and software, articles about computers, books and articles about the Internet, to mention only the most commonly known items. Translating computer subjects presents both an opportunity and a challenge. The opportunity is working in a fast-growing field. The challenge is the fact that computer subjects are changing and growing daily, and last year's computer dictionary is near-obsolete this year. Thus, to be a truly specialized computer translator, one needs to be in ongoing touch with computer publications and computer columns in the general press, and try out new equipment and programs. Like chemistry, computers represent one of the most active fields of translation, and cannot be ignored by anyone who wishes to develop a successful freelance business.

Electrical/Electronic Engineering

American companies play a dominant role in the global market of electrical and electronic products. As a result, there is a great need for translation of these subjects around the world. The translation of these documents requires a good understanding of the basic principles of electronics and the correct use of terminology. These documents follow well-established rules which must be adhered to very closely, and are typically full of acronyms and abbreviations, measurement units, scientific symbols, description of pieces of equipment, their components and all their pieces down to the smallest subcomponents. Fortunately, there are excellent dictionaries for these subjects both in English and in most major language pairs from/into English. Translators who work regularly with these subjects tend to develop extensive glossaries and are often known for their good terminology management, which is the key in this field. As a major technical area of translation, this area is definitely worth pursuing.

Environment

Environmental studies is a relatively new field, yet its importance around the world is quite evident. Unlike some of the other technical fields mentioned here, this subject is not well defined, and in effect encompasses several disciplines, such as biology, chemistry, forestry, hydrology, civil engineering, to mention only a few. It is not quite clear how one goes about specializing in translation of environmental subjects. My suggestion is, you shouldn't waste too much time trying to figure it out. You should only be aware of the fact that this is an important field, and if you should have the opportunity to work on translations related to environmental subjects, you will have to judge for yourself whether the particular document is within your area or areas of expertise.

Law

Translation of legal subjects is practically an inescapable feature of technical translation, just as all aspects of your daily life, from driving to getting married to buying a piece of property have legal implications. Nearly all the subjects discussed in this chapter get mixed with legal text (a chemical patent, a business contract, medical insurance, etc.) The law is one thing none of us can drop from our personal agenda, so we have to learn how to deal with it as best we can.

For translators, that means paying special attention to legal documents, and developing good legal reference resources. In addition, we have to be aware of the following aspects of legal translation: (a) The

---

How English is (Mis)used Around the World

In an Acapulco hotel: *The manager has personally passed all the water used here.*

In a Japanese hotel: *You are invited to take advantage of the chambermaid.*

In a Vienna hotel: *In a case of fire, do your utmost to alarm the hotel porter.*

In a Bangkok drycleaner: *Drop your trousers here for best results.*

In a Hong Kong dress shop: *Ladies have fits upstairs*

legal system of each country is different, therefore you cannot translate every legal term directly from one language to the next; (b) there are different specialties within the legal field, such as business law, patent law, criminal law, constitutional law, even computer law, and each has its own specialized terminology; (c) translations of legal documents can be used in court and are often used outside the court system (for naturalization, marriage etc.), and thus become legal documents in their own right, and therefore must be handled with extreme attention to accuracy and completeness.

Legal translation is by far one of the most if not the most common type of translation, not only in the U.S. but around the world. Most legal documents are not too difficult to translate, although some do tend to be turgid, or purposely ambiguous. Once you become regularly involved in a specific type of legal translation, such as contracts, depositions, divorce decrees etc., you find out that they invariably follow the same formula, and your work becomes much easier than when you first started out. In addition, legal translation requires good writing skills, and your command of your target language is being tested when you do this type of translation. Finally, while some types of legal translation may be tedious, many are quite interesting.

Medicine

Much of what was said before about chemical subjects also applies to medicine. Here too, we have a large number of subjects all grouped under the general heading of "medicine," which includes life sciences, pharmacology, even space medicine. Another major area related to medicine is health care, which has become a huge source of translations in the U.S., especially in Spanish. This field has its own jargon, with terms such as "copayment," "health care provider," "delivery," and so on. Mastering this jargon in both the source and target languages is time well spent.

One does not have to have a medical degree to translate in this field, but clearly terminology management is a key to effective translation in all biomedical subjects. The trend today in this field is TDB, or Terminology Database, which allow storing a vast body of information and manipulating it in a variety of ways. While physicians are notorious for their poor handwriting and hard-to-decipher transmission of medical information, the task of the translator is to render medically-related data in a clear and concise fashion, with the highest degree of accuracy.

The good news about medical translation is that the reference literature and the computerized TDBs are getting better every year, and there is nothing to prevent a translator in the world's major languages from developing good skills as a medical translator.

Military Subjects

Translation of military subjects has always been a huge industry. The trend in the world today is to move away from armed conflicts towards peaceful pursuits, but the world unfortunately is still far from being free from conflict, and the need for expert translators of military subjects is still very real. This field covers an enormous array of subjects, ranging from military history to military technology, the art of war, human issues involving the military, and much more. Most military materials are written in a concise and factual style which does not requires special literary skills. The underlying theme of military subjects is getting the job done quickly and efficiently. This is why much of military translation is done by people with a military background.

Over the years, the U.S. Department of Defense has been a major source of military-related translation in all languages. Many people have made a career of such translation work, and some still do. There is no one piece of advice for people who look to enter this field, since it is so broad and diffuse. But a general acquaintance with and understanding of military theory and operations is necessary to work in this field effectively. Thus, for example, a soldier does not "shoot" but "fires," and his or her personal weapon is not a "gun" but a "rifle." The military does have its own way of saying things, and like all professionals, they too insist on respect for their language.

Nautical Subjects

This field covers naval subjects, which are part of the military field, and civilian navigation, which includes anything from a small sailboat to huge oil tankers. Seafaring has one of the richest vocabularies in the English language, and people who are not directly involved in sailing and nautical activities can easily get lost in this linguistic environment.

Some areas of nautical translation, however, such as cartography, are not all that vocabulary-intensive, and can be mastered by "landlocked" translators. In approaching nautical subjects, one must first see how technical the particular document is, and whether one has sufficient background to handle it.

Patents

Patent translation is one of the main growth areas of translation around the world. This is particularly true if you are a Japanese-into-English translator, since the bulk of patent registration in the U.S. consists of Japanese patents. German and French come a distant second and third, with the rest of the major languages of the world trailing behind. Most patents relate to either medical, chemical or mechanical subjects. The legal part of the patent translation is fairly well-defined and straightforward, and does not require a great deal of training. The text itself can be difficult at times, and requires a certain degree of subject understanding. Most patents are only a few pages long, and make for a comfortable assignment—not too short to be unprofitable, and not too long to monopolize all your time. Many translators have developed a good system of doing patent translation, and the field is open to new players.

Social Sciences

This term is used here in the broadest sense, to include such areas as politics, international relations, and, basically, all social subjects which may be considered general rather than technical. For the most part, this type of translation, which includes books, newspaper and periodical articles, essays, speeches and so on, does not require specialized technical knowledge, but rather a broad education and a familiarity with the contemporary world. If you routinely translate, for example, articles concerning social and political events in Germany, you may want to subscribe to some German newspapers and magazines, to keep up with the latest trends in the German language. You should also read books about your subject, and take a personal interest in it beyond your translation assignments.

It should be pointed out that translations of this kind are not as prevalent as truly technical translations, and therefore a freelance translator who seeks to build his or her practice purely on this type of translation may find it difficult to secure a steady flow of assignments. Most technical translators look upon social sciences related translation as a bonus, an occasional opportunity to do something most of them enjoy doing, but do not expect to do on a regular basis.

Telecommunications

This subject is closely related to electronics, computers and, at times, marketing and advertising. The activity in this field around the world today is enormous, as giant telecommunications companies from the U.S., England, Germany, France and other countries compete for their share of the pie in the world markets. Here in the U.S., the competition among telecommunications companies is rather severe, as the laws regulating telecommunications services have been changing dramatically, and as the advent of the Internet has forced the traditional telephone companies to invest in looking for a share in this new world of communications. It is by no means an easy field to work in as a linguist, since there are new linguistic developments almost every week, and one needs to keep constantly abreast of all the new concepts and new terminology which this field keeps generating, not only in English but in other languages as well. But it is worth getting involved in and gaining expertise in, since its volume of translation is growing at a very rapid rate. A word of advice to those who get into this field: Stay in close touch with your client, and make sure the two of you have a good understanding as to the terminology you are expected to use, the degree of localization (adjusting the text to the particular country where it will be used), how much is to be left in the original language to avoid confusion, the use of acronyms, and the corporate style of the client which needs to be reflected in the translation. If you'll excuse the pun, in this type of work you certainly don't want to have any breakdown in communication.

For a successful translation career, the knowledge of two or more languages is not enough. One should also pursue a major technical area, such as law, medicine, business, etc...

---

10. HOW TO OPERATE SUCCESSFULLY AS A FREELANCE TRANSLATOR

So you've decided to try your hand at freelance translation. Congratulations! If this is indeed your calling, or your Karma, or your destiny, or whatever you choose to call it (as a translator you will always be compelled to choose the right word), stick to it, and your reward will be more than tangible. While not everyone may appreciate your work, since translation is—and has always been—one of the most misunderstood (sometimes even maligned) professions, if you maintain your professional integrity, you will always know your own self-worth and your reputation will grow.

But getting down to reality. Operating as a freelance translator allows the flexibility to work on projects of your choosing within a schedule of your own making under your own preferred conditions. However, this flexibility requires the mastery of many mundane technical details, if one is to operate successfully as a freelance translator. Here are some of the most important ones.

Financial Issues

Self-Employment. As a freelancer, you are self-employed, and have to pay your own taxes. Many freelancers tend to ignore this fact until they get their 1099 forms at the beginning of the new year and realize they have to pay taxes like everyone else. It is very important to set aside a

---

English Goes Abroad

Outside of a Paris dress shop: *Dresses for streetwalking.*

Hong Kong dentist advertisement: *Teeth extracted by the latest methodists.*

In a Tokyo bar: *Special cocktails for the ladies with nuts.*

---

portion of your income during the year and be ready for that infamous April 15th. Otherwise, you may find yourself paying interest to pay taxes, which is not the best way to manage your finances.

Financial Records. You may want to consult your accountant on what kind of expenses you can deduct from taxes, and keep records and receipts of those expenses. You will be able to deduct part of your house as an office, and all your phone, fax, office supplies and work-related room and board. The laws have been changing in recent years, and a good accountant is essential to maximizing your deductions.

Pricing Yourself. One of the first lessons a freelance translator learns is that not all translation jobs are created equal. By that I mean, like a good businessperson, you learn how to price each job, and either accept it or reject it. I have dealt with many freelance translators in many different languages who decide beforehand that—like a lawyer at a high-powered law firm —they will not offer their services for less than, say, a hundred dollars an hour or twenty cents per word. Now granted, there are a few translation and interpretation jobs around that will pay these high rates. But they are few and far between. I may be moving in the wrong circles, but quite frankly, while I have seen such rates being paid, they were quite exceptional, and I personally don't know any freelance translator who gets them on a regular basis.

The name of the game is earning money on a steady basis, not once in a blue moon. And to do so, one has to be flexible. Many a time I agreed to do a translation job for a client for less than it was worth, but my payoff often came when, soon thereafter, the same client, valuing the quality of my work and my near-fanatic adherence to deadlines, came back to me with another, often urgent job, and this time I charged a higher rate, which made up for the shortfall the first time around. In short, you quickly learn in this business that your potential clients—be they small or large companies, government agencies, academic institutions, it makes no difference who—are almost always looking for a bargain. While they may not argue with their doctor or lawyer or even plumber about their rates, you can rest assured they will argue with you, and will always try at least one or two of your competitors, hoping to get a better rate. You have to be prepared to do "creative rate structuring" if you are to get that coveted job.

How do you know how much to charge for your services? There is no easy answer to this question, as any professional translator knows. A lot depends on who your clients are. As a general rule, for-profit organizations will pay more than not-for-profit, or public and government agencies. The rule of thumb is supply and demand. If the client can get it cheaper, you may not get that job. You have to establish for yourself what one may call a realistic rate.

To begin with, written translation work is normally charged by the word. I have known good, fast translators who made a good living getting as little as 3 or 4 cents per word (time is the real measure of your translation earning. The more words per hour you can translate accurately, the more you will earn). Many translators will be shocked to hear this. They will call these rates "slave wages," and refuse to talk to me again. These days the range of 7 to 10 cents per word for translation from a foreign language into English, and 8 to 12 cents per words for translation from English into a foreign language is considered normal. In California the rates are usually somewhat higher than on the East Coast, but then again, they pay higher taxes out there. Rates have been changing in recent years, and will continue to change. Translation organizations in the U.S. are not allowed to set rates, or even suggest rates. To find out about going rates, you may want to talk to local colleagues or search online forums. ProZ.com also has a handy Translator Rates Calculator, which can give you a ballpark ideal rate based on your speed and skill, desired income, and related expenses.

To reiterate: Try to charge your better paying clients more, and those less capable of paying, less. Always look at the greater picture of your total yearly earnings, rather than getting yourself hung up on each case, giving the client and yourself a hard time. Flexibility is the secret weapon of the freelancer.

Getting Paid. Since most people do not have a good understanding of what translation is all about, and that includes some of the largest corporations and law firms in the country, they may decide after you perform your translation that your work is not up to snuff, and they will either withhold payment or try to reduce it. If indeed you did a less than acceptable job, well, then, you have to bite the bullet and take a reduction in pay. But that often is not the case, and you can find yourself in the lurch. If you know and trust your client (you have worked with them before, or they are a very reputable entity in your community, etc.), then you just go ahead and do the work. But if you have the slightest doubt about getting paid, get something in writing from your client, such as a purchase order, or have the client sign a statement issued by you, stating your own terms, or even try to get some money down. Remember, you are now in business, not in a social or academic situation, and the business world is tough.

Equally important is keeping good records of your clients, and keeping notes on them, for two main reasons: First, you want to know a year or two from now if you had a problem with a client, so that you can act accordingly and not make the same mistake twice. Second, you want to keep in touch with your clients, letting them know you moved, or your phone number changed, or even drop them a card for the holiday season. Your goal is repeat business, which means steady income, and also validates your worth as a good translator.

Delinquent Accounts. Hopefully, you won't take on too many bad clients. But having some bad clients is a fact of life, and cannot be avoided. The question is what to do with those who, for no good reason, refuse to pay.

In the case of government agencies, the bad news is that they often take longer than they should to pay. But the good news is that eventually they do pay, unlike the private sector, where your client may go out of business. Since they make the laws, or are in charge of enforcing them, they cannot ignore them, and they pay. There are extreme cases—more than a few—when a payment drags on for months. My suggestion is that for the first three months you send friendly reminders and/or make friendly phone calls. After that, you have the recourse of contacting the office of your congressperson, who is usually very responsive in contacting the delinquent person or office, and invariably you will get your money within 30 days. You should only use this as your last resort, although, in some instances, you may be surprised to find out that a government employee would say to you, "My hands are tied, please feel free to contact your congressperson to make sure you get paid." Government never ceases to amaze those contractors who work with it.

In the case of private clients, you have the recourse of taking them to small claims court. While the judge cannot force the defendant to pay, the process usually does work well, since most people don't want to ruin their credit record or their business reputation. Then again, you may be dealing with a client who had just gone belly-up or skipped town. In this case you have a business loss and a tax writeoff.

Since a great deal of freelance translation is done for law firms, let me state that the great majority of law firms and lawyers do appreciate translation work and pay on time, although some prefer to pay in 60 rather than 30 days. But then there are those exceptions, usually the smaller operators, who either experience chronic cash-flow problems, or live high on the hog and are always short on cash. Some of those members of the bar either wait till their client pays them before they pay you, or make up an excuse to get out of paying altogether. You almost get the feeling they have learned a trick or two from their own clients. Now, as a freelancer, or an independent contractor, you should never accept the argument "I'll pay you when my client pays me." You have absolutely no responsibility for someone else's clients, especially when it comes to a lawyer, many of whose clients are less than upright citizens. You are entitled to your money, and a lawyer of all people should know this. You give the attorney 60 days, and then you pull out your final weapon. You let your client know that if you don't get paid within 3 working days you will contact the ethics committee of the bar association he or she happen to belong to. In most cases, you will get your money very quickly. If you still don't get your money, you call the bar, and rest assured they will take some action.

Incidentally, what often happens in this type of delinquent accounts, is that the lawyer may send you part of the payment with a note that this is "payment in full." Do not deposit or cash this check, since such action means that you agree with the letter and waive your right to the rest of the money. Finally, if it is clear to you that the lawyer in question has financial or cash-flow difficulties, you may want to suggest getting your money in the form of a few monthly payments.

Record Keeping. Many freelance translators are far from being well-organized individuals. I ought to know, since being disorganized was my problem for many years. Typically, you happen to wander into this type of work. You do an assignment, you find out you are good at it, so you do another one. The next thing you know it is next year, you have done a fair number of assignments, and now you need to refer back to some of them, find out how you translated a certain phrase, or check

Translation Log

Job No._____ Date Received_____ Due_____
Name of client_____
Address_____
Phone_____ Fax_____
e-mail address_____

Job description (special instructions, language, length, special problems, etc.)

_____
_____
_____
_____
_____
_____
_____

Date delivered_____
Word count_____ Rate per word _____
Total due_____
Paid on_____
Notes

_____
_____
_____
_____
_____

some administrative detail, but you either can't find it or you didn't keep any records.

By now you get the picture. No one taught us in school how to keep records as freelancers, and so we have to learn from our mistakes. But rather than learn from your own mistakes, you will save a great deal of time and trouble if you learn from mine. In short, as soon as it becomes clear to you that you have started doing translation assignments regularly, start keeping records. On the next page we have included a sample translation log you can keep, preferably on line with hard copies in an alphabetic file. Along with this form you should keep a hard copy of your original text and your translation, if at all feasible (some clients won't allow you to keep copies because of confidentiality, and some jobs may be too large and complex for you to be able to keep copies).

Good record keeping will yield countless benefits. Those benefits will fall into two categories—first, you will be building a library of your completed assignments, that will greatly facilitate your work in the future. Second, you will be able to measure your progress, plan ahead, keep track of clients, be aware of your strong points and your weaknesses and plan accordingly, see the trends and have a better idea what to go after. Do not be afraid to develop a whole system of records, even if some duplicate each other to some extent. There is no such thing as being overorganized, certainly not in this field. Given the fact that ours is not a highly standardized profession, and that we all have different ways of doing our work, it is equally important that each one of us has his or her way of organizing oneself to do the best job possible.

Budgeting Yourself. Bear in mind that a freelancer has no job security, no steady biweekly or monthly paycheck, no tenure. You are in business for yourself, as a consultant, or a contractor, or a subcontractor. As such, you will experience periods of either feast or famine, and you will have to learn how to handle both.

I once knew a translator who did a large job, earned a few thousand dollars in less than two months, and spent the entire sum on an expensive notebook computer with a high-resolution color monitor, built-in fax, modem, and extra memory chips. Soon he ran into a long dry spell, and he needed the money to pay his bills. He had to sell his super-duper gadget at a considerable loss. He learned his lesson the hard way. He could have made do with a notebook half as expensive, and kept at least two thousand dollars in the bank. This would have carried him through the dry spell, until things started to pick up again (which they did). I believe he is now operating more prudently, and doing quite well.

It seems all freelancers learn this lesson at some point. Like a squirrel, we stash away some of our acorns for a rainy day. We learn how to look farther down our professional road, and by the time we have to sit down and do our tax return we feel a sense of satisfaction knowing we have provided well for ourselves, and have put aside enough to pay Uncle Sam.

Translator/Client Relations

Cultivating and keeping clients is the key to freelance success. A freelance translator generally works with individual clients, companies, organizations, government agencies, and last but not least, translation agencies. Understanding your clients and their needs, and being able to give them what they need and to have good communication and understanding with them, is the basis on which you build your freelance practice. This is not to say that you must please your clients no matter how unreasonable and unfair they happen to be, and never be willing to give up a client, but at the same time it is very important in doing translation work not only to do the best job possible but also to educate your clients and win them over.

Translation is one of the least understood professions around. Some people do not even refer to the process of transferring a text from one language to another as translation, but rather call it by all sorts of names, such as "transcription," "conversion," or simply "changing." Even well-educated people do not always make the distinction between "translating" and "interpreting." And certainly few people have a true appreciation of what a translator has to go through each time he or she confronts a translation assignment. Certainly the advent of the computer has not helped matters. In the popular mind, computers will soon replace human translators altogether, and this profession will disappear just like the old-time secretary, phone operator, etc. Given this state of affairs, it is quite obvious why translators, unlike lawyers or physicians, have a unique task of explaining themselves and paying special attention to client relations.

Unrealistic Promises. Some freelancers, especially when they start out, tend to promise more than they can deliver. You are offered a lucrative assignment and you hate to give it up. So you commit yourself to a timetable which is unrealistic, hoping that you may get an extension, or make up an excuse at the other end of your timetable and get away with it. An experienced translator knows this is a sure prescription for losing a client and tarnishing one's reputation. Most translations in the business world are needed on time, and quite often even sooner. In extreme cases, you may be asking for legal trouble, since you may cause loss of business or clients to your client. The first cardinal rule in translator-client relations is never to promise what you can't deliver. The right thing to do is explain to your client that the timetable is not realistic, and try to negotiate for more time. If this is not possible, suggest splitting the job among two or more translators. If there is no way you can find an accommodation with your client, then you have no choice but to turn down the job.

Establishing Credibility. With a new client you have to establish credibility and gain the client's confidence in your work. If you have a potential major client, one who can give you steady work, you have to make every effort on that first assignment to do the best job possible, no matter how long it takes. If you have a problem with a term or a phrase, let the client know. Honesty is usually more appreciated than pretentiousness. If the term is indeed a problem which nearly any other translator will have trouble with, then your case is sound. You don't gain any points by sweeping the problem under the carpet.

Once you have established credibility, you have to keep up your quality assurance program. The client expects the best from you, not only the first time, but every time.

Keeping Up with Clients. Around the holidays it is always thoughtful to send your clients holiday greetings, to let them know you think of them. You want your clients to think of you as their source of translation services, who is always there when they need you. When you move, let them know. When you don't hear from them for an extended period of time, drop them a note, letting them know you have been doing some interesting work in their language or field, so as to show them you are still there for them. Establishing a personal relationship with your clients is the key to repeat business. Moreover, you will often work with companies and organizations where there is a turnover of personnel, and the person you worked with last time won't be there next time. You need to find out who your new contact person or potential contact person is, and either drop in on them to introduce yourself or say hello over the phone. A new person on the job usually appreciates that sort of attention, which makes her/his work easier, and shows them that you are interested in working with them.

Legal Issues

Several legal issues that affect translators, the two most prominent ones being the employment status of the translator in the 50 states, and translator liability. Here is a brief review of both issues.

Independent Contractor. The status of the freelance translator in the U.S. has never been clearly defined. Since employment and unemployment issues are handled at the state level, there have been several court cases in recent years in states such as California, Colorado, New York and New Jersey which involved the question of whether a freelance translator who provides translation services to a translation agency is an employee of that agency or an independent contractor. While a freelancer is in effect an independent contractor, and prefers to operate as a self-employed individual or entity, there have been instances where a freelancer was not able to generate new assignments from an agency, and chose to apply for unemployment insurance on the pretext of having been "laid off" by that agency. This would give rise to an audit of the agency by the state's unemployment office, resulting, in some cases, in that claimant being defined by the state as an employee of the agency, entitled to unemployment payments. Some agencies have taken this matter to court and won. Others have preferred to pay the unemployment tax and leave it at that. But in the final analysis, the interests of the freelancer are hurt, because no translation agency can survive by carrying a large number of freelancers on its books when, in effect, it is a small business engaged in a large variety of languages and subjects which require the services of many different individuals. This issue is far from resolved, and the best way to confront it is by maintaining professional integrity and not making false employment claims.

Liability Insurance. An even more worrisome issue for freelancers is that of liability. A medical interpreter, for instance, can find him or herself in the midst of a medical malpractice suit, in which an immigrant who does not speak English was given the wrong medicine because of poor translation, and now this person sues the doctor and the interpreter on the advice of his or her lawyer, figuring that they can win the case by proving one or the other to be at fault. The American Translators Association now offers liability insurance to its members. While translators have been clamoring for this type of insurance for a long time, so far there have been few takers. It is your call whether or not you feel the need for this kind of insurance.

In short, when it comes to legal issues, freelance translators are basically on their own. While the legal issues are very real and potentially dangerous, the answers are not quite there yet, and may be a long time in coming.

English Goes Abroad

In a Bucharest hotel lobby: *The lift is being fixed for the next day. During that time we regret that you will be unbearable.*

In a Leipzig elevator: *Do not enter the lift backwards, and only when lit up.*

In a Belgrade elevator: *To move the cabin, push button for wishing floor. If the cabin enter more persons, each one should press a number of wishing floor. Driving is then going alphabetically by national order.*

11. SOURCES OF TRANSLATION WORK

If you choose freelance translation, you should consider yourself a one-person translation company. Your main concern will be where to find work. The need for freelance translation is greater than anyone can estimate, and is clearly growing at a rapid rate. Worldwide, translation is a multibillion dollar industry. But finding translation work on your own is easier said than done. The main problem is that translation is hardly ever a steady, ongoing function of any particular work source, such as an embassy, a company, a government agency, or even a publisher. None of those needs translation every day of the year. Each of them may need a great deal of translation all at once (more than any one person can handle within the given timeframe), and then none for a long time. And, if any one of them needs translation on an ongoing basis, chances are a decision will be made to hire an in-house translator rather than farm out the work.

The fact remains, however, that a well-rounded freelancer can earn well over $50,000 a year, and, in the case of highly specialized technical translators in major languages like Spanish, German, Japanese or Russian, even $100,000 or more. The secret to all of this is establishing for yourself a good clientele. There are two ways of doing this. The first, and by far the hardest, is finding your own clients and working with them directly. You may want to contact embassies, law firms, publishers, government agencies and so on, and solicit work directly from them. Many companies also use freelance websites, such as **www.elance.com**, **www.freelancer.com**, and **www.freelanceswitch.com**, to find translators for specific projects. If you are fortunate enough to find some good steady clients on your own, you will be doing quite well. But the problem often lies in the word "steady." What seems to be a steady client today may not be so steady tomorrow.

This brings us to the second, and by far the safer option, which is translation agencies. There are hundreds of them in the United States, and they handle huge amounts of translation business every year. In this chapter we will discuss translation agencies, as well as direct sources of translation available to the freelancer.

Translation Companies

Translation companies, also known as translation agencies, or translation bureaus, are for the most part privately owned commercial establishments ranging in size from one or two employees to ten or more, but hardly ever more than ten. Some are divisions of larger companies, offering translation as a secondary function. Some specialize in one language only, such as Spanish, German, or Japanese. Most offer several languages, and quite a few bill themselves as offering "all languages." This last type is somewhat pretentious, since there are more languages in the world than any one person can identify. But what they really mean is that they will make the effort to find a translator in almost any language they may be called upon to translate.

As a general rule, translation agencies employ relatively few in-house translators, since the flow of work in any given language is usually uneven. Instead, they rely on the services of a network of hundreds of freelancers who can handle a great variety of subjects. Those freelancers are located all over the United States and even abroad. The ones who are most reliable and professional get the major share of the work, and some of them earn the above-quoted figures.

As a freelancer, you need to cultivate at least one such agency, preferably two or three. The problem in working with only one is that, with few exceptions, there may not be a steady flow of work coming out of any given agency in any given language, in subjects you are equipped to handle. Two or three will give you better coverage, and assure a better flow. On the other hand, you may find yourself in a situation where all three ask you to do something at the same time, and you may not be able to do it. You need to establish an understanding with your agencies that would make an allowance for such a scenario, so that you don't spoil your relationship with any one of them.

The worst thing you can do as a freelancer working with translation agencies is to overcommit yourself. Your most important personal asset is your reliability. Once you fail to meet deadlines (keep in mind—the agency stands to lose a client if deadlines are not met), your reliability becomes questionable, and if you do it once too often, you may soon

Translator and Interpreter Application

<== Return to **Schreibernet.com**

STI

Thank you for your interest in working with Schreiber Translations, Inc. In addition to receiving your resume, we are interested in finding out some specific details regarding your services. This information will enable us to better match our needs with your services.

STI specializes in highly technical translation in over 90 languages. Most of the time, we work under strict time constraints, and our deadlines are critical. To qualify as a freelancer, you need expertise in specific areas, native ability in your target language, current electronic equipment, and a commitment to deadlines and quality.

There are five sections of information on this form: **Contact, Translator, Interpreter, Equipment** and **Experience**. Please fill in as much information in each of the sections as you can and then click the Submit Resume button at the bottom of the form. Your information will be reviewed as soon as possible after receipt and we will contact you with any questions. Please note that submitting this application is in no way a guarantee that you will receive work form us, however by filling out the application completely you stand a better chance of expediting the approval process.

Thank you again and we look forward to the possibility of working with you.

STI

Application for freelance linguists posted on a translation company's Website, www.Schreibernet.com (see next page).

⌄Equipment

What type of equipment/software do you have access to? Please mark all that apply.

PC   MAC   Fax   WordPerfect   Word   PowerPoint

Desktop Publishing and   HTML editing software

Graphics   InDesign   Foreign Language Software (specify:)

Quark   PageMaker

Other software not listed:

⌄Experience

Please provide us with 3 professional references so that we can contact them regarding the quality of your work.

Company 1:

Attention:

Address:

City and State:

Country:

Postal Code:

E-Mail Address:

Phone:

Fax:

Company 2:

Attention:

Address:

Sample section of the application

SCHREIBER TRANSLATIONS, INC.
51 Monroe Street, Suite 101
Rockville, MD 20850
Phone: (301) 424-7737

WORK ORDER
Fax: (301) 424-2336
Modem: (301) 424-0877
E-Mail: Translation@schreiberNet.com

JOB NO. STI-24000   Date Assigned: 08/02/99   Date Due: **09/01/99**
12:00:00 PM

NAME	JOHN DOE
ADDRESS	1234 MAIN STREET
	WASHINGTON, DC USA

PHONE H: 202.555.1234   FAX:202.555.1234

SERVICES REQUIRED:
☒ Translation   ☐ Editing   ☐ Proofreading ☐ Formatting   ☐ Dictation
LANGUAGE (FROM) **SPANISH**   (TO)**ENGLISH**
NOTE: IMMEDIATELY CHECK MATERIAL RECEIVED FROM STI FOR ANY OMISSIONS.

REQUESTED   ☐ Hard Copy   ☒ Electronic Copy with file name 24000-SP.DOC
DELIVERABLE:
DELIVERY: ☒ E-Mail   ☐ Facsimile ☐ Modem   ☐ Overnight

SPECIAL INSTRUCTIONS:

NOTE: THIS DOCUMENT IS FOR BILLING PURPOSES ONLY. NOTES OR COMMENTS OF ANY KIND RELATING TO THIS JOB SHOULD BE RELAYED DIRECTLY TO THE PROJECT MANAGER. INCLUDING THEM HERE MAY DELAY PAYMENT.

GENERAL INSTRUCTIONS: (PLEASE READ CAREFULLY):
- The due date specified above is binding. If unable to meet deadline, inform STI immediately by phone so that appropriate action may be taken. Extensions will be granted whenever possible. Late delivery may result in adjustment of payment.
- All work is considered confidential and should not be discussed without STI authorization.
- Translator is responsible for providing a complete and accurate translation, free of spelling errors, omissions, and grammatically and idiomatically poor language. Translator is responsible for reproducing all numbers unless otherwise agreed. STI reserves the right to reject unacceptable work and/or request improvements prior to payment. An incomplete or inaccurate translation may result in adjustment of payment or, in extreme cases non-payment.
- Contractor is required to keep a backup file and/or hard copy of all jobs for up to one month following delivery.
Payment: Payroll is issued on the 15th of every month. All work submitted on or before the 15th of a given month will be paid on the 15th of the following month. Any work submitted to STI after the 15th will be paid on the second 15th thereafter. Payment for written translations is based on target language word count according to agreed program(s), unless otherwise agreed and specified. Payment for editing, proof reading or formatting will be agreed upon before acceptance of job.

THIS PORTION OF THE FORM MUST BE FILLED IN, THE BOTTOM MUST BE SIGNED, AND THE FORM MUST BE RETURNED TO STI FOR PAYMENT TO BE EFFECTED.

PLEASE CHECK THE FOLLOWING:
☐ DID YOU EDIT YOUR WORK?   ☐ DID YOU DOUBLE CHECK NUMBERS?
☐ DID YOU SPELL CHECK YOUR WORK?   ☐ DID YOU CHECK FOR OMMISIONS?
☐ DID YOU USE SPECIFIED FORMAT?   ☐ DID YOU NAME YOUR FILE 24000-SP.DOC?

TOTAL: WORDS/HOURS/PAGES   X $ (RATE) = $

THANK YOU FOR YOUR CONTINUED SUPPORT.

SIGNATURE OF CONTRACTOR   DATE SUBMITTED   APPROVED BY

THIS FORM MUST BE SIGNED AND RETURNED TO SCHREIBER TRANSLATIONS, INC. IN ORDER FOR PAYMENT TO BE EFFECTIVE

Translation agency work order

find out that those phone calls from the agency offering you work assignments stop coming.

Where do you look for translation agencies? Appendix 4 offers a listing of hundreds of such agencies. You can find more on the Internet, or through the ATA (American Translators Association), which has local chapters around the country. My suggestion is to start with those close to home. In this day and age of international electronic communications, distance has little meaning. But then again, close to home still works, because you can meet the people there, befriend them, and in some instances even avail yourself of their dictionaries and other resources.

Keep in mind that a translation company has overhead, and also needs to make some profit to stay in business. They do the hard work of finding translation assignments, and therefore share with you the profit from the job. You can usually make more money by going directly to the client, and if you have enough of your own clients you don't need a translation company to send work your way. But most freelance translators do need those companies, which invariably provide a more steady flow of work than what a freelancer can get on his or her own.

The two things all translation companies appreciate and reward in a freelancer are honesty and loyalty. If you agree to a deadline, stick to it. Don't renege on it at the last minute. That's a sure prescription to spoil your association with your company. Equally important is not to go behind the company's back and try to solicit its own clients directly. Some companies will make you sign an agreement to this effect. Others will rely on the honor system. Don't abuse their trust. It usually doesn't pay off.

Direct Sources of Work

Working with translation agencies usually does not stop you from finding your own clients, as long as there is no conflict of interest with the agency's clients. It would be impossible to list here all the potential sources of direct translation work, since they include practically the entire human race (everyone needs a document translated at some point). But there are some major sources which ought to be mentioned, and here are some of the more important ones.

Law Firms

Law firms are a major source of translation work. Some of the larger firms hire full-time translators or staff members who are bilingual, especially if they do business on a regular basis with a foreign entity. Most firms use translators on an as-needed basis. Legal translation is a specialized field in which you need to acquire experience working with legal documents. There are several legal specialties, such as patent law, international law, immigration, and so on. Each specialty has its own style and terminology, which a translator needs to become acquainted with. As a freelancer, adding legal translation to your list of specialties is an excellent idea. You will find out that your volume of translation will increase considerably by doing so.

Quite often, a law firm needs both document translation and interpretation. Keep in mind that interpretation is a discipline separate from translation, and that there is a big difference between one-on-one consecutive interpreting and simultaneous conference interpreting (see Chapter 15). If asked by a law firm to do both text translation and interpreting, be sure to find out first exactly what the assignments consist of.

Industry

Corporations doing business in other countries have to deal with documents originated in the languages of those countries or English documents that need to be translated into those languages. Here again we find the two approaches of either hiring translators or farming out work to freelancers and to translation services (or a combination of both). This field is perhaps the fastest growing source of translation in the new century. More and more major American companies are turning to international business as a way to offset the decline of business at home and to gain a share of the world market. Their need for translation is growing every day, and even those who have in-house translators are finding themselves using freelancers because of their volume of translation work (see Appendix 4).

If you are fortunate enough to form a relationship with a major company doing business overseas, you may find yourself in the enviable position of dealing with a major, steady source of translation.

How does one get work with major corporations? If you have a special expertise in their field of work, find out who handles outside vendors or services, and give them a call or drop them a note. It also helps to know someone in the company, who can do some of the legwork for you and put you in touch with the right people. As a general rule, this is not easy to do. But persistence does pay off some of the time, and even if only a few respond, it is worth the effort.

The U.S. Government

For several decades following World War II, translation in the federal government enjoyed a boom. The onset of the Cold War resulted in large-scale translation activities on the part of the U.S. Department of Defense (DoD), all the branches of the service (particularly the Army, Navy, and Air Force), and the Central Intelligence Agency (CIA). In addition, such multilingual organizations as the Voice of America (which started broadcasting in 1942 in 40 languages), sprang into being. These and other organizations employed a host of translators, and farmed out millions of words every year to be translated. Looking back, those were the feast years of government translation. During the nineties, however, a major shift has been taking place. Since 1992, there has been a sharp decline in government translations, and those translation agencies and freelancers who were dependent on government work for their bread and butter, were hurting. This is not to say that the U.S. Government is no longer a source of employment for translators. There are still many opportunities for translation in the government, offered by such bodies as the Language Services division of the U.S. Department of State (for in-house as well as freelance translators and interpreters), the Library of Congress, the U.S. Patent and Trademark Office, and so on (see list of U.S. Government Agencies, Appendix 4).

My translation company, Schreiber Translations, Inc. (STI), started out in life as a full-service translation company for the federal government. This was in the early eighties, when the boom was still on. We provided translation from and into over 50 languages and dialects, as well as interpreting, transcription, voice-over, graphics, and editing. Luckily for us, we realized early on that, as the world was changing, we were better off not being locked into government work, and we were able to develop a lucrative practice in the non-governmental sectors. At the same time, because we are located in the Washington, DC area, and because we have gained the trust of government agencies, we continue to get a great deal of government work.

What are the pros and cons of translating for the government? For many linguists over the years, the government has offered job security. I know some fine translators who have worked for the government for many years and had interesting and fulfilling careers. On the other hand, career translators in the government are not paid exceptionally high salaries. Quite a few freelance on the side in an effort to supplement their income. As for freelancers who contract with the government, here we have mixed results. Some have found themselves a cozy niche and are kept busy on a fairly regular basis. Others go through the "feast and famine" syndrome. Some have been frustrated by spending a long time hunting for government assignments, with little result. To freelance effectively for the government, one should, in most instances, work in one of the top languages the U.S. Government is interested in (Spanish, Russian, German, French and Japanese, and currently also Chinese and Arabic).

State and Local Government

Government at all levels, from the municipal to the federal, needs translation. At the local level we find more and more city and county government translating their pamphlets, brochures and other documents into the languages of their immigrant populations, notably Asian languages and Spanish. In addition, local government has an ongoing need for interpreters, mostly for the court system, but also for social services, hospitals, and other local institutions. At this time of tight budgets, this may not be the most lucrative field, but it is definitely worth exploring, since it is local, and mostly uses local linguists.

Major Organizations

Among the largest organizations that use a great deal of translation, one should mention the United Nations, The World Bank, the World Health Organization, the Organization of American States, to cite only some of the better-known ones here in the U.S. Surely there are more in Europe, such as the World Court, the European Community, and NATO. Most of these organizations use in-house linguists, and do not farm out translation work if they can help it. But quite often they have more documents to translate than they can handle in-house, and they look for outside help.

For a list of such organizations and how to contact them, see Appendix 4.

Publishers

Book publishers use freelance translators in many different ways. This is not an easy field to break into, particularly for the beginner. Many publishers turn to academia for translators, and if you are in academia and can translate from or into another language in your field of expertise, there is a chance you can get the work. Others turn to established translators with name recognition. But it is certainly worth trying to query publishers and find out if they need your services.

Software Localization Companies

A fast-growing area of translation is software localization, or translation of software-related text into other languages and adapting the text to the target culture. Software localization companies specialize in computer subjects and in English-into-foreign-language translation. They employ in-house translators, but they also use freelancers from time to time. Their work encompasses everything from computer manuals to localization of websites.

Networking

An excellent source of work for freelance translators is personal contacts with other translators. The ATA's local chapters are one place where translators meet and get to know each other. The annual conference of the ATA holds a networking session, which is very valuable. One also meets translators through personal contacts in the translation field.

The new way to meet translators is on the Internet. Language forums bring together translators from all over the world. All you need to do is post a message on one of those programs, and before you know it you get a response from someone in your own town or half way around the world.

Keeping in touch with other translators is a prime means of discovering work sources and assignments. There are clearly many advantages to networking in the translation field, and the more contacts one has, the better.

Professional translators need to know more than a source and a target language. They also have to develop expertise in the subject areas they translate.

12. A CAREER AS AN IN-HOUSE TRANSLATOR

Translators are not as visible to the general public as dentists or policemen, and therefore seem to be a rare breed. The fact is, thousands of translators work full-time in international corporations and organizations, the U.S. Armed Forces, U.S. Government agencies, law firms, medical organizations, and many other entities. I happen to know a large number of those translation professionals. Many of them seem to be quite happy and fulfilled in their career, and are paid respectable though not outrageous salaries.

If you would like to pursue a full-time translation career, there are several things to consider. Here are some of the most essential.

Level of Expertise

Besides being very proficient in both your source and target language, and having a good writing ability, you have to have expertise in the field you will be working in on a full-time basis. If, for instance, you become a full-time translator for the National Geographic Society, you will need a good background in geography, preferably a graduate degree in that field. Keep this in mind when you apply for an opening for a translator position in any given organization. Chances are they are looking for someone with a strong background in their field.

Translation Training

Potential employers will also be interested in your credentials as a professional translator. They may look for either a translation degree from an accredited institution, accreditation from an organization such as the ATA, or, in the case of U.S. Government employment, for both training and experience. For courses and programs for translators in colleges and universities, and for ATA accreditation, see Appendices 5 and 7.

I am not trying to imply that you cannot find full-time employment as a translator without the above training or accreditation. Unlike medicine or law, translation is not a fully regulated profession by any means. While the above are very helpful, they are not a must. You can find employment as a translator on your own personal merit, provided you can prove that you have an exceptional ability to translate and a thorough familiarity with your subject. The FBI, for instance, will test you to determine your exact level of expertise. Many a career translator started out in a totally different field, and somehow by virtue of his or her special skills in this field became recognized as a reliable and much-needed translator. This, of course, is up to you to discover about yourself.

The Right Language

If your language of expertise is Maltese (the language of the Island of Malta), your chances of finding full-time employment as a translator in the United States are very slim. In all my years as a translation agency manager, I only had one request for Maltese (it came from the FBI, and they later changed their mind about doing it). I did find one person in the U.S. who could translate Maltese, but as I expected it was not his full-time occupation.

Invariably, a full-time translation career is possible if you work in one of the major languages of the world, such as Russian, Spanish, German, French, Italian, Portuguese, Japanese, Chinese, or Arabic.

Multiple Languages

If you are fortunate enough to be fluent in several languages, particularly major ones, you may want to consider a full-time translation career. Many organizations look for individuals like yourself, not the least of which are international companies, law firms, government agencies, and the United Nations.

Pros and Cons

A full-time translation job means steady income, benefits, and

Some Tips on Sending out Resumes for Translation Jobs

1. Proofread your resume ten times. In this business, you cannot afford any typos, mistakes or poor language in your introductory written effort.

2. Put your language and area of expertise in the first paragraph of your resume. This is the first thing the reader wants to know, and there is no sense burying it somewhere on the bottom.

3. Know your potential employers. Be sure you have the right qualifications for what they are looking for.

4. Stick to the point. Don't tell them you like to play tennis or hockey. They are too busy to be bothered with your personal life.

5. Capitalize on your experience, especially if it is relevant to what they are looking for.

6. Don't write a "threadbare" resume. Make it substantial, but only include pertinent information.

7. Use good quality laser printing paper, preferably a grade about the usual 20 pound stock, and, if possible, a pleasing color, like light tan or beige.

8. Don't make it too fancy, just dignified and business-like.

9. If you add a sample translation, make it short (one or two paragraphs) and effective.

10. Make it easy to read, crisply printed, and bold key words, such as your subject areas.

everything else that goes with steady employment. But like all other jobs, it also has its drawbacks. Unlike the freelancer, you don't enjoy the same sense of freedom and flexibility. You become locked into one area and one subject, and at times you may find it quite repetitive and unchallenging. You are also part of an organization which, like all organizations, has its own politics which you may not always find to be to your liking. If you are fortunate enough to work for a congenial organization, you are lucky. But this is not always the case. Ultimately, the decision of which way to go is up to you.

Proverbs from Around the World

A proverb is a short sentence based on long experience.

—Cervantes

The man who is surrounded by dwarves looks like a giant.

—Jewish

Trust in Allah, but tie your camel.

—Arabic

If you scatter thorns, don't go barefoot.

—Italian

Even the lion has to defend himself against flies.

—German

Good luck beats early rising.

—Irish

Visits always give pleasure—if not the arrival, the departure.

—Portuguese

13. TRAINING PROGRAMS

Several institutions, including universities, U.S. Government agencies, and world bodies like the United Nations, provide translation education and training. Yet translator education in the United States is not nearly as advanced as it is in some other parts of the world. In fact, most working translators in America today were trained, so to speak, on the job. I happen to be one of them. My background includes five years of graduate school, but it was not in the field of translation (although in some ways related to it). I picked up translation on my own as a young teenager, as part of my lifelong flirtation with writing. During the past fifteen years I have worked with literally hundreds of translators, and I have watched many of them grow and develop on the job, as I took part in providing them with professional tips and practical advice. This handbook is part of my own effort to put all that experience into a book for the benefit of present and future translators and students of translation. So if you wonder whether you have to take a course or pursue a study program in order to become a translator, the answer is: not necessarily. There are, however, advantages to such programs, and if you have the opportunity to pursue them, you certainly should.

One very effective approach to translator education is to choose a practical field of knowledge where there is a growing need for translation, such as telecommunications, and get a degree in that field, while working on either a translation degree on improving your language and writing skills. There is always a need for a highly specialized technical translator in such a field, and if you establish a reputation for yourself as an authority in that area, you may find yourself very much in demand.

Appendix 5 provides a list of translator education programs around the country. The list is far from exhaustive, and you should consult your local college or university on this matter, since this type of program has been proliferating in recent years. You may also suggest to your local county or other type of government to invite a local senior translator to give an adult education class in translation, which can certainly benefit the community.

Bad Translation

Some years ago the Cincinnati Reds got to the World Series. The next day the following sign appeared all over town:

Darn tootin' we rootin'!

A newspaper reporter from a foreign country was in town that day. He didn't quite know what to make of this sign, and since he was too proud of his English expertise, rather than ask one of the locals to interpret, he came up with his own interpretation. He reported the event to his newspaper in these words:

Signs appeared yesterday all over
Cincinnati, Ohio, saying: "Damn
all those car horns! We are going
back to our roots, namely, to the
horse and buggy!"

---

14. ORAL INTERPRETATION

A field closely related to translation is oral interpretation. Many translators also work as interpreters, and many professional interpreters are known to do text translation as well. The two terms—translation and interpretation—are often confused, despite the fact that they represent two distinct ways of working with language. This handbook is primarily concerned with text translation, but a few words about oral interpretation are in order.

Oral interpretation is best suited for those who possess the following skills:

- Exceptional articulation
- A high comfort level speaking in front of an audience
- Public speaking experience
- Complete ease in both languages
- The ability to retain one or more points while listening to new information, and then reproduce the entire message accurately in the second language.
- The ability to summarize the main points of something that's being said
- Experience in one or more technical areas (not always necessary, but helpful)

Interpreting requirements—depending on the type of interpreting one is engaged in—can range from simple, general conversation, to highly technical exposés and discussions. Most interpreting falls into the general categories of:

- Consecutive interpreting
- Simultaneous interpreting
- Sight translation
- Signing (sign language)

Interpreting can take place in the following environments:
- Escort
- Meeting
- Phone
- Courtroom
- Conference

Consecutive Interpreting. This may be the most common form of interpreting, since it covers a wide variety of situations where the interpreter waits for the speaker to finish a sentence, and then renders it orally in the target language. Some of the most common types of consecutive interpreting are court interpreting, where the interpreter waits for the witness, or any other foreign speaker to finish each sentence or segment of presentation, and then repeats it in the language of the court; medical interpreting, in which the patient does not speak the target language, and needs someone to mediate linguistically between patient and doctor or nurse; business negotiations interpreting, where the two sides sit around the table with an interpreter who helps them communicate by listening to each side and interpreting for the other side.

Other scenarios requiring consecutive interpreting include telecon interpretation, factory/construction site tours, and foreign visitor escort services. Consecutive interpreting requires formal training, and, in such instances as court interpreting, certification as well. Court interpreting is a career that is growing in prominence in parts of the country that have large populations of non-speakers or minimal speakers of English, such as Miami, Los Angeles, Chicago and New York. It should be mentioned that federal and state exams for court interpreter certification require proficiency in simultaneous and sight modes of interpretation, in addition to the consecutive mode. If you find this type of work challenging and suitable to your temperament, you may want to look into training for it by either contacting the local court system or checking the various teaching programs (see Appendix 5).

Escort Interpreting. This is usually the easiest form consecutive interpreting, as it seldom involves very technical language. For the beginner, escort interpreting is a good place to start. A useful resource for learning more about government-related escort interpreting is the U.S. Department of State's Office of Language Services, which produces an

Escort Interpreter Manual. The *Manual* deals with the basic functions and responsibilities of escorts assigned to the U.S. Information Agency's cultural exchange program. To request a copy of the manual, call the OLS' administrative office at (202) 647-1102.

Over-the-Phone Interpreting (OPI). Interpreting over the phone is probably as old as the phone itself, but it has been brought into prominence in recent years by the Language Line service of AT&T. This is a 7-day-a-week, 24-hours-a-day interpreting service, purportedly in 140 languages. The service enables speakers of different languages to communicate by telephone via a three-way conference call including an interpreter. Several translation companies around the country have now entered this field. They hires freelance interpreters who are on call to perform this service, which is used mainly for businesses (such as customer service centers), for 911 calls for the local police, and for public institutions such as school systems. These companies claim to be able to provide an interpreter over the phone within 45 seconds, and that nearly all requests for interpreters are filled.

Simultaneous Interpreting. This is a highly specialized form of interpreting, which requires a special aptitude. True simultaneous interpreting can only be done with the appropriate equipment. There are a few different types currently used, all of which are based on the premise that what the speaker says is transmitted into the interpreter's ear, while the interpreter repeats it into a microphone in the second language. One has to be able to listen to the speaker and repeat the same words in a different language almost at the same time. This takes a great deal of training and experience, and is paid at a higher rate than consecutive. Everyone has seen heads of state on the news with an interpreter standing by, echoing every word uttered by the speaker in another language. No doubt this is a very challenging activity, and those who practice it deserve our admiration. It would not be advisable to undertake this type of interpreting without the proper training and experience. Examples of organizations that employ simultaneous interpreters are the United Nations and the U.S. Department of State.

Simultaneous interpretation may be required for such things as business or professional conferences, training seminars, or presentations. A simultaneous interpretation longer than two hours requires at least two interpreters to allow for rest periods.

Sight Translation/Document Comparison. During conferences and negotiations, there are often written documents that have to be explained, interpreted and/or translated on the spot, for immediate use. While it is understood that one cannot produce perfect translations under such conditions, nevertheless the interpreter on duty has to be able to provide a good working version of the text in question. This means that the interpreter in this particular situation has to be familiar with the subject matter of those documents, and not have to look up every other word in the dictionary. Sight translation can be very taxing at times, but there is little one can do about it. It comes, as they say, with the territory of the interpreting craft.

An interpreter or a translator may occasionally be called upon to compare documents in the source and target languages in order to verify that the two versions are fully identical. This happens most often in the case of legal documents, such as contracts involving private parties, corporations, or international agreements, treaties, etc., at various governmental levels. Discussion may take place in both languages, involving the interpreter, who now acts as a linguistic consultant. This is a highly responsible task which requires sensitivity and familiarity with both cultures and languages, and skills both as a translator and interpreter.

Another example of sight translation occurs when a client is faced with an overwhelming amount of material in a foreign language, and needs someone to review the material and determine which documents or parts of documents are useful and require translation.

Sign Language. This discipline has grown in importance in recent years, as American society has become more sensitive to the needs of the disabled. It is common today to see sign interpreters for the deaf in lectures, conferences and on television. Signing, at the same time, is an activity that has grown in popularity among American interpreters, and more are training for it now than ever before. As evidence of the field's growing pains, recent literature points to insufficient instructional materials and training programs for prospective sign interpreters.

Since it calls for working in the simultaneous mode, signing is a demanding form of interpretation. Nevertheless, this is undoubtedly one of the most rewarding forms of interpretation, as it helps an entire segment of the population participate in the normal activities the rest of us are engaged in. It speaks well for our society that sign language, which was first brought to this country in the last century by the Frenchman Gallaudet, has become a familiar sight to all of us through the mass media, and that there is a regular demand for it in the courts, hospitals, and nearly any other area of human activity.

The Pros and Cons of Interpretation

The field of interpreting can offer many challenges and rewards. It almost always puts the interpreter in an extremely high-pressure situation, both from the standpoint of having to come up with the correct way of saying something on a moment's notice, and because of the consequences of an error made on the part of the interpreter, which can be very serious.

A true commitment to an interpreting career, especially one in simultaneous interpreting, requires flexibility. One must be willing to do a lot of traveling, for example. Also, interpreting assignments are often required in the evenings, during dinners or functions, or on weekends, to meet or see off foreign visitors. A serious consideration with interpreting is the role that personality plays. Unfortunately, there are many instances where an interpreter is dismissed in the middle of an assignment, not because of any lack of skill, but simply because his or her personality rubs the client the wrong way. And yet, interpreting can present many exciting opportunities, including participation in world events, such as the Olympic Games, the launch of a spacecraft, the signing of a peace treaty, or meetings between world leaders.

When considering an interpreting assignment, keep several important factors in mind:

- Insist, and this cannot be emphasized enough, that you be given preparation materials. Whether the assignment is a business meeting or a technical presentation, the only way for you to familiarize yourself with the corporate- or industry-specific terminology in question is to review related materials beforehand. If the client absolutely cannot provide such materials, make sure to inform them that you will be operating at a disadvantage.
- Be sure to discuss fees ahead of time and to obtain some sort of contract from your client outlining these fees. If there is travel involved, there should be some sort of compensation for the travel time. If

the preparation requires an unusual amount of time, there should be some sort of compensation for this as well. There should ideally be some prearranged fee for last-minute cancellation, although if this work stems from the government this may not be possible.

- Confirm that your client is aware of the difference between simultaneous and consecutive interpreting, and if what they really need is simultaneous, they will be providing the appropriate equipment, and also the appropriate backup.
- Make sure you are given a single contact to report to. Often there is confusion when there are several people involved in a meeting or conference, and it is not always clear who has the authority to dismiss you.
- Make sure you are aware of any possible boundaries of your assignment. For example, if a foreign delegation member requests your help on a shopping trip after business hours, should you accompany this person? Will you be paid for your time?

Closing remarks

Interpreting requires a training different from written translation. I would encourage those who are interested in translation yet are more at ease speaking than writing to look into pursuing an interpreting career. To my knowledge, the professional field of interpreting is not nearly as vast as that of translation. But there are thousands of full- and part-time interpreters employed in the United States, mostly by the court system and by international bodies such as The United Nations, The World Bank, The International Monetary Fund, and various U.S. Government agencies, notably the U.S. Department of State. Since interpreters, unlike translators, regularly interact with people under less than easy conditions, it is important for interpreters to have a gregarious and pleasing personality, a good appearance, good manners, patience, social savvy, and a good sense of humor.

Bear in mind that people often confuse oral interpretation with written translation. Be sure, when requested to do interpreting, that they are not actually asking for translating.

The American Translators Association (ATA)

The ATA is to the freelance translator in the U.S. what the AMA is to physicians, or the bar associations to lawyers. While the ATA does not have the status and prestige enjoyed by the AMA or the bar, it is a friendly, vigorous and effective organization, where individual translators have a say and are able to grow together with their association as they work together on a better future for translators and for the translation profession. One may think I have a vested interest in the ATA, or that they paid me to say these things. Wrong on both counts. I am saying these things as someone who has never been active in ATA politics, and who by nature shies away from organizations. I am saying these things because during the past 34 years I have watched the ATA grow from 2,000 to over 11,000 members, with scant means, with little or no outside help, and I have watched its members work hard with a limited budget, producing, among other things, a great monthly professional periodical, the *ATA Chronicle* (which alone is worth the annual dues). Its working committees pursue issues of interest to translators, and its annual conference, which I have enjoyed for the past fifteen years, is arguably the single best opportunity during the year for translators to expand their horizons.

The ATA was established in 1959 by two hardy and idealistic translators in New York. When I joined in 1979 it was headquartered in a town on the Hudson River in New York, but a few years ago it moved to my "neighborhood," namely, the Greater Washington area (Alexandria, Virginia, to be precise). It has quite active regional chapters in North and South Carolina (Carolina Association: CATI), Atlanta (Atlanta Association: WAIT), Missouri (Mid-America: MICATA), Washington, DC (National Capital Area: NCATA), New York City (New York Circle of Translators: NYCT), Cleveland (Northern Ohio: NOTA), San Francisco (Northern California: NCTA), Los Angeles (Southern California: SCATIA), and Florida (Florida Chapter ATA: FLATA), cooperating groups in Colorado (Colorado Translators Association: CTA), Delaware (Delaware Valley Translators Association, DVTA), New Mexico (New Mexico Translators and Interpreters Association: NMTIA), and Seattle (Northwest Translators and Interpreters: NOTIS), and affiliated groups in Michigan (Michigan Association: Matin), and Utah (Utah Association: URIA). Every ATA officer, director, division administrator, chapter officer, and committee member is an unpaid volunteer. For addresses and additional information on ATA chapters, see Appendix 6. The ATA's Website (see address below) also lists unaffiliated regional translation and interpretation organizations.

The ATA accepts all translators as members, as well as translation agencies and organizations involved in translation, such as academic institutions and corporations, but it encourages its individual members to become ATA-accredited. Currently accreditation is available into English from Arabic, Danish, Dutch, Finnish, French, German, Hungarian, Italian, Japanese, Polish, Portuguese, Russian and Spanish, and from English into Chinese, Dutch, Finnish, French, German, Hungarian, Italian, Japanese, Polish, Portuguese, Russian and Spanish. Chinese and Hebrew are being added, and accreditation in the Nordic languages is being studied.

Membership is open to U.S. and foreign translators and translation students, as well as companies and institutions. For more information, please visit:

American Translators Association
225 Reinekers Lane, Suite 590
Alexandria, VA 22314
Phone: +1-703-683-6100
Fax: +1-703-683-6122
Website: www.atanet.org.
E-mail: ata@atanet.org

FIT (Fédération internationale des traducteurs/International Federation of Translators)

This international organization does not accept individual membership, but rather organizational. Its members include the ATA and similar translator organizations world-wide. See Appendix 6 for a list of addresses of FIT chapters and members.

Website: www.fit-ift.org

Other Organizations

There are several additional national, regional and local organizations of translators and interpreters or both in the U.S., and several foreign and international ones that have ties with U.S. translators. During my 27 years of intense involvement in translator affairs in the U.S. I have seen very little evidence of their impact on the affairs or welfare of translators in this country, but since this handbook is committed to giving translators as full a picture as possible of the translation scene in the U.S., I'll try to cover some of this ground.

National Association of Judiciary Interpreters and Translators (NAJIT)

Founded in 1978, NAJIT represents court interpreters throughout the U.S. who work in the federal and state court systems in both foreign and sign languages. It holds annual conferences and local workshops, and publishes a quarterly newsletter (*Proteus*), and other materials for interpreters. It helped design the federal certification exam mandated by the Court Interpreters Act of 1978. For more information, please visit:

NAJIT
1901 Pennsylvania Ave, NW, Suite 804
Washington, DC 20006
Phone: 202-293-0342
Website: www.najit.org

ALTA (American Literary Translators Association)

Operates out of the University of Texas at Dallas. It publishes the biannual *Translation Review.* For more information, please visit:

The University of Texas at Dallas

800 W. Campbell Rd., Mail Station JO51
Richardson, TX 75083-3021
Phone: (972) 883-2093
Fax: (972) 883-6303.
Website: www.utdallas.edu/alta/

PEN American Center

This is the world organization of poets, playwrights, editors and novelists, with an interest in literary translators. For more information, please visit:

PEN
588 Broadway, Suite 303
New York, NY 10012
Phone: (212) 334-1660
Fax: (212) 334-2181
Website: www.pen.org
E-mail: pen@pen.org

AMTA (Association for Machine Translation in the Americas)

Publishes *MT News International.* For more information, please visit:

AMTA
209 N. Eighth Street
Stroudsburg, PA 18360
Phone: +1-570-476-8006
Fax: +1-570-476-0860
Website: www.amtaweb.org
E-mail: business@amtaweb.org

16. TRANSLATION: A LIFELONG CAREER

The best thing about translation is that it is an activity you can pursue at different times of your life, and you can continue doing it or pick it up again even after you retire from your regular job. This has never been more true than today, in the age of digital communications. I wrote several parts of this handbook on the plane from Washington to San Diego, on the beach in Puerto Rico, and in other places I have lost track of, thanks to my six-pound notebook computer and my two-pound LaserJet printer, two small items which travel with me almost everywhere.

When I get up too early to go to the office, I do some translating. When I have some time to kill between engagements, I do some more.

Translation has put me in touch with more areas of human knowledge and endeavor than almost any other career is capable of doing. At one time or another, a translator becomes part of almost anything. During thirty years of providing translation for U.S. Government agencies, I started with the State Department and the FBI, moved on to the Defense Department, and at one time or another interacted with almost every federal department and agency. I can think of few other careers more challenging and fascinating.

But best of all, a translator never stops learning. Language keeps changing, knowledge keeps increasing, and the professional translator stays on top of it all. Once you have developed good translation habits, you will enjoy the continuous activity of learning new words and terms, and being part of the latest advances in many areas of human knowledge. It is, indeed, a privileged position.

I hope you have enjoyed reading this handbook as much as I have enjoyed writing it, and that you will benefit from translation as much as I have. If that is the case, then my reward will be great indeed. I have felt for many years that translators deserve a better break than they have been getting in our largely insular, monolingual society.

Most translators I have known were and are hard-working folk, decent and dedicated people, friendly and generous, and it has been a special privilege for me to be their colleague and friend, as well as teacher and provider of translation work. There is no doubt in my mind that ours is a profession that will become more and more prominent as the twenty-first century begins to unfold, and for several years now I have felt a sense of exhilaration knowing that I am part of one of the great adventures of our time.

APPENDICES

APPENDIX 1.

DICTIONARIES AND REFERENCE LITERATURE

For a general discussion of dictionaries and reference literature, see Chapter 8.

Translators use hundreds, perhaps thousands, of different dictionaries and reference books. The prices on these can vary significantly. It is not possible to list all of them, or to provide their current cost, but there are dictionaries and reference books that stand out, and a good number of those are listed here. Full reference information is provided wherever possible. Entries follow reverse chronological order, except where other-wise indicated, and especially useful works are followed by comments.

The languages listed are:

Afrikaans	French	Norwegian
Albanian	Georgian	Pilipino / Tagalog
Amharic	German	Polish
Arabic	Greek	Portuguese
Basque	Hebrew	Romanian
Bengali	Hindi	Russian
Bosnian	Hungarian	Serbian
Bulgarian	Icelandic	Slovak
Byelorussian	Indonesian	Slovene
Cambodian	Italian	Somali
Catalan	Japanese	Spanish
Chinese	Kazakh	Swahili
Creole	Korean	Swedish
Croatian	Kurdish	Tatar
Czech	Lao	Thai
Danish	Latin	Turkish
Dutch	Latvian	Ukrainian
Esperanto	Lithuanian	Uzbek
Estonian	Macedonian	Vietnamese
Farsi	Malay	Yiddish
Finnish	Nepali	Yoruba

A. GENERAL ENGLISH LANGUAGE REFERENCES

American English Dictionaries
Which is the best dictionary for American English? The answer, quite simply, is none. American English is long overdue for some truly comprehensive dictionary, not unlike the complete *Oxford Dictionary of British English*. In its absence, the following general American English dictionaries are recommended in order of preference:
Webster's Third New International Dictionary, Springfield, MA, 2003. *This is the traditional "major" American-English dictionary. Though dated, it is still good to have around.*
American Heritage Dictionary, 5th Ed., Boston: Houghton Mifflin Harcourt., 2011. *An excellent one-volume all-around dictionary, beautifully illustrated.*
Other large dictionaries of this kind are offered by Random House, Oxford University Press and others, but they do not improve on the above two.
For a smaller, very useful dictionary (of which there are many), we recommend:
Webster's New World Dictionary, Guralnik, D., New York: Simon & Schuster, many editions.
A book which complements the standard dictionaries is:
American English Compendium, 3rd Ed., Rubinstein, M., Rockville, MD: Schreiber Publishing, 2006. *It covers proverbs, expressions, U.S. slang, U.S. vs. British English, foreign words in American English, acronyms and abbreviations, and other "odds and ends."*

American English Reference Books
Most translations into English, particularly technical ones, require what is known as "good idiomatic English." There are general rules for what is considered good writing style and good usage. Here are some of the key books in this field:
ACS Style Guide: A Manual for Authors and Editors, Americal Chemical Society, 1998.
The Chicago Manual of Style, 16th Ed., Chicago: The University of Chicago Press, 2010. *More popular with editors than translators.*
Technical Editing: A Practical Guide for Editors and Writers, Tarutz, J., Addison Wesley Longman, 1992.
The Elements of Style, 4th Ed., Strunk, W. & White, E.B., New York: Macmillan, 1999. *A classic and a must.*
Modern American Usage, Follett, W., New York: Hill & Wang, 1998. *Old but useful. Many good tips on those English words, phrases and terms which are often misused.*
Roget's Thesaurus, Boston: Houghton Mifflin, many editions. *Beware of the thesaurus! It may be useful as an intermediate step in your search for the right word, but not as the final authority.*
Style Manual, U.S. Government Printing Office, Washington, DC, 2008. *A must for translators involved in U.S. Government translations. The Government has its own rules of American English usage, which should be adhered to in this type of work.*

Additional References
Random House Historical Dictionary of American Slang, Lightner, J.E., New York: Random House, 2002.

Acronyms, Initialisms, & Abbreviations Dictionary, Hall, L., Washington: Gale Cengage, 2009.
A Dictionary of American Idioms, Makkai, A., New York: Barron's, 2004.
The Handbook of Good English, Johnson, E.D., New York: Pocket Books, 1991.
The Elements of Grammar, Shertzer, New York: MacMillan, 1996.
The Elements of Editing, Plotnik, New York: Pearson, 1996.
Handbook of American Idioms & Idiomatic Usage, Prentice Hall, 1987.
Colloquial English, Collis, H., Prentice Hall, 1981.

General Reference
This type of book is hard to recommend. The field is so vast it would fill a separate volume. Here are some handy ones:
Encyclopedia Britannica, the flagship of all English-language encyclopedias, is now available on CD-ROM. Powered by Netscape and priced far below the hardcover set, it is a major, though not exhaustive, source of information.
Columbia Desk Encyclopedia, comes in different sizes, and can help you (not always) with names, dates and other bits of information.
Almanacs, many different kinds. Of limited use to translators.
Atlases, too many to enumerate. One of the best new ones is the **Times Atlas of the World.**

Business and Related Fields
Dictionary of Real Estate Terms, Friedman, J., New York: Barron's, 2008.
Dictionary of Insurance Terms, Rubin, H., New York: Barron's, 2008.
Dictionary of Business and Economic Terms, Friedman, J., New York: Barron's, 2012.
Dictionary of Finance and Investment Terms, Downes, J., New York: Barron's, 2010.
Dictionary of Banking Terms, Fitch, T., New York: Barron's, 2012.

Chemistry/Life Sciences
Hawley's Condensed Chemical Dictionary, 15th Ed., Wiley-Interscience, 2007.
In addition to the previous reference, you can find multivolume encyclopedias of chemistry in the public libraries that will answer many of your questions. But as your questions become more and more specific, you will need very specialized reference material in the many specialized areas of chemistry and life sciences, which are often published by government, public and private organizations, such as the World Health Organization (www.who.int), pharmaceutical companies, and many more.

Computers and the Internet
Here the field changes almost daily. For some quick, handy sources of basic computer terminology, you might try:
Webster's New World Dictionary of Computer Terms, 8th Ed., Pfaffenberger, B., New York: Macmillan, 2000.
Newton's Telecom Dictionary, 26th Ed., Newton, H., New York: Flatiron Publishing, 2011.
Computer Desktop Encyclopedia, Freedman, A., New York: McGraw-Hill, 2001.
Dictionary of Computer and Internet Terms, 10th Ed., Downing, D., and Covington, M., New York: Barron's, 2009.

Electric/Electronics
McGraw-Hill Electronics Dictionary, Sclater, N., New York: McGraw-Hill, 1997.
Standard Dictionary of Electrical and Electronic Terms, Jay, F., New York: Institute of Electric and Electronic Engineers, 1997.

Engineering
McGraw-Hill Concise Encyclopedia of Engineering, Parker, S., New York: McGraw-Hill, 2005.

Law
Black's Law Dictionary, 9th Ed., Black, H. C., St. Paul, MN: West Publishing, 2009. *The standard book in its field.*
Merriam-Webster Dictionary of Law, Springfield: Merriam-Webster, 1996. *A comprehensive guide to American law, including new terms, usage examples, and an appendix with an explanation of the American court system. Inexpensive.*
Dictionary of Legal Terms: A Simplified Guide to the Language of Law, Gifis, S., New York: Barron's, 2008.

Medicine
Stedman's Medical Dictionary, 28th Ed., Baltimore: Lippincott, Williams & Wilkins, 2006. *Highly recommended.*
Dorland's Illustrated Medical Dictionary, 32st Ed., Philadelphia: W.B. Saunders Co., 2011. *Also an excellent reference.*
Dictionary of Medical Terms, 6th Ed., Sell, R., Rothenberg, and Chapman, C., New York: Barron's, 2012.
Merck Manual, 19th Ed., Merck & Co., 2011 (see also **The Merck Index**).
The Bantam Medical Dictionary, 6th Ed., New York: Bantam, 2009.
Blakiston's Gould Medical Dictionary, McGraw-Hill, 1979. *Highly regarded.*

Military
For all military material, the Jane series (annual, London: Jane's Information Group) is the key source:
Jane's All the World's Aircraft
Jane's Fighting Ships
Jane's Weapon Systems

Also recommended:
Encyclopedia of Modern U.S. Military Weapons, Laur, T., New York: Berkley Publishing Group, 1998.
The Dictionary of Modern War, Luttwak, E., New York: HarperCollins, 1998.
Encyclopedia of the U.S. Military, Arkin, W., New York: Harper & Row, 1990.
The Harper Encyclopedia of Military History: From 3500 B.C. to the Present, Dupuy, R.E., New York: HarperCollins, 1993.

Science and Technology
Dictionary of Science & Technology on CD-ROM, Academic Press, 1996.

Van Nostrand Scientific Encyclopedia, 10th Ed., Considine, D., New York: Van Nostrand Reinhold, 2008.

McGraw-Hill Dictionary of Scientific & Technical Terms, 6th Ed., Parker, S., New York: McGraw-Hill, 2002. *One of the finest one-volume references covering all science and technology. A must for any technical writer or translator.*

Telecommunications

McGraw-Hill Illustrated Telecom Dictionary, Clayton, J., New York: McGraw-Hill, 2002.

Data & Telecommunications Dictionary, Petersen, J., CRC Press, 1999.

B. GENERAL AND SPECIALIZED DICTIONARIES IN LANGUAGES OTHER THAN ENGLISH

The following list is by no means exhaustive. Wherever we were able to examine a dictionary closely, we inserted a short comment. Otherwise, you should get additional information before purchasing a dictionary, to make sure it fulfills your needs.

AFRIKAANS

Afrikaans-English/English-Afrikaans Dictionary. Kromhout, Jan. Revised edition, Hippocrene Books, 2000.

Afrikaans: Engineering
Engineering Terms: Afrikaans-English/English-Afrikaans. Uys, J.R. New York: i.b.d., 1976.

Afrikaans: Legal
English-Afrikaans Legal Dictionary. Hiemstra, V.G. Gaunt, Inc., 1984.

ALBANIAN

Oxford Albanian-English Dictionary. Newmark, L. Oxford University Press, 2000.
Albanian-English/English-Albanian Standard Dictionary. Hysa, Ramazan. Hippocrene, 2004.

AMHARIC

Advanced Amharic Lexicon: A Supplement to Concise Amharic-English Dictionaries. Getahun, Girma. Lit Verlag, 2004.
Concise Amharic Dictionary. Leslan, W. University of California Press, 1996.
Phrase Book: English, Amharic, Tigrina & Arabic. Giorgis, A.G. 1998.

ARABIC

General Dictionaries
Arabic-English Dictionary: The Hans Wehr Dictionary of Modern Written Arabic. Wehr, H. Snowball, 2011. *This is one of the best general Arabic-English dictionaries around. Available in hardcover and paperback.*
Al-Mawrid: A Modern English-Arabic Dictionary. Baalbaki, M. Kazi Pubns, Inc., 2007. *Contains many modern words and idioms.*
Arabic-English Lexicon. 8 vols. Lane, E.W. French & European Publications Inc., 2003.
The Concise Oxford English-Arabic Dictionary of Current Usage. Doniach, N.S. Oxford: Oxford University Press, 1992.
Al-Fara'id al-Durriyah. Hava, G. Beirut: Dar al-Mashriq, 1982.
An Arabic-English Lexicon. 8 vols. Lane, E.W. Beirut: Librairie du Liban, 1980.
Al-Qamus al-'Asri. Elias, Elias A. Cairo: Modern Press, 1960.

Arabic: Dialects
NTC's Gulf Arabic-English Dictionary. Hamdi, A. Lincolnwood, IL: NTC Publishing Group, 1999.
A Dictionary of Post-Classical Yemeni Arabic. Piamenta, Moshe. Leiden, New York: EJ Brill, 1997.
al-Qamus al-Arabi al-Shabi al-Filastini. Barghuthi, A. al-Lahjah.
al-Filastiniyah al-Darijah. Birah: Jamiyat Inash al-Usrah, Lajnat al-Abhath al-Ijitimaiyah.
A Dictionary of Iraqi Arabic: English-Arabic/Arabic-English, Georgetown Classics in Arabic Language and Linguistics. Clarity, Beverly, ed. Stowasser, Karl, Wolfe, Ronald G., Woodhead, D.R. and Beene, W. Georgetown University Press, 2003.
Dictionary of Egyptian Arabic. Hinds, Martin. Beirut: Librairie du Liban, 1987. *Egyptian terms.*
An Arabic-English Dictionary of the Colloquial Arabic of Egypt. Spiro, S. Beirut: Librairie du Liban, 1980.
A Dictionary of Moroccan Arabic: Moroccan-English & English-Moroccan, Georgetown Classics in Arabic Language and Linguistics. Harrell, Richard, Sobelman, Harvey and Fox, Thomas, eds. Georgetown University Press, 2004.
A Dictionary of Syrian Arabic: English-Arabic, Georgetown Classics in Arabic Language and Linguistics. Stowasser, Karl and Ani, Moukhtar, eds. Georgetown University Press, 2004.

Arabic: Agriculture
Chihabi's Dictionary of Agriculture and Allied Terminology: Arabic-English & English-Arabic. Al-Khatib, A. 2000.

Arabic: Botany
Botany and Microbiology Dictionary: English-Arabic. Safat. Kuwait: Kuwait Foundation for the Advancement of Sciences, 1985.
Illustrated Polyglotic Dictionary of Plant Names. Bedevian, A. Cairo: Argus and Papazian Presses, 1936.

Arabic: Business and Related Fields
Arabic Business Dictionary. Sofer, M, and Ettayebi, A. Rockville, MD: Schreiber Publishing, 2006.
Islamic Economics and Finance: A Glossary. Khan, M.A. Routledge, 2007. *Arabic-English.*
The Office and Business Management Dictionary: English-Arabic, Arabic-English. Compiled by Multi-Lingual International Publishers Ltd. London: Oxford University Press, 1987.
English-Arabic Dictionary of Accounting and Finance. Abdeen, A. Beirut: Librairie du Liban, John Wiley & Sons, 1986.
A Dictionary of Economics, Business & Finance (English-Arabic). Ghattas, Nibah. New Impression edition. Librairie Du Liban Publishers, 2000.
Banking and Financial Dictionary: English, French, Arabic. El Assiouty, M.N. Cairo: Distributor, Investment Trustee Department, National Bank of Egypt, 1980.

Dictionnaire des Termes Economiques et Commerciaux. Henni, M. Beirut: Librairie du Liban, 1982. *English-French-Arabic.*

Arabic: Chemistry
Unified Dictionary of Chemistry Terms: English, French, Arabic. Tunis: Arab League Educational, Cultural and Scientific Organization, 1992.
Kuwait Science Encyclopedia, Chemistry Dictionary. Kuwait: Book & Author Programme, 1984.
Illustrated Dictionary of Chemistry in English with English-Arabic & Arabic-English Glossaries. Godman, A. Beirut: Librairie du Liban, 1984.

Arabic: Civil Engineering
Arabic Dictionary of Civil Engineering. Kay, E. London: Routledge & Kegan Paul, 1986.

Arabic: Communications
A Dictionary of Audio-visual Technology: English-Arabic. Sieny, M.E. Beirut: Librairie du Liban, 1987.
Dictionary of Mass Communications: English-French-Arabic. Badawi, A.Z. Cairo: Dar al-Kitab al-Masri, 1985.

Arabic: Computers
Arabic Encyclopedia of Library, Information, and Computer Terms: English-Arabic. Elshami, Ahmed M. al-Tab'ah: Academic Bookshop, 2001.
Computer Dictionary with CD-ROM (English-Arabic). Arab Scientific Publishers, 2001. *A computer dictionary of computer and software terms with CD-ROM which includes dictionary and Microsoft manual style for technical publications.*
Encyclopedic Dictionary of Computer Terminology. Elzohairy, Librairie du Liban, 1997.
Encyclopedia of Computer and Internet Terms: English-Arabic. Hammad, A.E. Hammad, 2008.
English-Arabic Computer Dictionary. Kashou, R., Reading, Berkshire, UK: University of Reading & Sagar Computers, Ltd., 1992.
An Illustrated Dictionary of Data Processing, Computing, and Office Automation: English-Arabic with English Index. Cusic, D. Beirut: Librairie du Liban, 1988.
Al-Kilani Dictionary of Computer & Internet Terminology, Arabic-English/English-Arabic. Kilani, Taiseer, and Mazen. Beirut: Librairie du Liban, 2004.
A Dictionary of Data Processing and Computer Terms: English-French-Arabic. Haddad, E.W. Beirut: Librairie du Liban, 1994.
Illustrated Dictionary of Computing Science. Quentin, R.D. Beirut: Librairie du Liban, 1996.
Arabic Computer Dictionary. Ghanayem, M.F. Texas: International House Publications, 1986. *Arabic-English.*

Arabic: Diplomacy
A Dictionary of Diplomacy and International Affairs: English-French-Arabic. el 'Adah, Samouhi Fawq. Librairie du Liban, 1996.

Arabic: Geography
Dictionary of Arabic Topography and Place Names. Groom, N. London: Librairie du Liban, 1983.
Glossary of Arabic Place Names. Arabian American Oil Company. s.l.: ARAMCO, 1978.

Arabic: Journalism
al-Qamus al-Ilami: Arabi-Inkilizi. Najm, A. Baghdad: Wizarat al-Thaqafah wa-a;-Ilam, 1982.

Arabic: Law
Arabic-English Law Dictionary. Amin, S.H. Glasgow: Royston, 1992.
Faruqi's English to Arabic Law Dictionary. 5th Rev. Ed. Faruqi, H. Beirut: Librairie du Liban, 2005.
Customs Dictionary: English-Arabic. Mahmoud, R. Cairo: published by author, 1984.
Faruqi's Arabic to English Law Dictionary. Faruqi, H. Beirut: Librairie du Liban, 2003.
Law Dictionary: English-Arabic. al-Wahab, D.I.I. Beirut: Librairie du Liban, 1988.

Arabic: Medicine
Marashi's Grand Medical Dictionary: English-Arabic. Marashi, Dr. Mohammed Oussama. Librairie du Liban Publishers, 2003.
Hitti's Pocket Medical Dictionary: English-Arabic. Hitti, Y.K. Beirut: Librairie du Liban, 2006.
A Modern Arabic Dictionary of Dental Terms: English-Arabic. Duyat, M. Amman: Dar al-Ibdaa, 1990.
Concise Medical Dictionary. Allah, J.& Fawzi, M. Cairo: University Book Centre, 1986.
Qamus Mustalahat Tibb al-Asnan. Mutayyam, K. S.N.: Matbaat al-Taqddum, 1984.
The New Medical-Pharmaceutical Dictionary. Oweida, A.M. Cairo: Dar al-Fikr al-Arabi, 1970.
Dictionary of Anatomy. Abadir, F.M. Princeton University Arabic Collection, Alexandria: Al Maaref Establishment, 1968.
The Unified Dictionary of Anatomy English-Arabic. World Health Organization, 2005.

Arabic: Military
Illustrated Military Dictionary: English Arabic. Hadary, Sherif Al. Madbouli, 2004.
Modern Military Dictionary, Kayyali, M.S. Arab Institute for Research and Publishing, Beirut, London: Third World Center for Research and Publishing, 1994. *Arabic-English-Arabic.*
Arabic Military Dictionary. Kay, E. London: Routledge & Kegan Paul, 1986. *English-Arabic-English.*
Pocket Book of Military Terms. 6th Ed. Badran, C. Cairo: Greater Egypt Publishers, 1982. *English-Arabic.*
Al-Mu'jam al-'Askari al-Muwahhid. Committee for Standardizing Military Terminology for Arab Armies, 1971. *Arabic-English.*

Al-Mu'jam al-'Askari al-Muwahhid. Committee for Standardizing Military Terminology for Arab Armies, Cairo: Dar al-Ma'arif, 1970. *English-Arabic.*

Arabic: Nautical
Elsevier's Maritime Dictionary. Bakre, M. Elsevier Science, Ltd., 1987. *English-French-Arabic.*

Arabic: Oil
A New Dictionary of Petroleum and the Oil Industry. Al-Khatib, A. Beirut: Librairie du Liban, 1990. *English-Arabic.*

Arabic: Psychology and Psychiatry
Mujam Ilm al-Nafs wa-al Tibb al-Nafsi: Injilizi-Arabi. Jabir, J. Cairo: Dar al-Nahdah al-Arabiyah, 1988.
Mujam Ilm al-Nafs, Inkilizi-Faransi-Arabi. Aqil, F. Beirut: Dar al-Ilm lil-Malayin, 1985.
Dictionary of Psychology: English-Arabic, Illustrated. Zahran, H. Cairo: Al Shaab Print House, 1972.

Arabic: Science and Technology
Mustalahat al-Duru. Amman: al-Majma al-Lughah al-Arabiyah al-Urduni, 1994. *Dictionary of explosives.*
al-Mujam al-Muwahhad Li-Mustalahat al-Riyadiyat wa-al-Falak: Injilizi, Faransi, Arabi. Tunis: al-Munazzamah, 1990.
Unified Dictionary for Terminologies of General and Nuclear Physics: English, French, Arabic. Tunis: Arab League Educational, Cultural and Scientific Organization, 1989.
A New English to Arabic Dictionary of Scientific and Technical Terms. Al-Khatib, A. Beirut: Libraire du Liban, 2005.
Mujam al-Hayawan. Maluf, A. Beirut: Dar al-Raid al-Arabi, 1980.
Dictionary of Zoological Terms, Unified Dictionary of Scientific Terms for General Education Levels, No.4. s.l.: Iraqi Academy Press, 1976.
Dictionnaire des sciences de la nature. Ghaleb, E. Beirut: Imprimerie Catholique, 1965. *Arabic-English-French.*
Space Dictionary. al-Laqqani, M. Cairo: Dar El-Hana Press, 1962.

AZERBAIJANI

Azerbaijani-English/English-Azerbaijani Dictionary and Phrasebook. Awde, N., Ande, N. and Ismailov, F., eds. Hippocrene, 1999.
Azerbaijani-English Dictionary. O'Sullivan, P., Kensington, MD: Dunwoody Press, 1995.
Azerbaijani-English/English-Azerbaijani Dictionary. Mamedov, S. New York: Hippocrene, 1995.

BASQUE

Basque-English/English-Basque Dictionary & Phrasebook. Conroy, J. New York: Hippocrene, 1998.

Basque-English/English-Basque Dictionary. Aulestia, G. and White, L. Reno: University of Nevada Press, 1992.

BENGALI

Samsad Bengali-English Dictionary. Biswas, S. Calcutta: Sahitya Samsad, 2008.
Dictionary of English, Bengali & Manipuri. French & European Publications, 1992.

BOSNIAN

Bosnian-English/English-Bosnian Compact Dictionary. Nikolina Uzacanin, N. New York: Hippocrene, 1996.

BULGARIAN

Bulgarian-English/English-Bulgarian Dictionary. Tchomakov, I. New York: Hippocrene, 1997.
Bulgarian-English Dictionary, 2 vols., Atanassova, T., et al. Sofia: 1997.

Bulgarian: Medical
Medical Dictionary:English-Bulgarian, Assen, G. 1998.

Bulgarian: Technical
Technical Dictionary: English-Bulgarian. Sofia: Technika EOOD, 1992.
English-Bulgarian Polytechnical Dictionary. French & European Publications, 1995.

BYELORUSSIAN

Hippocrene Concise Byelorussian-English/English-Byelorussian Dictionary. Ushkevich, A. and Zezulin, A. New York: Hippocrene, 1992.

CAMBODIAN

The New Oxford Picture Dictionary: English-Cambodian. Oxford: Oxford University Press, 1999.
Cambodian-English/English-Cambodian Dictionary. New York: Hippocrene, 1990.
Modern Cambodian Dictionary. Headley, R. Kensington, MD: Dunwoody Press, 1997.

CATALAN

Catalan-English/English-Catalan Dictionary. Sabater, M.S. and Freixenet, J.A. New York: Hippocrene, 2001.
Catalan Dictionary. London: Routledge, 1994. *English-Catalan/Catalan-English.*
Diccionari anglés-català. Oliva: Encyclopedia Catalana, 1989.

CHINESE

General Dictionaries
Far East Medium Chinese-English Dictionary. Shih-chiu, L. Taipei: Far East Book Company (Cheng & Tsui Co.), 2000.
Handbook of Chinese Synonyms with Bilingual Explanations. Beijing: China Today Press, 1992. *Simplified characters.*
Milet Bilingual Visual Dictionary. Corbeil, J.C. Milet, 2001.
English-Chinese Word-Ocean Dictionary, 2 vols. Wang Tungyi, Beijing Defense Industry Press, 1987.
Reverse Chinese-English Dictionary. Beijing: Commercial Press, 1999.
The Shogakukan Dictionary of New Chinese Words. Tokyo: Shogakuk-an, 1985.
Chinese Idioms and Their English Equivalents. Yongzhen, Chen, and Chen, Spring. Hong Kong: Commercial Press, 2002. *A must for anyone translating general Chinese text.*
The Pinyin Chinese-English Dictionary. Beijing Foreign Languages Institute, Chinese-English Dictionary Editorial Committee, Hong Kong: Commercial Press, 1984. *A very good mid-sized dictionary. Entries are arranged alphabetically but there is also a character index.*
A Dictionary of World Place Names. Shanghai: Shanghai Cishu Chubanshe, 1989.
A Classified and Illustrated Chinese-English Dictionary. Hong Kong: Joint Publishing Company, 1989.
Xin hua ci dian. Beijing: Commercial Press, 1980. *The most basic reference. Indispensable.*
Chinese Cihai. Shanghai: Shanghai Cishu Chubanshe, 2001. *The staple reference of Chinese translators for years.*
Xinhua Hanyu Cidian. Dictionary Editorial Department of the Chinese Academy of Sciences' Language Research Institute, Hong Kong: Commercial Press, 2004.
Chinese-English Dictionary of Contemporary Usage. Wen-shun, Chi. Berkeley: University of California Press, 1977.
Handbook of Chinese-English Phrases. Beijing: Waiwen Chubanshe, 1970.
Tung-Fang Kuo-Yu Tz'u-Tien. Taipei: Far East Book Company, 1970.

Chinese: Aerospace/Aviation
English-Chinese Aviation Dictionary. Renjie, Hue. Beijing: Shangwu Yinshuguan, 1983.
Chinese-English Rocketry Dictionary. 7602nd Air Intelligence Group, 1979.

Chinese: Agriculture
A Chinese-English Dictionary of China's Rural Economy. Broadbent, K., Farnham Royal, Bucks, England: Commonwealth Agricultural Bureau, 1978.

Chinese: Biology/Life Sciences
English-Chinese Dictionary of the Life Sciences. Beijing: Zhongguo Kexuejishu Chubanshe, 1992.

Chinese: Business and Related Fields
Chinese Business Dictionary. Sofer, M., Guo, R., eds. Rockville, MD: Schreiber Publishing, 2005.

Global Business Dictionary: English-Chinese-French-German-Japanese-Russian. Sofer, M., ed. Rockville, MD: Schreiber Publishing, 2005.
English-Chinese Dictionary of Finance. Adams, S.J., and Mathieson, T.I. AMCD Publishers, Ltd., Hong Kong University Press, 1992.
Dictionary of International Trade and Finance. Chung-hwa Cheng-hsin-swo Inc. Publishing Department, Taipei, Taiwan: 1989.
A New Century Chinese Dictionary of Economics and Trade. Commercial Press, 2002.
Chinese-English Dictionary of New Economic Terms used in contemporary China. Hong Kong: Commercial Press, 1993.
An English-Chinese Dictionary of Finance, Economics and Accounting. Jinchi, Chen. Beijing Economics Institute, Beijing: Zhong-guo Caizheng Jingji Chubanshe, 1987.
An English-Chinese Dictionary of Economics and Finance. Hu Xisen, Yu Jialai and Qu Wanfang. Beijing: Shiyou Gongye Chubanshe, 1986.
A Glossary of Economic and Commercial Terms (Chinese-English). Xie Zhenqing. Beijing: Zhongguo Duiwai Jingji Maoyi Chubanshe, 1997.
Nichi-Ei-Chu Boeki Yogo Jiten. Shangwu Yinshuguan, Toho Shoten. Tokyo: Toho Shoten, 1986. *Japanese-English-Chinese*
Accounting Terminology in Use in the PRC & the USA. Lou Er-Ying and Farrell, J.B. Hong Kong: Joint Publishing Co., and Shanghai: Shanghai Renmin Chubanshe, 1985.
A Chinese-English Textile Dictionary. Zhu Zhengdu, Lou Erduan, et al. Beijing: Fangzhi Gongye Chubanshe, 1985.
An English-Chinese Glossary of International Finance and Trade. Beijing: Zhong-guo Zhanwang Chubanshe, 1996.
An English-Chinese Lexicon of International Economy. Beijing: Zhongguo Shehui Kexue Chubanshe, 1984.
English-Chinese Economics Glossary. Chongqing: Zhongguo Shehui Kexue Chua-banshe, 1983.
English-Chinese Accounting Dictionary. Beijing: Shiyou Gongye Chubanshe, 1982. *Good, reputable reference.*
A Dictionary of Economic Management Terms. Changchun: Jilin Renmin Chuban-she, 1982.
Glossary of Foreign Exchange Terms. Caizheng Jingji Chubanshe, 1980. *Chinese-English-French-Russian-German.*
English-Chinese/Chinese-English Dictionary of Business Terms. Chu Hsiu-feng. Hong Kong: Chi Wen Publishing Co., 1973.
English-Chinese & Chinese-English Accounting Dictionary. Ji Zehua. Xiang gang wan li shu dian, 1995.

Chinese: Chemistry
English-Chinese Dictionary of Chemistry and Chemical Engineering, 4th Ed. Beijing: Kexue Chubanshe, 2000.
Chinese-English/English-Chinese Chemistry Dictionary on CD-ROM. Beijing: Chemical Industry Press.
Chinese-English-Japanese Glossary of Chemical Terms. Tokyo: Toho Shoten, Ltd.,

1980. *Far from complete, but there are very few other such sources available in this field. Entries are arranged by number of strokes in a character.*

Chinese: Civil Engineering
English-Chinese Dictionary of Civil and Architectural Engineering Terms. French and European Pubns, 1992.

Chinese: Computers
English-Chinese Computer Software Dictionary. Zhou Hanzong. Changsha: Hunan Kexue Jishu Chubanshe, 1986.
A Comprehensive IBM Computer Dictionary. Science Popularization Press, 1985.
English-Chinese Computer Dictionary. Beijing: Renmin Youdian Chubanshe, 1984.

Chinese: Electrical Engineering/Electronics
English-Chinese Dictionary of Data Communications Technology. Electrical Engineering Press, 1990.
Chinese-English Dictionary of Electronics Technology. Gan Dayon. Beijing: Dianzi Gongye Chubanshe, 1987. *A valuable reference.*
English-Chinese Dictionary of Electrical Engineering. Beijing: Kexue Chubanshe, 1987.
English-Chinese Dictionary of Television and Electronics. Beijing: Kexue Chubanshe, 1987.
English-Chinese Dictionary of Remote Sensing. Li Wenlan. Beijing: Kexue Puju Chubanshe, 1986.
English-Chinese Dictionary of Television and Video Recording. Beijing: Renmin Youdian Cidian, 1987.

Chinese: Environmental Sciences
Chinese-English Dictionary of Environmental Sciences. Beijing: Zhongguo Huanjing Chubanshe, 1993.

Chinese: Fiber Optics
English-Chinese Lightwave Communications and Optical Fiber Technical Dictionary. Zanyi Long. Beijing: Renmin Youdian Chubanshe, 1985.

Chinese: Geology
Geology Dictionary. Ministry of Geology and Mineral Resources, Beijing: Dizhi Chubanshe, 1983.
English-Chinese Comprehensive Geology Dictionary. Beijing: Kexue Chubanshe, 1980.

Chinese: Highway Engineering
English-Chinese Dictionary of Highway Engineering. Zhao, Zukang. Beijing: Renmin Jiaotong Chubanshe, 1991.

Chinese: Journalism
English-Chinese Glossary of Newspaper Terms. Hong Kong: Commercial Press, 1986.

Chinese: Laser/Infrared Technology
English-Chinese Dictionary of Lasers and Infrared Technique. Zhou Rongsheng. Beijing: Kexue Chubanshe, 1987.

Chinese: Medical
English-Chinese Medical Dictionary. Commercial Press, 1988.
An English-Chinese Medical Dictionary. Lu, Zai-ying. People's Medical, 2006.

Chinese: Military
English-Chinese Military and Technical Dictionary. Jiang Kang, Lu Zuokang. Luoyang: Yuhang Chubanshe, 1985.
Cihai, Military Supplement. Shanghai: Shanghai Cishu Chubanshe, 1980. *A must, as is the "Cihai" itself.*

Chinese: Science and Technology
The Chinese-English Dictionary of Scientific and Technical Glossaries (Hanying keji dacidian) 2 vol. Beijing: Kexue Jishu Wenxian Chubanshe, 1998. *A good comprehensive general technical dictionary.*
A Comprehensive Chinese-English Dictionary of Science and Technology. Beijing: Commercial Press, 2003.
Chinese-English Dictionary of Scientific and Technical Terms. Harbin: Heilongjiang Renmin Chubanshe, 1985. *One of the best, but unfortunately not available from the publisher.*
Comprehensive Chinese-English Dictionary of Science and Technology. Beijing: Kexue Chubanshe, 1988.
A Modern Scientific and Technical Dictionary. Shanghai: Shanghai Scientific and Technical Publishing House, 1980. *Highly recommended.*
An English-Chinese Dictionary of Technology. Qinghua University Specialist Group, Beijing: Guofang Gongye Chubanshe, 2002. *Recommended.*
A Modern Science and Technology Dictionary. Shanghai: Shanghai Kexue Jishu Chubanshe, 1980.

Chinese: Transportation
English-Chinese Dictionary of Railway Terms. Beijing: Renmin Tiedao Chubanshe, 1977.

CREOLE

Haitian Creole-English Dictionary. Targete, V. Kensington, MD: Dunwoody Press, 1993.
Creole-English/English-Creole Concise Dictionary. Ovide, Stephenic. New York: Hippocrene, 2006.
Haitian Creole-English-French Dictionary. 2 vols. Valdman, A. Bloomington, IN: Creole Institute, Indiana University, 1981.
English Haitian Creole Word to Word (Billingual Dictionaries). Vilsaint, Fequiere. Florida: Educa Vision, Inc., 2006.

Creole: Medicine
Haitian Creole-English Pocket Medical Translator. International Medical Volunteers Association, 1996.

CROATIAN, see Serbo-Croatian.

CZECH

General Dictionaries
Anglicko-český, česko-anglický: English-Czech and Czech-English Dictionary. 10th Ed. Poldauf, I. French & European Publications, 2001.
Czech-English Comprehensive Dictionary. Poldauf, I. New York: Hippocrene, 1998.
Czech-English/English-Czech Concise Dictionary. Trnka, N. New York: Hippocrene, 2009.
English-Czech Dictionary. 4 vols. Hais, K., et al. Prague Academia, 1997.
Slovník spisovného jazyka českého. 4 vols., Hais, K., et al. Prague: Academia, 1971.
Czech-English/English-Czech Dictionary. Chermak, A. Saphrograph Corp., 1963.

Czech: Chemistry
Anglicko-český a česko-anglický chemickotechnologický slovník. Jouklova, Z. Prague: SNTL, 1967.

Czech: Computers
English-Czech Dictionary of Data Processing, Telecommunications & Office Systems. New York: i.b.d. Ltd., 1994.
Anglicko-český a česko-anglický slovník výpo cetní techniky. 2 vols. Minihofer, O. New York: i.b.d., 1994.

Czech: Economics
Česko-anglický obchodní slovník. Zavada, D. Prague: Orbis, 1958.

Czech: Electronics
English-Czech and Czech-English Dictionary of Electrical Engineering & Electronics. Malinova, L. Prague: SNTL, 1992.

Czech: Nuclear Physics
Czech-English/English-Czech Dictionary of Nuclear Physics and Nuclear Technology. New York: i.b.d. Ltd., 1985.

Czech: Technical
Česko-anglický technický slovník. 4rd Ed. Stackova, V. Prague: SNTL-Nakladatelství technický literatury, 1986.
English-Czech Technical Dictionary. 4th Ed. Bazant, Z.P. French & European Publications, 1986.

DANISH

General Dictionaries
Danish-English Comprehensive Dictionary. Kjaerulft-Nielsen, B. New York: i.b.d. Ltd., 1994.
Danish Dictionary. Garde, A. London: Routledge, 1995.
Nye ord i dansk. Petersen, P. Copenhagen: Gyldendal, 1984. *Danish-Danish*
Nudansk ordbog. 2 vols. Becker-Christensen, C. Copenhagen: Politikens forlag, 2002.

Danish: Business and Related Fields
English-Danish Commercial Dictionary. Svensson, A.L. New York: i.b.d. Ltd., 1991.
Miniordbog i fanansietingsenggelsk: engelsk-dansk, dansk-engelsk. Norager, P. Copenhagen: Samfundslitteratur, 1987.
Dansk-engelsk handels-og fagordbog: for erhvervslivet, administrationen og forvaltningen. Bailey, I.E. Copenhagen: Det Schon-bergske Forlag, 1989.

Danish: Law
Retsplejeordbog (Legal Dictionary). Hjelmblink, S. Copenhagen: Munksgaard, 1991(Munksgaards ordboger).
Danish: Medicine
Medicinsk ordbog: dansk-engelsk, engelsk-dansk. Pilegaard, M. and Baden, M. Copenhagen: Munksgaard, 1994.

Danish: Technical
English-Danish Technical Dictionary. Clausens. New York: i.b.d. Ltd., 1995.
Danish/English Technical Dictionary. Christensen, A.O. New York: i.b.d. Ltd., 1995.
Teknisk ordbog: dansk-engelsk, udarbejdet i samarbejde med Fonden for Fagsproglig Liksikografi. Copenhagen: Fonden for Fagsproglig Leksikografi og Grafisk Forlag, 1990.
Dansk-engelsk teknisk ordbog. Warrern, A. Copenhagen: Clausen Boger, 1989.

DUTCH

General Dictionaries
NTC's Compact Dutch & English Dictionary. New York: McGraw-Hill, 1998.
Wolters Handwoordenboek Nederlands-Engels. 20th Ed. ten Brug-gencate, K. Utrecht: van Dale Lexicografie, 1997. *English-Dutch volume also published 1997.*
Wolters' Engels Woordenboek. 20th Ed. 2 vols. Gerritsen, J., et al. Wolters-Noordhoff, 1997.
Van Dale Dutch-English/English-Dutch Dictionary. Martin, W. and Tops, G.A.J. Utrecht, Van Dale Lexicografie, 2004.
The New Routledge Dutch Dictionary. Osselton, N. E. and Hempelman, R. London: Routledge, 2003.
Van Dale, Groot Woordenboek der Nederlandse Taal, 12th Ed. 3 vols. Geerts, G. & Heestermans, H. Van Dale Lexicografie, 1995.
Nijhoffs Zuid Nederlands Woordenboek. de Clerck, W. Antwerp: Martinus Nijhoff, 1981.

Jansonius Nieuw Groot Nederlands-Engels Woordenboek. 3 vols. Jansonius, H. Leiden: Nederlandsche Uitgeversmaatschappij, 1973.

Dutch: Business and Related Fields
The Banking and Insurance Lexicon (Dutch-English). Voeten, M.E.C.M., Van Den End, A. Gateway: 1996. *Excellent.*
English-Dutch Dictionary of Financial Management. 5th Ed. Van Amerongen, F. Samsom, 1992.
Passkey: Dutch-English Reference Book on Business Terminology. 10th Ed. Huit-inga, T. 1998.

Dutch: Computers
Woordenboek Informatics. van Steenis, H. Sybex uitgeverij, 2001.
Verklarend Informatica Woordenboek (Dutch-English). 2nd Ed. van Uitert, C. and Kaspers A.M. 1989.

Dutch: Law
The Legal Lexicon (Dutch-English). 3rd Ed. Van Den End., A. Gateway: 2005. *Excellent resource.*

Dutch: Medicine
Dutch to English and English to Dutch Medical Dictionary with CD ROM. Kerk-hof, P.L.M. 2006.

Dutch: Military
Dutch-English Dictionary of Military and Associated Terms. Brokling, L.G. Menlo Park, CA: published by the author, 1983.

Dutch: Technical
Dutch-English Great Polytechnic Dictionary. Schuurmans Stekhoven, G. New York: i.b.d. Ltd., 1997. *Recommended.*

ESPERANTO

Comprehensive English-Esperanto Dictionary. Benson, P. Esperanto League for North America, 1995.
Concise Esperanto and English Dictionary. Wells, J.C. Lincolnwood, IL: NTC Publishing Group, 1992.

ESTONIAN

General Dictionaries
Langenscheidt Picture Dictionary (Estonian/English). Langenscheidt, 1993.
Estonian-English/English-Estonian Concise Dictionary. Kyiw, K. New York: Hip-pocrene, 2002.
Estonian-English Dictionary. Saagpakk, P.F. New Haven: Yale University Press, 2000.

Estonian-English Dictionary. Silvet. New Jersey: French & European Publications, 1993.
Estonian: Business and Related Fields
English-Estonian/Estonian-English Business Dictionary. Aule, A., et al. Tallinn: TEA, 1993.

FARSI (PERSIAN)

Farsi-English/English-Farsi Concise Dictionary. Miandji, A. New York: Hippocrene, 2003.
The Larger English-Persian Dictionary. Haim, S. Tehran: Farhang Moaser, 2004. *English-Persian/Persian-English.*
A Dictionary of Common Persian And English Verbs: With Synonyms & Examples. Amuzgar, H. Ibex Publishers, 2005.
Combined New Persian-English and English-Persian Dictionary. Aryanpur Kashani, A. Costa Mesa, CA: Mazda Publishers, 1986.
Comprehensive Persian-English Dictionary. Steingass, F. London: Routledge, 2005.

FINNISH

General Dictionaries
NTC's Compact Finnish and English Dictionary. Sovijarvi, S. NTC Publishing Group, 1999.
Suomi-Englanti-Suomi: Sanakirj. 4th Ed. Reikiaro, I. and Robinson, D. Jy-väskylä: Gummerus, 2005.
Lyhennesanakirja. Helsinki: Otava, 1985.
Finnish-English General Dictionary. 14th Ed. Hurme, R., et al. Helsinki: Wer-ner Söderström, 2003.
Nykyslangin sanakirja. 3rd Ed. Karttunen, K. Osakeyhtiö: Werner Söderström, 1980.
Suomalais-englantilainen suursanakirja. Alanne, V.S. Porvoo: Werner Söderström, 1980.
30,000 Lyhennettä. Helsinki: Otava, 1970.

Finnish: Business and Related Fields
Stock Exchange Dictionary (Estonian-English-Finnish-German-Russian). Liivaku, U. New York: i.b.d. Ltd., 1994.
Finnish-English Technical and Commercial Dictionary. Talvitie, J.K. Frencb & European Publications, 2000.
Ajankohtainen sihteerin perussanasto. 8th Ed. Porko, L. Helsinki: Gaude-amus, 1988.

Finnish: Electronics
Finnish-English Dictionary of Electronics. Hukki, P. Ikaalinen: Hukki & Pakarinen 1995.

Finnish: Medicine
Medical & Scientific Terms Dictionary. Pesonar, N. New York: i.b.d. Ltd., 1987. *English-Finnish.*

Finnish: Military
Sotilaslyhennesanasto. Poroila, E. Kirjapaino: Mikkeli, 1960. *Finnish-English/ English-Finnish.*

Finnish: Technical
Englanti-suomi suuri kuvasanakirja: A visual glossary. Porvoo: Söderström, 1986.

FRENCH

General Dictionaries
Harrap's New Standard French & English Dictionary. 4 vols. London: George G. Harrap & Co Ltd., 1990. *This is the best French-English/English-French dictionary for all-around translation use, and perhaps one of the finest examples of lexicography in any language. One can only wish this kind of a dictionary existed in every language.*
Collins Robert French Unabridged Dictionary. 9th Ed. New York: HarperCollins, 2011. *Arguably the best one-volume French-English/English-French all-around dictionary for translators.*
Le Petit Larousse Illustré. Larousse, 2012.
Le Petit Robert de la Langue Francais. Paris: Robert, 2011. *French-French. Also available on CD-ROM.*
Nouveau Dictionnaire étymologique. 1st Ed. Jacquenod, R. Alleur, Marabout: 1996.
TERMIUM® for CD-ROM. The Government of Canada, Ottawa, Ontario: Public Works and Government Services Translation Bureau, 1995. *An electronic dictionary with over 3 million French and English terms covering many specialized subjects. Updated monthly for subscribers.*
Dictionnaire des faux amis. Van Roey, J., et al. Louvain-la-Neuve: Duculot, 2004. *French-English/English-French.*
Dictionnaire encyclopédique. 2 vols. Maubourguet, P., et al. 1994. *Includes illustrations and atlas.*
Oxford Hachette French-English/English-French Dictionary. 4th Ed. Correard, M.H. 2007. *Also available on CD-ROM. Highly recommended.*
Larousse grand dictionnaire anglais-français/français-anglais. Garney, F. Larousse, 2010.
Dictionnaire de l'argot, ais et de ses origines. Colin, J.P. Paris: Larousse, 2005.
Dictionnaire des mots contemporains. Gilbert, P. Paris: Robert, 1991.
Dictionnaire des néologismes officiels. Fantapie, A. Franterm, 1984. *French-English/ English-French.*
Dictionary of Modern Colloquial French. Herail and Lovatt, London: Routledge, 1996.
The Oxford-Duden Pictorial French-English Dictionary. 2nd Ed. Oxford: Clarendon Press, 1996.
Dictionnaire usuel illustré. Flammarion, 1983.
Lexique général. 4th Ed. New York: United Nations Publications, 1991. *English-French. Used by all United Nations translators.*
Dictionnaire des expressions et locutions figurées. Rey, A. and Chantreau, S. French and European Publications, 1990. *French-French.*
Lexis, Dictionnaire de la langue française. Larousse, 2003.

Dictionnaire français-anglais de locutions et expressions verbales. Dubois, M. Larousse, 1973.
A Dictionary of Colorful French Slang and Colloquialisms. Deak, E. and Deak, S. New York: Dutton, 1964.

French: Aerospace/Aviation
Aeronautics Abbreviations Glossary (French-English). Delol, J. Paris: la Maison du dictionnaire, 1997.
Technical Dictionary of Aeronautics (English-French/French-English). 4th Ed. Lambert R. 2001.
Dictionnaire de l'aéronautique et de l'espace/Dictionary of Aeronautics & Space Technology. Goursau, Henri. St. Orens-de Gameville: published by author. *French-English volume 1998; English-French 2007.*
Dictionnaire de télédétection aérospatiale. Paul, S. Paris: Masson, 1982. *French-English.*

French: Architecture
Dictionary of Architecture & Construction (French-English/English-French). 3rd Ed. Forbes, J. London: Editions Tec and Doc, 2003.

French: Automotive
Glossary of Automotive Terminology. Chrysler Corporation, Warrendale, PA: SAE Publications, 1978. *French-English/English-French.*

French: Business and Related Fields
French Business Dictionary: The Business Terms of France and Canada. Sofer, M., ed. Rockville, MD: Schreiber Publishing, 2005.
Global Business Dictionary: English-Chinese-French-German-Japanese-Russian, Sofer, M., ed. Rockville, MD: Schreiber Publishing, 2005.
Dictionary of Economics, Finance & Accounting Dictionary. Esposito, M., 2005. *French-English/English-French.*
French Dictionary of Business, Commerce and Finance. London/New York: Routledge, 1996. *French-English/English-French (CD-ROM 1999).*
Dictionary of Financial and Stock Market Terminology (English-French/French-English). Freeland, C. Published by author, 2009. *Highly recommended.*
Dictionnaire financier anglais-français. Whettem-Leysen, V. and Adams, S. Cheshire, England: AMCD (Publishers) Ltd., 1995.
Economic, Business & Finance Dictionary (French-English/English-French). 18th Ed. Marcheteau, M. 2009. *Small paperback, but still a good reference.*
Dictionary of Accounting (English-French). Ménard, L. 1994. *Excellent.*
Dictionnaire de banque et bourse. Crozet, Y. 1993.
Dictionnaire économique et juridique anglais-française. 3rd Ed. Baleyte, et al. Navarre, 1992.
Le Robert & Collins du Management (Commercial, Financier, Economique, Juridique), Péron, M. and Shenton, G. Paris: Dictionnaires Le Robert, 2002. *French-English/English-French. Very fine reference.*

Dictionary of Business: English-French, French-English. Collin, P.H. Teddington, Middlesex: Peter Collin Publishing, Ltd., 2002.
Economics Dictionary (French-English/English-French). Greenwald, D. 1987.
French-English/English-French Accounting, Fiscal and Finance Dictionary. de Saxcé, F. 2007.
Glossaire des communautés européennes. Conseil des communautés européennes, 1987.
Delmas/Harrap Business Dictionary. Delmas/Harrap, London: Harrap & Co Ltd., 1979.
Dictionnaire des affaires. Peron, M. Paris: Librairie Larousse, 1968.
Dictionnaire de la comptabilité. 3rd ed. Sylvain, F. Toronto: Institut Canadien des Comptables Agréés, 2011.

French: Chemistry
French-English Dictionary for Chemists. 3rd ed. Patterson, A.M. New York: Wiley & Sons, 1967.

French: Communications
French Dictionary of Telecommunications. New York: Routledge, 1997. *Also available on CD-ROM. French-English/English-French.*
Dictionnaire de multimédia/Multimedia Dictionary, 2nd Ed. Notaise, J. 1996.
Dictionary of Media & Multimedia (French-English/English-French). Chevassu, F. Presse Pocket, 1995.
English-French Dictionary of Telecommunications and the Internet. de Luca, Johanne, 2004.

French: Computers
Dictionary of Computing and Information Technology. 3rd Ed. Simon, C. London, 2004.
Dictionnaire d'informatique français-anglais. 7th Ed. Ginguay, M. Paris: Masson, 2001.
Dictionnaire de la microinformatique. Fantapie, A. Paris: Franterm, 1984. *French-English.*
Dictionnaire de l'informatique. Morvan, P. Paris: Librairie Larousse, 1996.
Harrap's French and English Dictionary of Data Processing. Camille, C. London: Harrap, 1990.

French: Electronics
Encyclopedic Dictionary of Electronics (English-French). Fleutry, L. 1991.
International Electrotechnical Vocabulary, General Index. Geneva: International Electrotechnical Commission, 1979. *English-French/French-English.*

French: Environment
French Dictionary of Environmental Technology. New York: Routledge, 1997. *French-English/English-French.*

French: Journalism
Newspaper French: A Vocabulary of Administrative and Commercial Idiom. Ritchie, A. University of Wales Press, 1993.

French: Law
Dahl's Law Dictionary French-English/English-French. St. Dahl, H. William S. Hein Co., 2008.
Vocabulaire juridique. 9th Ed. Cornu, G. Presse universitaire de France, 2011. *Excellent; covers civil and private law.*
L'Anglais juridique/Legal English. Dhuicq, B. Presse Pocket, 2008.
The Council of Europe Legal Dictionary (French-English). Bridge, F.H.S. Council of Europe Publicationss, 2002. *Highly regarded.*
Economic & Legal Dictionary (French-English/English-French). 5th ed. Baleyte, J., et al. 2000.
Dictionnaire juridique français-anglais. Quemner, Th. A. Paris: Editions de Navarre, 1977.
Dictionnaire juridique et économique. Doucet, M. Paris: La Maison du Dictionnaire, 1980.

French: Medicine
Dictionary of Medicine, French-English with English-French Glossary. 2nd Ed. Djordjevic, S.P. Rockville, MD: Schreiber Publishing, 2004.
The most complete and updated French into English medical dictionary available.
French to English and English to French Dictionary of Medical and Biological Terms and Medications. Hill, G.S. French and European Publications, 2005.
Dictionnaire anglais-francais des sciences medicales et paramedicales. 5th ed. Gladstone, W.J. 2002.
Dictionnaire médical du chirurgien dentiste. 1st Ed. Girard, P., et al. Masson, 1997.
Dictionary of Medical Terms (French-English). Garnier, M. Laurier, 2002. *Excellent.*
Medical Dictionary (French-English). Hamburger, J. Paris: Flammarion, 1994. *Also very useful.*
Dictionnaire français-anglais/anglais-français des termes médicaux et biologiques. Lepine, P. Paris: Flammarion Médecine-Sciences, 1993.
Medical Dictionary (French-English/English-French). Delamare, J. Maloine, 1992.
Dictionnaire de médecine. Hamburger, J. Paris: Flammarion, 1982.

French: Military
A French-English Military Technical Dictionary. Willcox, C. Ross & Perry, 2001.
Lexique militaire. Ottawa: Canadian Forces Headquarters, 1982. *English-French/French-English.*
Glossaire militaire. Imprimerie Nationale, 1982. *English-French/French-English.*

French: Mining
The Oxford-Duden Pictorial French-English Dictionary. Oxford: Clarendon Press, 1996.

French: Oil
Dictionary of Petroleum Technology (French-English/English-French). Moureau, M., and Brace, G., Editions Technip, 2008. *Recommended.*

French: Political
Dictionnaire Français-Anglais/Anglais-Français (Collection Saturne). Dubois, M. Paris: Larousse, 1993.

French: Technical
French Technical Dictionary. 2 vols. London: Routledge, 1997. *French-English/English-French. Very comprehensive. Also available on CD-ROM.*
Words Techniques: dictionnaire thématique anglais: industrie, technologies, ingénierie. Gusdorf, F. Ellipses, 2000.
Dictionnaire Général de la Technique Industrielle, Tome IX: French-English. Ernst, R. Wiesbaden: Brandstetter, 2009.
Dictionnaire international d'abbréviations scientifiques et techniques. Azzaretti, M. La Maison du Dictionnaire, 1978.
Dictionnaire Technique français-anglais. Malgorn, G. Dunod, 2003.

GEORGIAN

Georgian-English/English-Georgian Dictionary & Phrasebook. New York: Hippocrene, 2011.
Kartuli enis ganmartebiti leksikoni. Chikobava, A.S. Tbilisi: Georgian Academy of Sciences Linguistics Institute, 2007.
Inglisur-kartuli leksikoni, Gvarjaladze, T.& I. Tbilisi: Izd. Sabchota sakartvelo, 2003.

GERMAN

General Dictionaries
Langenscheidts Enzyklopädisches Wörterbuch (Der Große Muret-Sanders). 4 vols. Berlin: Langenscheidt, 2000. *The best all-around German-English, English-German dictionary. Quite expensive, but definitely a good investment for the German-English translator.*
Duden Deutsches Universal Wörterbuch. Mannheim: Dudenverlag, 2003. *German-German.*
Deutsches Wörterbuch. Wahrig, G. Gütersloh: Bertelsmann Lexikon-Verlag, 2008. *German-German. Excellent reference.*
Brockhaus-Wahrig-Deutsches Wörterbuch. Brockhaus, F.A. Wiesbaden: 1994.
Grosses Abkürzungsbuch. Koblischke, H. Leipzig: VEB Biblio graph-isches Institut Leipzig, 1994.
Collins German-English/English-German Dictionary. 5th ed. Terrell, P. New York: HarperCollins, 2005.
Collins Unabridged Dictionary (German-English/English-German). 5th ed. New York: HarperCollins, 2005.
Duden Wörterbuch der Abkürzungen. 4th Ed. von Werlin, J. Mannheim: Dudenverlag, 1999. *Recommended.*
Langenscheidts Grosswörterbuch. Messinger H. Berlin: Langenscheidt, 1999.
The Oxford-Harrap Standard German-English Dictionary. Jones, T. Oxford: Clarendon Press, 1978.

English-German/German-English Dictionary. 2 vols. Wildhagen Heraucourt, Wiesbaden: Brandstetter Verlag, 1972. *Though dated, it is still outstanding.*

German: Acoustics
Dictionary of Acoustics. Langenscheidt, 1998. *English-German/German-English.*

German: Advertising/Marketing
Standard Dictionary of Advertising, Mass Media and Marketing (German-English). Koschnick, W.J. 1986.
Dictionary of Advertising and Marketing. Gruber, C.M. 1986.

German: Aerospace/Aviation
Luftfahrt-Definitionen Englisch-Deutsch/Deutsch-Englisch/Glossary of Aeronautical Terms English-German/German-English 2nd ed. Cescotti, R. Stuttgart: Motorbuch Verlag, 1993.
Aeronautic & Space Technology Dictionary (Russian-German-English). Kotik, M. 1986.

German: Agriculture
Dictionary of Agriculture/Forestry/Horticulture. 2 vols. Langenscheidt. *Vol.1 (English-German) 2002; vol. 2 (German-English) 2002.*

German: Automotive
Pons Fachwörterbuch der Kfz-Technik. 2 vols. Schmitt, P. Stuttgart/Dresden: Ernst Klett, 1992. *German-English/English-German. Highly recommended.*

German: Biology
German Dictionary of Biology. 2 vols. Eichhorn, Routledge/Langenscheidt, 1999. *Vol. 1 (German-English, 1st ed.); vol. 2 (English-German, 2nd ed.) on CD-ROM 2005.*
Dictionary of Human Biology: English/German, German/English. Reuter, Peter. Birkhauser, 2001.

German: Business and Related Fields
German Business Dictionary. Sofer, M., ed. Rockville, MD: Schreiber Publishing, 2006.
Global Business Dictionary: English-Chinese-French-German-Japanese-Russian. Sofer, M., ed. Rockville, MD: Schreiber Publishing, 2005.
German Dictionary of Business, Commerce and Finance. London: Routledge, 2003. *German-English/English-German. Also on CD-ROM.*
Dictionary of Business & Economics (German-English/English-German). 5th ed. 2 vols. Schäfer, W. Vahlen F. Verlag, 1997 (German-English), 1996 (English-German). *Highly recommended; a condensed version is available on CD-ROM.*
Management & Marketing Dictionary (English-German/Geman-English). 2 vols. Schäfer, W. 1995. *Also available on CD-ROM.*
English-German Dictionary of Banking and Stock Trading. Zahn, H.E. 2012.
Financial Dictionary (German-English/English-German), Schäfer, W. DTV Verlag, 1999.

Dictionary of Banking & Finance: English-German (Bilingual Specialist Dictionaries). Collin, P.H, Torkar, E., Livesey, R. Peter Collins Publishing Ltd., 2005.
Dictionary of Legal, Commercial and Political Terms. Dietl, Erica, and Lorenz, Egon. Verlag C.H. Beck, 2010. *German-English/English-German. Highly recommended.*
Collins Business German. Clarke, S. New York: HarperCollins, 1992.
Financial & Economic Glossary (English-German). Zahn, H. 1989.
Wörterbuch Wirtschaftsenglisch. Hamblock, D. and Wessels, D. 2008 *German-English; English-German.*
Cambridge-Eichborn German Dictionary. Cambridge: Eichborn/Cambridge University Press, 1983. *German-English/English-German.*
Wörterbuch der Rechts-und Wirtschaftssprache. Romain, A. München: Verlag C.H. Beck, 2002. *German-English/English-German.*

German: Chemistry
English to German Dictionary of Chemistry and Chemical Technology. Technical University of Dresden Staff. 2003.
German Dictionary of Chemistry & Chemical Technology. Gross. 2 vols. Routledge/Langenscheidt. *Vol. 1 (German-English) 6th ed. 1997 vol. 2 (English-German) 5th ed. 1997; (also on CD-ROM 1998).*
German Dictionary of Analytical Chemistry. Knepper, et al. Routledge/Langenscheidt, 1997; CD-ROM 1998.
Dictionary of Chemistry (German-English/English-German). 2 vols. Wenske, G. German-English, 1993; English-German, 1992. *The best.*
Chemie und chemische Technik. Technische Universität, Dresden: VEB Verlag Technik, 1992. *German-English. Recommended.*
Dictionary of Chemical Engineering. Lydersen, A.L. and Dahl, I. New York: John Wiley and Sons, 1992. *English-German-Spanish-French.*

German: Civil Engineering
English to German Dictionary of Building and Civil Engineering. Gelbrich, Uli. French and European Publishers, 2004.
Dictionary of Building and Civil Engineering. 2 vols. Langenscheidt. *Vol. 1, English-German, 2000; vol. 2, German-English, 2001.*

German: Computers
Computer Dictionary German-English/English-German. Microsoft Pr Deutschland, 2000. *Book & CD-Rom edition.*
German Dictionary of Information Technology. London/New York: Routledge, 1996; CD-ROM, 1997.
Computer Englisch. Schulze, Hans Herbert. Hamburg: Zohwohlt Taschenbuch Verlag, 2001. *German-English/English-German.*
Lexikon Informatik und Datenverabeitung/Informatics and Data-processing Lexicon. 4th ed. Schneider, H.J. 1998. *German-English with English-German index.*
Dictionary of Computing (German-English/English-German). Ferretti, V. 2004. *Highly recommended.*
Dictionary of Artificial Intelligence. Langenscheidt, 1998. *English-German/German-English.*

Technische Kybernetik. Junge. Berlin: VEB Verlag Technik, 1982. *English-German/ German-English.*
Fachausdrücke der Text-und Datenverarbeitung. IBM Deutschland, 1978. *English-German.*
Fachwörterbuch Energie-und Automatisierungs-Technik. 4th Ed. 2 vols. Siemens, 1999. *German-English.*
Routledge German Dictionary of Information Technology (CD-ROM). Seeburger, U. London: Routledge, 1998.

German: Construction
German Dictionary of Construction. London/New York: Routledge, 1998.

German: Electronics
English to German Dictionary of Electrical Engineering and Automation. Bezner, Heinrich. French and European Publications, 2003.
German Dictionary of Electrical Engineering and Electronics. Budig, Peter-Klaus. 2 vols. Langenscheidt/Routledge, 1998. *Vol. 1, German-English* (5th ed.)*; vol. 2 (6th ed.). Also on CD-ROM.*
German Dictionary of Microelectronics. Bindmann, W. Routledge/Langenscheidt, 1999. *German-English/English-German.*
Dictionary of Electronics, Computers & Telecommunications (German-English/ English-German). 2 vols. Ferretti, V. Berlin: Heidelberg Springer, 2001.
Dictionary of Microelectronics & Microcomputer Technology. Attiyate, Y.H. and Shah, R. VDI Verlag, 1992.
Lexikon der Elektronik, Nachrichten und Elektrotechnik. Wernicke, H. Deisenhofen: Verlag H. Wernicke, 1985. *German-English-German.*

German: Environment
German Dictionary of Environmental Technology. London/New York: Routledge, 1997. *Also on CD-ROM.*
German Dictionary of Environmental Technology. Langenscheidt, 1998. *English-German/German-English.*

German: Food Technology
Dictionary of Food Technology (English-German). Bratfisch, R. Berlin/Paris: Verlag Alexandre Hatier, 1994.

German: Law
Rechtswörterbuch. Buch und CD-ROM. 20th ed. Creifelds, Carl. 2011.
Legal Terminology Handbook (Anglo-American-German). Heidinger, F. 1996. *Recommended.*
Dictionary of Legal & Commercial Terms. Romain, A. *German-English, 2004; English-German, 2000.*
Dictionary of Legal, Commercial and Political Terms. 2 vols. Dietl, Erica, and Lorenz, Egon. Verlag C.H. Beck, 2010. *German-English/English-German. Recommended.*

Der Grosse Eichborn Legal and Economic Dictionary. Eichborn, R. *German-English, 1986; English-German, 1981.*

German: Medicine
German Dictionary of Medicine. London: Peter Collin, 2002.
German Dictionary of Medicine. Nöhring, F-J. 2 vols. Routledge/Langenscheidt, 1997. *Vol.1, German-English;Vol.2 (English-German). Also on CD-ROM.*
Compact Dictionary of Clinical Medicine (English-German). Reuter, P. and Reuter. C. 1997.
Dictionary of Veterinary Medicine and Biosciences (English-German). 3rd ed. Mack, R. 2006.
Hexal Wörterbuch Medizin German-English/English-German. Walburga, R.B. 1995.
English-German Medical Dictionary. Reuter, P. and Reuter C. Berlin/New York: Springer, 2005.
Roche Lexikon Medizin. Urban & Fischer, 2003.
Medizinisches Wörterbuch. Unseld, D. 1996. *German-English/English-German.*
Wörterbuch für Ärtzte, (Dictionary for Physicians). Stuttgart: Georg Thieme Verlag, 1969. *German-English.*

German: Nautical
Schiffstechnisches Wörterbuch. Dluhy, R. Vincentz Verlag, 1999. *English-German/ German-English.*
Schiffahrts Wörterbuch. Hamburg: Horst Kammer, 1991. *German-English-French-Spanish-Italian.*

German: Nuclear Energy
Engineering. Freyberger, G.H. Stuttgart/New York; Georg Thiemig Verlag, 1979. *English-German/German-English.*
Wörterbuch der Kraftwerkstechnik: 1. Konventionelle Dampfkraft-werke, 2. Kernkraftwerke. Stattmann, F. Stuttgart/New York: Georg Thiemig Verlag, 1977.

German: Optics
Dictionary of Optics and Optical Engineering. 2nd ed. Langenscheidt, 1998. *English-German/German-English.*

German: Patents
Dictionary of Patent and Trademark Practice. Üxeküll, J-.D. 1998. *German-English/ English-German.*

German: Physics
German Dictionary of Physics. 2 vols. Sube, R. Routledge/Langen-scheidt. *Vol. 1 (German-English) 2001; vol. 2 (English-German) 2003. CD-ROM 1999.*

German: Technical
German Technical Dictionary/Universal-Wörterbuch der Technik Englisch. 2

vols. London/New York: Routledge, 2004. *German-English/English-German. Also available on CD-ROM and diskette.*

Fachwörterbuch/Technik und angewandte Wissenschaften German/English. 5th ed. Walther, R. Berlin/Paris: Verlag Alexandre Hatier, 1993.

Last Resort Dictionary for Technical Translators (German-English/English-German). Walker, B. 1992.

Dictionary of Engineering and Technology. Ernst, R. Oxford University Press, 1990. *Recommended.*

Fachwörterbuch Energie und Automatisierungstechnik. Bezner, H. Siemens Aktiengesellschaft, 1999. *German-English.*

The Oxford-Duden Pictorial German-English Dictionary. New York: Oxford University Press, 1997.

The Compact Dictionary of Exact Science and Technology. Kucera, A. Wiesbaden: Brandstetter Verlag, 1989. *English-German.*

Anglo-American and German Abbreviations in Science and Technology. Wennrich, P. New York: Bowker, 1976-78.

Solid-State Physics and Electronic Engineering. Bindman, W. 1972. *German-English/English-German.*

German-English Technical & Engineering Dictionary. 2nd ed. De Vries, L. and Herrmann, T. New York: McGraw-Hill, 1996. *A must for every serious student and translator.*

GREEK

General Dictionaries
Neo Lexiko tis Helliniki. Stafylidis, 1995. *Greek-Greek.*

Hyper Lexicon. Stafylidis, 2005. *Greek-English/English-Greek. Contains examples of use and information on the changes of meaning according to the field of use. Very accurate.*

Langenscheidt Greek (Modern) Standard Dictionary. Berlin: Langenscheidt, 2005.

Hellino-anglikon Evrilexikon. Tsambounara, P. Athens, 1987.

NTC's New College Greek & English Dictionary. Nathanail, P. NTC Publishing Group, 2006.

The Pocket Oxford Greek Dictionary. Pring, J. Oxford: 2002. *Greek-English English-Greek.*

Hyper lexiko tis Ellinikis Glossas. 5 vols. Pagoulatos, 1985. *Greek-Greek.*

Mega Sigkhronon Ellino-Anglikon Lixikon, Genikon kai Emborikon-Oikonomikon-Tekhnikon-Allilografias. Elevtherios Arkhondakis. 1974.

Mega Ellino-Anglikon Lexikon. Crighton, W. Athens: G.K. Elevtheroudakis A.E. *Supplement to the above, more up-to-date, but still not quite caught up with current coinage.*

Greek: Biology/Medicine
Mesh-HELLAS Vioiatriki orologia. Vita Iatrikes Ekdosis. Medical Studies Association, 1995. *The latest in biomedical terminology. Award winner.*

Lexiko tis Viologias. Malliaris Pedia. Harper Collins, 1994. *Contains explanations of terms and illustrations.*

Greek: Economics
Lexiko tis Iconomias. Malliaris Pedia. Harper Collins, 1994. *With explanations of terms and an introduction to economics.*

Greek: Law
Introduction to Greek Law. Kerameas, et al. Sakoulas Publications, 2008. *From the top publisher of legal literature in several languages. Great source of documentation in law, economics, commerce.*

Greek: Physics
Lexiko tis Fysikis. Malliaris Pedia. Harper Collins, 1994. *Contains explanations of terms and explanatory diagrams.*

Greek: Technical
Michigan Press Ellino-Anglikon (Lexikon) Epistimonikon Kai Tekh-nikon Oron. Giannakopoulou, E.S. Athens: Monotoniko, Ekdotikai Viomikhanikai Epikhirisis P. Koutsoumbos A.E., 1984.

HEBREW

General Dictionaries
The Oxford English-Hebrew Dictionary of Current Usage. Kahane, A. and Doniach, N. Oxford University Press, 2004.
Milon Hazuti/Visual Dictionary, Hebrew-English, (Hebrew edition). Sar'el, B. Jerusalem: Carta Publishing, 1998.
TEXTON Electronic Dictionary (English-Hebrew-English). Tel Aviv: Kravitz Technology, Ltd., 1991. *A hand-held electronic dictionary.*
Oxford Student's Dictionary for Hebrew Speakers, (English-English-Hebrew). 2nd Ed. Hornby, A.S. and Reif, J. Tel Aviv: Kernerman Publishing Ltd., 1993. *Intended for Hebrew speakers. Entries in English give English definitions and Hebrew equivalents.*
Dictionary of Israeli Slang *Milon ha-slang ha-makif.* Rosenthal, Ruvki. Jerusalem: Keter, 2006.
The Megiddo Modern Dictionary. Sivan, R. Tel Aviv: Megiddo, 1988. *English-Hebrew/Hebrew-English. Newer than the Alkalai, but not as good.*
The Complete English-Hebrew/Hebrew-English Dictionary. Alcalay, R. Tel Aviv: Masada, 2000. *Hebrew-English/English-Hebrew. Good general source.*
Milon Olami Le'ivrit meduberet. Ben-Amotz, D. Jerusalem: Levin-Epstein, 1982. *An excellent source of Israeli slang.*
Milon Ivri Shalem. 3 vols. Alkalai, R. Ramat Gan: Masada, 2006. *Hebrew-Hebrew. A good authority on contemporary Hebrew.*
Otzar Hasafa Haivrit. Stuchkov, N. New York: Schulsinger, 1968. *A major Hebrew thesaurus.*
Yad Halashon. Avineri, Y. Tel Aviv: Izraeel, 1964. *A treasury of Hebrew elucidations.*
Konkordantzya LaTanakh. Mandelkern, S. Tel Aviv: Schocken, 1969. *The guide to finding every word and phrase in the Bible.*
The Comprehensive Hebrew Calendar. Spier, A. New York: Feldheim, 1996. *The Hebrew and general calendars, 1900-2100.*

A Dictionary of the Targumim, the Talmud Babli and Yerushalmi, and the Midrashic Literature. Jastrow, M. New York: Pardes, 2007. *Hebrew-English. The guide to classical Hebrew and Aramaic.*

Hebrew: Computers
English-Hebrew/Hebrew-English Dictionary. New York: i.b.d. Ltd., 1992.
Dictionary of Electronic and Computer Terms. Bick, J. Bnei Brak: Steimatzky 1991. *Hebrew-English/English-Hebrew.*
The Up-to-Date Technical Dictionary. Bick, J. Tel Aviv: Sifri, 1998.

Hebrew: Economics
Milon Munakhim. Yakir, A. Tel Aviv: Heshev, 1989. *Hebrew-English.*

Hebrew: Law
Legal Dictionary. Shaked, E. Bnei Brak: Steimatzky, 2000.
Legal Dictionary. Moses, E. Tel Aviv, 2006.

Hebrew: Medicine
Dictionary of Medical & Health Terminology. New York: Simon & Schuster, 1997.

Hebrew: Military
Lexicon Dvir, Munakhim Tzvaiim. Burla, Y. Tel Aviv: Dvir, 1988.
Dictionary of Military Terms. Akaviya, A. Haifa: Magen, 1951.

Hebrew: Political
Diplomatic Hebrew: A Glossary of Current Terminology. Marwick, L. Washington, D.C.: Library of Congress, 1980.

Hebrew: Technical
Milon Lemunahim Tekhniyim. Be'er, H. Hata'asiya Hatzva'it, 1984.
The Technical Dictionary. 2 vols. Gafni, H. Jerusalem: Keter Publishing House, 1978. *Hebrew-English/English-Hebrew.*
Technical Dictionary. 6th Ed. Ettingen, S.G. Tel Aviv: Yavneh, 1983. *Hebrew-English-French-German-Russian.*

HINDI

General Dictionaries
The Oxford Hindi-English Dictionary. Verma, S. K. Oxford University Press, 2009.
Hindi-English/English-Hindi Standard Dictionary. Raker, J. New York: Hippocrene, 2002.
Hippocrene Practical Hindi-English/English-Hindi Dictionary. Tiwari, U. New York: Hippocrene, 1991.
A Practical Hindi-English Dictionary. 32nd Ed. Chaturvedi, M. and Tiwari, B.N. New Delhi: National Publishing House, 2009.
Angrezi-Hindi Kosh, (English-Hindi), C. Bulcke, S., New Delhi: Chandra & Co. Ltd. Publishers, 1987.

Hindi: Business and Related Fields
Glossary of Audit & Account Terms, (English-Hindi). 2nd Ed. New Delhi: Office of the Comptroller & Auditor General of India, 1987.

Hindi: Political
Rajniti Vigyan Kosh. Gauba, O. P. Delhi: B.R. Publishing Corporation, 1982. *English-Hindi.*

HUNGARIAN

General Dictionaries
Hungarian-English Dictionary. Akademiai Kiado. *Book & CD-ROM edition, 2006.*
Hungarian Practical Dictionary: Hungarian-English English-Hungarian. Szabo, E. Hippocrene, 2005.
NTC's Hungarian-English Dictionary. Magay, T. and Kiss, L. Lincolnwood, IL: NTC, 1998.
English-Hungarian Deluxe Dictionary. Orszagh, L. Arthur Vanus Co., 1992.
Magyar-Angol Szotar. 2 vols. Orszagh, L. Budapest: Akademiai Kiado 2002.
Idegen szavak es Kifejezesek szotara. Bakos, F. Budapest: Akademiai Kiado, 2007.

Hungarian: Business and Related Fields
Angol-Magyar Bank es Tozsdeszotar. Nagy, Peter. Budapest: Akademiai Kiado, 1993.
Longman Dictionary of Business English, Longman Angol-Magyar Business Szotar. J. Adam, Czobor Zsuzsa. Budapest: Akademiai Kiado, 1993.
Angol-Amerikai Kozgazdasagi Kifejezesek Ertelmezo Szotara. Budapest: Muszaki Fordito Vallalat, 1992.
Magyar-Angol Kereskedelmi, Penzugyi es Bankszotar. Budapest: Muszaki Fordito Vallalat, 1992.
Negynyelvu kozgazdasagi szotar. Kelen, B. Budapest: Kozgazdasagi & Jogi Kiado, 1974.

Hungarian: Computers
Hungarian-English Dictionary of Computer Technology. Kovacs, M. New York: i.b.d. Ltd., 1991.
Az adatfeldolgozas Fogalommeghatarozasai es Tobbnyelvu Szotar. Budapest: Magyar Szabvanyugyi Hivatal, 1982.
Adatfeldogozas, computerek, irodagepek. Verlag Technik. Berlin: Verlag der Ungarischen Akademie.

Hungarian: Geography
Magyar Helysegnev-Azonosito Szotar. Lelkes, G. Budapest: Balassi Kiado, 2011.
Magyar Neve Hatarokon tuli helysegnev-szotar. Sebok, L. Budapest: Arany Lapok, 1990.

Hungarian: Law
Magyar-Angol Jogi Szotar. Mora, I. Budapest: Muszaki Fordito, Vallalat, 1997.

Hungarian: Medical
English-Hungarian Medical Dictionary. Veghelyi, P. Budapest: Terra., 1991.

Hungarian: Technical
Angol-Magyar Muszaki es Tudomanyos Szotar I-II. Magay, T., Kiss, L. Budapest: Akademiai Kiado, 2005.
English-Hungarian Technical Dictionary. Nagy, E. Budapest: Akademiai Kiado, 1990.
Elektronika: Hiradastechnika, Vacuum-technika. 2 vols. Oldal, R. Budapest: Akademiai Kiado, 1983.
Magyar-Angol Muszaki Szotar. 6th ed. Budapest: Akademiai Kiado, 1990.
Angol-Magyar Muszaki Szotar. 7th ed. Budapest: Akademiai Kiado, 1990.
English-Hungarian Dictionary of Science and Technology on CD-ROM. Magay, T.

ICELANDIC

General Dictionaries
English-Icelandic Dictionary. Mladen, D. New York: Hippocrene, 1996.
Icelandic-English Dictionary. Sigurdsson, A. Reykjavík : Orðabækur Ísafoldar, 1999.

Icelandic: Mathematics
English-Icelandic Mathematical Dictionary. Axelsson, Reynir. University of Iceland Press, 1997.

INDONESIAN

Tuttle's Concise Indonesian Dictionary. Kramer, A.L.N. Rutland, VT: Charles S. Tuttle Co., 2007.
An Indonesian-English Dictionary. Echols, J.M. New York: Cornell University Press, 1995.

ITALIAN

General Dictionaries
Cassell's Italian Dictionary: Italian-English English-Italian. Rebora, P. New York: Wiley, 2002.
Il Nuovo manuale de stile. Lesina, R. Bologna: Zanichelli, 2009.
The Firefly Italian/English Visual Dictionary. Corbeil, J.C. Buffalo: Firefly, 2010.
Sansoni-Harrap Italian-English/English-Italian Dictionary. 4 vols. Macchi, V. London, 1991. *Extensive, expensive.*
HarperCollins Sansoni Italian Unabridged Dictionary. Kramer, A.L.N. Rutland, Vermont: Charles Tuttle, 2005.
Dizionario Italiano Ragionato. Gianni, A. Florence: Sintesi, 1988.
Grande Dizionario Hazon Garzanti. Garzanti Editore S.p.A., 2007. *English-Italian/ Italian-English*
Il nuovo Zingarelli vocabolario della lingua italiana. Zingarelli, N. Bologna: Nicola Zanichelli, 1991. *Italian-Italian.*
La nuova enciclopedia universale. Garzanti, 1982. *Italian-Italian.*

Collins/Sansoni Italian Dictionary. 4th Ed. Macchi, V. Glasgow/Firenze: Collins, 2004. *Italian-English/English-Italian.*
Dizionario della lingua italiana. Devoto, G. Firenze: Le Monnier, 2004. *Italian-Italian. Excellent reference.*
Prontuario dei termini politici, economici, sociali in uso in Italia. Ferrau, A. Roma: Zingarelli Editore S.p.A., 1974.
Il Ragazzini/Biagi Concise Dizionario. Ragazzini, G; Biagi, A. Bologna: Nicola Zanichelli, 2007. *English-Italian/Italian-English.*
Streetwise Italian Dictionary/Thesaurus. McGraw-Hill, 2005.

Italian: Business and Related Fields
Italian Business Dictionary. Sofer, M., ed. Rockville, MD: Schreiber Publishing, 2006.
Nuovissimo dizionario commerciale. Ragazzini, G. and Gagliardelli, G. Milan: Mursia 1992. *English-Italian/Italian-English.*
Italian-English/English-Italian Finance & Commercial Dictionary. Picchi, F. Zanichelli, 1990.
Dictionary of Commerce (Italian-English/English-Italian). Motta, G. Milan: Carlo Signorelli Editore, 1978.
Italian-English/English-Italian Dictionary of Economics and Banking. Codeluppi, L. New York: i.b.d. Ltd., 2001.

Italian: Law
Dizionario Giuridico. de Francis, F. 1996. *English-Italian (based on British Law), Italian-English (based on American Law). Very fine reference.*

Italian: Medicine
New English and Italian Dictionary of the Medical Sciences, Biology and Biotechnology. Italian-English and English-Italian/Il Nuovo Medicina e Biologia: Dizionario Enciclopedico di Scienze Mediche e Biologiche e di Biotecnologie Inglese-Italiano e Italiano-Inglese. French and European Publications, 2003.
Medical & Biological Dictionary (Italian-English/English-Italian). Delfino, G. Zanichelli, 1996.
Italian-English/English-Italian Medical Dictionary. Petrelle, M. Le lettere, 2007.
Italian-English/English-Italian Medical Dictionary. Lucchesi, M. Cortina Rafaello 1987.
English-Italian Dictionary of Medical Phraseology. Marino, V. New York: i.b.d. Ltd., 1985.
Dizionario medico. 5th Ed. Lauricella, E. Firenze: Sadea, 1997. *Italian-Italian.*

Italian: Military
Military Dictionary: English-Italian. U.S. Government Staff. Ross & Perry, 2002.

Italian: Nautical
Grande dizionario di Marina. Silorata, M.B. Cava dei Tirreni: Di Mauro, 1970. *English-Italian/Italian-English.*

Italian: Technical
Technical Dictionary. 13th Ed. Marolli, G. Milano: U. Hoepli, 2005. *English-Italian/ Italian-English. Excellent reference, now on CD-ROM.*
English-Italian/Italian-English Technical Dictionary. Ragazzini, G., et al. Milano: Mursia, 1983.
Dizionario tecnico. Denti, R. Milano: Ulrico Hoepli Editore, 1996. *Italian-English/ English-Italian.*
McGraw-Hill Zanichelli Dizionario enciclopedico scientifico e tecnico. Bologna: Nicola Zanichelli, 2004. *English-Italian/Italian-English.*

JAPANESE

General Dictionaries
Kodansha's Furigana English-Japanese Dictionary. Yoshida, M. and Nakamura, Y. New York: Kodansha America, Inc., 1999.
Kojien. Shinmaru, Izuru. Tokyo: Iwanami Shoten, 2008.
Waei Hon'yaku Handobukko. Murata, S. Tokyo: The Japan Times, Ltd., 1991.
Japanese Family Names in
Chinese Characters: A Guide To Their Readings. Nihon Seimei, Yomifuri Jiten Sei no Bu. Tokyo: Nichigai Associates, 1990. *This or a similar name dictionary is a must.*
Japanese Given Names in Chinese Characters; A Guide To Their Readings, Nihon Seimei, Yomifuri Jiten Mei no Bu. Tokyo: Nichigai Associates, 1990. *See note above.*
Shin Gijutsu Ryakugo Jiten. Aoyama, K. Tokyo: Kogyo Chosakai Publishing Co., 1985.
Torendo Nichibei Hyogen Jiten. Iwazu, K. Tokyo: Shogakukan, 2007.
Shin Eiwa Daijiten. Takebayashi, S. Tokyo: Kenkyusha, 2002.
Shin Waei Daijiten. Watanabe, T. Tokyo: Kenkyusha, 2007. *Highly recommended. Includes many examples of usage.*
Nichibei Kogo Jiten. Seidensticker, E. Tokyo: Asahi Shuppansha, 1978.
Nandoku Seishi Jiten. Ono, S. and Fujita, Y. Tokyo: Tokyodo, 1985.
Iwanami Kokugo Jiten. Nishio, M. Tokyo: Iwanami Shoten, 2011.
Nihon Chimei Hatsuon Jiten. Kyokari, N. H. Tokyo: Nihon Hoso Shuppan Kyokai, 1961.

Japanese: Business and Related Fields
Japanese Business Dictionary. Sofer, M., ed. Rockville, MD: Schreiber Publishing, 2005.
Global Business Dictionary: English-Chinese-French-German-Japanese-Russian. Sofer, M., ed. Rockville, MD: Schreiber Publishing, 2005.
Japanese Business Language. Mitsubishi Staff. London: Routledge, 1994.
A Dictionary of Japanese Financial Terms. Williams, D. University of Hawaii Press, 1995.
Advanced Business English Dictionary. Rev. ed. Kobayashi, H. Tokyo: Pacific Management Consultants, Global Management Group, 1987
New Japanese-English Dictionary of Economic Terms. Tokyo: The Oriental Economist, 2000.
Keizai Yogo Jiten. Hasegawa, H. Tokyo: Fujishobo, 1998.

Japanese Directory of Professional Associations. 3rd Ed. Tokyo: Intercontinental Marketing KK, 1995. *After the third edition, the Japan Publications Guide Service switched to publishing solely online. It can be accessed at http://jpgsonline.com*
Nihon Shoko Keizai Dantai Meibo. Tokyo Shoko Kaigisho, 1982.
Waei Keizai Eigo Jiten. Hanada, M. Tokyo: The Japan Times, Ltd., 1978.
Seikai Kancho Jinjiroku. Tokyo: Toyo Keizai Shinposha, 1987.

Japanese: Computers
English-Japanese/Japanese-English Dictionary of Computers and Data-Processing Terms. Ferber, G. MIT Press, 1989.
Japanese-English Dictionary of Computers. Tokyo, Nichigai Associates, 1989.

Japanese: Medicine
Suteddoman Igaku Jiten. Medical View, 2002. *Translation of Stedman's Medical Dictionary.*

Japanese: Technical
Kagaku Gijutsu 35-Mango Daijiten. 2 vols. 3rd ed. Tokyo: Interpress, 1996. *A most comprehensive general purpose Japanese technical dictionary. A reliable source of scientific terms.*
Kagaku Daijiten. Zaidan, K. K. S. Tokyo: Maruzen, 2005.
Nikkei High-Tech Dictionary. Tokyo: Nihon Keizai Shimbunsha, 1988.
Magurokiru Kagaku Gijutsu Yogo Daqiten: McGraw-Hill Science and Technology Dictionary. 3rd Ed. Tokyo: Nikkan Kogyo Shimbunsha, 1997.

KAZAKH

Kazakh (Qazaq)-English Dictionary. Krippes, K.A. Kensington, MD: Dunwoody Press, 1995.

KOREAN

General Dictionaries
NTC's Compact Korean Dictionary. Rhie, G. and Jones, B.J. Lincolnwood, Illinois: NTC, 2002.
Essence Hanyong Sajon, Korean-English Dictionary. Kim Chol-hwan. Seoul: Minjung Sorim, 2001.
The New World Comprehensive Korean-English Dictionary. Seoul: Sisa Yong-osa, 1989.
Essence Yonghan Sajon. Kim Myong-hwan & Kim Chol-hwan. Seoul: Minjung Sorim, 1984.
Hyondae Choson-mal Sajon. Seoul: Taejegak, 1991. *Korean-Korean.*
Kugo Taesajon. Li Hui-sung. Seoul: Minjung Sorim, 1998. *Korean- Korean.*
Choson Munhwa-o Sajon. Pyongyang: Linguistics Research Institute, Academy of Social Sciences, 1973.

Korean: Business and Related Fields
Korean Business Dictionary. Sofer, M. Rockville, MD: Schreiber Publishing, 2006.

Kyongje Sino Sajon. Seoul: Maeil Kyŏngje Sinmunsa, 2010.

Korean: Nuclear Energy
Wonjaryok Yongo Sajon. Seoul: Hanguk Wonjaryok Sanop Hoeui Chulpansa, 1983.
English-Korean/Korean-English.

Korean: Technical
Kigye Yongojip. Seoul: Tongmyongsa, 1976. *Korean-Chinese-English/English-Korean-Japanese.*
Kigye Yongo Sajon. Seoul: Songan-dang, 1982. *English-Korean/Japanese-Korean/Korean-Japanese-English.*

KURDISH

Kurdish-English/English-Kurdish Dictionary. Amindarov, A. New York: Hippocrene, 2006.

LAO

Lao-English Dictionary. Kerr: White Lotus, 1992.
English-Lao/Lao-English Dictionary. Marcus, R. Rutland, VT: Charles E. Tuttle, 2001.

LATIN

Cassell's Latin Dictionary. Simpson, D.P. New York: MacMillan, 2003.
Langenscheidt Pocket Dictionary (Latin-English/English-Latin). Berlin: Langenscheidt, 2005.
Latin Dictionary. Lewis, C.T. and Short, C. Oxford: Clarendon Press, 2005.

LATVIAN

Practical Latvian-English/English-Latvian Dictionary. Sosare, M. New York: Hippocrene, 2000.
Latvian-English Dictionary. Turkina, P. E. Riga: Avots, 1991.
Renyi Bilingual Picture Dictionary Latvian. Forest House Publishing, 1994.

LITHUANIAN

English-Lithuanian Dictionary. Piesarkas, B. Vilnius: Alma Littera, 2004. *Lithuanian-English/English-Lithuanian.*
Lithuanian-English Dictionary. Vilnius: Mokslas, 1979.
Lithuanian-English/English-Lithuanian Concise Dictionary. Martsinkyavishute, V. New York: Hippocrene, 2008.

MACEDONIAN

Macedonian Dictionary. Mircevska, S. New York: Routledge, 1998.

Anglisko-makedonski recnik. Crvenkovski, D. Skopje: Venecija, 2007.
Makedonsko-angliski recnik na idiomi. 3rd Ed. Murgoski, Z. Skopje: Tabernauka, 2002.
Macedonian-English/English-Macedonian Concise Dictionary. Wermuth, J. New York: Hippocrene, 1997.

MALAY

Comprehensive Malay Dictionary. Pelanduk, 2004.
English-Malay/Malay-English Dictionary. French & European Publications, 1992.
Standard Malay-English/English-Malay Dictionary. Rev. ed. Coope, A.E. New York: Hippocrene, 1993.

NEPALI

A Practical Dictionary of Modern Nepali. Schmidt, R. L, Singh M. Delhi: Ratna Sagar, 2005.
Nepali-English/English-Nepali Dictionary. Prakash, A.R. New York: Hippocrene, 2003.
Concise Nepali-English/English-Nepali Dictionary. Raj, P.A. New York: Hippocrene, 1992.

NORWEGIAN

General Dictionaries
Norwegian Dictionary (Norwegian-English/English-Norwegian). 2nd Ed. London: Routledge, 2006.
Aschehoug og Gyldendals store norske ordbok. Guttu, T. Oslo: Kunnskapsforlaget, 2005.
Engelsk-norsk ordbok. 2nd ed. Svenkerud, H. Cappelen, 2004.
Norsk-engelsk administrativ ordbok: Navn og termer fra offentlig virksomhet. Chaffey, P. Oslo: Universitetsforlaget, 1999.
Norsk-engelsk ordbok, stor utgave. Kirkeby, W.A. Oslo: Aschehoug-Gyldendal, 1986.
Bokmålsordboka. Definisjons-og rettskrivningsordbok. Landrø, M.I. and Wangensteen, B. Oslo: Universitetsforlaget, 2007. *Norwegian-Norwegian.*
Definisjons- og rettskrivingsordbok. Høvdenak, M., et al. Oslo: Det Norske Samlaget, 2006. *Norwegian-Norwegian. This book and the above are the most comprehensive, single-volume N-N dictionaries.*
ADNOM: norsk-engelsk glossar. Oslo: Universitetsforlaget, 1984.
Norwegian-English Dictionary. 4th Ed. Haugen. Madison: University of Wisconsin Press, 1996.
Norsk slang. Tryti, T. Oslo: Universitetforlaget, 2009. *Norwegian-Norwegian. Government administration and private association names and terms.*
Nyord i norsk, 1945-1975, Nor.-Nor. Norsk Språkråd, Oslo: Universitetsforlaget, 1982. *Contains cross-references among Danish, Norwegian and Swedish.*
Norsk-engelsk handelsordbok. Gabrielsen, E.D. Oslo: Kunnskapsforlaget, 1978.

Norwegian: Agriculture
Norsk landbruksordbok: utgitt av Nemnda for Norsk land-bruksordbok. Rømmetveit, M. Oslo: 1979.

Norwegian: Automotive
Norwegian-English/English-Norwegian Dictionary of Motor Vechicle and Traffic Terminology. Kirkeby, W.A. New York: i.b.d. Ltd., 1978.

Norwegian: Business and Related Fields
English-Norwegian Dictionary in Social Economics. Hansen, E. Scandinavian Press, 1992.
Norwegian English Commercial Dictionary. Gabrielsen, E.D. New York: i.b.d. Ltd., 1987.

Norwegian: Law
Norsk-engelsk juridisk ordbok: strafferett, straffeprosess og andre termer; med engelsk-norsk register. Chaffey, P. and Walford, R. Oslo: Universitetsforlaget, 1999.
Norsk-engelsk juridisk ordbok. Craig, R.L. Oslo: Universitetsforlaget, 1999. *Contract law.*
Norsk-engelsk juridisk ordbok: sivilrett og strafferett. Lind, A. Oslo: Bedriftsøkonomens Forlag, 2007.

Norwegian: Medical
Norwegian-English/English-Norwegian Medical Dictionary. Kåss, E. New York: i.b.d. Ltd., 1993.

Norwegian: Military
English-Norwegian Military Dictionary. Ark, O.J. Oslo: J. W. Cappelens, 2002.
Engelsk-amerikansk-norsk militær ordbok. Marm, I. Oslo: Fabritius, 1977.
Norwegian: Oil
Petroleums-ordliste: engelsk-norsk, norsk-engelsk. Utarbeidet ved Norsk termbank. Oslo: Universitetet i Bergen, 1988
Olje Ordliste, Rådet for Teknisk Terminologi Norsk Språkåd. Universitesforlaget, 1992.

Norwegian: Technical
Engelsk-Norsk teknisk ordbok. 6th rev. ed. Ansteinsson & Reiersen, F. Bruns bokhandels forlag, 1999.
Miljøleksikon: energi, helse, natur, økologi. Pleym, H. Bekkestua: NKI, 1991.
Norsk teknisk fagordbok. Hjulstad, H. and Norevik, B. Bergen: Universitetsforlaget, 1984.
Norsk dataordbok. 5th ed. Norsk språkråds komité for dataterminologi. Bergen: Universitetsforlaget, 1993. *Norwegian-English.*
Teknisk, illustrert ordbok. Arleij, R., oversatt av Hacheim, O., and Eidnes, T. Oslo: Yrkesopplæring, 1983. *Contains English, French, Spanish, Finnish, Polish, Serbo-Croatian, Turkish, Vietnamese, and Urdu equivalents.*
Ordbok for automatiseringsteknikk. Rådet for teknisk terminologi. Oslo: 1986.

PILIPINO/TAGALOG

Pilipino: General Dictionaries
Tagalog-English/English-Tagalog (Filipino) Standard Dictionary. Gavez Rubino, C. New York: Hippocrene, 2002.
Pilipino-English/English-Pilipino Phrase Book and Dictionary. New York: Hippocrene, 2006.
Vicassan's Pilipino-English. Santos, V.C. Manila: National Book Store, 2006.
Hippocrene Concise Pilipino-English/English-Pilipino Dictionary. Bickform, S. New York: Hippocrene, 2006.

Tagalog: General Dictionaries
English-Tagalog/Tagalog-English Pocket Dictionary. Enriques, L. Colton Book Imports, 2005.
Tagalog Dictionary. Ramos, T.V. Honolulu: University of Hawaii Press, 1997.
English-Tagalog Dictionary. English, L.J. Manila: Congregation of the Holy Redeemer, 2008.

POLISH

General Dictionaries
Polish-English Dictionary. Vol. 1-3. Pogonowski, I. New York: Hippocrene, 1996.
Collins Polish-English/English-Polish Dictionary. 2nd Ed. Glasgow: HarperCollins, 2012.
Mały słownik subkultur młodzieóowych. Peczak, M. Warsaw: Semper, 1992. *Youth, subculture, and slang idioms.*
Słownik języka polskiego. 3 vols. Warsaw: Państwowe Wyd. Naukowe, 1992. *Polish-Polish.*
Wielki słownik pol.-ang./ang.-pol. 2 vols. each. Stanisławski, J. Warsaw: Wiedza Powszechna, 1993.
Encyklopedia popularna PWN. Warsaw: Państwowe Wyd. Naukowe, 2007. *Polish-Polish.*
Słownik poprawnej polszczyzny. Doroszewski, W. Warsaw: Państwowe Wyd. Naukowe.
Słownik wyrazów obcych. Tokarski, J. Warsaw: Państwowe Wyd. Naukowe.
Mały słownik języka polskiego. Skorupka, S. Warsaw: Państwowe Wyd. Naukowe, 1968.
The Kosciuszko Foundation Dictionary. 2 vols. Bulas & Whitfield. New York: The KoÑciuszko Foundation, 2008. *Polish-English/English-Polish.*

Polish: Aerospace
Słownik lotniczo-kosmonautyczny (pol.-ang.-ros.). Czerni, S. Warsaw: Wyd. Komunikacji i Łączności , 1984.

Polish: Agriculture
Mała encyklopedia rolnicza. Warsaw: Wyd. Rolnicze i Leśne, 1964.

Polish: Business and Related Fields

Słownik handlu zagranicznego. Białecki, Klemens, et al. Warsaw: Państwowe Wydawnictwo Ekonomiczne, 1993.

Słownik pięciojęzyczny ekonomiczno-handlowy. Ratajczak, P. Zielona Góra: Kanion, 1993. *Multilingual. Has English, French, German, and Russian for Polish terms.*

Podręczny słownik menedóera. Woytowicz-Neyman, M. and Pu»awski, M. Warsaw: Państwowe Wydawnictwo Ekonomiczne, 1992. *English-Polish/Polish-English.*

Podręczny słownik polsko-niemiecko-angielski rachunkowości i bankowości. Jaruga, A. et al. Łódź: Towarzystwo Gospodarcze RAFIB, 1992.

Mi"dzynarodowy s»ownik finansów. Bannock, G. and Manser, W. Warsaw: Wydawnictwo Andrzej Bonarski, 1992.

Leksykon finansowo-bankowy. Jaworski, W., et al. Warsaw: Państwowe Wydawnictwo Ekonomiczne, 1991.

Słownik terminologii prawniczej i ekonomicznej angielsko-polski. Jaślan, J. & H. Warsaw: Wiedza Powszechna, 1991. *Designed for lawyers and economists.*

Mały słownik biznesmena. Rumowska, E. and Czerniawski, R. Warsaw: Poltext, 1991.

Słownik skrótów. Paruch, J. Warsaw: Wiedza Poszechna, 1990. *A listing of acronyms and abbreviations.*

Leksykon rachunkowości. Niewiadoma, M. Skierniewice: Centrum Kreowania Liderów, Bogusław J. Feder. *English-Polish.*

Pocket Business Dictionary, Polish-English/English-Polish. 2 vols. Woytowicz-Neyman, M. and Malec, J.

Słownik handlowo-ekonomiczny polsko-angielski. Đwieóewska, W. Warsaw: Państwowe Wyd. Ekonomiczne, 1970.

Mały słownik ekonomiczny. Drewanowski, et al. Warsaw: Polskie Wyd. Gospodarcze, 1958.

Polish: Computers

Terminóów I Komunikatóów Komputerowych. Sikorski, W. Warsaw: Mikom, 1995.

Dictionary of Computer Science (English-Polish). Marciniak, A., et al. Warsaw: Wydawnictwo Naukowe PWN, 1993.

Polish: Environment

Dictionary of Environmental Protection (Polish-English). Czekierda, K. 2010.

Polish: Law

Police and Legal Dictionary (Polish-English-French-German-Russian). Sostek, G. 1996.

Słownik prawniczy polsko-angielski. Cracow: Wyd. Polskiej Akademii Nauk, 1986.

Polish: Medicine

Polish-English/English-Polish Medical Dictionary. Słomski, P. New York: i.b.d., 2003.

Lexicon Medicum (Eng.-Rus.-Fr.-Ger.-Lat.-Pol.). Złotnicki. Warsaw: 1971.

Polish: Military

Leksykon wiedzy wojskowej. Warsaw: Wyd. Ministerstwa Obrony Narodowej, 1979.

Mała encyklopedia wojskowa. 3 vols. Wyd. Ministerstwa Obrony Narodowej, 1970.
Ilustrowany wojskowy słownik techniczny (Pol.-Rus.-Eng.-Fr.). Zlomanov, A.A. Wyd. Ministerstwa Obrony Narodowej, 1968.
Angielsko-polski słownik wojskowy. Wyd. Ministerstwa Obrony Narodowej, 1960.

Polish: Nautical
Maritime Dictionary (English-Polish/Polish-English). Milewski, S. Warsaw: Wyd. Naukowo-Techniczne, 1992.

Polish: Technical
Technical Dictionary (Polish-English/English-Polish). Reprint. Skrzynska, M., et al. 2010.
Angielsko-polski słownik skrótów-elektronika, informatyka, teleinformatyka. Bosakirski, B. Warsaw: Wydawnictwo Naukowo-Techniczne, 1992.
Słownik naukowo-techniczny polsko-angielski/angielsko-polski. 2 vols. Czerni, S. and Skrzyńska, M. Warsaw: Wyd. Naukowo-Techniczne, 1992.
Leksykon naukowo-techniczny. Warsaw: Wyd. Naukowo-Techniczne, 1983.

PORTUGUESE

General Dictionaries
The Oxford-Duden Picture Dictionary: (English- Brazilian Portuguese). Oxford University Press, 2008.
Dicionário de Expressões Populares Portugueses. Simões, G. A. Lisbon: Dom Quixote, 1993. *Portuguese-Portuguese,*
The New Michaelis Dictionaries. São Paulo: Edições Melhoramentos, 2000. *A series of dictionaries. The* Novo Michaelis *Portuguese-English/English-Portuguese is a good comprehensive dictionary.*
Dicionário Escolar de Português-Inglês /Dicionário Escolar de Inglês-Português. 2 vols. sold separately. Lisbon: Porto Editora, 2007.
Novo Dicionário Aurélio da Língua Portuguesa. 5th ed. Buarque de Holanda, A. Curitiba: Ed. Positivo, 2005. *Portuguese-Portuguese. Essential.*
A Portuguese-English Dictionary. Taylor, J. Stanford University Press, 1998.
A Dictionary of Informal Brazilian Portuguese. Chamberlain, B. Washington, D.C.: Georgetown University Press, 2003.
Webster Dicionário Inglês-Português. Houaiss, A. and Cardim, I. Rio de Janiero, Record, 2008.
Dicionário de Expressões Idiomáticas. Pugliesi, M. Editora Parma Ltda., 1981. *Portuguese-Portuguese.*
The New Appleton Dictionary of the English and Portuguese Languages. Houaiss, A. New York: Appleton-Century-Crofts, 1967.
HarperCollins Portuguese Concise Dictionary. 3rd ed. HarperCollins, 2010.
Dicionário Estrutural, Estilístico e Sintático da Língua Portuguesa. Ramalho, E. Porto: Lello & Irmão, 1999. *Though published in Portugal, it is still useful for Brazilian texts.*

Portuguese: Business and Economics
Portuguese Business Dictionary. Sofer, M., ed. Rockville, MD: Schreiber Publishing, 2006.
Dicionário de Termos de Negócios Inglês-Português/Português-Inglês. 3rd Ed. Pinho, Manuel Orlando M. Editora Atlas, 2007.
Michaelis Dicionário Executivo Inglês-Português. Melhoramentos, 1989.
Dicionário Bancário Português-Inglês. Correia da Cunha, A. Portugal: Publicações Europa-América, 1988. *Excellent but small.*
Dicionário de Economia e Gestão. Lima, G., et al. Porto: Lello & Irmão, Editores, 1984.
Dictionary of Economic and Commercial Terms. Cavalcante, J.C. Marques, 1982. *English-Portuguese.*
Dicionário Técnico Contábil. Altmann, M.R. 1990. *English-Portuguese/Portuguese-English.*

Portuguese: Computers
Computer Dictionary: English-Portuguese/Portuguese-English. French & European Publications, 1998.
Dicionário de Informática, Inglês-Português, Português-Inglês. Microsoft Press, Editora Campus, 1998.
Dicionário Enciclopédico de Informática. Fragomeni, A.H. 1987. *English-Portuguese/Portuguese-English.*
Dicionário de Informática. Society of Computer and Peripheral Equipment Users. Rio de Janeiro: 1985.
Dicionário de Informática. Lisbon: Publicacões Dom Quixote, 1984.

Portuguese: Law
Enciclopédia do Advogado. 5th ed. Soibelman, L. Rio de Janeiro: Luso-Brazilian Books, 1995. *Portuguese-Portuguese. Essential for legal translation.*
Noronha Legal Dictionary/Dicionário Jurídico. 6th Ed. de Noronha Goyos, D. Editora Observador Legal, 2006. *Portuguese-English/English-Portuguese. An absolute necessity.*
Dicionário Jurídico Português-Inglês/Inglês-Português. 9th Ed. Chavez, M. Rio de Janeiro: Barrister's Editora, 2011.
Vocabulário Jurídico. 2 vols. DePlacido e Silva. Rio de Janeiro: 2009. *Portuguese-Portuguese.*

Portuguese: Medicine
Medical Dictionary: English, Spanish, Portuguese. Notte-Schlegel, I. New York: Springer-Verlag, 2008.
Dicionário Médico. Paciornik, R. Rio de Janeiro: Editora Guanabara-Koogan, 1985.
Dorland (Pocket) Dicionário Médico. Sao Paolo: Roca, 2004.

Portuguese: Metallurgy
Dicionário Metalúrgico, Inglês-Português, Português-Inglês. Taylor, J.L. São Paulo: Assoc. Brasileira de Matais, 2004.

Portuguese: Technical
Dicionário Verbo de Inglês Técnico e Científico. Farinha dos Santos Tavares, J. Lisbon: Editorial Verbo, 2007. *English-Portuguese/Portuguese-English.*
Glossário de Termos Técnicos. Mendes Antas, L. São Paulo: Traco Editora, 1980.
DePina Dicionário Técnico (Inglês-Português/Português-Inglês). Araujo, Avelino de Pina. MAKRON Books, Editora McGraw-Hill, 1978.

ROMANIAN
General Dictionaries
Romanian-English/English-Romanian Dictionary. New York: Hippocrene, 2002.
NTC's Romanian and English Dictionary. Bantaş, A. Lincolnwood, IL: NTC, 1997.
Dicţionar de neologísme. Marcu, F. and Manca, C. Bucharest: Editura Academici, 1978.
Dicţionarul explicativ al límbii române. Coteanu, I. and Seche, L.& M. Bucharest: Academy of the Republic of Romania, 1975.
Dicţionar engléz-român. Leviţchi, L. Bucharest: Academy of the Republic of Romania, 1974.
Dicţionar român-engléz. 3rd ed. Leviţchi, L. Bucharest: Editura Stiinţifică', 1973.
Dicţionarul límbii române modérne. Macrea, D. Bucharest: Academy of the Romanian Republic, 1958. *Romanian-Romanian. Later editions may be available.*

Romanian: Business
Business Dictionary. London: Peter Collin, 1999.

Romanian: Technical
Dicţionar tehnic român-englez. Bucharest: Editura tehnic|, 1970.

RUSSIAN

General Dictionaries
The Oxford Russian Dictionary. Unbegaun, B. Oxford: Oxford University Press, 2007.
English-Russian/Russian-English Dictionary. 2nd ed. Katzner, K. New York: John Wiley & Sons, 1999. Also available on CD-ROM. *Good for American English.*
Russian-English Dictionary of Verbal Collocations and Translation. Benson, M. & E. Amsterdam/Philadelphia: John Benjamins, 1993.
Russian-English Translator's Dictionary. Vedeneeva, C. and Zimmerman, M. 1997.
Elsevier's Russian-English Dictionary. 4 vols. Macura, P. Amsterdam: Elsevier, 1999. *One of the major all-around Russian-English dictionaries. Expensive.*
Slovar russkogo yazyka. Ozhegov, S.I. Moscow: Russkiy yazyk, 2006. *Russian-Russian. A good one-volume general dictionary.*
Russian-English Dictionary of Interjections and Response Phrases. Kveselevich, D. I. and Sasina, V.P. Moscow: Russkiy yazyk, 1990.
New English-Russian Dictionary. Galperin, I.R. Moscow: Russkiy yazyk, 1993. *Reliable, one of the best in the field.*
Russko-angliyskiy slovar. Smirnitskiy. Moscow: Russkiy yazyk, 1989.
Krylatye slova. Ashukin, N.S. Moscow: Khudozhestvennaya literatura, 1999.
Dictionary of Russian Abbreviations. Scheitz, E. New York: Elsevier, 1986. *A must.*

Abbreviations and acronyms are a plague of the Russian language, and a translator's nightmare.
Russian-English Dictionary. Taube, A.M. Moscow: Russkiy yazyk, 1993.
The Oxford Russian-English Dictionary. Wheeler, M. Oxford: Clarendon Press, 2000. *Excellent, but not as extensive as the Elsevier.*
Slovar russkogo yazyka, Rus-Rus. 4 vols. Yevgenyeva, W.P. Moscow: Russkiy yazyk, 1981, 1983, 1984. *A first choice for many translators.*
Slovar russkikh lichnykh imen. Petrovski, N.A. Moscow: Russkiy yazyk, 1995.
Sovetski entsiklopedicheski slovar. Prokhorov, A.M. Moscow: Sovetskaya entsiklopediya, 1984.
Russian-English Dictionary of Abbreviations and Initialisms. Shipp, J.F. Philadelphia: Translation Research Institute, 1982. *Out of print.*
Slovar trudnostey russkogo yazyka. Rozental, D.E. Moscow: Russkiy yazyk, 1984. *Very helpful for translation into Russian.*
Solzhenitsyn's Peculiar Vocabulary: Russian-English Glossary. Carpovich, Vera V. New York: Technical Dictionaries Co., 1976.
Frazeologicheskiy slovar russkogo yazyka. Molotov, A.I. Moscow: Sovetskaya entsiklopediya, 1967.

Russian: Agriculture
Elsevier's Dictionary of Agriculture and Food Production. Rakipov, N. and Geyer, B. Elsevier Science B.V., 1994. *Russian-English.*
English-Russian Dictionary of Agriculture. Kozlovsky, V.G. and Rakipov, N.G. Moscow: Russkiy yazyk, 1997.
Russko-angliyskiy selskokhozyaystvenniy slovar. Ussovskiy, 1977.

Russian: Aviation/Aerospace
Elsevier's Dictionary of Civil Aviation. Beck, S. Aslezova. Elsevier, 2002.
Dictionary of Aeronautics and Space Technology. Goursau, H. and Novitchkov, N. Saint-Orens-de-Gameville, France: Goursau, 1994. *English-Russian.*
English-Russian Dictionary of Civil Aviation. Marassanov, V.P. Moscow: Russky Yazyk Publishers, 1989.
Aeronautics & Space Technology Dictionary (Russian-German-English). Kotik, M. 1986.
English-Russian Aviation & Space Dictionary. Murashkevich, A.M. Moscow: Voyenizdat, 1974.

Russian: Botany
Russian-English Botanical Dictionary. Macura, P. Columbus: Slavica, 1982.

Russian: Business and Related Fields
Russian Business Dictionary. Sofer, M., ed. Rockville, MD: Schreiber Publishing, 2005.
Global Business Dictionary: English-Chinese-French-German-Japanese-Russian. Sofer, M., ed. Rockville, MD: Schreiber Publishing, 2005.
Elsevier's Dictionary of Economics, Business, Finance and Law: Russian-English. Elsevier, 2007.

Russian-English, English-Russian Business Dictionary. Zagorskaya, A. and Petrochenko, N.P. New York: John Wiley, 1996.
Dictionary of Economics and Finance (English-Russian). Anikin, A. 2004.
Russian-English Foreign Trade and Foreign Economic Dictionary. Zhdanova, I.F. Moscow: Russkiy yazyk, 2002.
A Russian-English Social Science Dictionary. Smith, R.E.F. Birmingham: Institute for Advanced Research in the Humanities, 1990.
Ekonomiko-matematicheskiy slovar. Fedorenko, N.P. Moscow: Nauka, 1987.
Kratkiy ekonomicheskiy slovar. Belik, Yu. A. Moscow: Politizdat, 1989.
Ekonomicheskiy morskoy slovar-spravochnik. Kotlubay, M. Odessa: Izd. Mayak, 1976.

Russian: Chemistry
Elsevier's Dictionary of Chemistry (Russian-English). Macura, P. Amsterdam: Elsevier, 1993. *Recommended.*

Russian: Civil Engineering
Elsevier's Dictionary of Civil Engineering. Bhatnager, K.P. Amsterdam: Elsevier, 1988.

Russian: Computers
The Comprehensive Russian-English Dictionary of Computer Terms. Druker, P. IEEE Computer Society Press, 1999.
English-Russian Explanatory Dictionary of Abbreviations in the Field of Computer Terms. Sevastyanov, 1995.

Russian: Education
Lingvo-stranovedcheskiy slovar: narodnoye obrazovaniye v SSSR. Denisova, M.A. Moscow: Russkiy yazyk, 1978.

Russian: Electronics
Anglo-russkii slovar po radioelektronike. Lisovskiy, F.V. Moscow: Russkiy yazyk, 1999. *A valuable and comprehensive reference in the field. Contains a Russian index.*
Russian-English Dictionary of Electrotechnology and Allied Sciences. Macura, P. Melbourne, FL: Robert E. Krieger Publishing Company, 1986.
Anglo-russkij slovar po mikroelektronike. Prokhorov, K. Moscow: Russkiy yazyk, 1985.

Russian: Geography
English-Russian/Russian-English Geographical Dictionary. Gorskaya, M. Moscow, 1994.

Russian: Geology
Russko-angliyskiy geologicheskiy slovar. Sofiano, T. A. Alexandria: American Geological Institute, 1984.
Geologicheskiy slovar. 2 vols. Moscow, 1978. *Russian-Russian.*

Russian: Law
English-Russian dictionary of American criminal law. Clothier, G. Greenwood Press, 1998.
Legal Dictionary (Russian-English). Butler, W. E. 2001.
Legal Dictionary (English-Russian). Mamulyan, A.S. and Kashkin, S. 2005.
Encyclopedia of Soviet Law. Amsterdam: Martinus-Jijhoff Publishing Co. 1985.

Russian: Maritime
English-Russian Dictionary of Navigation, Hydrography and Oceanography. Sorokin, A.L. 1984.

Russian: Mathematics
Russian-English Dictionary of Mathematics. Efimov, Oleg. Boca Raton, FL: CRC Press, 1993.
Russian-English Mathematical Dictionary. Milne-Thomson, L. M. Ann Arbor, MI: University Microfilms International, 1991.
Russian-English Dictionary of the Mathematical Sciences. Lohwater, A.J. Providence, RI: The American Mathematical Society, 1990.

Russian: Medicine
Comprehensive Russian-English Medical Dictionary. Russo. 3rd ed. 2005.
Stedman's English-Russian Medical Dictionary. Moscow: Géotar, 1995. *Recommended.*
Russian-English Medical Dictionary & Phrase Book. Petrov, V., et al. 1993.
English-Russian Dictionary of Medical and Biological Abbreviations. Akzhigitov, G.N. Rockville, MD: Kamkin, 2001.
Anglo-russkiy slovar po immunologii i immunogenetike. Petrov. Moscow: Russkiy yazyk, 1990.
Anglo-russkiy slovar po biotekhnologii. Drygin. Moscow: Russkiy yazyk, 1990.
Anglo-russkiy meditsinskiy slovar. Akzhigitov, G.N. Moscow: Russkiy yazyk, 2000.
The above four dictionaries are an absolute must for translating medical texts.
Entsiklopedicheskii slovar meditsinskikh terminov. Petrovskiy. Moscow: Sovetskaya entsiklopediya, 1984. *Russian-Russian.*
Russian-English Medical Dictionary. Yeliseyenkov, Yu.B. Moscow: Russkiy yazyk, 1975.
Russian-English Biological-Medical Dictionary. Carpovich. New York: Technical Dictionaries, 1960.

Russian: Metallurgy
English-Russian Metallurgical Dictionary. Perlov, N.I., Isteyev, A.I., Tyurkin, V.A., et al. Moscow: Russkiy yazyk, 2002.

Russian: Military
Russian-English Glossary of Military Terms and Abbreviations. 2nd ed. Office of Naval Intelligence, 1993.
English-Russian Dictionary of Antimissile & Antisatellite Defense. Novichkov, N.N. Moscow: Voyenizdat, 1989.

English-Russian Military Dictionary. 3rd ed. Shevchuk, V.N. and Polyukhin, V.M. Moscow: Voyenizdat, 1987. *Classic. Contains media jargon on military themes.*
Voyennyy Entsiklopedicheskiy slovar. 2nd ed. Akhromeyev, S.F. Moscow: Voyenizdat, 1986.
Spravochnik ofitsera nazemnoy artillerii. 2nd ed. Lebedeb, V.Ya. Moscow: Voyenizdat, 1984.
Russian-English/English-Russian Military Dictionary. London: Her Majesty's Stationery Office, 1983. *British usages.*
Anglo-russkiy voyenno-morskoy slovar. Favorov, P. Moscow: Voyenizdaat, 1994.

Russian: Mining
Gornoye delo: terminologicheskiy slovar. 4th ed. Lidin, G.D., et al. Moscow: Nedra 1990.
English-Russian-English Dictionary on Mining Polyglossum 3.52 (on CD). V.P. Manyshev. ETS Publishing House, 2005.

Russian: Oil
Wavetech's Russian/English Oil & Gas Translator: Abbreviations, Parameters, and Unit. Pennwell, 1996.
Woods' Illustrated English-Russian Petroleum Technology Dictionary. Serednytsky, L., et al. Dallas/Kiev: Albion Woods Publisher, 1997.
Petrologicheskiy anglo-russkiy tolkovyy slovar. Marakushev, A. A. Moscow: Mir, 1986.
Russko-angliyskiy razgovornik dlya neftekhimikov i khimikov-neorganikov. Kuznetzov, Yu.I. and Sloushcher, V.M. Moscow: Russkiy yazyk, 1985.
Russko-angliyskiy neftepromyslovyy slovar. Stoliarov, D.E. Moscow: Russkiy yazyk, 1982.
Anglo-russkij slovar po chimii i pererabotke nefti. Kedrinskiy, V.V. Moscow: Russkiy yazyk, 1979.

Russian: Physics
Russian-English Physics Dictionary. Emin, I. New York: Wiley & Sons, 1963.

Russian: Technical
Dictionary of Science & Technology (Russian-English). 4th Ed. Callaham, L.I. 1996.
Elsevier Dictionary of Science and Technology. Chakalov, G.G. Amsterdam: Elsevier, 1996.
The Comprehensive English-Russian Scientific and Technical Dictionary. 2 vols. Barinov, S.M., et al. Moscow: Russkiy yazyk, 2007.
Science and Engineering Dictionary. Carpovich, Drs. E.A. & V.V. Technical Dictionaries Co., 1988. *Excellent, even indispensable.*
Russko-angliyskiy politekhnicheskiy slovar. Kuznetsov, B. V. Moscow: Russkiy yazyk, 2005.
Kratkiy illyustrirovannyy russko-angliyskiy slovar po mashinostroyeniyu. Shvarts, V.V. Moscow: Russkiy yazyk, 1983.
Anglo-russkiy slovar po sistemnomu analizu. Vyshinskaya Ye. V. 1982.
Politekhnicheskiy slovar. Ishlinskiy. Moscow: Sovetskaya entsiklopediya, 1980.

Anglo-russkiy slovar po nadezhnosti i kontrolyu kachestva. Kovalenko, E.G. Moscow: Russkiy yazyk, 1999. *A comprehensive work for anyone engaged in this field.*
Russko-angliyskiy tekhnicheskiy slovar. Chemukhin. Moscow: Voyenizdat, 1971.
Russian-English Scientific and Technical Dictionary. Alford & Alford. Oxford: Pergamon, 1981.

SERBIAN, See Serbo-Croatian

SERBO-CROATIAN
Note: While Serbian and Croatian are now being treated as two separate languages, most dictionaries for those languages are still known as Serbo-Croatian dictionaries. Serbian and Croatian dictionaries are included in this category.

General Dictionaries
Standard English-SerboCroatian/SerboCroatian-English Dictionary. Benson, M. Cambridge University Press, 1999.
Srpskohrvatsko-engleski recnik. 6th Ed. Benson, M. Nis: Zograf, 2005.
English-SerboCroatian and SerboCroatian-English Dictionary. Benson, M. Cambridge, UK: Cambridge University Press, 1990.
The New Standard Dictionary (English-Serbo-Croatian/Serbo-Croatian-English). Grujic, B. and Srdevic, I. 2008.
Serbo-Croatian-English/English-Serbo-Croatian Dictionary of Synonyms & Antonyms. 5th ed. Dajkovic, J. 1994.
The Oxford-Duden Pictorial Serbo-Croat & English Dictionary. Oxford: Clarendon Press, 1988.
Hrvatsko ili srpsko engleski rjecnik. Drvodelic, M. Zagreb: Skolska Knjiga, 1989.
Veliki rjecnik stranih rijeci. Klaic, B. Zagreb: Zora, 1974.
Recnik u slikama: Engleski i srpskohrvatski. Beograd, G. Zagreb: Naprijed, 2002.

Serbo-Croatian: Business and Related Fields
Croatian Dictionary of Business and Government. Ivir, V. Zagreb : Školska knjiga, 1998.
English-Serbo-Croatian and Serbo-Croatian-English Economic Dictionary. 6th Ed. Gligorijevic. Belgrade, 2003.

Serbo-Croatian: Law
English Grammar in Criminal Justice Studies and English-Croatian Criminal Justice Dictionary. 2nd Ed. Gacic, M. Zagreb: Ministarstvo unutarnjih poslova Republike Hrvatske, 1995.

Serbo-Croatian: Maritime
Serbo-Croatian-English Maritime Dictionary. Pricard, B. Zagreb: Školska knjiga, 1989.

Serbo-Croatian: Technical
Serbo-Croatian-English/English-Serbo-Croatian Dictionary of Naval Architecture, Mechanical Engineering and Nuclear Energy. Bartolic, L. Zagreb: Školska knjiga, 2005.

Recnik tehnickih izraza. Belgrade: Tehnicka knjiga, 1971.

SLOVAK

General Dictionaries
English-Slovak Dictionary. Haraksimova, E. Bolchazy-Carducci Publishers, 2001.
Slovak-English/English-Slovak Pocket Dictionary. New York: i.b.d. Ltd., 1995.
Krátky slovník slovenského jazyka. Kacala, J., et al. Bratislava: Veda, 2003.
Hippocrene Concise Slovak-English/English-Slovak Dictionary. Trnka, N. New York: Hippocrene, 2003.
Cesko-slovenský slovník. Horák, G. Bratislava: V da, 1981.
Slovak-English Phraseological Dictionary. Konus, J.J. Passaic, NJ: Slovak Catholic Sokol, 1969.
Slovensko-anglický slovník. Vilikovská, et al. Bratislava: SPN, 1991.
Anglicko-slovenský a slovensko-anglický vreckový slovník. Smejkalova, J. Bratislava: Slovenské padagogické nakladatel'stvo, 1991.

Slovak: Technical
Vreckový anglicko-slovenský a slovensko-anglický technický slovník. Novak & Binder, Slovenské vydavatel'stvo technickej literatúry, 1971.

SLOVENE

General Dictionaries
English-Slovene/Slovene-English Modern Dictionary. Komac, D. New York: Hippocrene, 2005.
Veliki Slovensko-Angleski Slovar. Grad, A. Ljubljana: Drzavna Zolozba Slovenije, 1982.

Slovene: Business
Slovene Business Dictionary. London: Peter Collin, 1999.

SOMALI

General Dictionaries
Somali: Somali-English, English-Somali Dictionary & Phrasebook. Awde. N. New York: Hippocrene, 2006.
English-Somali/Somali-English Dictionary. Korshel, M. New Delhi: Star Publications, 2009.

SPANISH

General Dictionaries
Diccionario de la lengua española. 22*nd* ed. Madrid: Real Academia de la Lengua Española, 2009. *Spanish-Spanish (Available in one volume hardcover deluxe edition, also 2-volume economic hardcover; CD-ROM edition). This is the official dictionary of the Spanish language. The new 22nd edition incorporates for the first time foreign-*

isms (mainly English) as well as many Latin American colloquialisms, making this dictionary a must for Spanish translators.

HarperCollins Spanish-English/English-Spanish Dictionary. Bradley, D. New York: HarperCollins, 2005. *Contains 230,000 references and 444,000 translations.*

The Oxford Spanish Dictionary. Jarman, B.G. and Russell, R. Oxford: Oxford University Press, 2008. Thumb indexed. *Spanish-English/English-Spanish. Also on CD-ROM. Very good.*

Diccionario internacional Simon and Schuster. de Gamez, T. New York: Simon & Schuster, 1997. *English-Spanish/Spanish-English Contains many Latin Americanisms.*

Multicultural Spanish Dictionary. 2nd ed. Sofer, M., ed. Rockville, MD: Schreiber Publishing, 2006. *Everyday Spanish words as they differ from country to country.*

Libro de Estilo "El País." 14th ed. 1998.

The Interpreter's Companion (Spanish-English/English-Spanish). Mikkelson, H. Acebo: 2001. *Compilation of terms not found in other dictionaries, covering legal, medical, drugs, weapons, profanity and slang terms.*

Diccionario de Ideas Afines. Corripio, F. 2011. *Recommended.*

Collins Spanish-English/English-Spanish Dictionary, Unabridged. 3rd ed. Smith, C. New York: HarperCollins, 2006. *Widely considered one of the best of its kind.*

Firefly Spanish/English Visual Dictionary. Corbeil, J.C. New York: Firefly, 2010.

Qué es qué (What's What), Enciclopedia visual bilingüe. Maplewood, NJ: Hammond, 1988. *A pictorial dictionary.*

The Collins Spanish Dictionary. Butterfield, J. London: Collins, 2010. *Good for Spanish for Spain.*

Diccionario de dudas y dificultades de la lengua española. Seco, M. Madrid: Espasa-Calpe, 2011.

Diccionario de uso del español. 2 vols. Moliner, M. Madrid: Editorial Gredos, 2012. *Spanish-Spanish. Excellent; also available on CD-ROM.*

Gran diccionario español-inglés. Garcia Pelayo y Gross, R. Ediciones Larousse, 2004. *Very comprehensive. European-oriented.*

2001 Spanish and English Idioms. Savaiano, E. and Winget, L. Woodbury, NY: Barron, 2008. *Not exhaustive, but quite useful.*

Diccionario de los idiomas inglés y español. Velázquez, M. Mexico: Prentice-Hall, 1994. *Spanish-English/English-Spanish.*

Sinónimos castellanos. Garcia, R. and Sopena, R. Buenos Aires: 1980. *Spanish-Spanish.*

Diccionario español de sinónimos y antónimos. Sainz de R., F.C. 2011. *Spanish-Spanish.*

Buenas y malas palabras. Orellana, M. Chile: Editorial Universitaria, 1998.

General Regional Spanish Dictionaries

Mexican Spanish. London: Lexus, 1999.

The Dictionary of Chicano Spanish. Galvan, R.A. Lincolnwood, IL: NTC, 1995.

La Traducción del Inglés al Castellano. Orellana, M. 2002.

Nuevo Diccionario Lunfardo. Gobello, J. 2008. *Colloquial language of Buenos Aires by a noted author on the subject.*

Lexicón de colombianismos. 2 vols. di Fillipo, M. A. Bogota: Biblioteca Luis-Angel Arango, 1983.

Diccionario de venezolanismos. Academia Venezolana de la Lengua, Universidad Central de Venezuela, Facultad de Humanidades y Educación, Caracas: Instituto de Filología Andrés Bello, 1993.
Bilingual Dictionary of Mexican Spanish. 3rd ed. Hamel, B. H. Beverly Hills: Bilingual Book Press, 2002.
Diccionario de americanismos. Steel, B. Madrid: Sociedad General Española de Libreria, 1990.
Diccionario de mejicanismos. Santamaria, F. Mexico City: Editorial Porrua, 1993. *Very useful for any Mexico-related translation.*

Spanish: Aviation/Aeronautics
Diccionario aeronáutico civil y militar inglés- español. Velasco, Madrid: Paraninfo, 1995.

Spanish: Business and Related Fields
Spanish Business Dictionary. 2nd Ed. Sofer, M., ed. Rockville, MD: Schreiber Publishing, 2005. *Multicultural business Spanish with varying terms from major Spanish-speaking countries such as Spain, Mexico, Venezuela, Chile and Argentina.*
Spanish Dictionary of Business, Commerce and Finance. London: New York, Routledge, 1997; CD-ROM, 1998.
Nuevo diccionario bilingüe de economía y empresa. Lozano, J.M. Madrid: Ediciones Piramide, 1996. *English-Spanish/Spanish-English.*
Dictionary of Business. Collin, P.H. Middlesex, UK: 2002. *English-Spanish/Spanish-English*
English-Spanish Banking Dictionary. Esteban, R.G. Madrid: Editorial Paraninfo, 2000.
Diccionario Enciclopédico Profesional de Finanzas y Banca. 3 vols. 1992.
World Bank Glossary (Spanish-English/English-Spanish). 1996.
Dictionary of Accounting (Spanish-English with S-E/E-S vocabulary). Kohler, E. 2005.
Harrap's Glossary of Spanish Commercial and Industrial Terms. Rodrigues, L. London: Harrap, 1990. *English-Spanish/Spanish-English.*
Diccionario comercial inglés-español/español-inglés. Giraud, A. Barcelona: Editorial Juventud, 1996.
Dictionary of Modern Business. Robb, L. Washington D.C.: Anderson Kramer Associates, 1960. *English-Spanish/Spanish-English.*

Spanish: Chemistry
Diccionario de química y de productos químicos. Sax, I. Barcelona: Ediciones Omega, 2006. *Best of its kind.*

Spanish: Communications
Spanish Dictionary of Telecommunications. Castro, E. London/New York: Routledge, 1998. *Spanish-English/English-Spanish.*
Diccionario del video inglés-español. Perales, Madrid: Paraninfo, 1992.
Diccionario para Electrónica, Telecomunicaciones e Informática. Buenos Aires: EMEDE, S.A. 1986.

Diccionario Terminológico de los medios de comunicación. Prieto, F. Marid: Ediciones Piramide, 1991. *English-Spanish.*

Spanish: Computers
Dictionary of Information Technology (Spanish-English/English-Spanish). Vollnhals, O. 1997. *Very good.*
English-Spanish/Spanish-English Dictionary of Electrical and Computer Engineering. Kaplan, S. New York: John Wiley, 2001.
Computer Dictionary (English-Spanish). Freedman, A. 1999.
Diccionario comentado de terminología informática. Aguado, G. Madrid: Editorial Paraninfo, 1996.
Diccionario de informática inglés-español/español-inglés. Madrid: Ediciones Diaz de Santos, 1993.
Diccionario de informática inglés-español. Olivetti, Barcelona: Editorial Paraninfo, 1993. *Rather small and limited.*
Dictionary of Computer Terms. Chiri, A. New York: Hippocrene, 1993.
Diccionario microinformática (inglés-español). Tapias, R. Barcelona: Editorial Noray, 1985. *Old but useful.*

Spanish: Electronics
Diccionario de electrónica (español-inglés/ inglés-español). Amós, Madrid: Paraninfo, 1995.
Diccionario de electrónica y técnica nuclear. Markus, J. 1993. *Spanish-English.*

Spanish: Engineering
Electrical and Computer Engineering Dictionary. Kaplan, S. New York: John Wiley & Sons, 2001. *English-Spanish/Spanish-English.*
Diccionario técnico inglés-español. Malgorn, G. Madrid: Paraninfo, 2006.
Dictionary of Environmental Engineering. J. Villate. Miami: Ediciones Universal, 1979.
Engineers' Dictionary. Robb, L. New York: 2009. *English-Spanish/Spanish-English. Still considered one of the best.*

Spanish: Environment
Spanish Dictionary of Environmental Technology. London/New York: Routledge, 1998. *Spanish-English/English-Spanish.*
Spanish-English Dictionary of Environmental Science and Engineering. Headworth, H. New York: John Wiley, 1998.

Spanish: Law
English-Spanish, Spanish-English Legal Dictionary. Kaplan, S. New York: John Wiley, 2008.
Legal Dictionary (Spanish-English/English-Spanish). Alcarez Varo, E. 2008. *Highly recommended.*
Diccionario Jurídico Inglés-Español. Saint Dahl, Henry. McGraw Hill. 2004.
Bilingual Dictionary of Criminal Justice Terms. Benaman, V; Connolly, N; and Loos, S. Longwood, FL: Gould Publications, Inc. 1996. *English-Spanish. Small but good.*

Diccionario de Derecho. 4th Ed. Duran, R. Barcelona: Bosch, 2012.
El Inglés Jurídico Norteamericano. Alcarez Varo, E. 2008.
Diccionario Jurídico. Moro, T. Madrid: Espasa-Calpe, 2007.
Diccionario Jurídico Español-Inglés. Cabanellas, G. & Hoague, E.C. Buenos Aires: Heliasta, 2010. *Spanish-English/English-Spanish. Highly recommended; complements the Alcarez Varo (see previous).*
Dictionary of Law, Economics and Politics. Ramon La Casa Navarro. Madrid: Editoriales de Derecho Reunidas, 1991.
Diccionario de Derecho. de Pina, R. and de Pina Vara, R. Mexico City: Editorial Porrua, 2010.
Diccionario de términos legales. Robb, L. Mexico: Editorial Limusa, 1995.
Diccionario de ciencias jurídicas, políticas y sociales. Ossorio, M. Heliasta S.R.L, 2010.

Spanish: Maritime
Nautical Dictionary (Spanish-English/English-Spanish). Malagón Ortuondo, J.M. 2007.
Diccionario marítimo y de construcción naval. Perez, J.A. Barcelona: Ediciones Garriga, 1976.

Spanish: Medicine
Medical Dictionary: English, Spanish, Portuguese. Nolte-Schlegel. New York: Springer-Verlag, 2008.
English-Spanish/Spanish-English Medical Dictionary. Rogers, G. New York: McGraw-Hill, 2007.
The Delmar English-Spanish Dictionary for Health Professionals. Kelz, R.K. Delmar Publishers, 1996.
Medical Dictionary (Spanish-English/English-Spanish). McElroy, O.H., et al. 2012. *Good, small paperback.*
Mosby's Medical Dictionary (Spanish-English with E-S/S-E Vocabulary). De Teran Bleiberg, E. 2003. *Extensive explanations and illustrations.*
Bilingual Glossary for Medical and Healthcare Translators: Oncology, Hematology, and Radiotherapy: English-Spanish-English. Albin, V. and Coggins, M. Houston: PCM Translation Resources, 1994.
Medical Encyclopedic Dictionary (Spanish-English). 2 vols. Dorland, 1992. *Excellent.*
Diccionario de términos médicos. Torres, R. Madrid: Alhambra, 2011. *Spanish-English/English-Spanish.*
Diccionario de los Términos Técnicos de Medicina. Garnier, M. and Delamare, V. 1981.

Spanish: Military
Diccionario técnico militar. Gomez, A. Madrid: Ediciones Agullo, 1980.
Diccionario moderno de tecnología militar. Wells, R. Fairfax, VA: Lexicon Press, 1977.

Spanish: Mining
Glossary of Mining Terms (Spanish-English/English-Spanish). Diaz Preto, P. 1995.

Spanish: Psychiatry
Glossary of Psychiatric Terms (Spanish-English/English-Spanish). Nemiah, J.C. 1996.

Dictionary of Psychology and Psychiatry (Spanish-English/English-Spanish). Kaplan, S. New York: Routledge, 2011.

Spanish: Real Estate
Dictionary of Real Estate Business. Salles, M. Chicago: Real Estate Education, 1997.

Spanish: Technical
Polytechnic Dictionary of Spanish and English Languages. Rev. ed. Beigbeder Atienza, F. 2009. *Highly recommended.*
Routledge Spanish Technical Dictionary. 2 vols. London/New York: Routledge, 1996. *Vol. 1, Spanish-English; vol. 2, English-Spanish. CD-ROM, 1998.*
The Contractors Dictionary of Equipment, Tools and Techniques. Webster, L. F. New York: John Wiley, 1996.
Technical Glossary for Bilingual Technical Writers and Translators: English-Spanish/Spanish-English. Rodríguez, H. Published by author, 1996.
Diccionario técnico. Garcia Diaz, R. Mexico: LIMUSA, S.A., 2007.
Glosario Internacional para el Traductor (Spanish-English/English-Spanish). Orellana, M. 2005. *Very useful for translators.*
Diccionario de términos científicos y técnicos. 5 vols. Barcelona: McGraw-Hill Boixarev, 1981. *A translation of the excellent McGraw-Hill Dictionary of Science and Technology (see General References).*
Spanish-English/English-Spanish Encyclopedic Dictionary of Technical Terms. 3 vols. Collazo, J.L. McGraw-Hill, 1992.
Glosario español-inglés de términos técnicos. 5 vols. Thomann, A. E. Armco Steel Corporation, 1980. *Spanish-English/English-Spanish.*

SWAHILI

General Dictionaries
Swahili-English, English/Swahili Practical Dictionary. Awde, Nicholas. Hippocrene, 2007.
Concise Swahili and English Dictionary. Perrot, D.V. Sevenoaks: Hodder and Stoughton Ltd., 1992.

SWEDISH

General Dictionaries
English-Swedish Comprehensive Dictionary. New York: Hippocrene, 1997.
Norstedts stora englesk-svensk/svensk-englesk ordbok. Andra uppla-gan, Petti, V. Rider, I.H., Berglund, B.M., Martinsson-Visser, Y., Swedenborg, L. and Wiman, M. Stockholm: Norstedts Förlag, 2004. *Recommended.*
Svengelsk ordbok (Acta Wexionensia. Ser.3, Language & Literature;1). Selten, B. Stockholm: Almquist & Wiksell International, 1993. *English loanwords and words with English elements with correct Swedish spellings and definitions in Swedish.*
Fökortningsordbok: åtta tusen svenska och internationella förkortningar med förklaringar. Collinder, B. and Svenblad, R. Andra utökade upplagan, Malmo: Liber, 1987. *Acronyms and abbreviations.*

Nyord i svenskan fran 40-tal till 80-tal; Svenska spraknamnden; textredigering. Swedenborg, L. Stockholm: Esselte Studium, 2001. *Swedish-Swedish.*
Svensk ordbok/utarbetad vid språkdata. Göteborgs universitet, Sture, A., vetenskaplig ledare, Solna: Esselte Studium, 1990. *Swedish-Swedish.*
A Modern Swedish-English Dictionary (Swedish-English/English-Swedish). 2 vols. 4th rev. ed. Stockholm, Prisma, 1989.
Stora engelsk-svenska ordboken. Santesson, R. Stockholm: Esselte Studium, 1984.

Comprehensive.
Svensk-engelsk ordbok. Santesson, R. Stockholm: Esselte Studium, 1975.
Bonniers svenska ordbok. Malmström, S., Györki, I., and Sjögren, P. Stockholm: Albert Bonniers Förlog, 2011. *Swedish-Swedish.*
Svensk slangordbok. Andra Upplagan, Gibson, H. Stockholm: Esselte Studium, 1988.
Nusvensk ordbok, 5 vols. Östergren, O. Stockholm: Wahlström & Widstrand, 1982. *Swedish-Swedish.*
Nya förkortningordboken. Larsson, W. Halmstad: Bokförlaget Spektra AB, 1975.
Illustrerad svensk ordbok. Molde, et al. Natur och Kultur, 1970. *Swedish-Swedish.*

Swedish: Business and Related Fields
Dictionary of Business: English-Swedish. Collin, P.H. Malmström, L. and Fox, R. Teddington, Middlesex: Peter Collin Publishing Ltd., 1998.
755 Svenska organisationer pa fyra språk: Engelska, franska, tyska, finska. Heyum, J. Stockholm: Addax Språkförlag, 1987.
Ekonomi ordbok: svensk-engelsk fackordbok for ekonomifunktionen med begreppsförklaringar. Edström, N.F. and Samuelson, L.A. Stockholm: P.A. Norstedt & Söners Forlag, 1987.
Svensk-engelsk affärslexikon. Stockholm: J. Sanders och Affärsförlaget, 1980.
Svensk-engelsk fackordbok. 3rd rev. ed. Gullberg, P.A. Norstedts & Söner Förlag, 2000.

Swedish: Law
Juridisk ordbok: Svensk-engelsk fackordbok. Martinger, S. Stockholm: Norstedts Förlag, 1987.

Swedish: Nuclear Energy
Karneergiordlista. Stockholm: Tekniska nomenklaturcentralen och Sveriges Mekanstandardisering, 1990. *Nuclear energy terms--Swedish, English, French and German equivalents.*

Swedish: Technical
Norstedts dataordbok. Darcy, L. and Boston, L., compilers. Schroder, J., translator. Stockholm: P.A. Norstedt & Söners Förlag, 1987.
Svensk-engelsk teknisk ordbok (Swedish-English/English-Swedish). 2 vols. 10th ed. Engström, E. AB Svensk Trävarutidning Förlaget, 1997.

TATAR

Concise Tatar-English/English-Tatar Dictionary. Shahmayer, S. New York: Hippocrene, 1994.

THAI

General Dictionaries
Thai-English/English-Thai Dictionary & Phrasebook. Higbie, J. New York: Hippocrene, 2012.
The Oxford-Duden Pictorial Thai and English Dictionary. Oumah, C. New York: Oxford University Press, 1998.

TURKISH

General Dictionaries
Turkish-English/English-Turkish Dictionary. New York: Hippocrene, 2002.
The Oxford Turkish Dictionary. Fahir, I., et al. Oxford: Oxford University Press, 1992.
Turkish Grammar. Lewis, Geoffrey. Oxford University Press, 2001.
Redhouse Yeni Turkce-Ingilizce Sozluk. Istanbul: Redhouse Press, 1992.
Buyuk Turkce-Ingilizce Sozluk. Tuglaci, P. Ankara: ABC, 1991.

Turkish: Computers
Dictionary of Information Technology: Turkish-English/English-Turkish. French & European Publications, 1999.

Turkish: Technical
Dictionary of Technical Terms: Turkish-English. French & European Publications, 1999.

UKRAINIAN

General Dictionaries
English-Ukrainian/Ukrainian-English Dictionary. Bikhovets, N., et al. Rockville, MD: Kamkin, 1995.
Hippocrene Practical Ukrainian-English/English-Ukrainian (with Menu Terms). Hrabovsky, L. New York: Hippocrene, 2006.
English-Ukrainian Dictionary. Toronto: University of Toronto, 1990.
Hippocrene Standard Ukrainian-English/English-Ukrainian Dictionary. New York: Hippocrene, 1994.
Ukrayinsko-anhliyskyy slovnyk. Zhluktenko, Yu.O., et al. Kiev: Radyanska Shkola, 1987.
Ukrayinsko-anhliyskyy slovnyk. Andrusyshen, C.H. Toronto: University of Toronto Press, 1981.
Slovnyk ukrayinskoyi movy. 11 vols. Academiya nauk, Keva: Naukova dumka, 2001.
Slovnyk inshomovnykh Sliv. Melnychuk, O.S. Kiev: URE, 2000.
Slovnyk Ukrayinskykh idiom. Udovychenko, G.M. Kiev: Radyanskyy pysmennyk, 1968.

Ukrainian: Business
Ukrainian-English Dictionary of Business. Kronglov, A. McFarland, 1997.

UZBEK

Uzbek-English/English-Uzbek Dictionary. Awde, N. New York: Hippocrene, 2002.
Uzbek-English Dictionary. Waterson, N. Oxford: Oxford University Press, 1980.

VIETNAMESE

NTC's Vietnamese-English Dictionary. Nguyen, D. Lincolnwood, IL: NTC, 1995.
Vietnamese-English/English-Vietnamese Dictionary. Le-Ba-Khanh. New York: Hippocrene, 1991.
Tu Dien Tieng Viet. Hanoi: Vien Khoa Hoc Xa Hoi Viet Nam, Vien Ngon Ngu Hoc, Trung Tam Tu Dien Ngon Ngu, 1992. *Vietnamese-Vietnamese.*
Tu Dien Viet-Ahn. Bui Phung. Hanoi: Hanoi University, 1986.
Tu Dien Tieng Viet. Van Tan. Hanoi: Nha Xuat Ban Khoa Hoc Xa Hoi, 1986.
Thanh Ngu Tieng Viet. Nguyen Luc. Hanoi: Nha Xuat Ban Khoa Hoc Xa Hoi, 2009. *Contains correct rendition of proverbs.*
Tu Dien Anh Viet. Huu Chi, et al. Hanoi: Nha Xuat Ban Khoa Hoc Xa Hoi, 1975. *English-Vietnamese.*
Tu Dien Hoc Sinh [Cap II]. Nguyen Luong Ngoc. Hanoi: Giao Duc, 1971.
Vietnamese-English Student Dictionary. Nguyen Dinh Hoa. Carbondale: Southern Illinois University, 1972.
Vietnam Tu Dien. 2 vols. Le Van Duc. Saigon: Khai tri, 1970. *Available in U.S.*
Tu Dien Thanh Ngu Dien Tich. Dien Huong. Saigon: Khai Tri, 1992.

YIDDISH

Yiddish-English-Hebrew Dictionary. Harhavy, A. New York: Schocken Books, YIVO Institute for Jewish Research, 2005. *Reprint of 1928 expanded 2nd ed.*
English-Yiddish/Yiddish-English Dictionary. Harduf, D.M. Brookline, MA: Israel Book Shop, 2003.
Modern English-Yiddish/Yiddish-English Dictionary. Weinrich, U. New York: Schocken Books, 2006.

YORUBA

Yoruba-English/English-Yoruba Concise Dictionary. Yai, O.B. New York: Hippocrene, 1996.

Given today's technology, printed dictionaries are still dominant. It is possible that at some point in the future online dictionaries will become so comprehensive and accurate that they will force the printed dictionaries to take a back seat. But this may not happen for some time.

Dictionaries are becoming ever more available in general bookstores and in bookstore chains such as Barnes & Noble and on the Internet via amazon. com, barnesandnoble.com, and more. The following is a partial list of book sources that specialize in dictionaries, particularly hard-to-find technical ones. Some will order a great many technical dictionaries for you from sources in both the U.S. and abroad. Some of the British, European and other overseas bookstores listed here are excellent and well worth contacting.

The best way these days to shop for dictionaries is on the Internet.

U.S. SOURCES OF DICTIONARIES

Cheng & Tsui Co., Boston, MA	www.cheng-tsui.com
China Books & Periodicals, Inc., San Francisco, CA	www.chinabooks.com
French & European Publications, Inc.	www.frencheuropean.com
Hippocrene Books, New York, NY	www.hippocrenebooks.com
John Wiley & Sons, Hoboken, NJ	www.wiley.com
Kinokuniya Bookstores, San Francisco, CA	www.kinokuniya.com
Kinokuniya Bookstores, New York, NY	www.kinokuniya.com
McGraw Hill, New York, NY	www.mcgraw-hill.com
Polish Bookstore and Publishing, Brooklyn, NY	www.polbook.com
Rizzoli International Book Store, New York, NY	www.rizzoliusa.com
Routledge, New York, NY	www.routledge.com
Schoenhofs Foreign Books, Cambridge, MA	www.schoenhofs.com
Schreiber Publishing, Rockville, MD	www.SchreiberLanguage.com
Szwede Slavic Books, Redwood City, CA	www.szwedeslavicbooks.com
Western Continental Book, Inc., Denver, CO	www.continentalbook.com
YBP Library Services, Contoocook, NH	www.ybp.com

FOREIGN DICTIONARY SOURCES

Argentina
Editorial Planeta, www.editorialplaneta.com.ar

Australia
Kinokuniya Bookstores, www.kinokuniya.com

Chile
Editorial Universitaria, Santiago, Chile www.universitaria.cl

France
La Maison du Dictionnaire, Paris, France www.dicoland.com
Editions du CNRS, Paris, France www.cnrseditions.fr
Editions Klincksieck, Paris, France www.klincksieck.com

Germany
Kubon & Sagner, Munich, Germany www.kubon-sagner.de
Lagenscheidt, www.langenscheidt.com

Hong Kong
Joint Publishing Company, Central District, Hong Kong www.jointpublishing.com

Mexico
Editorial Planeta, www.editorialplaneta.com.mx

Malaysia
Kinokuniya Bookstores, www.kinokuniya.com

Singapore
Kinokuniya Bookstores, www.kinokuniya.com

Spain
Editorial Planeta, www.editorial.planeta.es

Sweden
Tekniska Litteratursallskapet, Stockholm, Sweden www.tls.se

Thailand
Kinokuniya Bookstores, www.kinokuniya.com

United Kingdom
B.H. Blackwell Ltd, Oxford, United Kingdom   www.blackwell.co.uk
Grant & Cutler, London, UK www.grantandcutler.com
Multilingual Matters, www.multilingual-matters.com
Oxford University Press, Oxford, UK www.oup.co.uk

APPENDIX 3.
FOREIGN LANGUAGE SOFTWARE SOURCES

This appendix is designed for translators who translate documents *from* English *into* another language. Word processing software in languages other than English is produced both in the U.S. and in the country of the target language. Translators in the U.S., however, have to be aware of the compatibility of the software with U.S. word processing software. Microsoft's dominance in English language word processing extends to its localized products, which have the obvious advantage of being compatible with their English versions and with one another, in addition to the considerable number of languages they cover. We start, therefore, with a listing of Microsoft foreign language products, followed by other sources. This is by no means an exhaustive listing, but rather a sampling of sources to help translators who have a need for software in a given language to start the process of looking for the product that best meets their needs.

Microsoft Foreign Language Software and Product Support
(Website: microsoft.com/worldwide)

Arabic
Microsoft Egypt, Smart Village, Kilo 28, Cairo/Alex Desert Road Abou Rawash, Cairo, Egypt
Phone: +202 35393333 Fax: +202 35390303

Chinese
Microsoft (China) Co., Ltd, 19/F, Millennium Tower, 38 Xiaoyun Road, Chaoyang, Beijing 100027, P.R. China
Phone: 011-86-10-8453-8989 Fax: 011-86-10-8453-8509

Croatian
Microsoft Hrvatska d.o.o., Turinina 3/IV, HR - 10010 Zagreb, Croatia
Phone: 385 1 4802 500 Fax: 385 1 4802 525

Czech
Microsoft s.r.o., BB Centrum, budova Alpha, Vyskocilova 1461/2a, 140 00 Praha 4, Czech Republic
Phone: +420 2611 97 111 Fax: +420 2611 97 100

Danish
Microsoft Danmark ApS, Tuborg Boulevard 12, 2900 Hellerup, Denmark
Phone: (45) 44 89 0100 Fax: (45) 44 68 5510

Dutch
Microsoft B.V., Evert van de Beekstraat 354, 1118 CZ Schiphol, Netherlands
Phone: +31 (0)20-5001500   Fax: +31 (0)20-5001999

French (Canadian)
Microsoft Canada Co., 1950 Meadowvale Blvd, Mississauga, Ontario L5N 8L9
Phone: (877) 568-2495 Fax: (800) 933-4750

French
Microsoft France, 18 Avenue du Québec, Zone de Courtaboeuf 1, 91957 Courtaboeuf Cedex, France
Phone: (33) 825 827 829   Fax: (33) 1 64 46 06 60

Finnish
Microsoft OY (Suomi), Keilaranta 7, 02150 Espoo, Suomi
Phone: 358 (0) 9 525 501 Fax: 358 (0) 9 878 8778

German
Microsoft Deutschland GmbH, Konrad-Zuse-Str. 1, D-85716 Unterschleißheim (Munich), Germany
Phone: +49/(0)89/3176-0 Fax: +49/(0)89/3176-1000

Greek
Microsoft Hellas S.A., 221 Kifisias Ave., 151 24, Athens, Greece
Phone: +30 211 1206 000 Fax: +30 211 1206 003

Hebrew
Microsoft Israel Ltd., Ha'Pnina st. 2, Ranana 43107, Israel
Phone: 972-9-7625400 Fax: 972-9-7625200

Hungarian
Microsoft Magyarorszag Kft., Graphisoft Park 3 (Zahony u.), 1031 Budapest, Hungary
Phone: +36 1 437 2800 Fax: +36 1 437 2899

Italian
Microsoft, Centro Direzionale San Felice, Palazzo A, Via Rivoltana 13, 20090 - Segrate (MI), Italy
Phone: 39 02 70 398 398 Fax: 39 02 70 392 020

Japanese
Microsoft Company, Limited, Odakyu Southern Tower 2-1, Yoyogi 2-Chome Shibuya-ku, Tokyo 151-8583, Japan
Phone: 81-3-4332-5300

Korean
Microsoft Korea, 6th Floor, POSCO Center, 892 Daechi-Dong, Kangnam-Gu, Seoul, 135-777, Korea

Phone: 82-2-531-4500 Fax: 82-2-555-1724

Norwegian
Microsoft Norge AS, Postboks 43, Lilleaker, 0216 Oslo, Norway
Phone: (47) 22 02 25 00 Fax: (47) 22 95 06 64

Polish
Microsoft Sp. z o.o., Al. Jerozolimskie 195a, 02-222 Warszawa, Poland
Phone: (+48) 22-594-1000 Fax: (+48) 22-594-1002

Portuguese
MS Portugal, Edifício Qualidade C1- C2, Av. Prof. Doutor, Aníbal Cavaco Silva, Tagus
Park, 2744-010 Porto Salvo, Portugal
Phone: (351) 21 440-92-00 Fax: (351) 21 441-21-01

Russian
Microsoft Russia, 17 Ul. Krylatskaya, 121614, Moscow, Russia
Phone: +7 (495) 9678585 Fax: +7 (495) 9678500

Serbian and Montenegrin
Microsoft Software d.o.o., Makedonska 30/VI, 11000 Belgrade, Serbia
Phone: +381 11 330 66 00 Fax: +381 11 330 66 01

Slovene
Microsoft d.o.o., Ljubljana, Smartinska c. 140, SI - 1000 Ljubljana, Slovenia
Phone: +386 (0)1 5 846 100 Fax: +386 (0)1 5 846 122

Spanish (Mexican)
Microsoft Mexico, S.A. de C.V., Paseo de Tamarindos 400 A Piso 29, Col.Bosques de
las Lomas, Mexico D.F. C.P. 05120, Mexico
Phone: +52 (55) 5267-2000 Atencion a clientes: 01800 5272000
Fax: +52 (55) 5258-0225

Swedish
Microsoft AB, Box 27, S-164 93 Kista, Sweden
Phone: +46 8 7525600 Fax: +46 8 7505158

Tagalog
Microsoft Philippines, Inc., 16th Floor, 6750 Ayala Office Tower, 6750 Ayala Avenue,
Makati City 1200, Philippines
Phone: (63 2) 860 8989 Fax: (63 2) 860 8920

Thai
Microsoft (Thailand) Limited, 37th Floor, Unit No. 1-7, CRC Tower, All Seasons Place,
87/2 Wireless Road, Lumpini, Pathumwan, Bangkok 10330, Thailand
Phone: 66-2257-4999 Fax: 66-2257-0099

Turkish
Microsoft Bilgisayar Yazilim, Hizmetleri Limited Sirketi, Barbaros Plaza Is Merkezi, 145-C, Kat 21, Emirhan Caddesi, Dikilitas, Besiktas 80700, Istanbul, Turkey
Phone: 90-212-326-5000 Fax: 90-212-258-5954

Vietnamese
Microsoft Vietnam, 9th Floor, Hanoi Tung Shing Square, 2 Ngo Quyen, Hanoi, Vietnam
Phone: +844-825-1955 Fax: +844-826-1222

Printed or Digital Dictionaries?

Are printed dictionaries about to be replaced by digital ones (on CD, online, etc.)? Probably not. Digital books are dependent on a transmission medium, such as computer or a listening device, which is not always readily available. A printed book is a self-contained medium, which can be kept nearby and taken along. It should be around for some time to come, until the day when most reading will be done on digital media.

APPENDIX 4.
SOURCES OF TRANSLATION WORK

There are three major sources of translation work in the United States: the government sector, the public sector, and the private sector.

The government sector includes the city, county, and state governments in addition to the federal government. All of them need translation work on a fairly regular basis, and all of them are worth contacting. It is not always easy to find the right person or office to contact, but perseverance does pay off. One good place to start your search is the procurement or contracting office of any given government entity. They usually know who in the system needs what, and they can often tell you whether they've heard lately of someone in the system needing translation. Again, you need to have a great deal of patience with these folks, who are not known for their alacrity.

The U.S. Government, or the "Government" with a capital G, is a huge source of translation. It is hard to put a dollar figure on it, but it cer-tainly goes into the many millions of dollars per year. Government translation requests come in three main forms:

a. Translation contracts. Various government agencies issue a re-quest for a bid on a one- to five-year translation contract. Those usually require several languages, and most freelancers cannot handle them on their own. To find out about those contracts, read the government publication *Commerce Business Daily* (found on line at http://cbdnet.gpo.gov). You may want to monitor the contract office handling the particular contract, and have them tell you (under the Freedom of Information Act) which company is awarded the contract. You can then contact that company and offer your services in your particular areas of expertise.

b. Translation requirements in a non-translation contract. The Government may need a company to monitor drug dealers who speak Spanish. It contracts with a company specialized in electronic monitoring. That company will then subcontract the translation portion of its prime contract to a translation company. Here again you can follow this process, and offer your services.

c. One-time translation order. The Department of Energy may need to translate a Russian book on power plants. It will look for someone who has a good knowledge of Russian and English, and experience in this kind of technical translation. They usually turn to a translation company, but they may also contract with an individual. This type of assignment is very hard to find, since the agency will rarely advertise what they call a "small purchase" (which to a freelancer can be quite big), and will instead contact an established translation company.

The **public sector** includes many organizations, academic institutions, foundations, and so on. All of them, at one time or another, need translation work. The question is how to find out who needs what and when. I wish I had the answer, but I don't. The same holds true for the **private sector,** which consists of commercial and industrial entities, law firms, and individuals.

All of which leaves you with the **translation companies**, who in effect act as a broker between you and the work sources. They develop many contacts, they bid on contracts, they advertise in the media and in the Yellow Pages, and they provide millions of dollars worth of translation work for freelancers every year.

The following is a list, arranged alphabetically, of translation companies. It is followed by a state-by-state regional index. A word of caution: not all of them are financially sound, and they do not always pay on time or treat freelancers with the professional respect they usually deserve. **Inclusion in the ensuing list does not mean in any way that we endorse any of the companies listed**. We leave it to you to check out any company you may be interested in, draw your own conclusions, and establish your own relation-ship with them.

The information contained in the following list is based on survey questionnaires sent to translation agencies. The amount of detail cor-responds to the amount of information given us by those agencies that responded and does not reflect any judgment on the editors' part as to the quality of those agencies. We have attempted to fill in as much information as we could for those agencies that did not to respond to our survey.

4.1 U.S. TRANSLATION COMPANIES

—A—

A Foreign Language Service, 40 W Baseline, #202, Mesa AZ 85210
Phone: (480) 813-4242 Fax: (480) 323-2324
E-mail: bill@aflscorp.com Website: www.aflscorp.com
Contact: Bill Peters. Member: ATA
A-Z Friendly Languages, Inc., 3818 Brookdale Circle, Brooklyn Park, MN 55443
Phone: (763) 566-4312 Fax: (763) 503-3977
E-mail: azfl@friendlylanguages.net
Contact: Natasha Geilman, President. Member: ATA
A2Z Global Language Solutions, 230 E. Cuthbert Blvd, Haddon Township NJ 08108
Phone: + 1 856 833 0220 Fax: +1 856 854 0491
Mobile: +1 609 968 6699
E-mail: tlandgren@a2zglobal.com Website: www.a2zglobal.com
Member: ATA
Contact: Theodora Landgren (only for executive issues or sales)
Full service LSP offering worldwide services for: translation, editing, publishing, proofreading, narration, interpreting, in most languages. Strengths especially in all aspects of engineering for Asian languages, audio files, high quality only. Languages often needed: Scandinavian, European, and all Asian languages. Subject matter mostly: medical devices, all aspects of Defense contracts, IT. Types of material: Marketing, technical, software and legal materials to support the product.
ABC Worldwide Translations & Interpretations
8306 Wilshire Boulevard, Ste. 200, Beverly Hills, CA 90211
Phone: (310) 260-7700 Fax: (310) 260-7705
E-mail: info@wordexpress.net Website: www.wordexpress.net
Contact: Muriel Redoute. Member: ATA
ABS Translation & Interpreting Service, 7814 Elm Ave, Wynnwood, PA 19038
Phone: (215) 233-3000 Fax: (215) 240-4980
E-mail: aram@abstrans.com Website: www.abstrans.com
Contact: Aram Sarkisian. Member: ATA
Academy of Languages Translation & Interpretation Services
216 First Ave. South, Ste. 330, Seattle, WA 98104
Phone: (206) 521-8601 Fax: (206) 521-8605
E-mail: translate@aolti.com Website: www.aolti.com
Contact: Olivier Fabris. Member: ATA
Accent on Languages, 2418 Fifth Street, Suite B, Berkeley, CA 94710
Phone: (510) 644-9470 Fax: (510) 644-9590
E-mail: services@accentonlanguages.com Website: www.accentonlanguages.com
Contact: Francine Kuipers, Treasurer. Member: ATA
Access 2 Interpreters, LLC, 4094 Pathfield Drive, Columbus, OH 43230
Phone: (614) 402-0258 Fax: (609) 939-1187
E-mail: jobs@accesstointerpreters.com

Contact: Yana Schottenstein, General Manager. Member: ATA
AccessOnTime, 3210 Lake Emma Road, Ste 3090, Lake Mary, FL 32746
Phone: (888) 748-7575 Fax: (407) 330-7959
E-mail: blima@accessontime.com Website: www.accessontime.com
Contact: Anabela Lima, Human Resources Director
Accu Trans, Inc., 4517 Minnetonka Boulevard, Ste 200, Minneapolis, MN 55416
Phone: (952) 927-7277 Fax (952) 925-4772
Website: www.proz.com/pro/51070
Contact: Nadia Oparista. Member: ATA
Accurapid Translation Services, Inc., 806 Main St., Poughkeepsie, NY 12603 Phone:
(845) 473-4550 Fax: (845) 473-4554
E-mail: info@accurapid.com Website: www.accurapid.com
Contact: Gabe Bokor, President
Founded 1978. Member: ATA. Translates German, Spanish, French, Hungarian,
Portuguese, Russian, Chinese and Japanese both from and into English. Emphasis on
Engineering, Patents, Law, Business and Finance translation. Prospective translators
should demonstrate competence and a professional attitude. Resumes are filed for future
reference. The company pioneered the use of technological tools in the industry. The
company maintains a pool of over 600 professional freelance translators from Europe,
Asia, and the Americas.
ACCUWORLD, LLC, 200 West Madison St., Ste. 930, Chicago, IL 60606
Phone: (312) 641-0441 Fax: (312) 641-7370
E-mail: accuworld@accuworld.com
Contact: Human Resources Department
Founded 1968. Member: ATA. Translates all languages, both from and into English.
Covers all areas, with specialties in foreign language voice-overs, health care, phar-
maceuticals, insurance, and technical manual translation. Resumes are compiled in
a database according to area of expertise. The company, headquartered in Hartford,
Connecticut has over 300 worldwide locations. It provides language training, cul-
tural training, translation/interpretation services, and foreign language typesetting and
voiceovers. Maintains a pool of 800+ translators.
ADA Inc., 2401 Shannon Place SE, Washington DC 20020
Phone: (202) 889-0123 Fax: (202) 678-2770
E-mail: lguzman@adainc.net Website: www.adainc.net
Contact: Leonid Guzman, Project Director. Member: ATA
Adams Globalization, 10435 Burnet Road, Ste. 125, Austin TX 78758
Phone: (512) 821-1818 Fax: (512) 821-1888
E-mail: info@adamsglobalization.com Website: www.adamsglobalization.com
Contact: Allan W. Adams, Pres /Mark Brown, Sales. Member: ATA
Advanced Communication and Translation, Inc., (ACT)
4332 Montgomery Avenue, Suite A, Bethesda, MD 20814
Phone: 301-654-2890 Fax: 301-654-2891
E-mail: act@act-translate.com Website: www.act-translate.com
Contact: Monique-Paule Tubb. Member: ATA
Advanced Language Translation Inc., 25 N. Washington St, Rochester, NY 14614
Toll Free: (800) 218-9024 Phone: (585) 697-0462 X18 Fax: (585) 697-0467
E-mail: info@advancedlanguage.com Website: www.advancedlanguage.com

Contact: Scott Bass, President Member: ATA
AE, Inc. - Translations, 15995 N Barkers Landing, Ste. 111, Houston, TX 77079
Phone: (281) 870-0677 Fax: (281) 556-9737
E-mail: translations@aetrans.com Website: www.aetrans.com
Contact: Stephen D. Ross. Member: ATA
Affinity Language Services, 101 S. Fairview Ave., Wind Gap, PA 18091
Phone: (610) 863-3955 Fax: (610) 863 8571
E-mail: info@affinity-languages.com Website: www.affinity-languages.com
Contact: Michelle Zuccarini
Founded 1998. Member: ATA. Works in Spanish, German, French, Italian, and Dutch.
Also in Japanese. Main areas: Technical, sci-tech, legal, medical, and business. Also
provides interpretation, editing, proofreading, transcription, and copywriting. Uses
translators worldwide.
Affordable Language Services, Ltd., 8944 Blue Ash Road, Cincinnati, OH 45242
Phone: (513) 745-0888 Fax: (513) 793-4755
Email: lelfers@affordablelanguages.com
Website: http://www.affordablelanguageservices.com
Contact: Lynn Elfers Member: ATA
Agencia Internacional, 599 Central St., Lowell, MA 01852
Phone: (978) 452-2934 Fax: (978) 441-0346
Contact: Manuel Melo, Owner. Member: ATA
Agnew Multinlingual, 741 Lakefield Rd., Ste. C, Westlake Village, CA 91361
Phone: (805) 494-3999 Fax: (805) 494-1749
Email: i.agnew@agnew.com Website: www.agnew.com
Contact: Irene Agnew
Founded 1986. Member: ATA, NAWBO, WBENC, WITI. Translates Spanish, Chinese,
French, German, Japanese, Russian, Vietnamese, etc. from English. Also scripts and
voiceover. Covers all technical areas. Prospective translators should have a B.A. degree
or higher and 2-3 years experience. Resumes received via E-mail, reviewed, graded
and scheduled for a translation test. The company is a full-service translation bureau,
as well as providing desktop publishing, Website design, multimedia, and audiovisual
services. Maintains a pool of 300-400 translators.
aiaTranslations LLC, P.O. Box 5255, Clinton, NJ 08809
Phone: (908) 955-5201 Fax: (908) 955-0210
Websites: www.aiaTranslations.com or www.aiaLifeSciences.com
E-mail: molly.naughton@aiaTranslations.com
Contact: Molly Naughton, MBA, President
Founded 1995, Member ATA. Agency focuses on healthcare and pharmaceutical-related
translations in all languages. Requires translators with medical and marketing expertise.
Freelancers are asked to complete online form at: www.aiatranslations.camp7.org in
lieu of sending resume.
Alamex Translation Services LLC, 301 Randolph Avenue, Ste. 200, Huntsville, AL
35801, Phone: (256) 532-4050 Fax: (256) 536-1834
E-mail: alamex@alamexllc.com Website: www.alamexllc.com
Contact: Patrick Castle. Member: ATA
Alanguage Bank, Inc., 159 West 25 St.., 6th Floor, New York, NY 10001
Phone: (212) 213-3336 Fax: (212) 343-2940

E-mail: info@alanguagebank.com Website: www.alanguagebank.com
Contact: Pei Wen Shih. Member: ATA
Albors and Associates, Inc., P.O. Box 5516 Winter Park, FL 32793
Phone: (800) 785-8634 Fax: (407) 657-7004
E-mail: rene@albors.com Website: www.albors.com
Contact: René A. Albors, President
Founded 1996. Member: ATA, NAJIT, Hispanic Chamber of Commerce, Orlando
Chamber of Commerce. Translates Spanish, French, Portuguese, Japan-ese, German,
Chinese, Russian, Polish, Arabic and Italian, both from and into English. Emphasis on
Legal, Medical and Business translations. Prospective translators should be experienced,
expert with terminology, and prompt in their delivery of finished work. Accepts
unsolicited resumes for translation and inter-pretation. Resumes are computer-filed, and
a letter of thanks is sent to acknowledge receipt. Maintains a pool of 5300 translators.
ALC Inc./AllWorld Language Consultants, Inc, 172 Rollins Ave., Rockville, MD
20852, Phone: (301) 881-8884 Fax: (301) 881-6877
Email: hr@alcinc.com Website: www.ALCINC.com
Contact: Carlos A. Scandiffio. Member: ATA
Alexandria Translations, 8827 Fort Hunt Rd., Alexandria, VA 22308
Phone: (703) 799-7606 Fax: (703) 799-7607
E-mail: info@alexandriatranslations.com Website: www.alexandriatranslations.com
Contact: Lidia Terziotti Member: ATA
Translates and edits documents in a variety of languages.
All Global Solutions International, PO Box 3634, Lantana, FL 33465
Phone: (561) 889-6488 Fax: (530) 658-4882
E-mail: alexm@allgsi.com Website: www.allgsi.com
Contact: Alexandre Monot, Founder & President. Member: ATA
All Language Translations, 2214 Garden Dr., Niskayuna, NY 12309
Phone: (518) 857-2848 Fax: (518) 372-6804
E-mail: cezary@ix.netcom.com
Contact: Cezary Drzymalski. Member: ATA
Allslavic Translation Services; 4930 NW 84th Ave., Ft. Lauderdale, FL 33351
Phone: (800) 775-5504 Fax: (954) 741-3898
E-mail: info@slavprom.com Website: www.allslavictranslations.com
Contact: Stanka Moskov. Member: ATA
Alpha Tech Communications, 4440 Chastant St, Suite E, Metairie, LA, 70002
Phone: (504) 454-6554 Fax: (504) 454-6717
E-mail: alphaTC@aol.com
Website: www.alphatechtranslations.com or www.ustranslations.com
Contact: Claudia Adamcewicz, Director of Sales & International Language Services
Founded in 1998. Member: ATA. Alpha Tech Communications translates many
languages including English into Spanish, French, German, Portuguese, Chinese and
Arabic. Along with translating English into those languages they translate them back
into their respective language. They also translate Italian-English, Japanese-English,
Greek-English, Russian-English, etc. Their main subjects of translation are medical
handbooks and legal documents. They deal with a wide variety of documents, from
journal articles to technical documents. They do accept resumes and they do use
freelance. The resumes are reviewed, evaluated, classified and kept in their data files

to contact freelancers when necessary. They require you to have a good command of the language pair(s) you work with. Experience, commitment and responsibility. Computer programs and internet tool skills. They have one in-house translator and about 20 freelancers.They also offer interpreting equipment rental/sales, video narration, transcription, proofreading/editing and ESL training.

ALTA Language Services, 3355 Lenox Rd. NE, Ste. 510, Atlanta, GA 30326
Phone: (404) 920-3838   Fax: (404) 920-3839
E-mail: translations@altalang.com
Contact: Hannah Lodge
Founded 1980. Member: ATA, AAIT. Uses freelance translators and interpreters. Accepts unsolicited resumes. Resumes are filed by language. Requires outstanding translation skills. Main languages (both ways) are Spanish, German, French, Japanese, Portuguese, Dutch, Italian, Chinese, Korean, and Russian. Main subjects are legal, medical, and general. Does multilingual typesetting in addition to translation and interpretation. Engages around 300 translators.

ALTCO Translations, 1426 Ridgeview Rd., Columbus, OH 43221, USA
Phone: (614) 486-2014   Fax: (614) 559-6682
E-mail: trudypeters@sbcglobal.net
Contact: Trudy E. Peters, Owner.
Founded 1982. Member: ATA. Uses freelancers for translation and interpretation. Only experienced translators' applications accepted. Main languages: all European languages. Main subjects are patents, business, IT, manuals, brochures, advertising, medical/pharmaceutical.

Alticor, Inc., 7575 Fulton Street East, Ada, MI 49355-0001
Phone: (616) 787-7372   Fax: (616) 787-7956
Website: www.alticor.com
Contact: Tieu O'Brien.   Member: ATA

Always Ready Translation Services, 11026 Ventura Blvd., Room 10, Studio City, CA 91604,   Phone: (800) 240-6601   Fax: (818) 755-8959
E-mail: language@worldnet.att.net
Contact: Dan Prescott, President
Founded 1985. Accepts resumes. Translates Spanish, Asian languages, Russian, Armenian, and other European languages.

American Bureau of Professional Translators (ABPT),
6060 Richmond Ave, Ste. 250, Houston, TX 77057
Phone: (713) 789-2500   Fax: (713)789-8920
E-mail: nancy@abpt.com or abpt@abpt.com   Website: www.abpt.com
Contact: Nancy Ehlinger, Project Manager
Member: AATIA, ALC, ATA, BBB, HITA, NCTA

American Education Research Corp., P.O. Box 996, West Covina, CA 91793
Phone: (626) 339-4404   Fax: (626) 339-9081
E-mail: aerc@verizon.net   Website: www.aerc-eval.com
Contact: Martha Alvarez.   Member: ATA

American ESL, Inc., 15 Main Street, Ste 222, Watertown, MA 02472
Phone: (781) 963-1114   Fax: (781) 767-7871
E-mail: info@myaesl.com   Website: www.myaesl.com
Contact: Kenneth Paquette, President.   Member: ATA

American Evaluation and Translation Service, Inc.,
407 Lincoln Rd., Ste. 11-J, Miami Beach, FL 33139
Phone: (786) 276-8190   Fax: (786) 524-0448
E-mail: info@aetsinternational.com Website: www.aetsinternational.com
Member: ATA
American International Business and Associates, Inc.,
4693 W Flager St., Miami, FL 33134
E-mail: abc1021@aol.com
Contact: Rita Benet, Vice President.   Member: ATA
American Language Technologies Inc.,
3941 Legacy Drive, #204, PMB 199A, Plano, TX 75023
Phone: (972) 517-2700   Fax: (469) 429-0020
E-mail: Jay@americanLT.com   Website: www.americanLT.com
Contact: Jay Forte, CEO.   Member: ATA
Based out of Dallas, TX but servicing nationally, American Language Technologies,
Inc is a full service translation and interpreting company providing translations, inter-
preting, and voice talent in 95 different languages. Work focuses on but is not limited
to the human resources departments (especially operations, ethics and HR manuals),
marketing, and legal departments. We also provide transcription services. Our main
client is the U.S. Federal Government and we continually search for DEA and DHS
cleared monitors for T3 lines.
American Translation Partners, Inc., 175 Pairmount Drive, Raynham, MA 02767
Phone: (508) 823-8892, (888) 443-2376, (617) 350-9988   Fax: (508) 823-8854
E-mail: info@americantranslationpartners.com
Website: www.americantranslationpartners.com
Contact: Scott Crystal
Founded 1998. Member: ATA, NAJIT, FIT, AIIC, ITI, CCHI, IMIA, LISA, ATC,
National Council on Interpreting in Health Care. Accepts resumes with details on
language proficiency and experience as well as computer proficiency. Is an international
network of language professionals assisting government, legal, medical, insurance,
technical, financial, internet, software and various other markets with translators,
interpreters, project managers and linguists in more than 200 language pairs. Core
competencies in business, legal, government, medical and insurance industries, also
numerous global industries. Services offered: document translation; consecutive/
simultaneous interpreters; software localization; website globalization & audio
transcription.
Americlic, LLC, 200 Eagle Rd., Ste. 106, Wayne, PA 19087
Phone: (877) 254-2587   Fax: (484) 654-1041
E-mail: kmaynard@americlic.com
Contact: Karin Maynard, VP Operations.   Member: ATA
APS International Ltd; 7800 Glenroy Rd., Minneapolis, MN 55439
Phone: (952) 831-7776   Fax: (952) 831-8150
E-mail: trans@civilactiongroup.com
Contact: Ann Mickow.   Member: ATA
Arabic Dialects, 8117 S Lemont Rd., #1, Darien, IL 60561
Phone: (773) 406-1234   Fax: (630) 427-1224
Website: www.arabic-interpreter.com   E-mail: ashraf@egypttours.com

Contact: Ashraf Michael, President. Member: ATA

ArchiText, a division of Translations.com,
23 Main St., 3rd Floor, Andover, MA 01810
Phone: (978) 409-6112 ext. 116 Fax: (978) 409-6096
E-mail: jdoyle@architext-usa.com Website: www.architext-usa.com
Contact: John J. Doyle

Argo Translation, Inc., 2420 Ravine Way, Ste. 200, Glenview, IL 60025
Phone: (847) 901-4070 Fax: (847) 901-4075
E-mail: sales@argotrans.com Website: www.argotrans.com
Contact: Jacqueline LaCarelli
Founded 1995. Member: ATA. Uses freelance translators and interpreters. Accepts unsolicited resumes. Works in all languages and subjects, viz., medical, technical, legal, commercial. Always on the lookout for professional translators. Has 575 translators.

Around The World, Inc., 23612 West 52nd Street, Shawnee, KS 66226
Phone: (913) 422-1030 Fax: (913) 422-1032
E-mail:atwtranslation@sbcglobal.net Website: www.atwtranslation.com
Contact: Gary West
Founded 1998. Member: ATA, BBB. Translates all languages, mainly technical, advertising, business and legal. Translates and typesets for private and business sectors. Utilizes over 5000 translators.

Arthur International, Inc., 900 IDS Center, 80 S 8th St., Minneapolis, MN 55402
Phone: (952) 474-3300
E-mail: sales.usa@arthurint.com Website: www.arthurint.com
Contact: Pierre deShasta. Member: ATA

Artra International Corp, 1 E Broward Blvd., Ste. 700, Fort Lauderdale, FL 33301
Phone: (877) 517-7727 Fax: (877) 517-8568
E-mail: mail@ARTRAinternational.com Website: www.artrainternational.com
Contact: Natalie Zlochevsky. Member: ATA

ASET International Services Corporation,
2009 North 14th St., Ste. 214, Arlington, VA 22201
Phone: (703) 516-9266 Fax: (703) 516-9269
E-mail: Khendzel@asetquality.com Website: www.asetquality.com
Contact: Kevin S. Hendzel, Director of Language Services
Founded 1987. Member: ATA. Translates in over 100 languages, both from and into English. Emphasis on Equipment Manuals, Pharmaceuticals and Medical Equipment, Software Localization, Nuclear, Chemical, Industrial and Structural Engineering, Law and Legislation, Regulations and Codes, Education and Consumer Goods translation. Prospective translators are required to have 10 years professional translating experience and formal technical training in a specialty area. Resumes are archived in database and assignments given when appropriate match arises. Resumes *must be faxed or submitted by E-mail.* The company also works with engineering drawings and specifications and possesses full AutoCad and full-color printing capabilities. They provide interpreting services and are an authorized Master Distributor for the Bosche interpreting equipment series.The company also handles rentals, sales and repair of Bosche interpreting equipment as well as customized installations of interpreting equipment. Aset also has a full-scale in-house audio/video production

studio and extensive expertise in complete localization of software, courseware and Web materials, including computer-based training. In-house staff of 83. Welcomes voice-over talent. Welcomes voice-over talent. Maintains a pool of 2000+ translators, interpreters, testers and voice talent.

Asian Link Corp., 1108 W Valley Blvd., Ste. 4, Alhambra, CA 91803
Phone: (626) 300-9191   Fax: (626) 300-8955
E-mail:sophia@asialink.com
Contact: Sophia N. Yang.   Member: ATA
Asian Pacific Development Center-Colorado Language Connection
1544 Elmira St., Aurora, CO 80010
Phone: (303) 365-2959 x 114 Fax: (303) 344-4599
E-mail: CLC@apdc.org   Website: www.apdc.org
Contact: Julia S. Vang   Member: ATA
Asian Translation Service, 392 North 1410 East, Lehi, Utah 84043
Phone: (801) 565-8281   Fax: (801) 365-6560
E-mail: ats@asiantranslation.com   Website: www.asiantranslation.com
Contact: Steve Stevens
Founded 1992. Member: ATA. Translates English into Hmong, Vietnamese, Cambodian, Thai, Korean, Japanese, Chinese, Tagalog, Malay, and Indonesian, mainly health-related, business, personal documents, and product catalogues. Provides full range of translation and interpretation. Uses about 30 translators.
ASIST Translation Services, 4663 Executive Drive, Ste. 11, Columbus, OH 43220
Phone: (614) 451-6744   Fax: (614) 451-1349
E-mail: asist@asisttranslations.com
Contact: Elena Tsinman, President
Founded 1983. Member: ATA. Uses freelance translators and interpreters. Accepts unsolicited resumes. All resumes are entered in a database. If qualified, translator is contacted immediately. Applicant must be experienced, native speaker, and have a university degree. Main languages are English into French, Spanish, Chinese, Japanese, Russian, Arabic, German, Somali, Portuguese and Italian. Additional languages are Dutch, Swedish and Danish. Does 2-3 million words a year. Does also typesetting, Website translation, software translation, localization, audio-visual productions, and desktop publishing. Maintains pool of 2000 translators.
Atlantic International Translators, Inc., 4956 Vermack Rd., Atlanta, GA 30338
Phone: (770) 350-9050   Fax: (770) 350-9051
E-mail: atlanticit@aol.com   Website: www.atlanticitinc.com
Contact: Rogelio Cipriano.   Member: ATA
Atlas Language Services, Inc., 161 North Clark Street, 47th Floor, Chicago, IL 60601, Phone: (312) 372-1600   Fax: (866) 816-0578
E-mail: info@AtlasLS.com   Website: www.atlasls.com
Contact: Kevin J. McQuire.   Member: ATA
Atlas Language Services, Inc., 820 East Terra Cotta Ave., Ste. 132, Crystal Lake, IL 60014, Phone: (815) 479-1600   Fax: (866) 816-0578
E-mail: info@AtlasLS.com   Website: www.atlasls.com
Contact: Kevin J. McQuire.   Member: ATA
Atlas Translation Services, 515 N. Central Ave, Ste. B, Glendale, CA 91203
Phone: (818) 242-2400   Fax: (818) 242-2475

E-mail: translations@atlaspvs.com
Contact: Sorina Kalili
Founded 1993. Uses freelancers for translation. Accepts unsolicited resumes. Main languages (both ways) are Farsi, German, Spanish, French, Arabic, Chinese, and Japanese. Main subjects are legal, business, and scripts. Also does legal interpretation.

ATS - Acclaim Technical Services, 101 Main St., Ste.400, Huntington Beach, CA 92648, Phone: (714) 596-8704 Fax: (714) 596-8734
E-mail: info@acclaimtechnical.com Website: www.acclaimtechnical.com

Audio To Go, Inc., 42 West 89th St. Apt. E, New York, NY 10024
Phone: (212) 721-1183 Fax: (212) 721-1273
E-mail: info@a2g.com Website: www.a2g.com
Contact: Gayle Goldfarb
Founded 1991. Member: NYCT. Accepts resumes. Requires certification, experience, native speakers in target language. Translates all languages. Translates audio and video programs with narrators in their native language.

Auerbach International Inc./dba Translations Express,
64 Mercedes Way, San Francisco, CA 94127
Phone: (415) 592-0042 Fax: (415) 592-0043
E-mail: translations@auerbach-intl.com Website: www.auerbach-intl.com
Contact: Philip Auerbach. Member: ATA

Auracom International, Inc., PO Box 779, Stowe, VT 05672
Phone: (888) 671-8911 Fax: (802) 253-7322
E-mail: info@auratrans.com Website: www.auratrans.com
Contact: Gordon McDermott Member: ATA, Founding Member ALC

Avantpage, 1138 Villaverde Lane, Davis, CA 95618
Phone: (530) 750-2040 Fax: (530) 750-2024
E-mail: luis@avantpage.com Website: www.avantpage.com
Contact: Luis Miguel, CEO
Founded 1996. Member: ATA, ALC. Accepts resumes. Requires 3 years exp., certification/accreditation where available. Translates English into Spanish, Japanese, Chinese (simplified and traditional), Korean, French, German, Vietnamese, Arabic, Hebrew, Italian, and Portuguese. Also Farsi, Thai, Tagalog, and MORE!. Main areas are healthcare, education, government, marketing, etc

Avantext, 2991 Shattuck Avenue, Ste. 200, Berkeley, CA 94705
Phone: (510) 644-3490 Fax: (510) 644-3492
E-mail: info@avantext-usa.com Website: www.avantext-usa.com

Avantgarde Translations, 5960 Fairview Road, Ste. 400, Charlotte, NC 28210
Phone: (704) 858-2127 Fax: (800) 575-8262
Website: www.avantgardetranslations.com
Contact: Memuna Williams. Member: ATA

Avid Translation, 235 E. 3rd Avenue, Ste 202, San Mateo, CA 94401
Phone: (650) 525-9896 Fax: (650) 525-9822
Website: www.avidtrans.net

Avid Translation, 5000 Birch Street, Ste 3000, Newport Beach, CA 92660
Phone: (800) 858-1146 Fax: (650) 525-9822
Website: www.avidtrans.net

—B—

Babel Trans-Media Center,
1720 Ala Moana Blvd., Tradewinds, Suite A5 Honolulu, HI 96815
Phone: (808) 946-3773   Fax: (808) 946-3993
E-mail: tmc@babeltmc.com   Website: www.babeltmc.com
Contact: Tomoki Hotta.   Member: ATA
Babel Tower, Inc., P.O. Box 25186, Ft. Lauderdale, FL 33320
Phone: (954) 240-8488
E-mail: information@babeltowerinc.com   Website: www.babeltowerinc.com
Contact: Sandra Fernandez
Founded 1996. Member: ATA. Interpreters/Translators.
Back to Basics Learning Dynamics, Inc., 1300 Paper Mill Road, Newark, DE 19711
Phone: (302) 594-0754 x209 Fax: (302) 421-9479
E-mail: beverly@backtobasicslearning.com
Website: www.backtobasicslearning.com
Contact: Beverly Stewart, M.Ed., President/Director.   Member: ATA
Founded 1985. Winner of many local, regional, and national awards and recognition
Education and Business Consultant.
Back to Basics Learning Dynamics, Inc., 6 Stone Hill Rd., Wilmington, DE 19803
Phone: (302) 594-0754 x209 Fax: (302) 421-9479
E-mail: beverly@backtobasicslearning.com
Website: www.backtobasicslearning.com
Contact: Beverly Stewart, M.Ed., President/Director.   Member: ATA
Founded 1985. Winner of many local, regional, and national awards and recognition
Education and Business Consultant.
Barinas Translation Consultants, Inc. 800 Hop Tree, San Antonio, TX 78260
Phone: (210) 545-0019   Fax: (210) 545-3735
E-mail: info@barinas.com   Website: www.barinas.com
Contact: Sonia Barinas, President
Company founded 1980. Member: MPI, AAHA, TSHE, SATC, San Antonio Chamber
of Commerce, GSHMA, ISMP, THMA. Uses freelance translators and interpreters.
Accepts unsolicited resumes. Resumes are checked for quality and experience,
then filed by language and areas of expertise. Please submit sample with resume,
and indicate degree in translation and/or interpretation. Degree in law, medicine
etc. is a plus. Main language pairs are Spanish/English, French/ English, French/
Spanish, Portuguese/English, German/English, Chinese/English, Japanese/English.
Main subjects are legal, medical, technical, telecom. Specializes in simultaneous
interpretation for meetings and conventions. Does about 350 projects a year. Uses
hundreds of freelancers.
Baystate Interpreters, Inc., 32 Pleasant Street, Gardner, MA 01440
Phone: (978) 632-1662   Fax: (978) 632-1772
E-mail: service@baystateinterpreters.com Website: www.baystateinterpreters.com
Contact: Darrin Brooks   Membership: ATA
Beacon Worldwide, 30 S Wacker Dr., 22nd Flr., Chicago IL 60606
Phone: +1 (312) 466-5671   Fax: +1 (312) 466-5601
E-mail: info@beacon-ww.com   Website: www.beacon-ww.com

Berkeley Scientific Translation Service, Inc, P.O.Box 150, Berkeley, CA 94701
Phone: (510) 548-4665   Fax: (510) 548-4666
E-mail: info@berksci.com   Website: www.berksci.com
Contact: Dr. Marlo R. Martin
Founded 1974. Member: ATA. Translates Japanese and the major European languages. Majority of work involves patent translations into English. Emphasis on Mechanical, Automotive, Chemical and Chemical Engineering, Computers and Software, Electronics, Biotechnology, Pharmaceuticals, and Physics translations. Prospective subject-qualified translators should be able to produce authoritative translations into their native language within their subject areas. Resumes are screened for educational background and technical knowledge as related to translation experience. The company was founded by a physicist and engineer and seeks translators with similar qualifications. Maintains a pool of 40-80 translators.

Betmar Languages, Inc., 6260 Highway 65 NE, Ste. 308, Minneapolis, MN 55432
Phone: (763) 572-9711   Fax: (763) 571-3467
E-mail: best@betmar.com
Contact: Elizabeth A. Loo.   Member: ATA

Better Communications, 3700 Wilshire Blvd., Ste. 490, Los Angeles, CA 90010
Phone: (213) 387-1166   Fax: (213) 387-1163
E-mail: info@bettercomm.com   Website: www.bettercomm.com
Member: ATA

Bilingual Professional Agency, Inc., 1663 E 17th St., Brooklyn, NY 11229
Phone: (718) 339-5800   Fax: (718) 339-8433
E-mail: translations@comprehensivenet.com Website: www.comprehensivenet.com
Contact: Leah Schlager.   Member: ATA

BioMedical Translators, 3477 Kenneth Drive, Palo Alto, CA 94303
Phone: (650) 494-1317   Fax: (650) 494-1394
E-mail: biomed@biomedical.com
Contact: Monique Vazire
Founded 1992. Member: ATA, NCTA. Main languages translated are French, German, Italian, Spanish, Dutch, Swedish, Portuguese, Danish, Japanese, and Chinese. Emphasis is on Medical and Biological translation, including equipment, studies and software. Prospective translators should possess at least one year experience, have knowledge of the medical field, and have access to medical dictionaries. Their equipment should include a PC and modem or E-mail; software should include Word and WordPerfect. Resumes are reviewed by the recruiting department and responded to with a test translation, which is then evaluated. The company specializes exclusively in the medical field and its peripherals. Their services also include desktop publishing. Maintains a pool of 500+ translators.

Bizzy Box Translation Services, 16060 Ventura Blvd., Ste. 105, Encino, CA 91436
Phone: (818) 728-1288   Fax: (818) 728-1286
E-mail: mail@bizzy-box.com   Website: www.bizzy-box.com
Contact: Nancy Afshar (Ponamarenko).   Member: ATA

Bloomberg L.P., 731 Lexington Ave, New York, NY 10022
Phone: (212) 318-2000 Fax: (212) 893-5371
Website: www.bloomberg.com

Bridge-Linguatec Language Services, 915 S. Colorado Blvd., Denver, CO 80246

Phone: (303) 777-7783   Fax: (303) 777-7246
Website: www.bridge.edu
Contact: Eric Clawson
Founded 1981. Translates mainly Spanish, French, German, Arabic, Dutch, Russian and Portuguese. Emphasis on legal and medical. Prospective translators should, by preference, be native speakers. Resumes are filed by language and translators contacted by need. The company also provides ESL training for executives, foreign language instruction, and interpretation services. Maintains a pool of 150-200 translators.

Bromberg & Associates, 3320 Caniff St, Hamtramck, MI 48212
Phone: (313) 871-0080   Fax: (888) 225-1912
E-mail: jinny@brombergtranslations.com   Website: www.brombergtranslations.com
Contact: Jinny Bromberg   Member: ALC,NAJIT, NCIHC, MiTIN

Bruce International, Inc., 4800 SW Griffith Dr., Ste 100, Beaverton, OR 97005
Phone: (503) 643-8448   Fax: (503) 643-7174
E-mail: info@bruceinternational.com   Website: www.bruceinternational.com
Contact: Rogelio Avalos, Vice-President   Member: ATA

Burg Translation Bureau, Inc., 29 South LaSalle, Ste. 936, Chicago, IL 60603
Phone: (312) 263-3379   Fax: (312) 263-4325
E-mail: burg@burgtranslations.com   Website: www.burgtranslations.com
Contact: Lodovico Passalacqua, President
Founded 1936. Member: ATA. Emphasis on technical translation. Translators carefully "screened." Strong Project Management and QC with ISO 9001:2000 certified by TÜV Rheinland. Translation and Typesetting. 60 language pairs translated using both in-house staff and external translation professionals having minimum 5 years experience.

—C—

Carmazzi Global Solutions, Sacramento, CA 95624
Phone: (888) 452-6543 Fax: (866) 648-3431
Email: info@carmazzi.com Website: www.carmazzi.com
Founded 1998. Provides interpretation (including Sign Language and over the phone interpretation) and translation services to many legal, healthcare, corporate, government, education, and insurance-related companies.

Carolina Polyglot, Inc., PO Box 36334, Charlotte, NC 28236
Phone: (704) 366-5781   Fax: (704) 364-2998
E-mail: wdepaula@carolinapolyglot.com   Website: www.carolinapolyglot.com
Contact: Dr. William DePaula
Company founded 1971. Member: ATA, CATI. Accepts unsolicited resumes. Resumes are filed by language pair. E-mail and fax filed electronically. Requirements for applicants include academic degree, previous experience, professional affiliation/ accreditation, references. Main languages (both ways) are French, Spanish, Italian, Portuguese, Romanian, German, Dutch, Arabic, Chinese, Vietnamese, and Japanese. Also translates Turkish, Farsi, Africaans, Hindi, Danish, Norwegian, Swedish, and Finnish. Main subjects are immigration, education, law, business, medicine, insurance, theology, ecology, literature, and computers. Uses over 30 translators.

Cascades Technologies, Inc.,
505 Huntmar Park Drive, Herndon Plaza, Ste 225, Herndon, VA 20170

Phone: (703) 793-7222 Fax: (703) 935-0061
E-mail: info@cascadestech.com Website: www.cascadestech.com
Caterpillar, Inc., Dealer Capability Dept., Corp Translation
501 SW Jefferson Ave., Peoria, IL 61630
Phone: (309) 494-5216 E-mail: opherk_jorg@CAT.com
Contact: Dr. Jorg Opherk. Member: ATA
CC Scientific, Ltd., P.O. Box 1135, Palm Desert, CA 92261
Phone: (760) 464-2150 Fax: (760) 341-7514
E-mail: casellas@ccscientific.com Website: www.cccsientific.com
Contact: Dr. Jaime R. Carlo-Casellas. Member: ATA
Certified Languages International,
4724 SW Macadam Ave., Ste 100, Portland, OR 97239
Phone: 800-362-3241 Fax: 800-362-2941
E-mail: Kristin@certifedlanguages.com Website: www.certifiedlanguages.com
Contact: Kristin Quinlan Member: ALC, ATA, CHIA, MMIA, NCIHC, NOTIS
Certified Translation Services, One Harbison Way, Ste. 105, Columbia, SC 29212
Phone: 1 (803) 781-7017 Fax: 1 (803) 781-5052
Email: email@certifiedtranslationservices.com
Website: www.certifiedtranslationservices.com
Contact: Ed Crosby. Member: ATA
CETRA Language Solutions
7804 Montgomery Avenue, Ste. 10, Elkins Park, PA 19027
Phone: (215) 635-7090 Fax: (215) 635-6610
E-mail: info@cetra.com Website: www.cetra.com
Contact: Terry Adams
Founded in 1997. All languages and subjects. CETRA does use freelance and they do accept resumes. The resumes are reviewed and filed together with information provided by the vendor via online form. You may fill out a form at http://info.cetra.com/contact-us
China Communications Consultants, P.O. Box 163, Bloomfield, CT 06002
Phone: (860) 614-1428 Fax: (860) 519-1238
E-mail: fzhou@chinacommunicationsconsultants.com
Website: www.chinacommunicationsconsultants.com
Contact: Feng Zhou, Interpreter/Translator. Member: ATA
Choice Translating, Inc., 121 West Trade Street, Ste. 2650, Charlotte, NC 28202
Phone: (704) 717-0043 Fax: (704) 717-0046
E-mail: translating@choicetranslating.com
Website: www.choicetranslating.com
Contact: Translating Project Manager. Member: ATA
CinciLingua, Inc., 322 East Fourth St., Cincinnati, OH 45202
Phone: (513) 721-8782 Fax: (513) 721-8819
E-mail: inquire@cincilingua.com Website: www.cincilingua.com
Contact: Michael Sum
Founded 1972. Member: ATA, ASME. Translates to/from more than 25 languages including: Spanish, French, German, Chinese, Japanese, Korean, Russian, Portuguese, etc. Prospective translators should have college degree, professional experience in a specific area (i.e. technical, medical, legal, business) and references. Must have

competency in MSWord and Excel, and should know PowerPoint, and translation memory tools. Resumes are reviewed by the Project Manager and databased. Qualified candidates may be asked to translate a short sample for additional information.

Cititran.com LLC, 11077 Biscayne Blvd., Ste 211, Miami, FL 33161
Phone: (305) 892-0181   Fax: Call First!
Website: www.cititran.com

Clark Translations, P. O. Box 452 Exeter, CA 93221
Phone: (559) 592-2918   Fax: (866) 639-4771
Website: www.clarktranslations.com   E-mail: info@clarktranslations.com
Contact: Bianca Clark.   Member: ATA

CLS Communication, Inc., 1500 Harbor Blvd., Weehawken, NJ 07086
Phone: 1 (877) 425-7266   Fax: (201) 223-0674
E-mail: info-ny@cls-communication.com   Website: www.cls-communication.com

Columbia Language Services
11818 SE Mill Plain Blvd., #307, Vancouver, WA 98684
Phone: (360) 896-3881 Fax: (360) 896-4074
E-mail: mail@columbia-language.com   Website: www.columbia-language.com
Contact: Sveltana Linchuk.   Member: ATA

CommGap International Language Services
7069 So. Highland Drive, Suite 201, Salt Lake City, UT 84121
Phone: (801) 944-4049   Fax: (801) 944-4046
E-mail: info@commgap.com   Website: www.commgap.com
Contact: Lelani P. Craig.   Member: ATA,ALC, IMIA, NAJIT

Communicaid Inc., 1550 The Alameda, #155, San Jose, CA 95126
Phone: (408) 287-8853   Fax: (408) 516-5266
E-mail: info@communicaidinc.com   Website: www.communicaidinc.com
Contact: Paula Madden.   Member: ATA

Community Interpreter Services, Catholic Charities
275 W. Broadway, South Boston, MA, 02127
Phone: (617) 464-8100   Fax: (617) 464-8151
E-mail: cis_request@ccab.org   Website: www.ccab.org/cis
Contact: Dragica Samardzic, Program Manager
Founded in 1986. Member: ATA, MMIA, NETA. Accepts resumes for rare languages only at this time. Translates Haitian Creole, Spanish, Cape Verdean Creole, Vietnamese, Russian, Portuguese, Cantonese/Mandarin Chinese, Vietnamese, Polish, Farsi, Bosnian and Albanian. Also Somali, Swahili, Italian, French, Arabic, Khmer and Laotian. They translate to/from a total of 70 languages. Emphasis on Personal Document translation. Prospective translators and interpreters should live in Massachusetts or a bordering state, and possess at least a Bachelor's degree, past translating experience, and fluency in at least two languages. Qualified resumes are responded to with an interview appointment. They are a nonprofit service operated by Catholic Charities. Maintains a pool of 200 translators and interpreters.

ComNet International, 501-I S Reino Road #358, Newbury Park, CA 91320
Phone: (818) 991-1277   Fax: (805) 498-9955
E-mail: agel@comnetint.com   Website: www.translationstogo.com
Contact: Dr. Elias Agel
Founded 1989. Member: ATA. Translates all languages, in all subjects. Prospective

two departments - programs and services. Programs is a language school providing small group and private language instruction. Services comprise translation, typesetting, formatting, interpretation, voiceovers and subtitling. Maintains a pool of 300 translators.

Cross Cultural Communications Systems, Inc.,
PO Box 6401, Manchester, NH 03103
Phone: (781)729-3736 Fax: (781) 729-1217
E-mail: info@embracingculture.com Website: www.embracingculture.com
Contact: Vonessa Phillips; Member: ATA

Crossword Translation & Interpreting, 1530 Avenue C, Katy, TX 77493
Phone: (281) 391-3534 Fax: (281) 391-7043
E-mail:language@crosswordtranslation.com
Contact: Office Staff
Founded 1997. Member: ATA. Accepts resumes. Translates and interprets most languages in all fields. Uses many translators and interpreters.

Cybertec USA, Inc., 227 Dermody Street, Roselle, NJ 07203-2318
Phone: (908) 245-3305 Fax: (908) 245-5434
E-mail: mail@cybertecusa.com Website: www.cybertecusa.com
Contact: Joseph Nunes
Technical Translation Bureau founded in 1990. Member: ATA, NYCT. Uses in-house and freelance professional translators. Accepts unsolicited resumes. Resumes are filed by language and specialty. Translators are required to be experienced, professional translators, preferably with language or other diploma and accreditation/certification. Translates mainly Portuguese (Euro, African and Brazilian) and Western European and American languages. Specializes in technical and commercial subjects, including many industries, petroleum, medical devices, imunology, and biotech. Does over 4 million words per year. Over 100 translators in company's pool. Offices in the USA and Portugal.

CyraCom International Inc., 5780 N. Swan Road, Tucson, AZ 85718
Phone: (520) 745 9447 x 0   Fax: (520) 745-9022
Email: info@cyracom.com Website: www.cyracom.com
Contact: Paul Burns
Company founded 1997. Member: ATA. Provides telephonic interpretation services on demand 24 hours a day, 7 days a week in about 150 languages. Has a secure system that provides rapid access to interpreters.

—D—

DTS Language Services, Inc.,
7780 Brier Creek Parkway, Ste. 335, Raleigh, NC 27617
Phone: (800) 524-0722 Fax: (919) 942-0686
E-mail: contact@dtstrans.com Website: www.dtstrans.com
Contact: Lucia Apollo Shaw
Founded 1972. Member: ATA, DIA, STC. Accepts resumes only electronically. Requires 5 years min. professional technical translation experience with related degree. Translates mainly Portuguese, French, Spanish, German, Italian, Czech, Vietnamese, Japanese, and Korean. Also Dutch, Finnish, Norwegian, Swedish. Mainly technical, medical, marketing, patents.

DocuTrans, Inc., 4712 S. 2675 W, Roy, UT 84067
Phone: (801) 916-3924   Fax: (801) 776-4027
E-mail: translate@docutrans.com   Website: www.docutrans.com
Contact: Gabriele H. Johnson.   Member: ATA, BBB of Utah
Dynamic Language Center, 15215 52nd Ave. S, Ste 100, Seattle, WA 98188
Phone: (206) 244-6709   Fax: (206) 243-3795
E-mail: web@dynamiclanguage.com   Website: www.dynamiclanguage.com

—E—

Echo International, Three Gateway Center, Floor 14 W, Pittsburgh, PA 15222
Phone: (412) 261-1101   Fax: (412) 261-1159
E-mail: ldutka@echointernational.com
Contact: Les Dutka, CEO
Eiber Translations, Inc. 55 Northern Blvd., Great Neck, NY 11021
Phone: (718) 463-2900   Fax: (718) 359-4073
E-mail: eibertrans@aol.com
Contact: Edna H. Eiber
eLocale, Inc., PO. Box 1806, Boulder, CO 80306
Phone: (877) 806-6060
E-mail: info@elocale.com   Website: www.elocale.com
Eriksen Translations Inc., 32 Court St., 20th Fl., Brooklyn, NY 11201
Phone: (718) 802-9010   Fax: (718) 802-0041
E-mail: info@erikseninc.com   Website: www.erikseninc.com
Contact: Natasha Bonilla, Vendor Manager
Founded 1986. Member: ASTD, ATA, GALA, NAJIT, NCIHC, NYCT, STC. Translates
into and from all major languages. Emphasis on Legal, Financial, Advertising,
Education, Pharmaceutical and Health Care. Translators are encouraged to register on
Website. The company also provides typesetting services and Website globalization.
Maintains a pool of 6000 translators.
Escalante Translations, 1930 Village Center Circle #3-930, Las Vegas, NV 89134
Phone: 1-888-262-3468 (USA only) or   (702) 302-7676   Fax: (303) 388-2255
E-mail: info@escalante.com   Website: www.escalante.com
Contact: Desiree Blum, Senior Vice President
Eurasia Translations, Inc., 16530 Ventura Blvd., Ste. 206, Encino, CA 91436
Phone: (818) 907-9718   Fax: (818) 907-9763
E-mail: viola@eurasia-usa.com   Website: www.eurasia-usa.com
Contact: Violetta Mordukhay
Founded 1993. Member: ATA. Accepts resumes. Translates mainly Spanish, German,
Hebrew, Russian, French, Arabic, Farsi and Indonesian. Also Romanian, Slovak, Malay,
Japanese, Polish, Czech and Chinese. Mostly immigration, legal, and book publishing.
Pool of over 200 translators.
Eureka-Foreign College Evaluators & Translators,
6034 W. Gunnison St, Ste 100, Chicago, IL 60630
Phone: (773) 545-1700   Fax: (773) 545-1716
E-mail: EurekaTranslator@aol.com   Website: www.polishtranslations.com
Contact: Maria Beata Kapelski, Executive Director

Founded 1992. Member: ATA, The Translators and Interpreters Guild. Translates Polish, both from and into English, and German and Spanish into English. Emphasis on University Admission Documents, Immigration & Naturalization, Labor Department, Business, Technical, Medical and Legal translation. Prospective translators should have IBM-compatible PC, Word or Word Perfect, Windows, minimum Bachelor's Degree. Resumes are reviewed, and qualified persons contacted. The company specializes in credential evaluation and Polish-American consulting services for business cooperation, cultural and marketing advisement, and is currently looking for Polish translators and interpreters. Maintains a pool of 10 translators.

EuroNet Language Services, 295 Madison Ave., 45th Fl., New York, NY 10017
Phone: (212) 271-0401   Fax: (212) 271-0404
E-mail: euronet@mindspring.com
Contact: Anouk, HRM
Founded 1989. Member: NYCT, ATA. Uses freelance translators and interpreters. Accepts unsolicited resumes. Translates Spanish, French, Portuguese, Italian, Dutch, German, Swedish, and other European languages, both from and into English. Translates all subjects. Prospective translators must be native speakers with bilingual capacity in English and possess a university degree. Resumes are reviewed and added to a database. Maintains a pool of 300 translators.

ExactLingua, LLC, P.O. Box 5201, Williamsburg, VA 23188
Phone: (757) 564-3065   Fax: (757) 564-8666
E-mail: rromero@exactlingua.com Website: www.exactlingua.com
Contact: Dr. Ralph Romero
Member: ATA. ExactLingua specializes in technical, manufacturing, legal, medical and financial translations in all language combinations. The company boasts a strong network of translators, editors and desktop publishers located across the US that guarantee the highest quality content and document delivery. ExactLingua also provides spoken word interpretation in all languages, and language and cultural sensitivity training.

Excel Translations, Inc., 114 Sansome Street, Suite 925, San Francisco, CA 94104
Phone: (415) 434-4224   Fax: (415) 434-4221
E-mail: info@xltrans.com   Website: www.xltrans.com
Contact: Hervé Rodriguez
Founded 1995. Offices in California, Pennsylvania and Spain. Member: ATA, NCTA, STC, HTML Guild. ISO 9001:2000 certified. Translates into and from all major European and Asian languages. Emphasis on Software Localization and Life Sciences. Prospective translators should have three years' translation experience and a specialty field. They should be native speakers and have access to the Internet. Most translations done using TM tools. Applicants will need to take a test. Resumes are screened and entered into a database if test is successful. Applicants are notified by postcard. The company works with both freelancers and in-house translators and provides full DTP services. Maintains a pool of 1,000 translators.

Executive Linguist Agency, Inc.
500 S. Sepulveda Blvd., Ste. 300, Manhattan Beach, CA 90266
Phone: (310) 376-1409   Fax (310) 376-9285
E-mail: mail@executivelinguist.com   Website: www.executivelinguist.com
Contact: Ronald R. Randolph
Expert Translators, 5975 Sunset Drive, Ste 705, Miami, FL 33143

Phone: (305) 665-9459   Fax: (305) 665-8704
E-mail: info@experttranslators.com   Website: www.experttranslators.com
Contact: Emily Correal or Angela Greiffenstein

—F—

FLS, Inc., 3609 A-5 Memorial Parkway SW, Huntsville, AL 35801
Phone: (256) 881-1120   Fax: (256) 880-1112
E-mail: info@flstranslation.com   Website: www.flstranslation.com
Contact: Judith H. Smith/ Caroline S. Myers
Company founded 1979. Member: ATA. Uses freelance translators and interpreters.
Unsolicited resumes accepted. Translates most languages. Over 200 translators. Also
places bilingual personnel for temporary or permanent positions, mostly Japanese.
Federal News Service, 1120 G Street NW, Ste 990, Washington, DC 20005
Phone: (202) 347-1400   Fax: (202) 393-4733
E-mail: info@fednews.com   Website: www.fednews.com
Contact: Carina Nyberg
Founded 1987. Accepts resumes. Requires college degree. Translates/transcribes to
and from over 70 languages. The company is a news wire that provides government
transcripts, online newsclipping, news monitoring services, and translations in almost
any language.
Fluent Language Solutions, PO Box 563308, Charlotte, NC 28256-3308
Phone: (888) 225-6056   Fax: (704) 532-7429
E-mail: info@fluentls.com   Website: www.fluentls.com
Contact: Daniel Roux

—G—

GES Translation Services, 776A Manhattan Avenue, Room 105, Brooklyn, NY 11222
Phone: (718) 389-8453   Fax: (718) 389-4442
E-mail:ges@gests.us
Contact: Bozena Brzozowski
Garcia-Shilling International, 400 S. Zang Blvd. Ste 1218, Dallas, TX 75208
Phone: (214) 942-4425   Fax: (214) 428-4458
E-mail: acento@swbell.net
Contact: Charlie Garcia Shilling
Garden & Associates Inc., 4301 Highway 7, Ste 140, St. Louis Park, MN 55416
Phone: (952) 920-6160   Fax: (952) 922-8150
E-mail: info@gardentranslation.com Website: www.gardentranslation.com
Contact: Tom Garden, CEO
Garden & Associates, Inc. Specializes in medical, legal, technical translation and
interpretation services with 800 interpreters speaking over 115 languages including
"Rare Dialects." The ability to provide rare languages and dialects puts us in a unique
position to satisfy the growing global needs of our clients.
Gazelle Globalization Group (g3), 451 Park Avenue South, New York, NY 10016
Phone: (212) 889-5077   Fax: (212) 686-5114
E-mail: info@g3translate.com   Website: www.g3translate.com
Contact: Nancy Cearley/John Labati

Member: ATA. Works with both freelance and in-house linguists and is open to receiving resumes from translators. g3 handles projects in over 100 languages and is specialized in the following fields: Market Research, Medical/Pharmaceutical/Healthcare, Financial Services, Government, Legal, Travel & Tourism. In addition to translation g3 provides cultural consulting, Website and software localization, foreign language transcription, interpreting, audio/video adaptation, subtitling and typesetting services.

Gene Mayer Associates, 9 Depot St., 2nd Fl., Milford, CT 06460
Phone: (203) 882-5990 Fax: (203) 882-5995
E-mail: gma@genemayer.com Website: www.genemayer.com
Founded 1985. Member: ATA, AIGA, Design Management Institute, National Investor Relations Institute, CT Art Directors Club. Provides graphic design, translation and production of complex printed material used by global corporations. Emphasis on business (employee information, annual reports, marketing brochures, corporate policy manuals). The firms handles translation, design, book layout and production in 30 languages. Prefers to work with agencies or with translators with a qualified track record with large corporate clients.

Geneva Worldwide Inc; 265 West 38th Street, 10th Floor, New York, NY 10018
Phone: (212) 255-8400 Fax: (212) 255-8409
E-mail: resumes@genevaworldwide.com Website: www.genevaworldwide.com
Contact: Craig Buckstein, COO
Member: ATA, GSA, NAJIT, NYCT, OGS, RID. Geneva Worldwide was founded in 1903. They translate Spanish, Creole, Chinese (T+S), Arabic, Polish, Korean, Bengali, Urdu, Russian, Albanian. In addition they also translate 180 more languages. Their main subjects are business, medical, legal, general, technical, and financial. They specialize in various types of translation. They do accept freelance along with resumes. The resumes are filed by language and coded by experience and SME. Requirements for applicants are professional resumes. Geneva Worldwide provides face to face interpretation and document translation in over 180 different languages. They provide multilingual services to many Federal, State, City and Private agencies. They have several hundred translators in their pool.

The Geo Group, 6 Odana Court, Ste. 205, Madison, WI 53719
Phone: (608) 230-1000 Fax: (608) 230-1010
E-mail: translation@thegeogroup.com Website: www.thegeogroup.com
Contact: Translation Manager
Founded 1991. Accepts resumes. Requires min. 3 years translation/interpreting experience. Main languages are Arabic, British English, Bulgarian, Chinese (Simplified), Chinese (Traditional), Czech, Danish, Dutch, Estonian, Finnish, Flemish, French, German, Greek, Hmong, Hungarian, Italian, Indonesian, Japanese, Korean, Latvian, Lithuanian, Maltese, Norwegian, Polish, Portuguese, Romanian, Russian, Serbian, Slovak, Slovene, Spanish, Swedish, Thai, Turkish, Ukrainian, Vietnamese. Also other Asian and European languages. Main subjects are medical and medical equipment, automotive, marketing, computers, dairy equipment, legal and audio/video. Uses a pool of over 650 translators.

Geotext Translations, 259 West 30th Street, 17th Floor, New York, NY 10001
Phone: (212) 631-7432 Fax: (212) 631-7778
E-mail: translations@geotext.com Website: www.geotext.com
Contact: Randon Burns

German Language Services, 4752 41st Ave., SW, Seattle, WA 98116
Phone: (206) 938-3600   Fax: (206) 938-8308
E-mail:maia@GermanLanguageServices.com
Website: www.GermanLanguageServices.com
Contact: Maia Costa
Founded 1979. Member: ATA, NOTIS, GACC. Accepts resumes only in electronic form. Requires formal training in translation or interpretation and 5 years experience. Only translates German.
Global Institute of Languages and Culture, Inc.,
73681 NW 5th St., Plantation, FL 33317
Phone: (954) 327-1662   Fax: (954) 327-8116
Email: antonietamercado@theglobalinstitutes.com
Website: www.theglobalinstitutes.com
Contact: Antonieta Mercado
Member: ATA. Translates Spanish, Portuguese, Italian, French, German, etc., both from and into English. Emphasis on General, Computer, Medical and Legal translation. Prospective translators should have a college degree, experience, and should be native speakers of the target language. Resumes are responded to based on the applicant's qualifications and the company's needs. Maintains a pool of 20 translators.
Global Languages & Cultures, Inc., 400 N. May Street, Ste. 101, Chicago, IL 60622
Phone: (312) 275-0465   Fax: (312) 275-0470
E-mail: edilia@e-translation.com   Website: www.e-translation.com
Contact: Edilia Sotelo
Global Language Solutions, Inc., 25 Enterprise, Ste 500, Aliso Viejo, CA 92656
Phone: (949) 798-1400   Fax: (949) 798-1410
E-mail: info@globallanguages.com   Website: www.globallanguages.com
Contact: Inna Kassatkina
Global Translation Systems Inc.,
910 Martin Luther King, Jr., Blvd., Chapel Hill, NC 27514
Phone: (919) 967-2010   Fax: (919) 929-1333
E-mail: mike@globaltranslation.com   Website: www.globaltranslation.com
Contact: Michael Collins.   Member: ATA
Global Visions INC., PO Box 2402, Virginia Beach, VA 23450-2402
Phone: (757) 479-1156   Fax: (757) 479-2555
E-mail: globalvisions48@msn.com
Contact: Kristi Emerson.   Member: ATA

—H—

Health Outcomes Group, 525 Mariposa Ave, Mountain View, CA 94041
Phone: (655) 691-9810   Fax: (650) 691-9811
E-mail: david_himmelberger@healthoutcomesgroup.com
Website: www.healthoutcomesgroup.com
Contact: David Himmelberger
Heartland's Cross-Cultural Interpreting Services,
4753 N. Broadway Ave., Suite 400, Chicago, IL 60640
E-mail: ccists@heartlandalliance.org   Website: www.heartlandalliance.org/ccis

Contact: Helder Weil
Founded in 1996, Cross-Cultural Interpreting Services is a program of Heartland Alliace, a highly regarded Human Rights organization in Chicago. We offer translation services in over 70 languages and evolve with the ever-changing needs in Chicago. Our primary fields are healthcare, education, law and social service.
HighTech Passport Limited, 1590 Oakland Rd., Ste. B202, San Jose, CA 95131
Phone: (408) 453-6303   Fax: (408) 453-9434
E-mail: info@htpassport.com   Website: www.htpassport.com
Contact: Anne-Marie Aubrespy, Director of Marketing
Founded 1992. Member: ATA, NCTA, GALA. Translates mostly from English into 60 languages. Emphasis on IT, web, medical, scientific (UI, documentation, marketing localization). Complete range of language services: internationalization, localization, linguistic and functional testing. The company also provides language engineering, multilingual desktop publishing, voiceover, and customized development. Maintains a pool of 2,000 qualified and specialized linguists.
Honda R&D North America, Inc., 21001 State Route 739, Raymond, OH 43067
Phone: (513) 645-6164   Fax: (513) 645-6341
E-mail: knason@oh.hra.com
Contact: Kay T. Nason

—I—

IDEM Translations, 550 California Ave., Ste. 310, Palo Alto, CA 94306
Phone: (650) 858-4336   Fax: (650) 858-4339
Email: info@idemtranslations.com   Website: www.idemtranslations.com
Contact: Mariam Nayiny. Member: ATA
ION Translations, LLC 2980 College Avenue, Ste 8, Berkeley CA 94705
Phone: (510) 841-5000   Fax: (510) 841-5003
E-mail: info@iontranslations.com   Website: www.iontranslations.com
Contact: R. Blair Sly
Founded 2005. Member: ATA, NCTA. Uses freelance translators and interpreters. Accepts unsolicited resumes. Work samples and resumes submitted by E-mail are reviewed and graded. Translates all major Asian and European languages. Focuses on patents and other technical, scientific, pharma/biotech, and legal subjects.
ISI (Interpreting Services International Inc.),
6180 Laurel Canyon Blvd., #245, N. Hollywood, CA 91606
Phone: (818) 753-9181   Fax: (818) 753-9617
E-mail: info@isitrans.com
Contact: Cathi Rimalower
ITW Interpreting Services, Inc., P.O. Box 70040, Pasadena, CA 91117
Phone: (626) 303-5192   Fax: (626) 359-8053
E-mail: gordon@itwservices.com   Website: www.itwservices.com
Contact: Gordon Lemke
Founded 1985. Memeber: ATA. Provides telephone interpreting with a focus on the insurance industry. Has an active pool of 130 interpreters speaking 34 languages.
INAWORD
1601 Cloverfield Boulevard, 2nd Floor, South Tower, Santa Monica, CA 90404

Phone: (310) 460-3200   Fax: (800) 805-7994
E-mail: info@inaword.net   Website: www.inaword.net
Contact: Stella Fridman.   Member: ATA
Inline Translation Services, Inc., 100 West Broadway, Suite 520, Glendale, CA 91210,
Phone: (818) 547-4995   Fax: (818) 547-4013
E-mail: info@inlinela.com   Website: www.inlinela.com
Inlingua Translation Service, 95 Summit Ave., Summit, NJ 07901
Phone: (908) 522-0622   Fax: (908) 522-1433
E-mail: summit@inlingua.com
Contact: Erica Alicea
Founded 1968. Uses freelance translators and interpreters. Accepts unsolicited resumes. Resumes are kept on file for future jobs. Applicants must have computer, fax, and modem. Ten top languages are Spanish, French, Italian, Portuguese, Russian, German, Chinese, Japanese, Danish, and Polish. Also translates Korean and Romanian. Main areas are lincenses, birth certificates, and transcripts. Has pool of some 30 translators. Operates as language school with translation services.
Inlingua, Inc., 171 East Ridgewood Ave., Ridgewood, NJ 07450
Phone: (201) 444-9500   Fax: (201) 444-0116
E-mail: ridgewood@inlingua.com
Website: www.inlingua.com, 2nd Website: www.inlinguaMetroNY.com
Contact: Sandra Stern, Translation Services Coordinator
Founded 1977. Member: ATA. Accepts resumes from translators and interpreters. Requires ATA accreditation. Main languages are Spanish, French, Portuguese, German, Italian, Chinese, Japanese, Russian, and Arabic. Also Hindi, Hungarian, Polish, Romanian and Dutch Czech, Serbo-Croation, Haitain-Creole, French Canadian. Mainly legal, pharmaceutical, financial. Additional subjects that we translate: Websites, medical, cosmetics,electronics subjects, tape transcriptions. Uses some 150 translators.
Intermark Language Services Corporation
735 Broad Street, Ste. 30B, Chattanooga, TN 37402
Phone: (423) 305-1413   Fax: (770) 444-3002
Website: www.intermarkls.com
Contact: Tom West
Founded 1995. Member: ATA. Accepts resumes. Interested in translators with with a law or business degree. Translates mainly French, Spanish, German, Portuguese and Swedish. Emphasis is on Law and Business translation. Prospective translators *must* provide a sample translation in every combination they wish to translate; ATA accreditation is preferred.
InterNation, Inc., 299 Broadway, Ste. 1400, New York, NY 10007
Phone: (212) 619-5545   Fax: (212) 619-5887
E-mail: info@internationinc.com Website: www.internationinc.com
Founded 1990. Member: ATA, NYCT. Uses freelance translators and interpreters. Accepts unsolicited resumes. Prospective translators are invited to register themselves in the online database at www.internationinc.com. All applicable database forms must be filled out completely. Translates from and into all major languages, but predominantly works with Spanish, Portuguese, Italian, French, German, Japanese, Chinese, Russian, Korean, Arabic, Polish, Dutch and the Scandinavian languages. InterNation specializes in foreign language voiceovers and subtitling for corporate sales, image, training, safety,

advertising videos and infomercials as well as documentaries. Maintains a state-of-the-art digital recording studio in-house and has an online voice talent database with audio samples of 400 native language voice actors in over 40 languages. Employs narrators and character actors mainly in the New York City area. Also translates commercial, financial, legal, technical, scientific, medical, pharmaceutical, PR material and advertising copy. Maintains a pool of some 5,000 translators.

International Bureau of Translations, Inc., PO Box 532189, Indianapolis, IN 46253
Phone: (317) 679-4666   Phone (interpreters): (317) 590-3546 Fax: (317) 571-1509
E-mail: ibtinc@ibtworld.com   Website: www.ibtworld.com
Contact: Demetria Gecewicz
Founded 1976. Indiana WBE status. Member: Indianapolis Chamber of Commerce. Provided 67 languages last year. Emphasis on Medical, Technical, Legal, Business and Marketing translation. In addition to translation and desktop publishing, the company does foreign videos, court interpretation, cultural presentations, and conducts language classes. They research the cultural acceptability of company names, product names and slogans, and are the official translators for the International Violin Competition. Prospective translators should be native speakers with access to a computer, modem, or fax. They should send a rate chart with their resume. Translators are contacted as the need arises. Maintains a pool of 150 translators.

International Communication by Design, Inc.,
13040 W. Lisbon Road, Brookfield, WI 53045
Phone: (262) 781-1644 Fax: (262) 781-1645
E-mail: info@icdtranslation.com   Website: www.icdtranslation.com
Contact: Catherin Potter
Founded 1991. Member: ATA, Wisconsin World Trade Center, STC. Translates mainly Italian, Spanish, French, German, Portuguese, Dutch, Arabic, Greek, Japanese and Chinese. Also Korean, Russian and Swedish. Emphasis on Technical Manuals, medical and Legal translation. Also, substantial work with Website localization. Prospective translators must be native speakers and ATA accredited, with a specific area of expertise. Resumes are filed and used as a resource for new translators, interpreters and typesetters. We are translation service company with a wide range of clients, from large corporations to smaller clientele. The company is actively involved within the translation community. Maintains a pool of over 1500 translators.

International Contact, Inc., 351 15th St., Oakland, CA 94612
Phone: (510) 836-1180 Fax: (510) 835-1314
E-mail: info@intlcontact.com Website: www.intlcontact.com
Contact: Carla Itzkowich. Member: ATA

International Effectiveness Centers, 360 Pine St., 3rd Floor, San Francisco, CA 94104
Phone: (415) 788-4149 Fax: (415) 788-4829
E-mail: iec@ie-center.com Website: www.ie-center.com
Contact: Taryk Rouchdy
Founded 1972. Member: ATA, NCTA. Translates Spanish, Chinese, Russian, and Portuguese, both from and into English, French and Vietnamese from English, and Japanese into English. Emphasis on Legal, Technical and Children's Book translation. Uses freelance translators and interpreters. Accept unsolicited resumes. Prospective translators must have at least 3 years experience and be tested unless they hold current ATA accreditation. Resumes are screened for qualifications and appropriate equipment

and, if qualified, entered into a data base The company also does desktop publishing in all languages, as well as voiceovers, dubbing, promotional work, crosscultural and language training, and international business consulting. Maintains a pool of 7000 translators in its data base, 170 of whom are used regularly.

International Institute of Metro St. Louis,
3654 South Grand Blvd St. Louis, MO 63118
Phone: (314) 773-9090　Fax: (314) 773-2279
Email: info@iistl.org Website: www.iistl.org
Contact: Language Services Dept.
Founded: 1919. Member: ATA, NAJIT, MICATA Provides interpretation and translation services in 40+ languages.

International Institute of Wisconsin,
1110 North Old Third Street, Suite 420, Milwaukee, WI 53203
Phone: (414) 225-6220 Fax: (414) 225-6235
E-mail: info@iiwisconsin.org Website: www.iiwisconsin.org

International Language Center, 1416 S. Big Bend Blvd., St. Louis, MO 63117
Phone: (314) 647-8888　Fax: (314) 647-8889
E-mail: ilc@ilcworldwide.com Website: www.ilcworldwide.com
Contact: Dede S. Brunetti

International Language Services, Inc.,
5810 Baker Rd., Ste. 250, Minnetonka, MN 55345
Phone: (952) 934-5678　Fax: (952) 934-4543
E-mail: bsichel@ilstranslations.com Website: www.ilstranslations.com
Contact: Barb Sichel, Director of Business Development
Founded 1982. Translates Spanish, French, German, Italian, Portuguese, Japanese, Swedish, Dutch, Danish, Chinese and most other languages from English. Emphasis on Medical, Technical, Business, Manufacturing, Legal translation. Prospective translators should have ATA accreditation, references, a minimum 3-5 years experience, and be native speakers of the target language. Resumes are read and filed by language. Maintains a pool of over 300 translators.

International Language Source, Inc., P.O. Box 338, Holland, OH 43528
Phone: (419) 865-4374　Fax: (419) 865-7725
E-mail: info@ilsource.com Website: www.ilsource.com
Contact: Ryan Stevens, Account Manager
Founded 1981. Member: TAITA, ATA. Uses freelance translators and interpreters. Accepts unsolicited resumes. Prospective translators should have a specialty area and the appropriate resources for projects in that area. Resumes are kept for 6 months in an active database. Contact may involve the paid translation of a short sample. Translates mainly French, Spanish, German, Italian and Chinese. Also Japanese, Portuguese and Hebrew. Emphasis on Glass Manufacturing and Retail, Automotive OEM and Aftermarket, Furniture, Legal, Industrial and Healthcare translation. In addition to translation services, the company provides video and interactive CD-ROM translation and voiceovers. The company is willing to consider internships and cooperative projects with other translation companies.

International Translating Company,
4144 N. Central Expressway, Ste. 600, Dallas, TX 75204
Phone: (877) 483-7480　Fax: (214) 540-4973
E-mail: language@itc4you.com Website: www.itc4you.com

Contact: Syed Rayees
Founded 1969. Member: Greater Dallas Chamber of Commerce. Translates Spanish, Chinese, French, German, Arabic, Russian, Japanese, Portuguese, Korean, Vietnamese, Bulgarian, Cambodian, Serbo-Croatian, Czech, Danish, Dutch, Farsi, Finnish, Greek, Gujarati, Hebrew, Hindi, Indonesian, Kurdish, Latin, Norwegian, Polish, Punjabi, Romanian, Hungarian, Swedish, Tagalog, Thai, Turkish, Ukrainian, and Urdu, both from and into English. Emphasis on Petroleum, Electronics, Legal, Business, Advertising, Food Export, Chemical, and Civil Engineering translations. Prospective translators must accept work *only* from translation companies, and *never directly from end users*. They must have either IBM or Macintosh computers, a modem and a fax. Resumes are filed until a need arises. In addition to translation, the company also provides high-resolution typesetting in most languages. Maintains a pool of 200 translators.

International Translating Bureau Inc,
16125 West 12 Mile Rd., Southfield, MI 48076-2912
Phone: (248) 559-1677   Fax: (248) 559-1679
E-mail: itbinc@itbtranslations.com   Website: www.itbtranslations.com
Contact: Mariano Pallarés, President
Founded 1977. Translates all language pairs. Emphasis on Automotive, Engineering, Machine Tool, Legal, Medical, and Public Relations translation. Prospective translators should be native speakers of the target language, have at least 5 years residence in the source-language country, and have academic training or on-job experience in a specialized field. Candidates must have computer, fax and current software, particularly Word for Windows for PC or Mac. Resumes are scanned for qualifications in which the company is interested and filed for future use. The company offers accurate, native-like translations. Maintains a pool of 250 translators.

International Translation Service, P.O. Box 188331, Sacramento, CA 95818
Phone: (530) 753-7482   Fax: (530) 753-7482
E-mail: its_worldwide@yahoo.com   Website: www.geocities.com/its worldwide
Contact: Garry Pratt
Founded 1970. Uses freelance translators and interpreters. Accepts unsolicited résumés. Prospective translators must be experienced in both their languages and specialty fields, and should possess a variety of means of communications, including phone, fax and E-mail; they should have computers with the appropriate language fonts. Résumés are filed by language. Translates mainly Scandinavian, German, Spanish, and French, and also Estonian, Irish, Italian, Russian, Finnish, Portuguese, Polish, Dutch and more. Translates mainly legal, scientific, commercial, and medical. Maintains a pool of some 80 translators.

Interpretations, Inc., 8665 W. 96th St., Ste. 201, Overland Park, KS 66212
Phone: (913) 782-9449   Fax: (913) 782-9559
E-mail: interp@exactwords.com   Website: www.exactwords.com
Contact: Gloria J. Donohue
Founded 1991. Member: ATA, MICATA, International Trade Club, International Relations Council, Women's Resources Network. Translates mainly Spanish, French, German, Portuguese, Russian, Dutch, Swedish and Italian. Also Danish, Finnish and Korean. Emphasis on Instructional and Technical, Legal, Advertising, Video Script and Educational Materials translation. Prospective translators must be native speakers and have five years' experience; ATA accreditation is a must. They should be up-to-date

on hardware and software. Resumes are reviewed and filed; a select number are asked to provide samples of their work and/or translate short paragraphs. The company also provides interpreters for meetings, conferences and telephone conferencing. Maintains a pool of about 100 translators.

InterSol, Inc.,Three Point Drive, Ste. 301, Brea, CA 92821
Phone: (714) 671-9180   Fax: (714) 671-9188
E-mail: solutions@intersolinc.com   Website: www.intersolinc.com
Contact: Susana Turbitt
Founded 1996. Member: ATA. Accepts resumes. Translates mainly French, Italian, German, Spanish, Portuguese, Japanese, Chinese, Danish, Swedish and Finnish. Mostly medical, electronics, computers, automotive, general business, travel and sports. Also software localization. Uses some 30 translators.

Interspeak Translations, Inc., 777 Sixth Avenue, Ste 19F, New York, NY 10001
Phone: (212) 679-4772   Fax: (646) 553-2975
E-mail: info@interspeaktrans.com   Website: www.interspeaktrans.com
Contact: Silvia Zehn.   Member: ATA

intránsol (International Translation Solutions)
321 West 48th Street, Minneapolis, MN 55419
Phone: +1 (612) 339-4660   Fax: (800) 850-1773
E-mail: translate@intransol.com   Website: www.intransol.com
Contact: Jason Wood, Managing Director (jason@intransol.com)
Founded in 1989 as JKW International, Inc., now doing business as (d/b/a) intránsol. Corporate member of ATA. intránsol translates to/from over 200 languages and dialects. Emphasis on commercial, medical, legal, technical, B2B, B2C, advertising and marketing materials. intránsol also provides multilingual typesetting and desktop publishing, multicultural marketing and design for global markets, simultaneous and consecutive interpreters, interpretation equipment sales and rental for meetings and conferences, transcription services, multilingual audio-visual and foreign language voiceover services. intránsol works with over 5,000 language professionals around the globe. Prospective freelancers should submit resumes to translate@intransol.com.

IRU Language & Translation Services,
2909 Hillcroft Ave., Ste. 538, Houston, TX 77057
Phone: (713) 266-0020   Fax: (713) 266-1716
E-mail: IRU2000@aol.com   Website: www.iru-services.com
Contact: Elke Krause
Member: AATG, ATA, GACC, HITA, NACT, and Houston-Leipzig Sister City Association. Founded In 1989. IRU specializes in the translation and interpretation of English, German, Spanish, French, Italian, Portuguese, Russian, Chinese, Korean and Indonesian in addition to many other languages. The different fields/subjects of their expertise include, but are not limited to: legal, commercial, medical, technical, general and personal. IRU does use freelance and they do accept resumes. Once a resume is received and the information is verified it is then added to their freelance database. IRU requires that translators hold a translation degree or equivalent, and that interpreters be court certified and that teachers hold a degree for foreign language education. The average work load is over 1,500 translations per year, with about 40 translators in the database/pool. IRU is a well-established company, serving not only the greater Houston area, but also Baytown, Clear Lake, Orange and Freeport, Texas. Some more of their

services include foreign language and ESL classes, private language tutoring with an emphasis on German, cross-cultural seminars and tour guiding/chaperon services for visitors. They offer prompt, accurate and confidential services at competitive prices. IRU is also listed in the membership directory of the German American Chamber of Commerce, the Yellow Pages and other directories.

Italian Translations Company, LLC,
5225 Pooks Hill Rd. Ste. 504-S, Bethesda, MD 20814-2014
Phone: (301) 404-0439 Fax: (240) 465-1140
E-mail: ItalTranslations@gmail.com, italiantranslations@live.com
Website: http://italiantranslationscompany.weebly.com/, www.facebook.com/ItalianTranslationsCompanyLlc
Contact: Mark L. Pisoni
Founded 1991. Member: ATA. Accepts resumes. Only translates Italian. Main subjects are economics and finance, legal, business, marketing and medical. Uses 15 translators.

Iverson Language Associates, Inc., 1661 N. Farwell Ave, Milwaukee, WI 53202
Phone: (414) 271-1144 Fax: (414) 271-0144
Website: www.iversonlang.com
Contact: Steven P. Iverson, President
Founded 1986. Member: ALC, ATA, STC, ASTD. Translates French, Spanish, Japanese,Italian, Arabic, Dutch, and Korean from English, and Portuguese, German, Polish, Chinese and all other languages, both from and into English. Emphasis on technical manuals (large machines), Medical Operators' Manuals, Spec Sheets, Financial, Software, Advertising Packaging, and Legal translations. Prospective translators should have computer, fax, current software, E-mail. Must be native speakers in the target language, with a technical background and formal training in a specific field of concentration. Three years experience in the industry and good writing skills are preferred. Resumes are reviewed internally for the required criteria. Interested translators should complete the translator listing format http://www.iversonlang.com/contact/translator.asp. The company provides translation, interpretation, typesetting and video narration services in most major languages, as well as technical writing and illustration. Typesetting capabilities include Chinese and Japanese. Maintains a pool of 600 translators. Iverson Language Associates is a long-standing member of the American Translators Association, and a Founding Member of the Association of Language Companies.

—J—

JLS Language Corporation, 135 Willow Rd., Menlo Park, CA 94025
Phone: (650) 321-9832 Fax: (650) 329-9864
E-mail: info@jls.com Website: www.jls.com
Contact: Ms. Rikko Field, President
Founded 1977. Member: ATA. Translates Japanese, Chinese, German, French and Spanish, both from and into English, with other languages on request. Emphasis on High Tech translation. Prospective translators should have ATA accreditation, education and industry experience. Resumes are screened and filed, and the promising applicants tested. In addition to High Tech, the company also does Agribusiness, Biomedical and Patent translations, and provides Chinese and Japanese desktop publishing. Maintains a pool of "hundreds" of translators.

JTG, Inc., 8245 Boone Boulevard, Ste. 402, Vienna, VA 22182
Phone: (703) 548-7570   Fax: (703) 548-8223
E-mail: info@jtg-inc.com   Website: www.jtg-inc.com
Contact: Muriel Jérôme-O'Keeffe.   Member: ATA
Japan-America Management, Ltd.,
2020 Hogback Rd., Ste. 17, Ann Arbor, MI 48105
Phone: (734) 973-6101   Fax: (734) 973-1847
E-mail: jamltdmi@ameritech.net
Contact: Landon Bartley Member: ATA
Japan Communication Consultants, LLC
The Empire State Building, 350 Fifth Ave., 59th Floor, New York, NY 10118
Phone: (212) 759-2033   Fax: (212) 759-2149
E-mail: jcc@japancc.com   Website: www.japancc.com
Contact: Mariko Numaguchi, Allan O'Hare   Member: ATA
Japan Pacific Publications, Inc., 519 6th Ave. S., Ste. 220, Seattle, WA 98104
Phone: (206) 622-7443   Fax: (206) 621-1786
E-mail: andrewt@japanpacific.com   Website: www.japanpacific.com
Contact: Andrew Taylor, President
Founded 1983. Member: ATA. Uses freelance translators and interpreters. Accepts unsolicited resumes. Resumes are entered into database and evaluated for skills and experience. Main language is Japanese. Also translates Chinese and Korean. Main areas are agriculture, business, bio-med, tourism, marketing, software and wood products. Translation, DTP, pre-press, Also publishes bi-weekly Japanese language newspaper and annual Japanese language visitor guide to Seattle.
John Benjamins Publishing Company, 763 N 24th St, Philadelphia PA 19130
Phone: (215) 769-3444   Fax: (215) 769-3446
E-mail: paul@ benjamins.com   Website: www.benjamins.com
Contact: Paul Peranteau Member: ATA
Publish books and journals for translators
Employment for Translator: None
Josef Silny & Associates, Inc., 7101 SW 102 Ave. Miami, FL 33173
Phone: (305) 273-1616   Fax: (305) 273-1984
E-mail: translation@jsilny.com   Website: www.jsilny.com
Contact: Marisa di Giovanni Member: ATA

—K—

Korean Consulting & Translation Service, Inc., PO Box 154773, Irving, TX 75015
Phone: (972) 255-4808   Fax: (214) 853-5374
E-mail: sbammel@koreanconsulting.com   Website: www.koreanconsulting.com
Contact: Steven S. Bammel, President
Member: ATA, founded in 1999. Only translates into and out of Korean, handling many different subjects. K>E freelance translators must be native English speakers. To apply, send resume with rates and be prepared to review brief training materials before doing a short translation test.
Kramer Translation, 893 Massasso St., Merced, CA 95341
Phone: (209) 385-0425 Fax: (209) 385-3747

E-mail: keith@kramertranslations.com   Website: www.kramertranslations.com
Contact: Keith & Marisa Ensminger.   Member: ATA

—L—

LRA Interpreters, Inc., 5455 Wilshire Blvd., #1015, Los Angeles, CA 90036
Phone: (323) 933-1006   Fax: (323) 933-1153
E-mail: LA@Lrausa.com   Website: www. Lrausa.com
Contact: Abel Plockier.   Member: ATA
LangTech International, 5625 SW 170th Ave., Aloha, OR 97007-3320
Phone: (503) 649-2478   (to fax, call first)
E-mail: langtech.international@yahoo.com Website: www.langtechinternational.com
Contact: Douglas Foran, Owner
Founded 1994. Active member: ATA, NOTIS. Does not accept resumes. Translates French (European and Canadian), Spanish, Italian and Portuguese (Brazilian and Lusitanian), both from and into English. Emphasis on Scientific/ Technical, Mechanical, Electronics, Automotive, Agricultural, Legal, Health Care/Medical and Employee Relations translation. Also interpretation and audio/visual narration.
The Language Bank, 875 O'Farrell St., San Francisco, CA 94109
Phone: (415) 885-0827   Fax: (415) 885-1304
Contact: Philip Nguyen, Manager
Founded 1987. Uses freelance translators and interpreters. Accepts unsolicited resumes. Resumes are screened for qualifications. Main languages are Spanish, Chinese, Vietnamese, Russian, Tagalog, Thai, Laotian, Cambodian, and French. Emphasis on social services. Pool of more than 100 translators.
The Language Bank, Inc., 34W056 Wagner Road, Batavia, IL 60510
Phone: (630) 406-1277 or (888) 852-1444 Fax: (603) 406-0917
E-mail: angela@language-bank.com   Website: www.language-bank.com
Contact:Angela Merritt
The Language Center, 25 Kennedy Blvd., Suite 400, East Brunswick, NJ 08816 -7077,   Phone: (732) 613-4554 Fax: (732) 238-7659
E-mail: tlc@thelanguagectr.com   Website: www.thelanguagectr.com
Contact: Mary Majkowski
Founded 1967. Member: ATA, TCD. Accepts resumes. Translates all languages. Main areas are health care, pharmaceutical, banking, financial.
Language Company Translations, L.C., P.O. Box 721507, Norman, OK 73070
Phone: (405) 321-5380
E-mail: nthtranslations@cox.net
Contact: Nancy T. Hancock, Director
Founded 1982. Member: ATA. Translates all languages in all disciplines. Potential translators should have experience and total fluency. They should be able to produce translations on disk and pdf if needed. Resumes are acknowledged and filed. Freelancers are contacted when appropriate work comes in. The company can take materials through final printing, working with commercial printers and supervising production. They also accept resumes from freelance interpreters. Maintains a pool of 60 translators.
Language Direct, 9801 Westheimber, Ste. 302, Houston, TX 77042
Phone: (713) 917-6870 Fax: (713) 917-6806

E-mail: translation@langdirect.com   Website: www.langdirect.com
Contact: Jylan Maloy.   Member: ATA
The Language Exchange, Inc., P.O. Box 750, Burlington, WA 98233
Phone: (360) 755-9910   Fax: (360) 755-9919
E-mail: Langex@langex.com   Website: www.langex.com
Contact: Jaye Stover.   Member: ATA
The Language Group, P.O. Box 68425, Virginia Beach, VA 23471
Phone: (757) 431-9004   Fax: (757) 431-0447
E-mail: info@thelanguagegroup.com   Website: www.thelanguagegroup.com
Contact: Giovanni Donatelli
Founded 1999. Member: ALC. Accepts resumes via E-mail. Translates mainly Chinese, Croatian, Czech, French, German, Italian, Japanese, Norwegian, Polish and Spanish. Mostly technical, engineering, finance and marketing. Uses some 150 translators.
Language Innovations, LLC, 1725 I St. NW, Ste. 300, Washington, DC 20006
Phone: (202) 349-4180   Fax: (202) 349-4182
E-mail: info@languageinnovations.com   Website: www.languageinnovations.com
Contact: Brian S. Friedman.   Member: ATA
Language Intelligence, Ltd., 16 North Goodman Street, Rochester, NY 14607
Phone: (585) 244-5578
Email: hr@languageintelligence.com   Website: www.languageintelligence.com
Language Line Services, One Lower Ragsdale Drive, Bldg. 2, Monterey, CA 93940
Phone: (831) 648-7436   Fax: (831) 648-7436
E-mail: dhansman@languageline.com   Website: www.languageline.com
Contact: Dale Hansman
LanguageOne, 2305 Calvert St. NW, Washington DC 20008
Phone: (202) 328-0099   Fax: (202) 328-1610
Website: www.languageone.com
Member: ATA
Language Plus,4110 Rio Bravo, Ste. 202, El Paso, TX 79902
Phone: (915) 544-8600   Fax: (915) 544-8640
E-mail: speak@languageplus.com   Website: www.languageplus.com
Contact: Connie Gyenis.   Member: ATA
Language Services Associates, Inc.,
607 North Easton Rd., Building C, Willow Grove, PA 19090
Phone: (215) 657-6571   Fax: (215) 659-7210
E-mail: lschriver@lsaweb.com   Website: www.lsaweb.com
Contact: Laura T. Schriver
Founded 1991. Member: ATA, DVTA, NAJIT, CHICATA, NOTA. Uses freelance translators and interpreters. Accepts unsolicited resumes. Resumes are acknowledged, kept, and used when needed. Applicants should have ATA accreditation. Main languages (both ways) are Spanish, German, French, Chinese, Japanese, Korean, Vietnamese, Russian, Hindi, Italian, and Tamil. Also Cambodian, Arabic, Farsi, Hebrew, Dutch and more. Emphasis on Legal and Medical translation. Maintains a pool of 745 translators. We have 4,000 subcontractors.
Language Services Consultants, Inc., P.O. Box 412, Ardmore, PA 19003
Phone: (610) 617-8962   Fax: (610) 617-9108
E-mail: ruth.karpeles@verizon.net   or   lsctranslations@msn.com

Website: www.lsctranslations.com
Contact: Ruth S. Karpeles
Founded 1992. Member: ATA, DVTA. Accepts resumes. Translates 80+ languages and Braille. Mostly medical, health, business, education and social services. Uses some 200+ translators.
Language Source, P.O. Box 13114, Wauwatosa, WI 53213
Phone: (414) 607-8766   Fax: (414) 201-0014
Website: www.langsource.com
Contact: Elizabeth Brudele-Baran
Language Training Center, Inc.
5750 Castle Creek Parkway, Ste 487, Indianapolis, IN 46250
Phone: (317) 578-4577   Fax: (317) 578-1673
E-mail: mgeorge@languagetrainingcenter.com
Website: www.languagetrainingcenter.com
Contact: Martin George, President
Member: BBB, TOEIC, ATA, TESOL, INTESOL, IFLTA, PAADS, ICVA, IRC, CIASTD, SHRM. Founded in 1993. The Language Training Center is a full-service language provideroffering translation, interpreting, language training, and cross cultural training. A leader in the translation field for over 20 years, LTC uses a team approach utilizing a project manager, translator, editor, and proofreader. LTC translates to and from English, Spanish, German, French, Simplified and TraditionalChinese, Japanese as well as many other languages. LTC specializes in corporate documents translation including, but not limited to, websites, handbooks, formal correspondence, legal contracts, marketing materials, etc. LTC uses freelance translatorsand accepts applications for subcontract works on an ongoing basis. Applicants will be contacted on an as needed basis. It is required that all LTC translators have some kind of past experience in translation and are members of a translation organization. LTC has more, than 100 translators that they currently utilizing with this number expanding.
The LanguageWorks, Inc., 1123 Broadway, Ste. 201, New York, NY 10010
Phone: (212) 447-6060   Fax: (212) 447-6257
E-mail: resources@languageworks.com   Website: www.languageworks.com
Contact: Resources.   Member: ATA
Languages Translation Services, 34726 31st Ct SW, Federal Way, WA 98023
Phone: (253) 835-0107   Fax: 775-993-7988.
E-mail: info@advancedtranslationservices.com
Website: www.advancedtranslationservices.com
Contact: Daniel Shamebo Sabore
Translation, interpretation, editing, proofreading, voice over, transcription, localization, film subtitling, voiceover, instruction and consulting through timely and reliable manner in more than 200 languages globally. Recruits qualified linguists and accept unsolicited mails. Some of the languages provided: Acehness, Adarigna, Afarigna,
Larisa Zlatic Language Services, 11411 Toledo Dr., Austin, TX 78759
Phone: (512) 626-3854   Fax: (512) 338-9384
E-mail: larisaz@serbiantranslator.com   Website: www.lztranslation.com
Contact: Larisa Zlatic, Ph.D.
Founded 1991. Provides Slavic languages to meet the demands of globalization and outsourcing in emerging East and Central European markets. In addition to translation

and software localization, it offers other language services, such as interpretation, voice over, editing and proofreading, international marketing and branding evaluation, computational linguistics consulting, Serbian language teaching, and more.

Lazar & Associates, 1516 South Bundy Drive, Ste. 311, Los Angeles, CA 90025
Phone: (310) 453-3302   Fax: (310) 453-6002
E-mail: languages@lazar.com   Website: www.lazar.com
Contact: Elaine Lazar
Founded 1995. Member: Corporate members of ATA and Association of Language Companies. General Services Administration certified. Accepts resumes for all languages. Mostly government, medical, pharmaceutical, IT, business, legal and technical equipment manuals. Has a pool of over 3000 translators, interpreters, transcribers, etc.

Legal Interpreting Services, Inc., 26 Court Street, Ste 2003, Brooklyn, NY 11242
Phone: (718) 786-7890
E-mail: AGerenburd@lis-translations.com   Website: www.lis-translations.com
Contact: Alexandra Gerenburd

Leggett & Platt, Inc., PO Box 757, Number 1 Leggett Road, Carthage, MO 64836
Phone: (417) 358-8131   Fax: (417) 359-5767
Website: www.leggett.com
Contact: Employment Manager
Member: ATA

LetSpeak, Inc., 2400 First Street, Ste 204, Fort Myers, FL 33901
Phone: (239) 274-5700   Fax: (239) 274-9709
E-mail: info@letspeak.com   Website: www.letspeak.com
Contact: Allendy Doxy. Member: ATA

The Lexiteria Corporation, 2459 Smoketown Road, Lewisburg, PA 17837
Phone: (570) 522-0122   Fax: (570) 522-5053 Toll Free: 877-939-9992
E-mail: translation@lexiteria.com   Website: www.lexiteria.com
Contact: Robert Beard
Founded 2000. Member: ATA since 2002. Uses native-speaking freelance translators in the target-language country and translates from virtually any language to any language in any format. Accepts unsolicited resumes. We match translators to the customer and refer all jobs from matched clients to their regular translator(s). Much experience in automotive, financial, medical, insurance, children's literature, and marketing fields.

Lingo Systems, 15115 SW Sequoia Pkwy, #200, Portland, OR 97224
Phone: (503) 419-4856   Fax: (503) 419-4873
E-mail: info@lingosys.com   Website: www.lingosys.com
Contact: Jeff Williams
Translates into 100 plus languages.

Lingotek, Inc., 15 West Scenic Point Drive, Ste 325, Draper, UT 84020
Phone: (801) 705-9310   Fax: (801) 705-9311
E-mail: services@lingotek.com   Website: www.lingotek.com
Contact: Jeff Labrum, Silvia Carvalho
Member: ATA, Gala, Lisa, TAUS; Lingotek was founded in January of 2001. Lingotek offers translation work to and from any language in the world. Lingotek uses freelance professional translators and are always accepting new resumes from translators. Please provide your resume to services@lingotek.com and list your qualifications and rates or

go to www.lingotek.com for more information. Lingotek has also developed proprietary software enabling collaborative translation and the ability to capture, grow, and re-use linguistic assets.

Lingua Communications Translation Services,
9321 Lavergne, Ste. 101, Skokie, IL 60077
Phone: (847) 673-1607   Fax: (847) 673-1669
E-mail: lingua@cifnet.com
Contact: Alex Babich, General Partner
Founded 1989. Member: ATA, MASA Uses 285 language combination. Prospective translators should possess experience, speed and quality at market-level pricing. Resumes are filed against need; translators are then contacted. Lingua maintains a pool over 500 translators.

Linguistic Systems, Inc., 201 Broadway, Cambridge, MA 02139
Phone: (877) 654-5006   Fax: (617) 528-7491
E-mail: info@linguist.com   Website: www.linguist.com
Contact: Martin Roberts, President
Founded 1967. Member: ATA. Uses freelance translators and interpreters. Applicants should have relevant education and experience. Translates all languages, all subjects. The company provides translation, interpretation, voiceover, and post-editing of machine translation. Maintains a pool of about 4000 translators.

—M—

M/C International, P.O. Box 506, Chagrin Falls, OH 44022
Phone: (440) 543-5652   Fax: (216) 820-4329
E-mail: mcinternational@stratos.net   Website: www.translationHQ.com
Contact: Mrs. E. Marchbank
Founded 1969. Accepts resumes. Translates Spanish, French, German, Italian, Portuguese, Russian. Translates mainly French, German, Dutch, Italian, Portuguese, Spanish, Arabic, Chinese and Japanese, but covers most languages of the world through our affiliates in the UK, Canada, South America, Europe, Africa, Asia, the Orient, Russia, the Ukraine, etc. Emphasis on technical, legal and commercial translation. The company is a full-service translation bureau. It also provides in-house technical manual preparation in English and all foreign languages, including on-the-premise Technical Illustration, Graphic Design, DTP, Photo retouching and Digital Photography.

MGE Lingual Services, 136 36th St. Drive SE, Ste. A-4, Cedar Rapids, IA 52403
Phone: (319) 366-1038   Fax: (319) 366-1047
E-mail: mike@mge-lingual.com   Website: www.mge-lingual.com
Contact: Michael G. Elliff.   Member: ATA

MTS Multinational Translating Service, 928 Connetquot Ave, Central Islip, NY 11722
Phone: (631) 581-8956   Toll Free: (800) 864-5069   Fax: (631) 224-9435
E-mail: info@mtsinc.us   Website: www.mtsinc.us
Contact: Lisa Alesci.   Member: ATA

MAGNUS International Trade Services Corp.
1313 North Grand Ave., #280, Walnut, CA 91789
Phone: (800) 594-5818   Fax: (800) 730-0380 or (800) 730-3080
Email: info@magnuscorp.com Website: www.manuscorp.com

Contact: Richard Antoine
Member: ATA, PCLA, HPRMA, LA-FTA, NOTA. Translates Spanish, Chinese, Vietnamese, Tagalog, Korean, Portuguese, French, German and Russian from English, as well as Hindi, Farsi, Armenian, Hmong, Lao and Arabic. Emphasis on Healthcare, Medical, Pharmaceutical, Engineering, Legal, Technical, and General Business translation. Prospective translators should have certification (if possible), appropriate education and field experience. Resumes are responded to with a standard contract, and contractors called as needed.

Marion J. Rosley Secretarial, Transcription & Translation Services
41 Topland Rd., Hartsdale, NY 10530
Phone: (914) 682-9718   Fax: (914) 761-1384
E-mail: mrosley@rosley.com   Website: www.rosley.com
Contact: Marion J. Rosley, President
Founded 1977. Member: NYCT, World Trade Council of Westchester, Westchester County Assn., Westconn. Translates all languages. Emphasis on Legal, Medical, Technical, and Business Correspondence translation. The company provides interpreting services in all languages. Prospective translators should have excellent skills and reasonable prices. Resumes are filed for future use. Maintains a pool of "hundreds" of translators. The company provides secretarial, transcription and translation services, including cassette transcription of conferences.

MasterWord Services, Inc., 303 Stafford, Ste. 204, Houston, TX 77079
Phone: (281) 589-0810   Fax: (281) 589-1104
Email: masterword@masterword.com Website: www.masterword.com
Contact: Mila Rusakova
Founded 1993. Member: ATA, Azeri Translators Association. Translates Russian, Spanish, Azeri, Brazilian Portuguese and Chinese, both from and into English. Emphasis on Oil and Gas, Drilling, Legal and Medical translations. Prospective translators should have significant translation experience, especially in the oil/gas or legal areas, and show quality performance on the company's certification exam. All resumes are acknowledged, and after prescreening, approximately 10% are sent an in-house certification exam, primarily in Russian or Spanish. They are then phoned for an in-person interview. The company also has offices in Baku, Azerbaijan, and is involved in ongoing projects in Europe, South America and Asia.They also have affiliates in Washington, DC, New York, London and Moscow. Maintains a pool of 35-50 translators.

McElroy Translation, 910 West Avenue, Austin, TX 78701
Phone: (512) 472-6753   Fax: (512) 472-4591
E-mail: marketing@mcelroytranslation.com   Website: www.mcelroytranslation.com
Contact: Susan Andrus
Founded 1968. Certified ISO 9001:2008, WBENC and HUB. Translates mainly German, Japanese, French, Spanish, Italian, Portuguese, Russian, Chinese, Dutch and Korean. Mostly engineering, technical, medical, legal, pharmaceutical, chemical, patents, localization and high tech.

M.E. Sharpe, Inc., 80 Business Park Drive, Armonk, NY 10504
Phone: (914) 273-1800   Fax: (914) 273-2106
E-mail: journals@mesharpe.com   Website: www.mesharpe.com
Contact: C. P. Chetti.   Member: ATA

Mercury Marine, W6250 West Pioneer Rd., Fond du Lac, WI 54936

Phone: (920) 929-5040 Fax: (920) 929-5893
Contact: Gary Fenrich. Member: ATA
Merrill Translations, 225 Verick St., New York, NY 10014
Phone: (212) 367-5970 Fax: (212) 367-5969
E-mail: translations@merrillcorp.com Website: www.merrillcorp.com
Resumes: resumestrans@merrillcorp.com
Contact: Thomas Alwood
Member: ATA, ITI; Founded in 1998. Translates mainly English to Spanish, French, German, Italian, Portuguese, Japanese, Chinese, Korean, Swedish and Russian. They work in 64 different languages. Subjects translated are legal, financial, advertising, medical and technical. They primarily focus on document translation. They also do some interpreting. Merrill Translations does use freeland and they do accept resumes. The resumes are all reviewed and qualified candidates are contacted to continue the registration process. They are mainly interested in applicants with college education and experience in legal and financial work. Merrill Translations is the foreign language services division of Merrill Corporation, a diversified document services company. They have offices in over 50 locations in the US and Europe. Merrill Translations production offices, located in New York and London, offer a full range of foreign language services, focused on the financial, life sciences, advertising, advertising and legal industries as well as general corporate clients. In addition to translation, localization, interpreting and foreign language typesetting services they also coordinate services with Merrill Corporation's other document management solutions, including printing and distribution anywhere in the world. They have more than 2,000 translators in their pool.
Metropolitan Interpreters and Translators Worldwide, Inc.,
110 E. 42nd St., Ste. 802, New York, NY 10017
Phone: (212) 986-5050 Fax: (212) 983-5998
E-mail: Dgrote@metlang.com Website: www.metlang.com
Contact: Daniel Grote, Vice President of Sales
Founded 1990. Member: ATA, NYCT, NAJIT, IAFL, RID. Uses freelance translators and interpreters. Accept unsolicited resumes. Resumes are entered in a database. Translates all languages. Emphasis on legal and law enforcement. About 500 in translator pool.
Monti Interpreting & Translation Services, Inc.,
1535 N. Maitland Ave, Maitland, FL. 32751
Phone: (888) 686-6007 Fax: (407) 379-9926
E-mail: caroline@montitrans.com Website: www.montitrans.com
Contact: Caroline Montalvo
Founded 1998. Member: ATA. Accepts resumes. Translates mainly Spanish, Creole, Vietnamese, French, Chinese, Arabic, Bosnian, Croatian, Cambodian, Portuguese and Turkish. Mostly medical, legal and corporate literature. Maintains a pool of 50 translators and 500 interpreters.
Morales Dimmick Translation Service, Inc.
1409 W. South Slope, Emmett, ID 83617, Phone: (208) 365-2622
E-mail: projects@mdtranslation.com Website: www.mdtranslation.com
Contact: Chris
Founded 1989. Member: ATA, IMA. Accepts resumes. Main languages are Spanish, Bosnian, Laotian, Vietnamese and Arabic. Mostly business, medical, legal and insurance. Maintains a pool of 65 translators.

The Multi-Lingual Group, 8 Faneuil Hall Marketplace, 3rd Floor., Boston, MA 02109
Phone: (617) 973-5077   Fax: (617) 213-5408
Email: info@themultilingualgroup.com   Website: http://themultilingualgroup.com
Contact: Felice Bezri
Founded 1994. Member: NAJIT. Translates Spanish, French, Italian and Portuguese, both from and into English, German, Swedish, Arabic and Cantonese into English, and Japanese and Mandarin from English. Emphasis on Medical Studies, Computer, Legal and Military translation. Prospective translators should be ATA members with extensive experience in written translation and specialization in one or more fields. Resumes are reviewed on a regular basis with a particular eye to the experience of the candidate. The company also provides simultaneous interpreting in over 50 languages and offers cross-cultural consulting. Maintains a pool of approximately 320 translators.

MultiLing International, Inc.
180 North University Avenue, Third Floor, Provo, UT 84601
Phone: (801) 377-2000   Fax: (801) 377-7085
E-mail: request@multiling.com   Website: www.multiling.com
Contact: Michael V. Sneddon
Founded 1988. Member: ATA, STC, Utah Information Technology Assn., Software Publishers Assn. Translates into 80+ languages, including Spanish, French, Dutch, German, Italian, Japanese, Chinese, Swedish, Danish, and Russian, both from and into English. Emphasis on Intellectual Property, Patents, and High-Tech Product Localization and the translation of related documents. Prospective translators must be native speakers of the target language with an undergraduate and, preferably, a master's degree, with an area of special expertise. They should have a good software and desktop publishing background and several years of experience and accreditation. The company works in all areas of translation, including working with translation software and aiding in its further development. Maintains a pool of 1,400 translators.

Multilingual Communications Corporation, PO Box 7164, Pittsburgh, PA 15213
Phone: (412) 621-7450   Fax: (412) 621-0522
E-mail: mktg@mccworld.com   Website: www.mccworld.com
Contact: Cathy Rosenthal
Founded 1977. Member: ATA. Translates Spanish, French, German, Chinese, Japanese, Russian, Italian, Korean, Portuguese, Arabic and Korean, both from and into English. Emphasis on Technical, Legal and Medical Software translation. Prospective translators should possess native proficiency and background in a specialized field. Resumes are evaluated on receipt, then contacted and tested. Their services include software localization. Maintains a pool of 500 translators.

Multilingual Solutions, 22 West Jefferson St., Ste. 402, Rockville, MD 20850
Phone: (301) 424-7444   Fax: (301) 424-7331
E-mail: mlsinc@MLSolutions.com   Website: www.mlsolutions.com

Multilingual Word, Inc, 1431 West 32nd St., Minneapolis, MN 55408
Phone: (612) 929-4203
E-mail: multilingualword@aol.com   Website: www.multilingualword.com
Contact: Michelle Livon.   Member: ATA

—N—

N.O.W. Translations, 23054 Covello St., West Hills, CA 91307
Phone: (818) 716-9112   Fax: (818) 888-6962
E-mail: thomasc@nowtranslations.com   Website: www.nowtranslations.com
Contact: Thomas Clement.   Member: ATA
Narragansett Translations & Interpreting, Inc.,
37 Chaffee Street, Providence, RI 02909
Phone: (401) 274-4077
E-mail: narragansett@usa.net   Website: www.narragansetttranslations.com
Nelles Translations, 20 North Wacker, Chicago, IL 60606
Phone: (312) 236-2788   Fax: (866) 615-8606
Email: info@nellestranslations.com Website: http://www.nellestranslations.com
Contact: Don Hanley
Founded 1956. Member: ATA, Chicagoland Chamber of Commerce, Chicago
Convention & Tourism Bureau. Translates Spanish, French, German, Italian,
Portuguese, Polish, Russian, Japanese, Chinese, Korean and numerous other languages,
both from and into English. Emphasis on Patent, Print Advertising, Legal, Brochures
and Manuals, and Personal Document translation. Prospective translators should be
experienced with references. They may be tested at the discretion of the company.
Resumes are acknowledged and promising applicants are contacted. The company
provides interpreting and voiceover services in addition to translation.
NetworkOmni Multilingual Communications,
4353 Park Terrace Drive, Westlake Village, CA 91361
Phone: (818) 706-7890   Fax: (818) 735-6305
E-mail: support@networkomni.com   Website: www.networkomni.com
Founded 1978. Member: ATA. Translates French, Italian, German, Spanish, Chinese,
Korean and Japanese, both from and into English. Handles a variety of subjects.
Excellence is the primary requirement for prospective translators. Resumes are
followed up with a call and a registration skills packet. The company has five separate
divisions: Interpretations, Translations, Tele-interpretations, Transcriptions and Video-
interpretations and all are supported by Omni's Quality Control staff. Maintains a
pool of 800 translators.
New England Translations, 185 Devonshire Street, Ste 900, Boston, MA 02110
Phone: (617) 426-1299   Fax: (617) 426-2283
E-mail: info@newenglandtranslations.com
Website: www.newenglandtranslations.com
Contact: Ken Krall, Director
Founded 1986. Member: ATA. Uses freelance translators and interpreters. Accepts
unsolicited resumes. Resumes are entered into databse by language and specialty.
Requires experience. Translates Spanish, Portuguese, French, German, Italian, Chinese,
Vietnamese, Korean and Japanese from English, and Spanish into English. Emphasis
on Finance, Legal, Marketing, Industrial and Medical translation, with specialties in
Financial and Medical. Prospective translators should have PC or Mac, fax, modem.
A small sample translation should be sent with the resume. Resumes are entered into
a database by language pair and technical specialty after qualifications are reviewed.

The company is dedicated to the translation of all major languages. It also provides instruction in Spanish only. Maintains a pool of 800 translators.

Newtype, Inc., 447 Route 10 East, Ste 14, Randolph, NJ 07869
Phone: (973) 361-6000   Fax: (973) 361-6005
E-mail: mporto@newtypeinc.com   Website: www.newtypeinc.com
Contact: Mark Porto. Member: ATA
Foreign language translations and complete graphic arts services in over 130 languages.

Northern Virginia Area Health Education Center (NVAHEC),
2 Herbert Street, Alexandria, VA 22305
Phone: (703) 549-7060   Fax: (703) 549-7002
E-mail: info@nvahec.org   Website: www.nvahec.org
Contact: Dallice Joyner (Executive Director)
Founded in 1996. Member: ATA. Provides interpretation and translation services for a wide array of assignments, ranging from health, mental health, human/social services, educational, business, legal and conferences. It also offers training classes for future interpreters, as well as continuing education sessions. Services are offered in the Metropolitan area and in the Montgomery County (MD) in more than 30 different languages, including Spanish, Vietnamese, Korean, Amharic, Farsi and Arabic.

Northwest Interpreters, Inc., PO Box 65024, Vancouver, WA 98665
Phone: (360) 566-0492   Fax: (360) 566-0453
E-mail: info@nwiservices.com   Website: www.nwiservices.com
Contact: Vic Marcus
Over 1,000 interpreters and translators available in over 100 languages.

NovaTrans Enterprises, Inc., P.O. Box 3903, Boca Raton, FL 33427
Phone: (561) 368-2485   Fax: (954) 255-5161
Email: mail@novatrans.net
Contact: Janet T. Aliaga. Member: ATA

—O—

Omega Translation Services, PO Box 745, Iowa City, IA 52244-0745
Website: www.omegatranslationservices.com
Contact: Timothy C. Parrott, M.A.

OmniLingua Worldwide, LLC., 306 6th Ave SE, Cedar Rapids, IA 52401
Phone: (319) 365-8565 Fax: (319) 365-7893
E-mail: info@omnilingua.com   Website: www.omnilingua.com

1-800-Translate, 865 United Nations Plaza, New York, NY 10017
Phone: (800) 872-6752   Fax: (212) 818-1265
E-mail: info@1-800-Translate.com   Website: www.1-800-Translate.com
Contact: Ken Clark

1-Stop Translation USA, LLC,
3700 Wilshire Blvd., #630, Los Angeles, CA 90010
Phone: (213) 480-0011   Fax: (213) 232-3223
E-mail: info@1stoptr.com   Website: www.1stoptr.com
Contact: Francesca Riggio
Founded in 1994. Member: ATA, ALC, GALA. Offices in the USA, China, and Korea.

Asian languages specialist, providing clients a direct link to Asia. Primary languages include Chinese (Traditional & Simplified), Japanese, Korean, Vietnamese, Thai, Malay, Indonesian, and Tagalog. Only employs translators who are experienced in providing the highest levels of quality and reliability to our list of over 400 clients. Areas of specialty are wide-ranging and resumes for qualified translators will be accepted.

OneWorld Language Solutions, 2909 Cole Ave., Ste. 120, Dallas, TX 75204
Phone: (214) 871-2909   Fax: (214) 871-2907
E-mail: ghayes@oneworldlanguage.com   Website: www.oneworldlanguage.com
Contact: Gabriele Hayes, Director
Founded 1990. Member: ATA, META. Uses freelance translators and interpreters. Accepts unsolicited resumes. Requires experience, prefers ATA members. Resumes are entered in database and applicants are contacted when the need arises. Translates (both ways) mainly Spanish, French, German, Italian, and Russian. Also Japanese, Dutch, and Chinese. Provides interpretation and language training. Maintains a pool of over 400 translators.

—P—

Pacific Dreams, Inc., 25260 SW Parkway Ave., Ste. D, Wilsonville, OR 97070
Phone: (503) 783-1390   Fax: (503) 783-1391
E-mail: info@pacificdreams.org   Website: www.pacificdreams.org
Contact: Ken Sakai   Member: ALC, ATA
Pacific Interpreters, Inc., 707 SW Washington, Ste 200, Portland, OR 97205
Phone: (877) 272-2434   Fax: (503) 445-5501
E-mail: recruitment@pacificinterpreters.com   Website: www.pacificinterpreters.com
Contact: Jennifer Ruden
Founded 1992. Member: ATA, SOMI, NOTIS, NAJIT, ASTM.
Pacific Ring Services, Inc., 1143 Christina Mill Drive, Newark, DE 19711
Phone: (302) 369-1518   Fax: (302) 369-1618
E-mail: pacific@dca.net   Website: www.pacificring.com
Contact: Motoko Yuasa, Registered US Patent Agent
Member: ATA. Pacific Ring Services, Inc. specializes in patents and patent litigation support.
Paragon Language Services Inc.
5657 Wilshire Blvd., Ste. 310, Los Angeles, CA 90036
Toll Free: (800) 499-0299   Phone: (323) 966-4655   Fax: (323) 651-1867
E-mail: info@paragonls.com   Website: www.paragonls.com
Contact: Hanne R. Mintz.   Member: ATA, ALC
Peritus Precision Translations, Inc., 3165 La Mesa Drive, San Carlos, CA 94070
Phone: (650) 394-4724 Fax: (650) 745-1083
E-mail: dagmar@peritusls.com Website: www.peritusls.com
Contact: Dagmar Dolatschko Member: ATA
Phoenix Translations, 2110 White Horse Trail, Ste E, Austin, TX 78757
Toll-free: (877) 452-1348   Phone (512) 343-8389   Fax (512) 343-6721
E-mail: service@phoenixtranslations.com   Website: www.phoenixtranslations.com
Contact: Sharon Quincy
Precision Translating Services,
150 West Flagler St., Museum Tower Penthouse II, Miami, FL 33130

Phone: (305) 373-7874   Fax: (305) 381-7874
E-mail: info@pretran.com   Website: www.pretran.com
Contact: Vicente J. de la Vega.   Member: ATA
Princeton Technical Translation Center, 333 Bolton Rd., East Windsor, NJ 08520
Phone: (609) 477-9983
Email: pttcllc@gmail.com   Website:http://www.princetontranslations.com
Contact: Charles Teubner, Director
Founded 1982. Member: ATA, STC. Translates French, German, Spanish, Italian, Portuguese, Chinese, Japanese, Russian and Scandinavian languages, both from and into English. Prospective translators should have advanced technical degrees and be proficient in Word/WordPerfect and related software.
Professional Translating Services Inc.,
Courthouse Tower Building, 2850 South Douglas Road, Coral Gables, FL, 33134
Phone: (305) 371-7887   Fax: (305) 371-8366
E-mail: info@protranslating.com   Website: www.protranslating.com
Contact: Luis A. de la Vega, Ph. D.
Founded 1973. Member: ATA. Accepts resumes. Translates into any language. Translations are in legal, technical, financial and advertising. Has a pool of over 1,000 translators.

—Q—

Quantum, Inc., 240 S. 9th St., Philadelphia, PA 19107
Phone: (215) 627-2251   Fax: (215) 627-5570
Email: info@quantumtranslations.com   Website: http://www.quantumtranslations.com

—R—

RIC International, Inc., 1035 Cambridge Street, Suite 11, Cambridge, MA 02141
Phone: (800) 240-0246   Phone 2: (617) 621-0940   Fax: (617) 621-2552
E-mail: info@ricintl.com   Website: www.ricintl.com
Member: ATA
R.R. Donnelley-Translation Services, 75 Park Place, New York, NY 10007
Phone: (212) 658-5033   Fax: (212) 341-7506
Email: translations@rrd.com Website: http://www.rrdonnelley.com
Contact: Aouck F. Le Fur.   Member: ATA
Rancho Park Publishing, Inc., 8601 Little Creek Farm Road, Chapel Hill, NC 27516
Phone: (919) 942-9493   Fax: (919) 942-9396
E-mail: ranchopark@gmail.com   Website: www.ranchopark.com
Contact: Stan Cheren
Founded 1988. Specializes in multilingual typesetting for translation agencies and their clients. All major languages, all major applications, Mac and PC.
Rapport International LLC, 93 Moore Rd., Sudbury, MA 01776
Phone: (978) 443-2540
E-mail: rapport@rapportintl.com   Website: www.rapportintl.com
Contact: Wendy Pease.   Member: ATA
Rennert Bilingual Translations, 216 East 45th St., 17th Fl. New York, NY 10025
Phone: (212) 867-8700   Fax: (212) 867-7666

E-mail: translations@rennert.com Website: www.rennert.com
Contact: Chad Orr, Director
Founded 1973. Member: ATA, New York Circle of Translators. Translates all languages. Emphasis on all aspects of Patent Law, Marketing, Public Relations, Business and Finance, Videos and Educational Material translation, and Website localization. Prospective translators should possess training and experience in the specific fields. Resumes are reviewed for education and experience, and a Rennert application is sent to the translator for completion. Maintains a pool of 3000 translators.
Rescribe, P.O. Box 503981, San Diego, CA 92150-3981
Phone: (800) 870-6639 Fax: (858) 487-5292
E-mail: erin@rescribe.com Website: www.rescribe.com
Contact: Erin Berzins
Founded 2001. Member: ATA. Accepts resumes. Translates into Spanish, French, Chinese, Vietnamese, Japanese, Italian, Dutch, German, Korean, Russian and Tagalog, as well as other languages. Wide variety of subject areas.
Richard Schneider Enterprises, Inc.,
27875 Berwick Drive, Suite A, Carmel, CA 93923
Phone: (800) 500-5808 Fax: (408) 904-5199
E-mail: service@idioms.com Website: www.idioms.com
Contact: Richard A. Schneider. Member: ATA
RussTech, 1338 Vickers Rd., Tallahassee, FL 32303
Phone: (850) 562-9811 Fax: (850) 562-9815
Website: http://www.russtechinc.com

—S—

SH3, Inc., 7101 College Blvd., Ste 500, Overland Park, KS 66210
Phone: (913) 747-0410 Fax: (913) 747-0417
E-mail: chubbard@sh3.com Website: www.sh3.com
Contact: Cathy Hubbard, Owner/General Manager
Founded 1980. Member: ATA, GALA, STC. Translates all major languages. Emphasis on Agricultural and Industrial Equipment, and Consumer Equipment translation. Prospective translators must be proficient with SDL 2011 and Across Language Server CAT tools, and demonstrate experience in engineering, electronic and industrial areas. Resumes are reviewed by subject specialty, experience, language, tools, and flagged for a future contact. Does around 50 million words a year. The company deals in high volume, highly technical manuals. Maintains an active pool of 250 translators.
Sajan, Inc., 625 Whitetail Boulevard, River Falls, WI 54022
Phone: (715) 426-9505 Fax: (715) 426-0105
E-mail: info@sajan.com Website: www.sajan.com;
Contact: Angel Zimmerman, Director of Operations
Member: ATA; Founded in 1997. They translate English in to most languages, Accepts freelance resumes (contact language@sajan.com for details on how to submit resumes). They require 5 or more years translating experience and translating in particular fields. Also ATA accreditation or equivalent in target language country. Their annual work-load is about 20 million words per year. They have 1200 active translators and about 7000 translators in their pool.

SARJAM Communications, Ltd., 1008 NE 122nd Ave., Portland, OR 97230
Phone: (503) 287-9277   Fax: (503) 252-9220
E-mail: sarjam@sarjam.com
Contact: Seth A. Reames
SARJAM Communications provides Japanese-English and English-Japanese translation, interpretation, and consultation to the entertainment media and media technology industries. Highly experienced translators, interpreters, and specialized consultants (Japanese/English only) are encouraged to provide their CV for consideration for participation in translation projects, interpreting assignments, and consultative business.

Schreiber Translations, Inc., 51 Monroe St., Ste. 101, Rockville, MD 20850
Phone: (301) 424-7737   Fax: (301) 424-2336
E-mail: translation@schreibernet.com   Website: www.schreibernet.com
Contact: Milton Shattuck, COO
Founded 1984. Member: ALC, ATA. Uses freelance translators and interpreters. Accepts unsolicited resumes only on Website. Translates (both ways) mainly Japanese, Russian, German, French, Spanish, Chinese, Italian, Arabic, Korean, Vietnamese, Hebrew, Polish, and Dutch, and close to 90 additional languages and dialects. Emphasis on patents, aerospace, law, medicine, communications, computers, engineering, public relations, military and maritime subjects, chemical subjects, and business and finance. Maintains a pool of over 1300 translators - 350 active, and 200 of those very active. In addition to translation and interpretation, the company produces multilingual brochures and advertisements, prints manuals and business literature in a variety of multinational fonts, and does voiceovers for video and films. Maintains a pool of over 1300 translators—350 active, and 200 of those very active.

Speak Easy Languages, 757 South Main St., Plymouth, MI 48170
Phone: (734) 459-5556   Fax: (734) 459-1460
Email: selanguages@earthlink.net Website: http://speakeasylanguages.com/
Contact: Cristina Clark
Founded 1980. Member: ATA. Translates all major language pairs. Emphasis on Automotive business, Brochure, Advertising and Legal translation. Prospective translators should be ATA accredited and possess fax and modem capabilities. Resumes are filed and the applicant called upon as the circumstance arises. The company also provides talent for voiceover work. Maintains a pool of 100.

STG, Inc., 12011 Sunset Hills Road, Ste 1200 Reston, VA 20190
Phone: (703) 691-2480   Fax: (703) 691-3467
Website: www.stginc.com
Contact: Duncan Sutton

Superior Translations, 1924 Minnesota Ave., Duluth, MN 55802
Phone: (218) 727-2572   Fax: (612) 454-4995
E-mail: info@superiortranslations.com   Website: www.superiortranslations.com
Contact: Elisa A. Troiani
Founded 1993. Member: ATA. Uses freelance translators and interpreters. Accepts unsolicited resumes. Resumes for translation should be e-mailed. Applicants are carefully screened and required to submit samples, references, and tests. Requirements are honesty, accuracy, editing/proofing skills, reasonable rates, punctuality, and an eye for detail. Translates mainly Spanish, French, German, Japanese, Chinese, Russian,

Portuguese, Italian, Polish and Hmong. Emphasis on all subject areas. Has 500-600 translators in its pool.

Suzuki, Myers & Associates, Ltd., P.O. Box 852, Novi, MI 48376
Phone: (248) 344-0909   Fax: (248) 344-0092
E-mail: office@suzukimyers.com   Website: www.suzukimyers.com
Contact: Kumiko Oh
Founded 1984. Member: ATA, MITN, Japan-America Society. Translates Japanese and Korean only, both from and into English. Emphasis on Manufacturing-related translation (Autos, Engineering, Quality Design, Robotics, Plastics, Assembly, Electronics, Paint, Contracts, Product Liability). Prospective translators should be competent and diligent. Resumes are responded to with a phone call. The company provides translation, interpretation, and consultation services in North American-Japanese relations. They also provide DTP services. Maintains a pool of about 40 translators.

—T—

Techno-Graphics and Translations, Inc.,
1451 East 168th St., South Holland, IL 60473
Phone: (708) 331-3333   Fax: (708) 331-0003
E-mail: techno@wetrans4u.com   Website: www.wetrans4u.com
Contact: Dave Bond or Pinay Gaffney
Founded 1972. Member: ATA. Uses freelance translators and interpreters. Accepts unsolicited resumes. Resumes are entered in database. Requires native ability and technical background. Translates (both ways) mainly European, Asian, Scandinavian and Middle Eastern languages. Main areas are industrial, agriculture, automotive, medical and telecommunications. Worldwide pool of 200 translators.

TechTrans International, Inc., 2200 Space Park Drive, Ste. 410, Houston, TX 77058
Phone: (281) 335-8000   Fax: (281) 333-4396
E-mail: ehogan@tti-corp.com   Website: www.tti-corp.com
Contact: Eileen Still Hogan   Member: ATA

Techworld Language Solutions, 2760 Industrial Row, Troy, MI 48084
Phone: (248) 288-5900   Fax: (248) 288-7900
Email: info@techworldinc.com Website: www.techworldinc.com
Contact: Fred Meinberg.   Member: ATA

Telelanguage, Inc., 421 SW 6th Ave. Suite 1150, Portland, OR 97204
Phone: (888) 877-8353   Fax: (503) 246-6002
E-mail: info@telelanguage.com   Website: www.telelanguage.com
Contact: Andre Lupenko.   Member: ATA

Telelingua USA, Corp, 2 Madison Avenue, Larchmont, NY 10538
Phone: (914) 833-3305   or   (800) 930-0232
E-mail: lmellet@telelingua.com or hbaraona@telelingua.com
Website: www.telelingua.com
Contact: Lionel Mellet, CEO
Member: GALA. Telelingua is a private holding company whose aim is to invest in its subsidiaries and develop their activities in the multilingual translation market. Based in Brussels, and with offices in New York, Paris, Munich and ShenZhen, Telelingua

operates in the fields of medical/pharmaceutical and technical translation, software localization and website translations. Telelingua is consistently in the Top 30 per Common Sense Advisory. The Company has strategic alliances in Latin America, central Europe and Asia, thus providing it's customers with a global solution to its GILT requirements. Telelingua translates into over 65 languages including the traditional English to F.I.G.S. and all Asian languages. The main areas of subject matter expertise are Medical Devices, Pharmaceutics, software localization and manufacturing. Telelingua uses both in house and freelance translators which are pre-screened and qualified by a strict QA process. They do accept resumes, though you must be a certified professional with a minimum five years working experience to be considered. Telelingua is also recognized for its leadership in developing and integrating some cutting edge translation technologies. A robust Enterprise Project Management system is at the core of a set of integrated tools including a portal that brings customers, projects, language resources and technologies together in real-time to manage and build measurable efficiencies into the localization process. Other integrated tools are the On-line review tool, imbedded glossaries in the translator's environment and an on-line Query tool for project team members to share information rapidly and efficiently. Telelingua has over 4,500 translators in its pool of professionals.

Total Benefit Communications, Inc.
1117 Perimeter Center West, Ste. E202, Atlanta, GA 30338
Phone: (678) 579-9600   Fax: (678) 579-9595
E-mail: tbc@benefitprojects.com Website: www.benefitprojects.com
Contact: Representative.   Member: ATA

TransGlobal Connections, 925 B Peachtree Street NE., Ste 333, Atlanta, GA 30309
Phone: (800) 316-8439   Fax: (404) 241-2804
Website: http://www.transglobalconnections.com

TransACT Communications, Inc.,
5105 200th St SW, Suite 200, Lynnwood, WA 98036
Phone: (425) 977-2100   Fax: (425) 776-3377
E-mail: support@transact.com   Website: www.transact.com
Contact: Ms. Kelsye Nelson
TransACT is the premier provider of multilingual parent notification documents to school districts nationwide. TransACT solutions combine expert content with innovative RoadMap technology, personal training and support so you can achieve compliance with confidence.

Transemantics, Inc., 1337 Connecticut Ave., Fourth Floor, Washington, D.C. 20036
Phone: (202) 686-5600   Fax: (202) 686-5603
E-mail: translation@transemantics.com
Contact: M-L Wax Cooperman, Director.   Member: ATA
Translation, interpreting and related services.

Transfirex Translation Services, Inc.,
20423 Waters Point Lane, Germantown, MD 20874
Phone: (301) 528-1695   Fax: (301) 542-0185
E-mail: info@transfirex.com   Website: www.transfirex.com
Contact: Margaret Johnson
Founded 2001. Member: ATA. Accepts resumes. All languages, all subjects. Has a pool of 25 translators.

Transimpex Translations, 3100 Main St, Ste 299, Kansas City, MO 64111
Phone: (888) 877-4679   Fax: (816) 561-5515
Email: translations@transimpex.com Website: www.transimpex.com
Contact: Ingrid Pelger, Doris Ganser or Brian White
Founded 1974. Member: ATA, Board member International. Trade Club of Greater Kansas City. Uses freelance translators and interpreters. Accepts unsolicited resumes. Resumes are put in database until needed. Requires degree in linguistics or translation. Main languages translated are German, French, Spanish, Portuguese, Italian, Japanese, Russian, and Arabic. Translates all subjects, with long experience in localization. Has overall pool of some 5000 translators, with about 150 active ones.

Translate4me Inc., 9720 Wilshire Boulevard, Suite 205, Beverly Hills, CA 90212
Phone: (310) 274-9771   Fax: (310) 274-9431
E-mail: translation@translate4me.com   Website: www.translate4me.com
Contact: Heidi Fulford
Member: ATA, ITI, BBB, NAWBO. The main languages that they translate are English to French, German, Spanish and Italian. They also translate into over 100 languages. They translate into all subjects. Translate4me Inc does use freelance and they do accept resumes. You may send your resume to usa@translate4me.com. Suitable applicants are sent an application form, terms of business nad are reference checked. They require that applicants have graduated and have at least 5 years translation experience. They should also have professional translator's qualifications. They have about 3,000 translators in their pool.

Translation Aces, Inc., 29 Broadway, Ste. 2301, New York, NY 10006
Phone: (212) 269-4660 Fax: (212) 269-4662
Email: info@translationaces.com Website: www.translationaces.com
Contact: Serge Nedeltscheff
Founded 1937. Member: NY Circle, NY Chamber of Commerce. Providing translation, interpretating, and all other foreign language services from all languages into English and vice-versa, in all subjects, specializing in legal, patent, technical, medical, financial, scientific, engineering, advertising and all other subjects. Prospective translators should have "experience, experience, experience." The company has more than 75 years' experience in providing the legal, financial, advertising, medical and governmental communities with translation, interpreting, voiceover and consulting services. Maintains a pool of over 500 translators and interpreters.

Translation Company of New York, LLC, 8 South Maple Ave., Marlton, NJ 08053
Phone: (856) 983-4733   Fax: (856) 983-4595
E-mail: TCNY2000@cs.com Website: www.tcny2000.com
Contact: Jennifer C. Thompson or Liliana Stevcic
Founded 1983. Uses freelance translators and accepts unsolicited resumes. Translates mainly French, German,Spanish, Italian, Japanese, Portuguese, Dutch, Russian, Chinese and Swedish. Main areas are pharmaceutical, chemical, medical, engineering, electronics and tourism. Has active pool of 200 translators.

Translations International, Inc.
100 South Fifth Street, Ste 1900, Minneapolis, MN 55402
Phone: (800) 259-2774 Fax: (202) 330-5776
E-mail: contact@tiinc.com Website: http://tiinc.com

Translation Source, 8582 Katy Freeway, Suite 240, Houston, TX 77024

Phone: (713) 465-0225   Fax: (281) 966-1869
E-mail: maria.quintero@translation-source.com
Website: www.translation-source.com
Contact: Maria Quintero
Founded 2001. Member ATA and ALC. Uses freelance translators and accepts unsolicited resumes.

Translations Unlimited, 1455 Forest Hill SE, Grand Rapids, MI 49546
Phone: (616) 550-7057   Fax: (616) 526-8583
E-mail: translationsu@gmail.com
Contact: Leslie Mathews, Director
Founded 1980. Member: ATA. Accepts resumes. Main languages are French, Spanish, German, Japanese, Portuguese, Italian, Chinese and Korean. Main areas are patents, sales literature, contracts, employee handbooks, medical and legal documents, technical specifications. Translator pool of 25-30.

translations.com, Three Park Ave., 40th Floor, New York, NY 10016
Phone: (212) 689-1616   Fax: (212) 685-9797
E-mail: info@translations.com   Website: www.translations.com
Contact: Pamela Kraljevich
Founded 1999. Member: ATA. Accepts resumes. Translates mainly Spanish, French, German, Chinese, Japanese, Portuguese, Italian, Korean, Norwegian and Swedish. Mostly software, IT-Telecom, finance, travel and medical. Provides full suite of globalization services. Pool of 500 translators.

The Translators, Inc., PO Box 271, Boxford, MA 01921
Phone: (978) 887-9739
E-mail: info@thetranslatorsinc.com   Website: www.thetranslatorsinc.com
Contact: Jim Swift, Personnel Manager
Founded 1980. Accepts resumes. Translates all languages, mostly medical, patents, human resources, computer, sci-tech, legal, electronic and engineering. Unlimited translator pool.

TransLingua, 1445 Pearl St., Ste. 215, Boulder, CO 80302
Phone: (303) 442-3471   Fax: (303) 442-5805
E-mail: boulder@translingua.com   Website: www.translingua.com
Founded 1992. Member: ATA. TCA, CTA (Colorado Translators Association). Translates medical, technical, legal documents, patents, marketing material, in all languages. Has a pool of over 800 translators.

TransLingua, 211 E. 43rd Street, Ste 1404, New York, NY 10017
Phone: (212) 697-2020 Fax: (212) 697-2891
Email: nyc@translingua.com   Website: www.translingua.com
Founded 1992. Member: ATA. TCA, CTA (Colorado Translators Association). Translates medical, technical, legal documents, patents, marketing material, in all languages. Has a pool of over 800 translators.

Transperfect Translations International, Inc.
3 Park Ave., 39th Floor, New York, NY 10016
Phone: (212) 689-5555   Fax: (212) 251-0981
E-mail: info@transperfect.com   Website: www.transperfect.com
Contact: Information.   Member: ATA, GALA
Transtek Associates, Inc., 599 North Avenue, Door 9, Wakefield, MA 01888

Phone: (781) 245-7980   Fax: (781) 245-7993
Website: www.transtekusa.com
Founded 1964. Member: ATA. Uses freelance translators and interpreters. Accepts unsolicited resumes.
Trustforte Language Services, 271 Madison Ave., 3rd Fl., New York, NY 10016
Phone: (212) 481-4980   Fax: (212) 481-4972
E-mail: info@trustfortelanguages.com   Website: www.trustfortelanguages.com
Contact: Jackie Cordero
Founded 1992. Member: ATA. Accepts resumes. Works in most languages. Provides translators and interpreters to a variety of fields, from business to entertainment.

—U—

United Nations Translators & Interpreters, Inc.,
1906 E. Robinson Street, Orlando, FL 32803
Phone: (407) 894-6020   Fax: (407) 894-6693
E-mail: unti@unti.com   Website: www.unti.com
Contact: Fiona Como
Founded 1991. Member: ATA. Accepts resumes. Translates mainly Spanish, Creole, French, German, Arabic, Farsi, Italian, Portuguese and Vietnamese. Mostly legal, medical, technical and INS documents. Uses about 50 translators.
University Language Center, Inc.,
1313 Fifth St. S.E., Ste. 201, Minneapolis, MN 55414
Phone: (612) 379-3823   Fax: (612) 379-3832
E-mail: info@ulanguage.com   Website: www.ulanguage.com
Contact: Therese Shafranski, Translation Department Manager
Founded 1986. Member: ATA. Accepts resumes. Translates Spanish, French, German, Italian, Portuguese, Russian, Chinese, Japanese and Hmong, as well as Turkish, Indonesian, Arabic and all Southeast Asian languages. Emphasis in all technical areas. The company handles all phases of production from translation to camera-ready art, including cultural assessment of the source documents. Maintains a pool of 250 translators.
University Translators Services, LLC, PO Box 3768 Ann Arbor, MI 48106-3768
Phone: (734) 655-7295   Fax: (734) 655-1345
E-mail: lfinch@univtrans.com   Website: www.univtrans.com
Contact: Laurie Finch, Owner
Member: ATA. Founded in 1987. They do accept resumes. They prefer that you have experience as well as certification. Having work experience or a degree in a specialty area is a plus. They work with all languages. Subjects include: automotive & manufacturing of all types, patents, legal documents, consumer surveys, promotional brochures, court interpreting, subtitling/voice over, Website HTML pages and software localization. Their work load is about 50% written translation and 50% interpretation. University Translators Services is a woman owned agency operating in the capacity of a LLC Partnership.
U.S. Translation Company, 1893 E. Skyline Drive, Ste. 203, South Ogden, UT 84403
Phone: (801) 393-5300   Fax: (801) 393-5500
E-mail: info@ustranslation.com   Website: www.ustranslation.com
Contact: David Utrilla.   Member: ATA

—V—

Vital International Programs, Inc.,
34514 Dequindre, Ste. C, Sterling Heights, MI 48310
Phone: (586) 795-2500   Fax: (586) 795-5763
E-mail: LNespolo@protranslating.com   Website: www.vitalinternational.com
Contact: Lil Néspolo
Voiance, 5780 North Swan Road, Tucson, AZ 85718
Phone: (866) 743-9010 Fax: (520) 745-9022
Email: translation@voiance.com Website: www.voiance.com
Voices for Health, Inc., 2851 Michigan NE, Suite 104, Grand Rapids, MI 49506
Phone: (616) 233-6505   Fax: (616) 233-6522
E-mail: info@voicesforhealth.com   Website: www.voicesforhealth.com
Contact: Scott Van Til, Translations; Van Nguyen, Interpretation Coordinator.
Founded 1997. Member: ATA. Accepts resumes. Translates mainly Spanish,
Vietnamese, Chinese and Arabic. Mostly healthcare and social services. Uses
hundreds of linguists.

—W—

Welocalize, Inc., 241 E. 4th St., Ste. 207, Frederick, MD 21701
Phone: (301) 668-0330 Fax: (301) 668-0335
E-mail: info@welocalize.com Website: www.welocalize.com
Contact: E. Smith Yewell. Member: ATA
Word for Word, Inc., 325 W. Chickasaw Rd., Virginia Beach, VA 23462
Phone: (757) 557-0131 Fax: (757) 557-0186
E-mail: wrd4wrd@exis.net
Contact: Curtis Hovey. Member: ATA
Word Magic Software, Inc., c/o Translation Technologies Corporation - US Distributor
P.O. Box 689, Alief, TX 77411-0689
Phone: (281) 564-3022 Fax: (713) 559-8370
E-mail: info@wordmagicsoft.com Website: www.wordmagicsoft.com
Contact: Ricardo Arguello Jr.
Founded in 1989; Word Magic Software only translates English into Spanish. They
translate any subject. They do not use freelance and they do not accept resumes.
They have English-Spanish Translation Software, Dictionary, Thesaurus, Spell
Checker, Verb Conjugator. They also offer translation services in both languages,
English and Spanish. Now Word Magic Software offers iPhone, iPad and Android
dictionaries.
Worldwide Translations, Inc., 2994 Marble Cliff Ct., Henderson, NV 89052
Phone: (800) 293-0412 Fax: (800) 536-6995
E-mail: corporate@wwtranslations.com Website: www.wwtranslations.com
Contact: Robert Sansing, President
Founded 1994. Member: ATA, RAPS, FDLI, DIA, NAJIT. Accepts resumes. Translates
mainly French, Italian, German, Spanish, Dutch, Portuguese, Greek, Swedish, Japanese
and Chinese. Emphasis on Medical, Machinery Manufacture and Computer Products
translation. Prospective translators should be native_speaking ATA members with

5+ years technical translation experience and references. Resumes are responded to by telephone when work becomes available. The company is expert in the CE Mark and Medical Device areas and specializes in the translation of instructional manuals. They hold their translators to a high standard of accuracy. Maintains a pool of over 100 translators.

Wudang Research Association, 430 N. Pine Meadow Drive, DeBarry, FL 32713
Phone: (386) 753-0897
E-mail: info@wudang.com   Website: www.wudang.com
Contact: Terri Morgan

4.2 U. S. TRANSLATION COMPANIES BY LOCATION

ALABAMA
Huntsville Alamex Translation Service, FLS

ARIZONA
Mesa A Foreign Language Service
Tucson CyraCom International, Voiance

CALIFORNIA
Alhambra Asian Link
Aliso Viejo Global Language Solutions
Berkeley Accent on Languages, Avantext, Berkeley Scientific Translation, ION Translations
Beverly Hills ABC Worldwide Translations & Interpretations, Translate4me
Brea InterSol
Carmel Richard Schneider Enterprises
Davis Avant Page
Encino Bizzy Box, Eurasia International
Exeter Clark Translations
Glendale Atlas Translation Services, Coto, Inline
Hollywood ISI
Huntingon Beach ATS
Los Angeles Better Communications, Lazar & Associates, LRA Interpreters, 1-Stop Translation USA, Paragon Language Services
Manhattan Beach Executive Linguist Agency
Menlo Park JLS Language Corporation
Merced Kramer Translation
Monterey Language Line Services
Mountain View Health Outcomes Group
Newbury Park ComNet International
Newport Beach Avid Translation
Oakland International Contact
Orange Continental Interpreting Services
Palm Desert CC Scientific
Palo Alto BioMedical Translators, IDEM Translation
Padadena ITW Interpreting Services
Sacramento Carmazzi Global Solutions, International Translation Service
San Carlos Peritus Precision Translations
San Diego Rescribe
San Francisco Auerbach International, Excel Translations, International Effectiveness Centers, The Language Bank
San Jose Communicaid, Hightech Passport Limited
San Mateo Avid Translation
Santa Monica INAWORD
Simi Valley Continental Communications Agency

Studio City Always Ready Translation Services
Walnut MAGNUS International Trade Services
West Hills N.O.W. Translations
West Covina American Education Research Corp.
Westlake Village Agnew Multilingual, NetworkOmni Multilingual Communications

COLORADO
Aurora Asian Pacific
Boulder eLocale, Translingua
Denver Bridge-Linguatec, Continental Book Company

CONNECTICUT
Bloomfield China Communications Consultants
Millford Gene Mayer Associates

DELAWARE
Newark Back to Basics, Pacific Ring Services
Wilmington Back to Basics

DISTRICT OF COLUMBIA
Washington ADA, Federal News Service, Language Innovations, Language One, Transemantics

FLORIDA
Boca Raton NovaTrans Enterprises
Coral Gables Professional Translating Services
DeBarry Wudang Research Association
Ft. Lauderdale Allslavic Translation Services, Artra International, Babel Tower
Fort Myers LetSpeak
Lantana All Global Solutions International
Lake Mary AccessOnTime
Maitland Monti Interpreting & Translation Services
Miami American International Business Counsel, Cititran, Expert Translators, Josef Sliny & Associates, Precision Translating Services
Miami Beach American Evaluation and Translation Service
Orlando United Nations Translators & Interpreters
Plantation Global Institute of Languages and Culture
Tallahassee RussTech
Winter Park Albors & Associates

GEORGIA
Atlanta ALTA Language Services, Atlantic International Translators, Total Benefit Communications, TransGlobal Connections

HAWAII
Honolulu Babel Trans-Media Center

IDAHO
Emmett Morales Dimmick Translation Service

ILLINOIS
Batavia The Language Bank, Inc
Chicago ACCUWORLD, Atlas Language Services, Beacon Worldwide, Burg Translation Bureau, Cosmopolitan Translation Bureau, Eureka-Foreign College Evaluators & Translators, Global Languages & Cultures, Heartland Cross-Cultural Interpreting Services, Nelles Translations
Darien Arabic Dialects
Glenview Argo Translation
Peoria Caterpillar, Inc.
Skokie Lingua Communications Translation Services
South Holland Techno-Graphics

INDIANA
Indianapolis International Bureau of Translations, Language Training Center

IOWA
Cedar Rapids MGE Lingual Services, OmniLingua
Iowa City Omega Translation Services

KANSAS
Overland Park Interpretations, SH3
Shawnee Around the World

LOUISIANA
Metairie Alpha Tech Communications

MARYLAND
Bethesda Advanced Communication and Translation, Italian Translations Company
Crofton Compass Languages
Frederick Welocalize
Germantown Transfirex Translation Services
Rockville ALC Inc., Multilingual Solutions, Schreiber Translations

MASSACHUSETTS
Andover ArchiText
Boston Community Interpreter Services, The Multi-Lingual Group, New England Translations
Boxford The Translators
Cambridge Linguistic Systems, RIC International
Gardner Baystate Interpreters
Lowell Agencia internacional
Sudbury Rapport International
Wakefield Transtek

Watertown American ESL
MICHIGAN
Ada Alticor
Ann Arbor Japan-America Management, University Translators Services
Grand Rapids Translations Unlimited, Voices for Health
Hamtramck Bromberg & Associates
Novi Suzuki, Myers & Associates
Plymouth Speak Easy Languages
Southfield International Translating Bureau
Sterling Heights Vital International Programs
Troy Techworld Language Solutions

MINNESOTA
Brooklyn Park A-Z Friendly Languages
Duluth Superior Translations
Minneapolis Accu Trans, APS International, Arthur International, Betmar Languages, intránsol (International Translation Solutions), Translations International, University Language Center
Minnetonka International Language Services, Multilingual Word
St. Louis Park Garden & Associates

MISSOURI
Carthage Leggett & Platt
Kansas City Transimpex
St. Louis International Institute of Metro St. Louis, International Language Center

NEVADA
Henderson Worldwide Translations
Las Vegas Escalante Translations

NEW HAMPSHIRE
Manchester Cross Cultural Communications Systems

NEW JERSEY
Bridgewater Counterpoint Language Consultants
Clinton aiaTranslations
East Brunswick The Language Center
East Windsor Princeton Technical Translation Center
Haddon Township A2Z Global Language Solutions
Marlton Translation Company of New York
Randolph Newtype
Ridgewood Inlingua
Roselle Cybertec USA
Summit Inlingua Translation Services
Weehawken CLS Communications
West New York Continental Language Services and Educational Consultants

NEW YORK
Armonk M.E. Sharp, Inc.
Brooklyn Bilingual Professional Agency, Eriksen Translations, GES Translation Services, Legal Interpreting Services
Central Islip MTS Multinational Translating Service
Great Neck Eiber Translations
Hartsdale Marion J. Rosley
Larchmont Telelingua USA
New York City Alanguage Bank, Audio To Go, Bloomberg L.P, C.P. Language Institute, EuroNet Language Services, Gazelle Globalization Group, Geneva Worldwide Inc, Geotext Translations, InterNation, Inc., Interspeak Translations, Japan Communication Consultants, The LanguageWorks, Merrill Translations, Metropolitan Interpreters and Translators Worldwide, 1-800-Translate, R.R. Donnelley, Rennert Bilingual Translation, Translation Aces, translations.com, Translingua, Transperfect Translations International, Trustforte Language Services
Niskayuna All Language Translations
Poughkeepsie Accurapid Translation Services
Rochester Advanced Language Translation, Language Intelligence

NORTH CAROLINA
Chapel Hill DTS Language Services, Global Translation Systems, Rancho Park Publishing
Charlotte Avantgarde Translations, Carolina Polyglot, Choice Translating, Fluent Language Solutions

OHIO
Chagrin Falls M/C International
Cincinnati Affordable Language Services, CinciLingua, Inc., Conversa Language Center
Columbus Access 2 Interpreters, ALTCO Translations, ASIST
Holland International Language Source
Raymond Honda R&D North America

OKLAHOMA
Norman Language Company Translations

OREGON
Aloha LangTech International
Beaverton Bruce International
Portland Certified Languages International, Lingo Systems, Pacific Interpreters, SARJAM Communications, Telelanguage
Wilsonville Pacific Dreams

PENNSYLVANIA
Ardmore Language Services Consultants
Elkins Park CETRA
Lewisburg Lexiteria

Philadelphia   John Benjamins Publishing, Quantum
Pittsburgh   Confluent Translations, Echo International, Multilingual Communications Corporation
Wayne   Americlic
Willow Grove   Language Services Associates
Wind Gap   Affinity Language Services
Wynnwood   ABS Translation & Interpreting Service

RHODE ISLAND
Providence   Narragansett Translations & Interpreting

SOUTH CAROLINA
Columbia   Certified Translation Services

TENNESSEE
Chattanooga   Intermark Language Services Corporation

TEXAS
Alief   Word Magic Software
Austin   Adams Globalization, Larisa Zlatic Language Services, McElroy Translations, Phoenix Translations
Dallas   Garcia-Shilling International, International Translating Company, OneWorld Language Solutions
El Paso   Language Plus
Houston   AE Inc. Translations, American Bureau, IRU Language & Translation Services, Language Direct, MasterWord, TechTrans International, Translation Source
Irving   Korean Consulting & Translation Service
Katy   Crossword Translation & Interpreting
Plano   American Language Technologies
San Antonio   Barinas Translation Consultants

UTAH
Draper   Lingotek
Lehi   Asian Translation Service
Ogden   U.S. Translation Company
Provo   MultiLing International
Roy   DocuTrans, Inc.
Salt Lake City   CommGap International Language Services

VERMONT
Stowe   Auracom International

VIRGINIA
Alexandria   Alexandria Translations, JTG, N. Virginia Area Health Education Center
Arlington   ASET, Comprehensive Language Center
Herndon   Cascades Technologies
Reston   STG

Virginia Beach   Global Visions, The Language Group, Word for Word
Williamsburg   ExactLingua

WASHINGTON
Burlington   The Language Exchange
Federal Way   Languages Translation Services
Seattle   Academy of Languages, Dynamic Language Center, German Language Services, Japan Pacific Publications
Vancouver   Columbia Language Services, Northwest Interpreters

WISCONSIN
Brookfield   International Communication by Design
Fond du Lac   Mercury Marine
Little Chute   Connecting Cultures
Madison   Geo Group
Milwaukee   International Institute of Wisconsin, Iverson Language Associates
River Falls   Sajan
West Allis   C.P. Gauger

4.3 U.S. GOVERNMENT AGENCIES

All U.S. Government agencies need translation from time to time. The question is when and where. There is no simple way to find out, but persistence does pay off, and if you keep exploring by reading the *Commerce Business Daily* (http://www.cbd-net. com), and by following leads, you will find translation work with the government.

Another way to find out about translation in the government is by locating the companies that have translation contracts with federal agencies. The government can provide this kind of information, and you can contact those companies and offer your services.

A word of warning: most government agencies do not accept unsolicited resumes. However, they do post available positions, which are usually accessible through the voice mail menu when you call them. In addition, you may now find Websites for all the major agencies, as well as useful sites listing job opportunities throughout the entire government (see below).

Visit http://usajobs.opm.gov to check information on availability of jobs in the entire Federal Government and to guide youself through the federal job application process.

The following is a list of federal agencies and some comments about the translation needs of each agency.

Agency for International Development (AID), The Ronald Reagan Building, 1300 Pennsylvania Avenue, NW, Washington, D.C., 20523
Phone: (202) 712-5043   Website: www.usaid.gov
AID is in charge of the U.S. Foreign Aid program. As such, it works in practically every language. Much of the work is done either in-house or in the target country, but from time to time AID needs translation services, and is worth contacting.

Agriculture, U.S. Department of, 1400 Independence Avenue, SW, Washington, DC, 20250   Phone: (202) 720-2791   Website: www.usda.gov
This department, oddly enough, actually offers translation courses. We don't know much about its current translation needs, so feel free to find out for yourself.

Air Force, Department of the, The Pentagon, Washington, DC, 20330
Phone: (703) 545-6700   Website: www.af.mil
This is a huge organization. Over the years it has done an enormous volume of translation, and was a pioneer in machine translation. The present status is not clear. You can try them, but there is no telling whether you'll find out anything specific. Ask them to send you literature about their language and translation needs.

Army, Department of the, Personnel & Employment Service, 6800 Army Pentagon, Washington, DC 20310-6800,   Phone: (703) 545-6700   Website: www.army.mil
Like the Air Force, the Army too has done and still does a very large volume of translation. The problem is how to get to the sources, which are spread all over creation.

Knowing someone at the Pentagon or at any of the bases helps. You'll need to talk to the procurement people either locally or at the above number.

Central Intelligence Agency (CIA), Central Intelligence Agency, Office of Public Affairs, Washington, D.C. 20505
Phone: (703) 482-0623   Website: www.cia.gov
The CIA hires a good number of translators in a great variety of languages. If interested in a CIA language career, visit the website for positions of interest and apply online.

Citizenship and Immigration Service, U.S. (USCIS), 425 I Street, NW, Washington, DC, 20536,   Phone: (202) 205-2000   Website: www.uscis.gov
The CIS uses the services of interpreters in many languages in all of its court locations in the U.S. Call to inquire about participating in this program.

Commerce, Department of, 1401 Constitution Avenue, NW, Washington, DC, 20230
Phone: (202) 482-2000   Website: www.commerce.gov
They have an interesting Japanese program which you may want to inquire about. Otherwise, they translate when they have to. Some Commerce agencies that engage in translation are the Patent and Trademark Office, the International Trade, and the National Technical Information Service.

Congress, Library of (LOC), 101 Independence Avenue, SE, Washington, DC, 20540
Phone: (202) 707-5000   Website: www.loc.gov
The LOC employs full-time translators.

Defense, Department of (DoD), Department of Defense, Washington Headquarters Services, 1155 Defense Pentagon, Washington, DC, 20301-1155
Phone: (703) 604-6219   Website: www.defenselink.mil
Inquire about translation work with DoD agencies at the Defense Supply office at the Pentagon. You may want to stop over there to look at their records. DoD does a great deal of translation.

Drug Enforcement Administration (DEA), Drug Enforcement Administration, Office of Personnel, 2401 Jefferson Davis Highway, Alexandria, VA, 22301
Phone: (800) 882-9539   Website: www.dea.gov
Ask them about Spanish translation and/or interpreting. They do a great deal of this kind of work.

Education, Department of, 400 Maryland Avenue, SW, Washington, DC, 20202,
Phone: (800) 872-5327 (general inquiries)   Website: www.ed.gov

Energy, Department of (DOE), 1000 Independence Avenue, SW, Washington, DC, 20585,   Phone: (202) 586-9534 (the Energy Library)   Website: www.energy.gov
The technical library of the DOE needs translation from time to time, and usually contracts out translation work. Call to inquire.

Environmental Protection Agency (EPA), Ariel Rios Building, 1200 Pennsylvania Ave., N.W., Washington, DC 20460, Phone: (202)564-0300 Website: www.epa.gov
The EPA usually contracts out translation work.

Federal Bureau of Investigations (FBI), J. Edgar Hoover Building, 935 Pennsylvania Avenue, NW, Washington, DC, 20535-0001
Phone: (202) 324-3000 (main number) Website: www.fbijobs.gov
The FBI employs full-time translators both at its Washington headquarters and in its field offices. All FBI language employees must be U.S. citizens. (Some exceptions are made for rare or unusual languages; linguists must then be legal resident aliens). Call to inquire. (Ask for the Applicant Coordinator).

Federal Trade Commission (FTC), Human Resources Management Office, Room 723, 600 Pennsylvania Avenue, NW, Washington, DC, 20580
Phone: (202) 326-2222 Website: www.ftc.gov
The FTC is involved in trade with the newly independent nations of Europe. You may want to find out if they need any translation work in this area.

Foreign Broadcast Information Service (FBIS), PO Box 2604, Washington, DC 20013, Phone: (703) 521-5638
Traditionally, FBIS, operating also as JPRS (Joint Publications and Research Service), has provided employment for translators in many languages, and has farmed out translation to hundreds of freelancers. The volume is not what it used to be, but it is still worth inquiring, particularly if you work in languages like Arabic, Farsi, French, German, Russian and many less common languages.

Health and Human Services, Department of (HHS), 200 Independence Avenue, SW, Washington, DC, 20201
Phone: (202) 619-0257 Toll Free: (877)696-6775 Website: www.hhs.gov

Housing and Urban Development, Department of (HUD), 451 7th Street, SW, Washington, DC, 20410 Phone: (202) 708-1112 Website: www.hud.gov
HUD maintains a division of Immigrant Services, which involves both print and oral media and utilizes both translators and interpreters.

Inter-American Foundation, Personnel Department, 901 N. Stuart Street, 10th Floor, Arlington, VA, 22203, Phone: (703)306-4301 Website: www.iaf.gov
May have a need for Spanish translation.

Interior, Department of the, (DOI), 1849 C Street, NW, Washington, DC, 20240
Phone: (202) 208-3100 Website: www.doi.gov

Joint Publications and Research Service, PO Box 2604, Washington, DC, 20013
See Foreign Broadcast Information Service.
Justice, Department of (DOJ), 950 Pennsylvania Avenue, NW, Washington, DC, 20530-0001, Phone: (202) 514-2000 Website: www.usdoj.gov
The DOJ is a major source of translation and interpreting. If you are interested in

working for this department, you may want to do some research first and find out which agencies of the DOJ have been doing translation lately, and in what languages, and then find out who is doing the work (mostly farmed out) and contact those sources.

Labor, Department of (DOL), 200 Constitution Avenue, NW, Washington, DC, 20210, Phone: (202) 219-6677 (job openings)   Website: www.dol.gov
Two DOL agencies, namely, OSHA (Occupational Safety and Health Agency) and BLS (Bureau of Labor Statistics) have need for translation and interpretation in Spanish and other languages.

National Aeronautics and Space Administration (NASA), 300 E Sreet, SW, Washington, DC, 20546-0001
Phone: 1-877-NSSC123 (NASA Shared Services Center) Website: www.nasa.gov
NASA does a very large volume of translating and interpreting, but mostly through its major contractors, like Hewlett Packard, Lockheed, IBM, etc. You can contact NASA for data on those companies, and then contact them and ask to talk to their Small Business office for more information.

National Institutes of Health (NIH), 9000 Rockville Pike, Bethesda, MD, 20892
Phone: (301)496-4000   Website: www.nih.gov
The NIH translates medical materials in a variety of languages, mostly through contractors.

National Security Agency (NSA), Fort George G. Meade, MD, 20755
Phone: 1-866-672-4473 (recruitment and staffing)   Website: www.nsa.gov
NSA employs a large number of language specialists, mainly in the area of cryptography. They have an active recruitment program. Call to inquire.

National Virtual Translation Center, 935 Pennsylvania Avenue, NW, Washington, DC, 20535   Website: www.nvtc.gov
This organization provides translation services to many different government agencies. Applicants must be U.S. citizens. Applications may only be submitted on-line; see Website for more information.

Navy, Department of the, Chief of Information, ATTN: Dept. of the Navy, 1200 Navy Pentagon, Room 4B463, Washington, DC, 20350-1200
Phone: (703) 545-6700   Internet: www.navy.mil
The Navy as a whole does a large volume of translation. It is difficult, though, to locate the specific sources. If you are a Navy veteran, you have a better chance of getting assignments.

Nuclear Regulatory Commission (NRC), 11555 Rockville Pike, Rockville, MD, 20852-2738, Phone: (301) 415-7000 Website: www.nrc.gov
The NRC contracts out its translation needs. If interested, find out who their present contractor is and get in touch with them.

Peace Corps, 1111 20th Street, NW, Washington, DC, 20526

Phone: (800) 424-8580   Website: www.peacecorps.gov
The Peace Corps teaches a great many languages, and if you want to get involved in their language program call to inquire.

State, Department of, 2201 C Street, NW, Washington, DC, 20520
Phone: (202) 647-4000   Website: www.state.gov
The State Department employs translators and interpreters, and farms out a great deal of translation and interpreting work. To find out more about it, call the Language Services office and ask for information.

Transportation, Department of (DOT), 1200 New Jersey Avenue, SE, Washington, DC, 20590,   Phone: (202) 366-4000   Website: www.dot.gov
DOT does not have ongoing translation needs, but they do a translation project from time to time.

Veterans' Affairs, Department of (VA), 810 Vermont Avenue, NW, Washington, DC, 20420,   Phone: (202) 273-5400   Website: www.va.gov
The VA may need translation occasionally, especially in Spanish. If you are a veteran you may have a better chance to get assignments.

Voice of America, Language Services, 330 Independence Avenue, SW, Washington, DC, 20237,   Phone: (202) 619-0909 (job hotline)   Website: www.voa.gov
See Information Agency, U.S.

4.4 MAJOR ORGANIZATIONS

Inter-American Development Bank
1300 New York Avenue, NW, Washington, DC, 20577
Phone: (202) 623-1000   Fax: (202) 623-3096   Website: www.iadb.org
The bank hires French, Spanish and Portuguese translators, mostly translating *into* English, and farms out a great deal of work in these languages.

International Monetary Fund (IMF), 700 19th Street, NW, Washington, DC, 20431; 1900 Pennsylvania Ave NW, Washington, DC, 20431
Phone: (202) 623-7000   Fax: (202) 623-4661   Website: www.imf.org
The IMF employs translators and farms out translation work on such topics as finance, economic development, economic affairs in Third World countries, banking and insurance.

Organization of American States (OAS), 17th Street & Constitution Avenue, NW, Washington, DC, 20006,   Phone: (202) 458-6824   Website: www.oas.org
The OAS translates a good volume of Spanish and Portuguese and some French from and into English.

United Nations, 1st Avenue & E 44th Street, New York, NY, 10017
Phone: (212) 326-7000   Website: www.un.org
The UN employs a large number of translators and interpreters. If you are interested in a UN career, visit the Career Portal on their website, where you can also submit your application into the UN online recruitment system.

The World Bank Group, 1818 H Street, NW, Washington, DC, 20433
Phone: (202) 473-1000 Fax: (202) 477-6391 Website: www.worldbank.org
The World Bank employs translators and farms out translation work on such topics as finance, economic development, economic affairs in Third World countries, banking and insurance.

World Health Organization (WHO), Avenue Appia 20, 1211 Geneva 27, Switzerland
Phone: (+41 22) 791 21 11   Website: www.who.org
Compiles and translates medical data in different languages.

4.5 MAJOR COMPANIES

The following is a listing of major companies that conduct business on an international scale. They represent opportunities for translators with the right languages and technical specialties to market their skills.

Alcatel-Lucent, Inc., 600-700 Mountain Avenue, Murray Hill, NJ, 07974
Phone: (908) 508-8080 Fax: (908) 508-2576 www.alcatel-lucent.com
AT&T spinoff Lucent Technologies manufactures telecommunications equipment, operating in more than 90 countries.

Alcoa Company, 201 Isabella Street, Pittsburgh, PA, 15212-5858
Phone: (412) 553-4545 Fax: (412) 553-4498 Website: www.alcoa.com
Alcoa is the world's top producer of aluminum products and packaging plastics, with operations in 23 countries, and exploring new markets in Asia, Central and South America.

Allergan Incorporated, P.O. Box 19534, Irvine, CA, 92623
Phone: 714-246-4500 Fax: 714-246-6987 Website: www.allergan.com
Allergan is the second largest maker of contact lenses (after Bausch & Lomb) as well as other eyecare products. They also produce skincare products. Outside the US, the company operates in China, India, Latin America and Southeast Asia.

Allied Waste (used to be **Brownign-Ferris Industries**), 15880 N. Greenway-Hayden Loop, Suite 100, Scottsdale, AZ, 85260 Phone: 480-627-2700
Website: http://investor.alliedwaste.com
Browning_Ferris is a rapidly expanding waste disposal firm operating in 770 locations including Asia, Europe, the Middle East and North America.

American Express, American Express Tower, World Financial Center, 200 Vesey St., New York, NY 10285 Phone: (212) 640-2000 Fax: (212) 619-9802
www.americanexpress.com
AmEx operates in the US and more than 160 other countries worldwide, providing Travel Related Services (credit cards and traveler's cheques). A second arm of the company provides Financial Advisors Services in 36 countries.

Amerisource Bergen, 1300 Morris Dr, Suite 100, Chesterbrook, PA, 19087
Phone: (610) 727-7000 Website: www.amerisourcebergen.com
AmerisourceBergen began operations in August of 2001 following the merger of AmeriSource Health Corporation and Bergen Brunswig. Bergen Brunswig is a pharmaceutical distributor with most of its sales going to hospitals and managed care facilities. They operate primarily in the US, but do business in Mexico as well.

Amgen, Inc., 1 Amgen Center Drive, Thousand Oaks, CA, 91320
Phone: 805-447-1000 Fax: 805-447-1010 Website: www.amgen.com
Amgen is one of the world's largest biotechnology companies. It operates worldwide, with offices in the US, Canada, China, Japan, and several European countries.

AMR Corporation, P.O. Box 619616, DFW Airport, TX, 75261
Phone: 817-963-1234 Website: www.aa.com
American Airlines is the top US airline, serving more than 170 destinations worldwide. Hub offices include locations in the continental US and San Juan, Puerto Rico. In

addition, American has inaugurated a new route to Paris. AMR bought out Trans World Airlines in 2001.

Amoco/ BP, 28100 Torch Parkway , Warrenville, IL 60555
Phone: (630) 836-5000 Website: www.bp.com
Amoco is North America's largest natural gas producer and one of the world's largest chemical and oil companies, with offices in 40 countries, including the Middle East, South America, Eastern Europe, the North Sea region, and China.

Arthur Andersen LLP, 33 W. Monroe, Chicago, IL 60603
Phone: 1 312 580 0033 Fax: 1 312 507 6748 Website: www.arthurandersen.com
Andersen is the largest accounting firm in the US, with a highly developed management consulting service. It maintains more than 360 offices in 76 countries in all parts of the world.

Anheuser-Busch Companies, Inc., 1 Busch Place, St. Louis, MO, 63118
Phone: 1-800-342-5283 Website: www.anheuser-busch.com
Anheuser-Busch is the world's largest beer brewer, selling its products in over 70 countries.

AOLTimeWarner. 1 Time Warner Center, New York, NY 10019
Phone: (212) 484-8000 Fax: (212) 956-2847
Website: www.timewarner.com
Time Warner, the huge multimedia company, has sales in the US, Europe, the Pacific Rim and elsewhere, and is currently investing in Japan's cable TV industry. Time Warner and AOL merged in 2000 to make AOLTimewarner.

Apple Computer, Inc., 1 Infinite Loop, Cupertino, CA, 95014
Phone: (408) 996-1010 Fax: (408) 974-2113   www.apple.com
Apple is the world's #2 computer manufacturer. It has manufacturing facilities outside the US in Ireland and Singapore, and conducts business worldwide.

Aramark Corporation, 1101 Market Street, Philadelphia, PA, 19107
Phone: (215) 923-2853 Website: www.aramark.com
Aramark is a diversified service company, with dozens of business under its corporate ægis. Although most of its operations are in the US, it also operates in Canada, Belgium, Germany, the Czech Republic, Hungary, Spain, Mexico, Japan and Korea.

Archer-Danids-Midland Company, 4666 Faries Parkway, Decatur, IL, 62526
Phone: (217) 424-5200 Fax: (217) 424-6196   www.admworld.com
ADM is a processor of grain, seed, and vegetable products, with 200 plants and worldwide marketing and operations.

Armstrong World Industries,
2500 Columbia Ave (17603), P.O. Box 3001, Lancaster, PA, 17604
Phone: (717) 397-0611 Fax: (717) 396-2787   www.armstrong.com
Armstrong manufactures floor coverings, furniture and building products, producing and marketing its products worldwide. Twenty-three of its facilities are in 11 countries outside the US, mostly in Europe, but in other regions as well.

Asarco, 5285 E. Williams Circle, Suite 2000, Tucson, AZ, 85711
Phone: (520) 798-7500 Fax: (520) 798-7780 Website: www.asarco.com
Asarco is one of the world's leading producers of copper, lead, zinc, silver and gold. Outside the US, the company maintains mines in Mexico and Peru.

Ashland, Inc., 50 E. Rivercenter Blvd, P.O. Box 391, Covington, KY, 41012
Phone: (859) 815-3333 Website: www.ashland.com

Ashland is one of the US's largest refiners of petroleum and works in non-petroleum energy and chemical production as well. In addition to its US refineries, the company does resource exploration in Australia, Nigeria, and Morocco and has facilities in 16 foreign countries. It markets its products and services in more than 140 countries.

AT&T Corp., 32 Ave. of the Americas, New York, NY 10013-2412

Phone: (212) 387-5400 Fax: (212) 226-4935 www.att.com

AT&T provides communications, computer, and network services worldwide and has 92 manufacturing facilities around the globe.

Atlantic Richfield Company, 515 South Flower St., Los Angeles, CA 90071

Phone: (213) 486-3511 Fax: (213) 486-2063 Website: www.arco.com

Atlantic Richfield is the sixth largest US oil company. It drills for oil and gas in China, Dubai and Indonesia, and is developing projects in the former Soviet Union.

Automatic Data Processing, Inc., One ADP Blvd., Roseland, NJ 07068-1728

Phone: (201) 994-5000 Fax: (201) 994-5387 Website: www.adp.com

ADP is the #1 payroll and tax filing processor in the US with 53 processing centers in the US, one in Canada and 2 in Europe, and is continuing to expand internationally.

Avery Dennison, 150 North Orange Grove Blvd., Pasadena, CA 91103

Phone: (626) 304-2000 Fax: (626) 792-7312 Website: www.averydennison.com

Avery Dennison is the leading US producer of labels, as well as 40 software support programs. The company has 200 manufacturing facilities and sales offices in 33 countries worldwide, with Asian regional headquarters in Hong Kong.

Avis, 6 Sylvan Way, Parsippany, NJ, 07054

Phone: 973-496-3500 Fax: (516) 222-6677 www.avis.com

Avis is the US's second largest car rental and leasing company, with 4800 locations in 140 countries worldwide.

Avon Products, Inc., 1345 Avenue of the Americas, New York, NY, 10020

Phone: (212) 282-5000 Fax: (212) 282-6049 Website: www.avon.com

Avon is the world's leading direct seller of beauty products, manufacturing its products in 18 countries, with subsidiaries in 45 countries. Its operations extend from the Americas (with a large Brazilian market) to Europe and the Pacific region.

Baker Hughes, 2929 Allen Parkway, Suite 2100, Houston, TX, 77019

Phone: (713) 439-8600 Fax: (713) 439-8699 Website: www.bakerhughes.com

Baker Hughes produces equipment and materials for the oil drilling and mining industries, operating 63 manufacturing plants, 36 of which are outside the US, both in Europe and the Western Hemisphere.

Ball Corporation, 10 Longs Peak Dr, Broomfield, CO, 80021

Phone: (303) 469-3131 Fax: (303) 460-2127 Website: www.ball.com

Originally known for its glass jars, Ball is expanding into aluminum can and PET plastic manufacture. It has joint ventures operating in Brazil, China, the Philippines and Thailand.

The Bank of New York Mellon, 1 Wall Street, New York, NY, 10286

Phone: (212) 495-1784 Fax: (212) 495-2546 Website: www.bnymellon.com

The Bank of New York operates businesses throughout the US and in 29 other countries, primarily in Europe and Asia.

Bank of America Corporation, Bank of America Corporate Center

100 North Tryon Street, Charlotte, NC, 28255

Phone: 1.800.432.1000 Fax: (415) 622-8467   Website: www. bankofamerica.com
BankAmerica does business in 36 countries in all regions of the world.
Bausch & Lomb, 1 Bausch and Lomb Place, Rochester, NY, 14004
Phone: (585) 338-6000 Fax: (585) 330-6007 Website: www.bausch.com
Basch and Lomb is the largest manufacturer of contact lenses and their peripheral
products. The company's other products include skin care, sunglasses and hearing aids.
B&L products are sold in over 70 countries worldwide.
Baxter Healthcare Corporation, 1 Baxter Parkway, Deerfield, IL, 60015
Phone: (847) 948-2000 Fax: (847) 948-3642 Website: www.baxter.com
Baxter is a producer of medical specialty products and medical/laboratory products
and distribution with 71 manufacturing plants in 21 countries, 149 distribution centers
and 25 research facilities worldwide.
Bear Stearns Company, 383 Madison Ave, New York, NY, 10179
Phone: (212) 272-2000 Fax: (212) 272-8239 www.bearstearns.com
Bear Stearns is a leading securities trading, investment banking, and brokerage firm.
It has offices in Western Europe, South America (including Brazil), Pakistan, and the
Far East, as well as in the US, and is involved in a joint venture in Greece.
Bechtel Group, 50 Beale St, San Francisco, CA, 94105
Phone: (415) 768-1234 Fax: (415) 768-9038 Website: www.bechtel.com
Bechtel is a designer and builder of facilities for the power, petroleum, chemical,
mining and metals, and other major industries. They conduct business in more than
50 countries in Asia, Europe, the Middle East, Latin America and Africa, as well as
the US and Canada.
Becton, Dickinson, and Company, 1 Becton Dr, Franklin Lakes, NJ, 07417
Phone: (201) 847-6800 Fax: (201) 847-6475 Website: www.bd.com
Becton, Dickinson manufactures and sells medical supplies and devices and diagnostic
systems, primarily in the US and Europe, but also throughout the rest of the world. It
has offices in Brazil, France, Japan, Mexico, Singapore and Canada.
Black & Decker Corporation, 701 East Joppa Rd., Towson, MD 21286 Phone:
(410) 716-3900 Fax: (410) 716-2933 Website: www. blackanddecker.com
Black & Decker is the world's largest producer of power tools and accessories, and
electric lawn and garden tools, as well as other products, all of which are marketed in
over 100 countries. The market is primarily the US and Europe, but they also reach
other regions.
The Boeing Company, 100 North Riverside, Chicago, IL, 60606 Phone: (312) 544-
2000 Website: www.boeing.com
Boeing has been the world's #1 commercial aircraft maker for more than 30 years and
one of America's largest exporters, serving all areas of the world, with recent contracts
in Malaysia.
Borden, Inc., 180 East Broad St., Columbus, OH 43215
Phone: (614) 225-4000 Fax: (614) 225-3410 Website: www.bordenchem.com
Borden is a producer of dairy products, pasta, and chemicals, operating manufacturing
and processing facilities in the US and Puerto Rico, as well as Canada, Brazil and Latin
America, the Far East, and Western Europe.
Bristol-Myers Squibb Company, 345 Park Ave., New York, NY 10154-0037
Phone: (212) 546-4000 Fax: (212) 546-4020 Website: www.bms.com
Bristol-Myers Squibb is one of the largest pharmaceutical companies in the US, with

business in Europe, the Middle East, Africa, the Pacific region, and other countries in the Western Hemisphere. Its largest markets are in the US, France and Japan.
Browning-Ferris Industries, Inc., 757 North Eldridge, Houston, TX 77079
Phone: (713) 870-8100 Fax: (713) 870-7844 Website: www.bfi.com
Browning-Ferris is a rapidly expanding waste disposal firm operating in 770 locations including Asia, Europe, the Middle East and North America.
Brunswick Corporation, 1 North Field Court, Lake Forest, IL, 60045
Phone: (847) 735-4700 Fax: (847) 735-4765 Website: www.brunswick.com
Brunswick is a leisure services and manufacturing company, making sports equipment and operating bowling alleys and pizza restaurants. Outside the US, it maintains 5 facilities in Germany and Austria.
Burlington Industries, Inc., 3330 West Friendly Ave., Greensboro, NC 27410
Phone: (336) 379-2855 Fax: (901) 379-4504 www.burlington-ind.com
Burlington Industries manufactures fabrics for the apparel and home furnishings industries, operating primarily in the US, but with 3 plants in Mexico.

Caltex Petroleum Corporation,
125 East John Carpenter Parkway, Irving, TX 75602-2750
Phone: (972) 830-1000 Fax: (972) 830-1081 www.caltex.com
Caltex Petroleum, a joint venture between Texaco and Chevron, has operations in 61 countries, primarily in Africa, Australasia, Asia, and the Middle East.
Campbell Soup Company, 1 Campbell Place, Camden, NJ, 08103-1701
Phone: (856) 342-4800 ext. 2225 Website: www.campbellsoups.com
Campbell, a leading producer and distributor of brand-name food products, does its primary non-US business in Europe, although it now has joint ventures with several producers in Japan and recently acquired a German soup manufacturer.
Cargill Incorporated, P.O. Box 9300, Minneapolis, MN, 55440-9300
Phone: 1-800-227-4455 Website: www.cargill.com
Cargill, primarily a food company, also has its hand in finished steel and financial services, with 1000 foreign offices in 65 countries, including Mexico, the Philippines, and South Africa.
Case Corporation, 700 State St, Racine, WI, 53404 Phone: 262-636-6011
Phone: (414) 636-6011 Fax: (414) 636-5043 Website: www.casecorp.com
Case is North America's second largest manufacturer of farm equipment, with retail stores in the US and 150 countries, as well as plants in Brazil, Canada, France, Germany, and the UK.
Caterpillar Inc., 100 North East Adams Street, Peoria, IL, 61629
Phone: (309) 675-1000 Fax: (309) 675-5800 www.caterpillar.com
Caterpillar is the world's #1 manufacturer of machinery for construction, mining, and agriculture, with 38 plants in 12 countries and 187 dealerships in 128 countries in all parts of the world. It has set up a holding company in China.
Chevron Corporation, 6001 Bollinger Canyon Rd, San Ramon, CA, 94583
Phone: (925) 842-1000 Fax: (415) 894-0348 Website: www.chevron.com
Chevron is a fully integrated oil and gas company with operations in the US and about 100 other countries worldwide, and is involved in a joint venture in Saudi Arabia.
Chiquita Brands International, Inc., 250 East Fifth St., Cincinnati, OH 45202
Phone: (513) 784-8000 Fax: (513) 784-8030 Website: www.chiquita. com

Chiquita distributes its fruit and vegetable products worldwide.

Chrysler Corporation, 1000 Chrysler Drive, Auburn Hills, MI, 48326-2766
Phone: (248) 576-5741 Fax: (248) 512-2912 Website: www.chryslercorp.com
Chrysler Corporation not only produces motor vehicles, but also operates two car rental companies and a variety of financial, leasing and insurance services related to its products. In addition to its US manufacturing plants, it has facilities in Austria and Venezuela, and sells many of its products in over 100 countries throughout the world.

The Chubb Corporation, 15 Mountain View Rd., PO Box 1615, Warren, NJ 07059
Phone: (908) 903-2000 Fax: (908) 903-2027 Website: www.chubb.com
Chubb Corporation is a large property/casualty company operating throughout the US and in 25 other countries in Europe, Asia, and Latin America.

CIGNA Corporation, 2 Liberty Place, 1601 Chestnut Street, Philadelphia, PA 19192
Phone: (215) 761-1000 Fax: (215) 761-5515 Website: www.cigna.com
CIGNA is one of America's top insurance companies, operating in the US, Europe, Latin America and Asia.

Citicorp, 399 Park Avenue, New York, NY, 10043 Phone: (212) 559-1000
 Fax: (212) 559-5138 Website: www.citibank.com
Citicorp is the largest banking company in the US and the only global full-service consumer bank, with more than 3400 locations in 95 countries worldwide, primarily in Western Europe, the Asia/Pacific region, Latin America, Canada, and Japan.

The Clorox Company, 1221 Broadway, Oakland, CA 94612-1888
Phone: (510) 271-7000 Fax: (510) 832-1463 www.clorox.com
Clorox produces, in addition to cleaning products, Kingsford products (charcoal, insecticides, chemicals), and food products. Its products are sold in more than 90 countries and produced in more than 35 plants in Latin America (but not Brazil), South Korea, Canada, and the US.

The Coastal Corporation, Coastal Tower, 9 Greenway Plaza, Houston, TX, 77046
Phone: (713) 877-1400 Fax: (713) 877-6754 Website: www.thecoastalcorporation.com
Coastal Corporation is an energy company involved in oil and gas exploration, petroleum refining, coal mining, etc., with marketing and distribution operations around the world.

The Coca-Cola Company, P.O. Box 1734, Atlanta, GA 30301
Phone: (404) 676-2121 Fax: (404) 676-6792 Website: www.coca-cola.com
Coca-Cola, the world's largest soft-drink and beverage company, is a presence in nearly every region of the world.

Colgate-Palmolive Company, 300 Park Avenue, New York, NY 10022
Phone: (212) 310-2000 Fax: (212) 310-3405 Website: www.colgate.com
Colgate-Palmolive, a giant in the oral, personal and household care and pet food markets, operates 66 facilities in the US and 235 in over 60 other countries throughout the world.

Compaq Computer Corporation (see Hewlett Packard)

Computer Associates, One Computer Associates Plaza, Islandia, NY 11749
Phone: (631) 342-6000 Fax: 631-342-6800 Website: www.ca.com
Computer Associates integrates systems management software for small computers with mainframe software, offering over 300 software products. The company has over 100 offices in 30 countries.

ConAgra, 1 Conagra Drive, Omaha, NE, 68102 Phone: (402) 595-4000
Fax: (402) 595-4707 Website: www.conagra.com
ConAgra is a diversified food company with products ranging from agricultural sup-

plies to production to marketing brand-name food products, with international offices in 27 countries.

ConocoPhillips, 600 North Dairy Ashford, Houston, TX, 77079-1175
Phone: (281) 293-1000 Website: www.conocophillips.com
A fully integrated energy company, ConocoPhillips conducts exploration and production operations in the US, UK, Nigeria, and Norway, with most of its sales in those regions.

Consolidated Freightways, Inc., 805 Broadway, Suite 205, Vancouver, WA, 98660
Phone: (360) 448-4000 Website: www.cfwy.com
Consolidated Freightways is a freight and delivery company with operations in North America and 89 countries elsewhere in the world.

Continental Airlines, Inc., 1600 Smith Street, Houston, TX 77002
Phone: (713) 834-5000 Fax: (713) 834-2087 Website: www. continental.com
In addition to locations in the US, Continental flies to 58 destinations in Australasia, Europe and Latin America.

Continental Grain Company, 277 Park Ave., New York, NY 10172-0002
Phone: (212) 207-5100 Fax: (212) 207-2910 Website: www.contigroup.com
Continental Grain is one of the world's largest commodities traders, with offices and facilities in aboutg 60 countries, including Switzerland and Hong Kong.

Cooper Industries, Inc., 600 Travis Street, Suite 5600, Houston, TX, 77002
Phone: (713) 209-8400 Fax: (713) 739-8995 Website: www.cooperindustries.com
Cooper Industries manufactures and sells automotive and electrical products, hardware and tools throughout the world, primarily in Europe and the Americas, including Brazil and the North Sea region.

Corning Incorporated, One Riverfront Plaza, Corning, NY, 14831
Phone: (607) 974-9000 Fax: (607) 974-8091 www.corning.com
Corning is a major producer of glass products, including computer screens and optical fiber, with 41 plants in 8 countries and lab services in 10 countries, particularly in the US and Europe.

Crown Cork & Seal Company, 1 Crown Way, Philadelphia, PA, 19154
Phone: (215) 698-5100 Fax: (215) 676-7245 Website: www.crowncork.com
Crown Cork & Seal is a worldwide producer of caps and seals for glass metal, and plastic jars, bottles, and other containers, operating 70 plants in the US and 68 plants in other countries, primarily in Europe and the Americas.

Cummins Engine Company, Inc., Box 3005, Columbus, IN, 47202
Phone: (812) 377-5000 Fax: (812) 377-4937 Website: www.cummins.com
Cummins manufactures diesel engines, with manufacturing operations in 14 countries and markets in all parts of the world.

Cyprus Amax Minerals Company, 9100 East Mineral Circle, Englewood, CO 80112
Phone: (303) 643-5000 Fax: (303) 643-5049 Website: www.cyprusamax.com
Cyprus Amax is America's largest mining company, operating in the US and the UK, Australia, Sweden, the Netherlands, Russia, Chile and Peru.

Dana Corporation, 4500 Dorr St, Toledo, OH, 43615
Phone: (419) 535-4500 Fax: (419) 535-4643 Website: www.dana.com
Dana Corp. specializes in under-the-hood equipment for motor vehicles (axles, drive shafts, filters, valves, etc.), with 550 manufacturing, assembly, and distribution facilities in 33 countries, including Mexico, China, and Brazil.

Deere & Company, 1 John Deere Rd., Moline, IL 61265
Phone: (309) 765-8000   Fax: (309) 765-5772   Website: www.deere.com
Deere & Company is the world's largest manufacturer of farm equipment and a lead-ing producer of industrial and lawn care equipment, selling its products in more than 160 countries worldwide, including Europe and China. It has a new factory in Mexico.
Dell Computer Corporation, One Dell Way, Round Rock, TX 78682
Phone: (512) 338-4400 Fax: (512) 728-3653 Website: www.dell.com
Dell sells 64 computer systems in 7 product families as well as software and peripherals in more than 130 countries, mostly in the Americas and Europe.
Deloitte, 1633 Broadway, New York, NY, 10019
Phone: (212) 489-1600 Fax: (212) 489-1687 Website: www.deloitte.com
Deloitte operates accounting offices in more than 126 countries worldwide.
Delta Air Lines, Inc., 1030 Delta Boulevard, Atlanta, GA, 30320-6001
Phone: (404) 715-2600 Fax: (404) 715-2100 Website: www.delta-air.com
Delta serves the US and 30 other countries, including a hub in Germany.
DHL Worldwide Express,
1200 South Pine Island Road, Ste 600, Plantation, FL, 33324
Phone: (415) 593-7474   Fax: (415) 593-1689 Website: www.dhl.com
DHL is an international shipper operating out of separate headquarters in California and Brussels, with 19 hubs and 1900 offices in 224 countries. It has developed a new minihub in Panama.
Dole Food Company, Inc., P.O. Box 5132, Westlake Village, CA, 91359-5132
Phone: (818) 879-6600 Fax: (818) 879-6615 Website: www.dole.com
Dole is one of the world's largest distributors of fresh and processed fruits, vegetables, and nuts, with operations in the Americas, Asia, Africa and Europe, and markets worldwide.
Domino's Pizza, Inc., 30 Frank Lloyd Wright Drive, Ann Arbor, MI 48106-0997
Phone: (734) 930-3030 Fax: (303) 668-4614 Website: www.dominos.com
Domino's, the pizza delivery company, has stores in the US and Canada as well as Latin America (including Brazil), the Middle East, Western Europe, and the Far East.
The Dow Chemical Company, 2030 Dow Center, Midland, MI 48674
Phone: (517) 636-1000 Fax: (517) 636-1830 Website: www.dow.com
Dow Chemical makes and supplies more than 2500 product families, with 94 plants in the US and 30 foreign countries worldwide. It sells its products in 164 countries. **Dow Jones & Company, Inc.,** 200 Liberty Street, New York, NY, 10281
Phone: (212) 416-2000 Fax: (212) 416-4348 Website: www.dowjones.com
Dow Jones, a media company specializing in business news and information, reaches markets in all parts of the world in print, on-line, and by satellite, radio, TV, pager, and fax. It has new services in Latin America and Italy.
Dresser Inc., 15455 Dallas parkway, Addison, TX, 75001
Phone: (972) 361-9800   Fax: (972) 361-9903 Website: www.dresser.com
Dresser is one of the largest energy service companies in the world, with more than 100 manufacturing plants in 50 countries and facilities serving more than 80 countries, particularly in Asia, the Middle East, Latin America, and Africa.
The Dun & Bradstreet Corporation, 103 JFK Parkway, Shorthills, NJ, 07078
Phone: (973) 921-5500 Website: www. dnb.com
Dun & Bradstreet is the world's largest marketer of information, software and services for business decision making, with a worldwide clientele, primarily in the US and Europe.

E.I. DuPont de Nemours, 1007 Market St., Wilmington, DE 19898
Phone: (302) 774-1000 Fax: (302) 774-7321 Website: www.dupont.com
DuPont is the US's largest chemical company and operates in about 70 countries worldwide, primarily in the US and Europe, and is currently working on joint ventures with China.

Eastman Kodak Company, 343 State St, Rochester, NY, 14650
Phone: (585) 724-4000 Fax: (716) 724-1089 Website: www.kodak.com
Eastman Kodak does business worldwide, currently focusing on emerging markets in Brazil, China, India, and Russia.

Eaton Corporation, 1111 Superior Ave, Cleveland, OH, 44114
Phone: (216) 523-5000 Fax: (216) 523-4787 Website: www.eaton.com
Eaton is a manufacturer of highly engineered products from basic automotive components to electrical power grids, with 150 facilities in 18 countries, primarily in the US, Europe, Latin America and Canada. It has recently acquired companies in the Netherlands, Thailand and Brazil.

Electronic Data Systems Corp. (EDS), 5400 Legacy Drive, Plano, TX, 75024
Phone: (972) 604-6000 Fax: (972) 605-2643 Website: www.eds.com
EDS provides systems and management consulting in 37 countries, primarily in the US and Europe.

Eli Lilly and Company, Lilly Corporate Center, Indianapolis, IN, 46285
Phone: (317) 276-2000 Fax: (317) 277-6579 Website: www.lilly.com
Lilly researches, produces and markets pharmaceuticals with operations in 27 countries and markets in 117, especially in the US, Japan, the Middle East and Europe.

Emerson Electric Co., 8000 West Florissant Avenue, St. Louis, MO, 63136
Phone: (314) 553-2000 Fax: (314) 553-3527 Website: www. emerson.com
Emerson produces both commercial and industrial machinery, systems, and appliances in 360 facilities worldwide, including new ventures in China, India and Eastern Europe.

Equifax Inc., 1600 Peachtree Street NW, Atlanta, GA, 30309
Phone: (404) 885-8000 Fax: (404) 885-8055 Website: www.equifax.com
Equifax is a credit reporting agency with operations in the US, Australia, Canada, the Caribbean, Europe, and Latin America.

The Equitable Companies Inc., 1290 Ave. of the Americas, New York, NY 10014
Phone: (212) 554-1234 Fax: (212) 707-1755 Website: www.equitable.com
Equitable is an insurance company with a brokerage and investment banking subsidiary and commercial real estate development and management services which, although it operates solely in the US, is partnered with French insurance giant Axa.

Ernst & Young International, 5 Times Square, New York, NY, 10036
Phone: (212) 773-3000 Fax: (212) 773-6350 Website: www.ey.com
Ernst & Young, one of the Big 6 accounting firms, maintains more than 670 offices in over 130 countries around the world.

ExxonMobil Corporation, 5959 Las Colinas Blvd., Irving, TX 75039-2298
Phone: (972) 444-1000 Fax: (972) 444-1882 Website: www.exxonmobil.com
Exxon, the world's largest publicly owned integrated oil company, operates in the US and in over 100 other countries, with new drilling operations in Eastern Russia and other former Soviet states, China and West Africa.

FedEx Corporation, 942 South Shady Grove Road, Memphis, TN, 38120

Phone: (901) 369-3600 Fax: (901) 395-2000 Website: www.fedex.com
FedEx offers package delivery services throughout the US and in 192 foreign countries, with recent expansions into Guyana, Marshall Islands, Bhutan, Brunei, French Guiana, Micronesia, Palau and Suriname.
Fluor Corporation, 6700 Las Colinas Blvd., Irving, TX, 75039
Phone: (469) 398-7000 Fax: (469) 398-7255 Website: www.fluor.com
Fluor is the world's largest engineering and construction firm, with operations in more than 80 countries, especially in North America, Europe and the Asia/Pacific region with a new facility in Indonesia.
FMC Corporation, 1735 Market St, Philadelphia, PA, 19103
Phone: 215-299-6000 Fax: 215-299-6140 Website: www.fmc.com
FMC manufactures chemicals for the agriculture, food and pharmaceutical markets, and makes machinery for the defense, food processing, and trans-portation industries. It operates 100 facilities and mines in the US and 20 other countries, principally in Europe and the Americas.
Ford Motor Company, P.O. Box 6248, Dearborn, MI, 48126
Phone: (313) 322-3000 Fax: (313) 323-2959 Website: www.ford.com
Ford, the world's #2 automaker, has operations in 30 countries, including a joint project with Volkswagen in Portugal.
Freeport-McMoRan Copper & Gold Inc., 1 North Central Ave, Phoenix, AZ, 85004
Phone: (602) 366-8100 Fax: (602) 234-8337 Website: www.fcx.com
Freeport-McMoRan is the #1 international mining company with facilities in 25 countries with sales primarily in the Americas. A large portion of their operations is in South America.
Fruit of the Loom, 1 Fruit of the Loom Drive, Bowling Green, KY, 42102
Phone: (270) 781-6400 Fax: (270) 781-1754 Website: www. fruit.com
Fruit of the Loom, maker of underwear and activewear, has 61 manufacturing facilities in the US, UK, Ireland, Canada, Jamaica, and Honduras and El Salvador, with plans to move more of its production outside the US.

Gannett Co.,Inc., 7950 Jones Branch Drive, McLean, VA, 22107
Phone: (703) 854-6000 Fax: (703) 558-3506 Website: www.gannett.com
Gannett is the US's largest newspaper publisher, with facilities in the US, UK, Canada, Germany, Hong Kong, and Switzerland.
The Gap Inc., 2 Folsom Street, San Francisco, CA, 94105
Phone: (650) 952-4400 Fax: (650) 427-2795 Website: www.gapinc.com
The Gap, operator of 1508 casual clothing stores, does business in the US and Puerto Rico, the UK, Canada, and France, and most recently in Japan and Germany.
Gateway, Inc., 7565 Irvine Center Drive, Irvine, CA, 92618
Phone: (949) 471-7000 Fax: (949) 471-7041 Website: www.gateway.com
Gateway manufactures and is a direct marketer of computers, with facilities in the U.S., Australia, Canada, China, Europe, Japan, and Mexico.
Genentech, Inc., 1 DNA Way, South San Francisco, CA, 94080
Phone: (650) 225-1000 Fax: (650) 225-6000 Website: www.gene.com
Genentech markets biotechnology products in North America, Europe, and Japan, and licenses products worldwide.
General Electric Company, 3135 Easton Turnpike, Fairfield, CT, 06828

Phone: (203) 373-2211 Fax: (203) 373-3497 Website: www.ge.com
General Electric, the giant company that makes everything from light bulbs to jet engines, operates in the US and Puerto Rico, with 113 plants in 25 other countries. Its market is worldwide with locations in 160 countries.

General Motors Corporation, 100 Renaissance Center, Detroit, MI 48243
Phone: (313) 556-5000 Fax: (313) 556-5108 Website: www.gm.com
General Motors, the world's biggest company, extends its manufacturing and assembly operations beyond the US and Canada into the UK, Austria, Germany, Belgium, Brazil, Mexico and Spain.

General Re Corporation, 695 East Main Street, Stamford, CT 06904-2351
Phone: (203) 328-5000 Fax: (203) 328-6423 Website: www.genre.com
General Re is the largest property/casualty reinsurer in the US, with operations in the US and in over 23 other countries worldwide, primarily Germany.

The Gillette Company, 800 Boylston St, Boston, MA, 02199
Phone: (617) 421-7000 Fax: (617) 421-7123 Website: www.gillette.com
Gillette, manufacturer of shaving products and other toiletries, as well as personal and household appliances, sells its products in more than 200 countries and manufactures them in 24, primarily in Europe and Latin America, with newer markets in Japan.

The Goldman Sachs Group, L.P., 85 Broad St., New York, NY, 10004
Phone: (212) 902-1000 Fax: (212) 902-3000 Website: www.gs.com
Goldman Sachs is an equities and fixed income broker and underwriter, investment banker, asset manager, and commodities trader in Asia, Australia, Europe and North America.

The Goodyear Tire & Rubber Company, 1144 East Market St., Akron, OH 44316
Phone: (330) 796-2121 Fax: (330) 796-2222 Website: www.goodyear.com
Goodyear is the world's largest rubber manufacturer, with plants in the US and 26 other countries in Europe, the Americas, and Asia. It has recently become involved in joint ventures in India and China, with planned expansion into Brazil, Indonesia, Malaysia and Thailand.

Great A&P Tea Co., 2 Paragon Drive, Montvale, NJ, 07645
Phone: (201) 573-9700 Fax: (201) 930-8144 Website: www.aptea.com
Although A&P operates in the US and Canada, most of the company is owned by the German firm Tengelmann, which also plans to take the A&P name to the Netherlands.

Halliburton Company, Suite 2400, 1401 McKinney Street, Houston, TX, 77010
Phone: (713) 759-2600 Website: www.halliburton.com
Halliburton, an energy, engineering, and construction services company, conducts business in the US and in more than 100 other countries around the world, including Japan, China, Germany, and Vietnam. It conducts drilling operations in the Middle East and North Sea regions.

Hallmark Cards, Inc., 2501 McGee Trafficway, Kansas City, MO, 64108
Phone: (816) 452-6672 Fax: (816) 274-5061 Website: www.hallmark.com
Hallmark distributes its products in more than 100 countries.

H&R Block, Inc., 4400 Main Street, Kansas City, MO, 64111
Phone: (816) 753-6900 Fax: (816) 753-5346 Website: www.hrblock.com
H&R Block operates 9,577 offices in the US, Canada, Australia and Europe.

Harris Corporation, 1025 West NASA Blvd., Melbourne, FL, 32919
Phone: (407) 727-9100 Fax: (407) 727-9344 Website: www.harris.com

Harris is a defense electronics manufacturer that has branched out into semi-conductors, telecommunications systems, and radio and TV broadcasting equipment. It has 29 plants and about 400 offices worldwide, including Russia, Malaysia and Singapore.

Hasbro, Inc., 1027 Newport Avenue, Pawtucket, RI, 02861
Phone: (401) 431-8697 Fax: (401) 431-8535 Website: www.hasbro.com
Hasbro, the #2 toy company in the US, designs, manufactures and markets its products throughout the world with operations in 25 foreign countries.

HCA Healthcare, One Park Plaza, Nashville, TN, 37203
Phone: (615) 344-9551 Fax: (615) 320-2266 Website: www.hcahealthcare.com
Columbia/HCA is the operator of 320 hospitals in the US, UK and Switzerland.

The Hearst Corporation, 250 W 55th Street, New York, NY, 10019
Phone: (212) 649-2000 Fax: (212) 765-3528 Website: www.hearstcorp.com
Hearst, one of the world's largest diversified media companies, markets its products throughout the US and in more than 80 countries, with a newspaper in Russia and interest in a French Canadian cable television company.

Hercules Incorporated, 1313 N Market Street, Wilmington, DE, 19894
Phone: (302) 594-5000 Fax: (302) 594-5400 Website: www.herc.com
Hercules is in the large-scale chemical business, with subsidiaries and affiliates in 24 countries, primarily in Europe, but also including Mexico (serving customers in Central and South America). It has a new plant in Shanghai.

Hershey Foods Corporation, 100 Crystal A Drive, Hershey, PA, 17033
Phone: (717) 534-6799 Fax: (717) 534-6760 Website: www.hersheys.com
Hershey operates outside the US in Italy, Germany, Belgium, Japan and the Netherlands, with successful newer ventures in Russia and plans to expand into the Latin American and Chinese markets.

Hewlett-Packard Company, 3000 Hanover St., Palo Alto, CA, 94304
Phone: (650) 857-1501 Fax: (650) 857-5518 Website: www.hp.com
Hewlett-Packard, producer of computers and printers for home and office, operates facilities in the US and 16 other countries, with 600 sales and support offices in more than 120 countries.

Hilton Hotels Corporation, 9336 Civic Center Drive, Beverly Hills, CA, 90210
Phone: (310) 278-4321 Fax: (310) 205-4599 Website: www.hilton.com
Hilton owns, manages, or franchises hotels in the US, UK, Australia, Hong Kong, Ireland, Belgium, Hong Kong, and Turkey.

H.J. Heinz Company, 600 Grant Street, Pittsburgh, PA, ,15219
Phone: (412) 456-5700 Fax: (412) 237-6128 Website: www.heinz.com
Heinz operates 88 food processing plants in 21 countries, and has markets internationally, especially in Europe and the Asia/Pacific region.

Honeywell Inc., 101 Columbia Road, Morristown, NJ, 07962
Phone: (973) 455-2000   Fax: (973) 455-4807 Website: www.honeywell.com
Honeywell is one of the world's top manufacturers of control systems and components, operating in 95 countries, primarily in the US, Europe and the Pacific Rim.

Hormel Foods Corporation, One Hormel Place, Austin, MN, 55912-3680
Phone: (507) 437-5611 Fax: (507) 437-5489 Website: www.hormel.com
Hormel markets its products in more than 40 countries, such as Australia, the UK, Hong Kong, Japan, Korea, Mexico, Panama, and the Philippines.

Hughes Network Systems, LLC, 11717 Exploration Lane, Germantown, MD, 20876

Phone: (301) 428-5500 Fax: (301) 428-1868 Website: www.hughes.com
Hughes Electronics has worldwide operations on all continents and maintains a network of 18 communications satellites orbiting the earth.
Hyatt Hotels Corporation, Hyatt Center, 71 S. Wacker, Chicago, IL, 60606
Phone: (312) 750-1234 Fax: (312) 750-8550 Website: www.hyatt.com
Hyatt's international division is responsible for the company's worldwide network of hotels, with its most recent units in Saudi Arabia and Azerbaijan.

IBM Corporation, 1 New Orchard Road, Armonk, NY, 10504
Phone: (914) 765-1900 Fax: (914) 765-7382 Website: www.ibm.com
IBM, the world's top computer company (hardware and software), sells its products worldwide.
Illinois Tool Works Inc., 3600 West Lake Avenue, Glenview, IL, 60025-5811
Phone: (847) 724-7500 Fax: (847) 657-4261 Website: www.itwinc.com
Illinois Tool Works makes a large range of equipment for the automotive, construction, food and beverage, and general industrial markets, with major non-US plants and offices in the UK, Australia, Canada, Ireland, Belgium, Germany, Sweden, Switzerland, France, Italy, Spain, Japan, and Malaysia.
Ingersoll-Rand Company, 155 Chestnut Ridge Road, Montvale, NJ 07645
Phone: (201) 573-0123 Fax: (201) 573-3172 Website: www.ingersoll-rand.com
Ingersoll-Rand is a leading manufacturer of nonelectrical industrial machinery, with plants in the US, Canada, Europe, Asia, Latin America, and Africa, and worldwide sales, especially in Europe.
Intel Corporation, 2200 Mission College Blvd., Santa Clara, CA 95054
Phone: (408) 765-8080 Fax: (408) 765-6284 Website: www.intel.com
Intel, the #1 maker of integrated circuits, including the Pentium chip, has plants in the US and Puerto Rico, Ireland, Israel, Malaysia, and the Philippines, with sales in the US, Europe, and the Asia/Pacific region.
International Paper Company, 6400 Poplar Avenue, Memphis, TN, 38197
Phone: (901) 419-9000 Website: www.ipaper.com
International Paper has production facilities in 27 countries and distribution in 130, primarily in the US and Europe, and is hoping to increase its access to markets in South America and the Pacific Rim.
ITT Industries, Inc., 1133 Westchester Avenue, White Plains, NY, 10604
Phone: (914) 641-2000 Fax: (914) 696-2950 Website: www.ittind.com
ITT Industries, another spinoff from the ITT split, supplies automotive components and systems, high-tech electronics for commercial and defense markets, and pumps, valves, etc., for fluid handling. The company operates worldwide, primarily in the US, Canada, Western Europe, and the Asia/Pacific region. The Fluid Technology division has joint manufacturing ventures in Brazil and China.

John Hancock Insurance Company, 601 Congress Street, Boston, MA, 02210
Phone: (617) 572-6000 Fax: (617) 572-6451 Website: www. johnhancock.com
John Hancock has added financial services to its base insurance business, licensed throughout the US and Canada, with subsidiaries and affiliates in the UK, Belgium, Indonesia, Malaysia, and Thailand, and doing business in 46 countries worldwide, including opening a new office in Beijing.

Johnson and Johnson, 1 Johnson and Johnson Plaza, New Brunswick, NJ, 08933
Phone: (732) 524-0400 Fax: (732) 524-3300 Website: www.jnj.com
Johnson and Johnson manufactures and markets a complete range of health care products, with operations in 50 countries and sales in more than 175, including joint ventures in China and Japan, and recent entry into the Eastern European market.

Johnson Controls, Inc., 5757 North Green Bay Avenue, Milwaukee, WI, 53201
Phone: (414) 524-1200 Fax: (414) 228-2302 Website: www.jci.com
Johnson Controls' main markets are batteries, commercial facilities management, plastic containers, and vehicle seating, operating in more than 500 locations worldwide, primarily in the US and Europe, with the recent acquisitions of Czech and French companies.

J.P. Morgan & Co., Incorporated, 60 Wall Street, New York, NY, 10250-0060
Phone: (212) 483-2323 Fax: (212) 648-5193 Website: www.jpmorgan.com
J.P. Morgan, an international banking company, conducts banking and investment operations in the US and 30 countries worldwide, with new offices in China, Poland, the Czech Republic, and Mexico.

Kellogg Company, 1 Kellogg Square, Battle Creek, MI, 49016-3599
Phone: (616) 961-2000 Fax: (616) 961-2871 Website: www.kelloggscompany.com
Kellogg's food business has manufacturing facilities in 20 countries and distribution in 160, mostly in the US and Europe, and includes facilities in Russia, India, Argentina, and China.

Kelly Services, Inc., 999 West Big Beaver Rd., Troy, MI, 48084
Phone: (248) 362-4444 Fax: (248) 244-4154 Website: www.kellyservices.com
Kelly provides temporary workers in clerical, technical, light-industry, and personal care from over 1000 offices in the US, UK, Ireland, Australia and New Zealand, Canada, Denmark, Norway, France, The Netherlands, and Switzerland.

Kimberly-Clark Corporation, 351 Phelps Drive, Irving, TX, 75038
Phone: (972) 281-1200 Fax: (978) 281-1435 Website: www.kimberly-clark.com
Kimberly-Clark, recently merged with Scott, is a paper products giant, with plants in the US and 25 foreign countries and sales in 150, primarily in Europe, Asia and Latin America.

Kmart Corporation, 3100 West Big Beaver Road, Troy, MI, 48084
Phone: (810) 643-1000 Fax: (810) 643-5636 Website: www.kmart.com
Kmart has retail stores in the US and Canada, as well as in Puerto Rico, Mexico and Singapore.

Koch Industries, Inc., 4111 East 37th Street North, Wichita, KS, 67220
Phone: (316) 828-5500 Fax: (316) 828-5739 Website: www.kochind.com
Koch is in the energy business, with refineries, pipelines, chemical technology, and even cattle ranches and financial services. The company has operations in the US, UK, Canada, and Singapore.

KPMG Peat Marwick LLP, 3 Chestnut Ridge Road, Montvale, NJ, 07645
Phone: (201) 307-7000 Fax: (201) 930-8617 Website: www.kpmg.com
KPMG, one of the Big 6 accounting firms, does b of its business outside the US, with offices in 142 countries, including the former Soviet Union. The company's main headquarters is in the Netherlands.

Lands' End, Inc., 1 Lands' End Lane, Dodgeville, WI, 53595

Phone: (608) 935-9341 Fax: (608) 935-4260 Website: www.landsend.com
Lands' End catalog sales of apparel and soft goods recently launched a catalog business in Japan, as well as small mailings (through its UK distribution center) of native language, native currency catalogs in France, Germany, and the Netherlands. The company has plans to continue to expand internationally.

Lear Corporation, 21557 Telegraph Rd., Southfield, MI, 48086
Phone: (248) 447-1500 Fax: (248) 447-1722 Website: www.lear.com
Formerly Lear Seating, the company makes auto seats and other interior components. It operates joint ventures in China and Thailand and recently acquired a component manufacturer in Sweden.

Lehman Brothers Holdings Inc., 745 Seventh Avenue, New York, NY, 10019
Phone: (212) 526-7000 Fax: (212) 526-3738 Website: www. lehman.com
Lehman Brothers is a leading investment bank, with offices throughout the US, Latin America, Western Europe, the Middle East (including Israel), India and the Far East.

Levi Strauss Associates Inc., 1155 Battery Street, San Francisco, CA, 94111-1230
Phone: (415) 544-6000 Fax: (415) 544-3939 Website: www. levistrauss.com
Levi Strauss is the world's largest clothing maker with production/warehouse and distribution facilities around the world, and operations in 72 countries, primarily in the Americas, Europe, and the Asia/Pacific region.

Lexmark International Group, Inc., 740 New Circle Rd. NW, Lexington, KY 40550
Phone: (606) 232-2000 Fax: (606) 232-2403 Website: www. lexmark.com
Formerly part of IBM, Lexmark is a manufacturer of computer printers and supplies, as well as typewriters. Its products sell in over 100 countries worldwide.

Liz Claiborne, Inc., 5901 W Side Avenue, North Bergen, NJ, 07047
Phone: (201) 682-6000 Website: www.lizclaiborne.com
Liz Claiborne apparel is produced in more than 50 countries, mainly in the US, China, Hong Kong, Indonesia, South Korea, and Sri Lanka, with sales in Asia (excluding Myanmar), Latin America (including Brazil), and the Middle East.

Lockheed Martin Corporation, 6801 Rockledge Drive, Bethesda, MD, 20817
Phone: (301) 897-6000 Fax: (301) 897-6704 Website: www.lockheedmartin.com
Lockheed Martin is the nation's largest defense contractor with products such as missiles, navigational systems, spacecraft, and satellite communication systems. The company has contracts in the Netherlands and China.

LSI Logic Corporation, 1621 Barber Lane, Milpitas, CA, 95035
Phone: (866) 574-5741 Fax: (408) 954-3108 Website: www.lsi.com
LSI manufactures integrated circuits and owns Nihon Semiconductor (now LSI Logic Japan Semiconductor). Its products are sold in North America, Europe, Japan and the Pacific Rim.

Manpower, Inc., 100 Manpower Place, Milwaukee, WI, 53212
Phone: (414) 961-1000 Fax: (414) 961-7081 Website: www.manpower.com
Manpower is the world's largest temporary employment company, with 2400 offices in the US and Canada, the UK, Australia, Europe, Israel, Latin America, and Japan.

Marriott International, Inc., Marriott Drive, Washington, D.C., 20058
Phone: (301) 380-3000 Fax: (301) 380-3969 Website: www.marriott.com
Marriott is in the hospitality business, owning hotels, restaurants, cruise ships,etc., with units in 25 countries worldwide.

Mars, Inc., 6885 Elm Street, McLean, VA , 22101
Phone: (703) 821-4900 Fax: (703) 448-9678 Website: www.mars.com
Mars not only produces candy items, but also produces and markets, pet food, rice, and ice cream bars. It has over 60 operating plants in 31 countries world-wide, including Russia and other former Soviet states, Africa, the Middle East, India, and China.

Marsh & McLennan Companies, Inc.,
1166 Avenue of the Americas, New York, NY 10036-2774
Phone: (212) 345-5000   Fax: (212) 345-4808 Website: www.marshmac.com
Marsh & McLennan is a top insurance brokerage service, with operations in more than 80 countries, primarily in the US, Canada, and Europe.

Masco Corporation, 21001 Van Born Road, Taylor, MI, 48180
Phone: (313) 274-7400 Fax: (313) 792-6135 Website: www.masco.com
Masco is a major manufacturer of home furnishings, kitchen, and bath-room products, with plants in the US and 12 other countries, and sales primarily in the US and Europe. The company has acquired a firm in Germany and has expanded its distribution and business facilities into the Philippines.

Mattel, Inc., 333 Continental Blvd., El Segundo, CA 90245-5012
Phone: (310) 252-2000 Fax: (310) 252-2179 Website: www.mattel.com
Mattel has offices and facilities in 37 countries worldwide, with manufacturing plants in China, Indonesia, Malaysia, Italy, and Mexico, and markets its toys in 140 countries.

McDermott International, Inc., 777 N. Eldridge Parkway, Houston, TX, 77079
Phone: (281) 870-5901 Website: www. mcdermott.com
McDermott is in the marine construction business, producing power generating facilities and equipment, offshore pipelines, nuclear submarine services, and shipbuilding, with worldwide markets, including a joint venture with a former competitor in France. It is also part of a consortium developing oil and gas fields off Sakhalin.

McDonald's Corporation, 2111 McDonald's Drive, Oak Brook, IL, 60523
Phone: (603) 623-3000 Fax: (603) 623-5004 Website: www.mcdonalds.com
McDonald's has restaurants in 89 countries, mostly in the Americas, Japan, and Europe, but in all other parts of the world as well, with its most recent venture in India.

McGraw-Hill Companies, Inc.,
1221 Ave. of the Americas, New York, NY 10020-1095
Phone: (212) 512-2000 Fax: (212) 512-4871 Website: www.mcgraw-hill.com
McGraw-Hill produces educational and professional publications, information and media services, and financial services worldwide, including new branches in Hong Kong and Singapore.

McKesson Corporation, 1 Post Street, San Francisco, CA, 94104
Phone: (415) 983-8300 Fax: (415) 983-7160 Website: www.mckesson.com
McKesson is the largest wholesale drug distributor in the US and Canada, with additional operations in Mexico.

McKinsey & Company, 55 East 52nd Street, 21st floor, New York, NY, 10022
Phone: (212) 446-7000 Fax: (212) 446-8575 Website: www.mckinskey.com
McKinsey is a business consulting firm with 69 offices in 35 countries.

Mead Corporation, 8821 Washington Colony Dr, Dayton, OH, 45458
Phone: (937) 438-1817 Fax: (937) 461-2424 www.mead.com
Mead Corporation is a paper and packaging producer with plants and offices in the US, UK, Canada, Mexico, Western Europe and Japan.

Medtronic, 710 Medtronic Parkway, Minneapolis, MN, 55432-5604
Phone: (763) 514-4000 Fax: (763) 514-4879 Website: www.medtronic.com
Medtronic manufactures medical devices and is the #1 manufacturer of pace-makers.
It is building a new plant in China.
Merck & Co., Inc., 1 Merck Drive, Whitehouse Station, NJ, 08889-0100
Phone: (908) 423-1000 Fax: (908) 423-2592 Website: www.merck.com
Merck is the largest pharmaceutical company in the world, with global operations,
primarily in North America, Europe (including Cyprus), and the Asia/Pacific region.
There is a subsidiary in Peru and a joint venture in China.
Merisel, Inc., 127 West 30th Street, 5th Floor, New York, NY, 10001
Phone: (212) 594-4808 Website: www.merisel.com
Merisel is the world's #1 wholesale computer hardware and software distributor, with
offices in the Americas, Europe, and Australia.
Merrill Lynch & Co., Inc.,
4 World Financial Center, 250 Vesey St., New York, NY, 10080
Phone: (212) 449-1000 Fax: (212) 236-4384 Website: www.ml.com
Merrill Lynch combines retail brokerage and cash management with investment
banking, clearing services, retail banking, and insurance, with operations throughout
the world.
Metropolitan Life, 1 Madison Avenue, New York, NY, 10010-3690
Phone: (212) 578-2211 Fax: (212) 578-3320 Website: www.metlife.com
MetLife and its affiliates operate in the US, the UK, Canada, Mexico, Argentina, Por-
tugal, Spain, Hong Kong, South Korea, and Taiwan.
Micro Warehouse, Inc., 535 Connecticut Avenue, Norwalk, CT, 06854
Phone: (203) 899-4000 Fax: (203) 899-4203 Website: www.microwarehouse.com
Micro Warehouse is a catalog seller of computer products with distribution in 15
countries worldwide.
Microsoft Corporation, 1 Microsoft Way, Redmond, WA, 98052
Phone: (425) 882-8080 Fax: (425) 936-7329 Website: www.microsoft.com
Microsoft is active in all phases of the computer systems and software industry, most
recently in the Internet area, with support subsidiaries and marketing in nearly 50
countries and worldwide sales, mostly in the US and Europe.
Monsanto Company, 800 North Lindbergh Blvd., St. Louis, MO, 63167
Phone: (314) 694-1000 Fax: (314) 694-6572 Website: www.monsanto.com
Monsanto, an American chemical giant, has sales throughout the world. They also
deal with agricultural technologies on a worldwide basis.
Morgan Stanley Dean Witter, 1585 Broadway, New York, NY, 10036
Phone: (212) 761-4000 Fax: (212) 761-0086 Website: www.msdw.com
Morgan Stanley is an investment banking and brokerage firm with operates in the US,
throughout Western Europe and Asia.
Morton International, Inc., 123 North Wacker Drive, Chicago, IL, 60606
Phone: (312) 807-2000 Fax: (312) 807-2241 Website: www. mortonsalt.com
In addition to salt, Morton International produces packaging adhesives, liquid plastic
coating materials, electronic materials, and dyes. The company operates in the US, the
UK, the Bahamas, Canada, Mexico, France, Germany, the Netherlands, Italy, and Japan.
It is merging its airbag manufacturing operations with a those of a company in Sweden
Motorola, Inc., 1303 East Algonquin Road, Schaumburg, IL, 60196

Phone: (847) 576-5000 Fax: (847) 538-5191 Website: www.motorola.com
Motorola makes both communications equipment items and the components inside them, with manufacturing facilities in the US and 18 foreign countries and sales around the world. Recent joint ventures involve Japan and China.

NABISCO Holding Corp., 7 Campus Drive, Parsippany, NJ, 07054
Phone: (973) 682-5000 Fax: (973) 503-2153 Website: www.nabisco.com
The leading international producer of cookies and crackers, NABISCO sells its products in more than 85 countries worldwide.

National Semiconductor, 2900 Semiconductor Drive, Santa Clara, CA, 95052
Phone: (408) 721-5000 Fax: (408) 739-9803 Website: www.national.com
National Semiconductor's products include integrated circuits, mixed-signal control systems, and chip designs, produced in plants in the US, UK, the Philippines, Singapore, and Malaysia, and sold throughout the Americas, Asia, and Europe.

Navistar International Corporation,
455 North Cityfront Plaza Drive, Chicago, IL 60611
Phone: (312) 836-2000 Fax: (312) 836-3982 Website: www. navistar.com
Navistar is the US's largest manufacturer of heavy and medium-sized trucks, and the leading supplier of school bus chassis, with sales throughout North America and exports to more than 77 countries worldwide, including recent expansions into Mexico and South America.

NCR Corporation, 1700 South Patterson Blvd., Dayton, OH, 45479
Phone: (937) 445-1936 Fax: (937) 445-1682 Website: www.ncr.com
NCR manufactures point-of-sale terminals and barcode scanners, ATMs and other similar equipment. It operates 1000 offices and 50 development and manufacturing facilities in more than 130 countries.

New York Life Insurance, 51 Madison Avenue, New York, NY, 10010
Phone: (212) 576-7000 Fax: (212) 576-8145 Website: www.newyorklife.com
New York Life operates in the US, the UK, Bermuda, Mexico, Argentina, Indonesia, South Korea, Hong Kong, Taiwan, and China.

Newell Rubbermaid Inc., 10 B. Glenlake Pkwy., Suite 300, Atlanta, GA, 30328
Phone: (770) 407-3800 Fax: (770) 407-3970 Website: www.newellrubbermaid.com
Rubbermaid, manufacturer of gardening accessories, housewares, furniture, decorations, toys, office products, and leisure items, operates facilities in the US and 9 foreign countries, including Mexico and Japan, and sells its products worldwide, including Eastern Europe.

Newmont Mining Corporation, 1700 Lincoln Street, Denver, CO, 80203
Phone: (303) 863-7414 Fax: (303) 837-5837 Website: www.newmont.com
Newmont mines gold in Indonesia, Mexico, Peru and Uzbekistan and operates a joint venture with Japan in Indonesia.

Nike Inc., 1 Bowerman Dr, Beaverton, OR, 97005
Phone: (503) 671-6453   Fax: (503) 671-6300 Website: www.nike.com
Nike, manufacturer and purveyor of athletic shoes, apparel, and accessories, sells its products in 110 countries and maintains administrative offices in the US, Canada, Hong Kong, Austria, and the Netherlands.

Northwest Airlines Corporation, 2700 Lone Oak Pkwy, Eagan, MN, 55112-3034
Phone: (612) 726-2111 Fax: (612) 727-7617 Website: www.nwa.com

Northwest serves 80 countries worldwide, with hubs in the US and Japan, and recently entered a code-sharing agreement in Korea, as well as doubling its service to China.
Novell, Inc., 404 Wyman Street, Waltham, MA, 02451
Phone: (800) 529-3400 Website: www.novell.com
Novell's software is marketed worldwide through offices in the US and 56 foreign countries.
Nucor Corporation, 1915 Rexford Road, Charlotte, NC, 28211
Phone: (704) 366-7000 Fax: (704) 362-4208 Website: www.nucor.com
Nucor is a steelmaker with operations in the US and in the Republic of Trinidad and Tobago.

Occidental Petroleum, 10889 Wilshire Blvd., Los Angeles, CA, 90024
Phone: (310) 208-8800 Fax: (310) 443-6690 Website: www.oxy.com
Occidental Petroleum operates worldwide, with a recently established subsidiary in Japan, and drilling sites in the Middle East.
Olsten Corporation, 175 Broad Hollow Rd., Melville, NY, 11747-8905
Phone: (516) 844-7800 Fax: (516) 844-7011 Website: www.olsten.com
Olsten is the third largest temporary staffing agency and the leader in home healthcare services in the US, UK, Mexico, Argentina, Denmark, Germany and Sweden.
Omnicom Group Inc., 437 Madison Avenue, New York, NY, 10022
Phone: (212) 415-3600 Fax: (212) 415-3530 Website: www.omnicomgroup.com
Omnicom is the #1 advertising agency in the world, operating in more than 60 countries.
Oracle Corporation, 500 Oracle Parkway, Redwood Shores, CA, 94065
Phone: (415) 506-7000 Fax: (415) 506-7200 Website: www.oracle.com
Oracle is a leading vendor of software and a developer of database management systems, with operations in 90 countries worldwide, mostly in the US and Europe.

PACCAR Inc., 777 106th Avenue NE, Bellevue, WA, 98004
Phone: (425) 468-7400 Fax: (425) 468-8216 Website: www.paccar.com
PACCAR is the world's 3rd largest heavy-duty truck manufacturer, with plants in the US, UK, Canada, Australia, and Mexico, and has added sales in Central and South America.
Packard Bell NEC, Inc., 10850 Gold Center Dr, # 200, Rancho Cordova, CA, 95670
Phone: (916) 388-0101 Fax: (916) 388-1109 Website: www. packardbell.com
Packard Bell is the #1 seller of PCs in retail mass markets, with manufacturing and distributing centers in Brazil, France, Israel, Japan, Hong Kong and Singapore.
Parker-Hannifin Corporation, 6035 Parkland Blvd., Cleveland, OH, 44124
Phone: (216) 896-3000 Fax: (216) 896-4000 Website: www.parker.com
Parker-Hannifin makes fluid poser systems and components, with 158 plants and 102 offices, stores and warehouses worldwide.
Pennzoil Company, 700 Milam Street, Houston, TX, 77002
Phone: (713) 546-4100 Website: www.pennzoil.com
Pennzoil has drilling operations in the US, Canada, Indonesia, and Qatar, and sells its products in 60 countries. It owns and operates a sulfur terminal in Belgium, and has signed contracts for projects in Egypt. It has undeveloped acreage in Azerbaijan, Qatar and Venezuela.
PepsiAmericas, Inc., 60 South Sixth Street, Minneapolis, MN, 55402
Phone: (612) 661-4000 Fax: (612) 661-3737 Website: www.whitmancorp.com

Whitman's business consists of Pepsi bottling, muffler manufacture, and walk-in refrigerators, with the last items being produced in the US, UK, Canada, and Mexico, and joint ventures in Asia and Europe.

Pepsico, Inc., 700 Anderson Hill Road, Purchase, NY, 10577-1444
Phone: (914) 253-2000 Fax: (914) 253-2070 Website: www.pepsico.com
Pepsico's food and beverage products are sold worldwide, especially in North America and Europe.

Pfizer Inc., 235 East 42nd Street, New York, NY, 10017-5755
Phone: (212) 733-2323 Fax: (212) 733-7851 Website: www.pfizer.com
Pfizer's pharmaceutical products are manufactured in 30 countries and sold in more than 150 worldwide, including joint ventures in Hungary and Japan.

Philip Morris Companies Inc., 6601 West Broad Street, Richmond, VA, 23230
Phone: (804) 274-2000 Web Page: www.philipmorrisusa.com
In addition to tobacco products, Philip Morris is in the food and beer production business, with worldwide distribution of its products, primarily in the US and Europe.

Pitney Bowes Inc., 1 Elmcroft Road, Stamford, CT, 06926-0700
Phone: (203) 356-5000 Fax: (203) 351-6835 Website: www.pitneybowes.com
Pitney Bowes mailing equipment is sold worldwide, primarily in the US and Europe, with recent ventures in France, Germany, Mexico and China.

Polaroid Corporation, 300 Baker Avenue, Concord, MA, 01742-2131
Phone: (781) 386-2000 Fax: (617) 386-3924 Website: www.polaroid.com
Polaroid not only makes cameras, lenses, and film, but has also expanded into the electronic imaging market. Its products are sold worldwide, mostly in the US and Europe, and are manufactured in the US, UK, Mexico, and the Netherlands.

PPG Industries, Inc., 1 PPG Place, Pittsburgh, PA, 15272
Phone: (412) 434-3131 Fax: (412) 434-2448 Website: www.ppg.com
PPG is the US's leading glass manufacturer, with plants in the US, the UK, Canada, Mexico, Spain, France, Germany, the Netherlands, Italy, and Taiwan.

Premark International, Inc., 1717 Deerfield Road, Deerfield, IL, 60015
Phone: (847) 405-6000 Fax: (708) 405-6013 Website: www.primarkintl.com
Premark markets food storage containers, professional food products, small appliances, and fitness equipment, manufacturing in 15 countries and selling in over 100 throughout the world, with plans to expand into India in the near future.

Pricewaterhouse Coopers, 300 Madison Avenue, New York, NY, 10017
Phone: (646) 471-4000 Fax: (646) 471-4444 Website: www. pwcglobal. com
One of the Big 6 accounting firms, Price Waterhouse maintains offices in 119 countries, including Vietnam.

Procter & Gamble Company, 1 Procter & Gamble Plaza, Cincinnati, OH, 45201
Phone: (513) 983-1100 Fax: (513) 983-9369 Website: www.pg.com
Procter & Gamble is a household products company with international markets around the world.

The Prudential Insurance Company, 751 Broad Street, Newark, NJ, 07102-3777
Phone: (973) 802-6000 Fax: (973) 367-8204 Website: www.prudential.com
Prudential operates in the US, Italy, Spain, Taiwan, Japan, and Korea.

Quaker Oats Company (a unit of **Pepsico**), P.O. Box 049003, Chicago, IL, 60604
Phone: (312) 821-1000 Fax: (312) 222-8323 Website: www.quakeroats.com

Quaker products are mostly grain-based foods and non-carbonated beverages, with operations worldwide, and sales around the world, primarily in North America and Europe.
Quantum Corporation, 1650 Technology Drive, Suite 700, San Jose, CA, 95110
Phone: (408) 944-4000 Fax: (408) 894-4152 Website: www.quantum.com
Quantum is the world's leading supplier of hard disks, with manufacturing facilities in the US and Indonesia. Its affiliate, Matsushita-Kotobuki Electronics, has plants in Ireland, Japan, and Singapore. The company's products are sold internationally, primarily in the US and Europe.
Qwest, 180 California Street, Denver, CO, 80202
Phone: (800) 899-7780 Fax: (303) 992-1724 Website: www.qwest.com
Qwest provides combined cable TV/telephone services, with interests in Europe, South America and Asia.

Radio Shack Corporation, 300 RadioShack Circle, Fort Worth, TX, 76102-1964
Phone: (817) 415-3700 Fax: (805) 415-2647 Website: www.radioshack.com
Radio Shack is one of the world's leading electronics retailers, with stores in the US, Canada, and Europe and a manufacturing plant in China.
Ralston Purina Group, Checkerboard Square, St. Louis, MO, 63164
Phone: (314) 982-1000 Fax: (314) 982-2134 Website: www.purina.com
RPG's main lines are pet foods and soy protein technologies. The company also owns Eveready, the battery producer. RPG has 125 plants worldwide, and markets its products around the world.
Raytheon Company, 870 Winter Street, Waltham, MA, 02451
Phone: (781) 522-3000 Website: www.raytheon.com
Raytheon's operations fall into 4 categories: aircraft, appliances, electronics, and engineering and construction, with principle operations in the Americas, Europe, the Middle East, and the Pacific Rim.
The Reader's Digest Association Inc., Reader's Digest Rd., Pleasantville, NY,10570
Phone: (914) 238-1000 Fax: (914) 238-4559 Website: www.rd.com
The Reader's Digest is a global publishing and entertainment empire, and is moving into CD-ROM and online technologies. Its sales are international, with emphasis on Europe and the US.
Reebok International Ltd., 1895 JW Foster Blvd, Canton, MA, 02021
Phone: (781) 401-5000 Fax: (781) 401-7402 www.reebok.com
Reebok manufactures athletic shoes, apparel, and equipment, selling its products in 140 countries, primarily in the US, UK, and the rest of Europe, and with a new joint venture in China.
Reynolds American Inc., 401 North Main Street, Winston-Salem, NC, 27101-2990
Phone: (336) 741-2000 Fax: (336) 741-4238 Website: www. reynoldsamerican.com
RJR is divided into a food products division and a tobacco products division, and sells its products in more than 160 countries worldwide. Its tobacco processing plants include locations in Poland and Turkey.
Rockwell Automation, 1201 South Second Street, Milwaukee, WI, 53204-2496
Phone: (414) 382-2000 Fax: (414) 382-4444 Website: www.rockwellautomation.com
Rockwell is involved in all areas of technological support, manufacturing automation systems, chips, modems, etc., around the world, and with a recent joint venture agreement with China.

Rohm and Haas Company, 100 Independence Mall West, Philadelphia, PA 19106
Phone: (215) 592-3000 Fax: (215) 592-3377 Website: www.rohmhass.com
Rohm and Haas manufactures specialty chemical products, and is best known as the
maker of Plexiglas. It has worldwide operations and a joint venture in Germany.
Ryder System, Inc., 11690 NW 105th Street, Miami, FL, 33178
Phone: (305) 500-3726 Fax: (305) 500-4129 Website: www.ryder.com
Ryder provides both full-service leasing and short-term rental of trucks, tractors, and
trailers in the US, UK, Canada, Germany, Mexico, Argentina, Brazil and Poland.

Sanmina-SCI Corporation, 2700 North First Street, San Jose, CA, 95134
Phone: (408) 964-3555 Fax: (408) 964-3636 Website: www.sanmina.com
SCI manufactures electronics in the Americas, Europe and Asia.
Sara Lee Corporation, 3500 Lacey Road, Downers Grove, IL, 60515
Phone: (312) 726-2600 Fax: (312) 726-3712 Website: www.saralee.com
In addition to food products, Sara Lee's business includes personal and household
items, with plants in the US and 35 other countries, and sales worldwide, primarily in
the Americas, Europe, and Asia.
S.C. Johnson & Son, Inc., 1525 Howe Street, Racine, WI, 53403-2236
Phone: (414) 260-2000 Fax: (414) 260-2133 Website: www.scjohnsonwax.com
S.C. Johnson is one of the world's largest makers of consumer chemical specialty
products, operating in all global regions, including Africa and Ukraine.
Schering-Plough Corporation, 2000 Galloping Hill Roada, Kenilworth, NJ, 07033
Phone: (908) 298-4000 Website: www.sch-plough.com
Schering-Plough produces pharmaceuticals, with sales throughout the world, and new
plants starting in China, Mexico, and Singapore.
Schlumberger, Limited, 5599 San Felipe, 17th Floor, Houston, TX, 77056
Phone: (713) 513-2000 Website: www.slb.com
Schlumberger combines oil field services and exploration with an electronics and technology
business, operating in 100 countries, and with international sales areas including France.
Seagate Technology, Inc., 920 Disc Drive, Scotts Valley, CA, 95066
Phone: (408) 438-6550 Fax: (408) 438-7205 Website: www.seagate.com
Seagate manufactures hard drives and is moving into software. It has sales offices in
14 countries, with most sales in the US and the Far East. It manufactures its products
in the US, UK, China, Malaysia, Singapore, and Thailand.
Sears Holdings Corporation, 3333 Beverly Road, Hoffman Estates, IL, 60179
Phone: (847) 286-2500 Fax; (847) 286-7829 Website: www.sears.com
Sears has stores in the US, Canada, and Mexico.
Sherwin-Williams Company, 101 Prospect Avenue, NW, Cleveland, OH, 44115
Phone: (216) 566-2000 Fax: (216) 566-2947 Website: www.sherwin-williams.com
Sherwin-Williams paints, chemicals, and automotive coatings are licensed in 36 foreign
countries, with subsidiaries in Canada, Argentina, Brazil, the Caribbean, and Mexico.
Silicon Graphics, Inc., 1140 East Arques Avenue, Sunnyvale, CA, 94085
Phone: (650) 960-1980 Fax: (650) 961-0595 Website: www.sgi.com
Silicon Graphics makes graphics computers and software for both the professional and
consumer markets, with 130 offices in the Americas, Europe, and the Pacific region.
Smurfit-Stone Container Corporation, 150 North Michigan Ave., Chicago, IL 60601
Phone: (312)346-6600 Fax: (312) 580-2272 Website: www.stonecontainer.com

Stone produces paperboard and paper packaging, with plants in the US, UK, Canada, Australia, Germany, the Netherlands, Belgium, France, Costa Rica, Mexico, and Venezuela, with sales in the US, Canada, and Europe.

Snap-on Incorporated, 2801 80th Street, Kenosha, WI, 53143

Phone: (262) 656-5200 Fax: (414) 656-5577 Website: www.snapon.com

Snap-on is the top manufacturer of mechanics' hand tools, produced in the US and 9 other countries. The company has sales in Canada, Mexico, Japan, Germany, the Netherlands and Spain.

Spiegel Brands Inc., 711 3rd Avenue, New York, NY, 10017

Phone: (212) 986-2585 Fax: (212) 916-8281 Website: www.spiegel.com

Spiegel operates both catalog sales and retail outlets in the US, Canada, Germany, and Japan.

Sprint Corporation, 6391 Sprint Pkwy, Overland Park, KS, 66251-4300

Phone: (913) 624-6000 Fax: (913) 624-3088 Website: www.sprint.com

Sprint's telecommunications services have expanded to Mexico and China, as well as France and Germany.

Stanley Works, 1000 Stanley Drive, New Britain, CT, 06053

Phone: (860) 225-5111 Fax: (860) 827-3895 Website: www.stanleyworks.com

Stanley tools are manufactured and distributed throughout the US and in 17 other countries, with recent expansions into China, India, Eastern Europe, and Latin America.

Steelcase Inc., 901 44th Street SE, Grand Rapids, MI, 49508

Phone: (616) 247-2710 Fax: (616) 246-4041 Website: www.steelcase.com

Steelcase is the world's largest manufacturer of office furniture, with plants in the US, UK, Canada, France, Morocco, the Ivory Coast, Belgium, Germany, Spain, Portugal, and Japan. Its products are sold worldwide, with a recent joint venture in India.

Sun Microsystems, 4150 Network Circle, Santa Clara, CA, 95054

Phone: (650) 960-1300 Fax: (650) 969-9131 Website: www.sun.com

Sun Microsystems provides Internet solutions, distributing its products in more than 125 countries worldwide, most recently in South Africa.

Sunoco Inc., 1735 Market Street, Suite LL, Philadelphia, PA, 19103-7583

Phone: (215) 977-3000 Fax: (215) 977-3409 Website: www.sunocoinc.com

Sun is an oil company with operations in the US, the UK, and the North Sea region.

Tenet HealthSystem Medical, Inc., 13737 Noel Road, Dallas, TX, 75240

Phone: (469) 892-2200 Fax: (469) 893-8600 Website: www.tenethealthcare.com

Tenet is a healthcare provider with facilities in the US and Spain.

Texas Instruments Incorporated, 12500 TI Blvd, Dallas, TX, 75243

Phone: (972) 995-2011 Fax: (972) 995-4360 Website: www.ti.com

TI manufactures computer chips, computers, defense electronics, calculators and printers, etc., with operations in 17 countries, and sales primarily in the US, East Asia, and Europe.

Textron Inc., 40 Westminster Street, Providence, RI, 02903

Phone: (401) 421-2800 Fax: (401) 421-2878 Website: www.textron.com

Textron, a major defense contractor, makes such varied products as helicopters, windshield washers, and watchbands, as well as providing financial services and insurance. It operates in the US and abroad, with sales in the US, Canada, Europe, the Asia/Pacific region, and Mexico.

Time Warner Inc., 1 Time Warner Center, New York, NY, 10019-8016
Phone: (212) 484-8000 Fax: (212) 956-2847 Website: www.timewarner.com
Time Warner, the huge multimedia company, has sales in the US, Europe, the Pacific
Rim and elsewhere, and is currently investing in Japan's cable TV industry.
Transamerica Corporation, 600 Montgomery St., 23rd Fl., San Francisco, CA 94111
Phone: (415) 983-4000 Fax: (415) 983-4400 Website: www.transamerica.com
Transamerica's insurance business operates in the US and Canada, but its leasing
business has branches in 47 countries (including Japan), and its commercial finance
business is in 6 countries.
TRW Inc., 1900 Richmond Road, Cleveland, OH, 44124
Phone: (216) 291-7000 Fax: (216) 291-7629 Website: www.trw.com
TRW provides advanced technology products and services, with manufacturing, R&D,
and other facilities in the US and 22 other countries, and sales primarily in the US and
Europe. The company has recently begun joint ventures in China, India and Turkey.
Tyco International Ltd., 9 Roszel Road, Princeton, NJ, 08540
Phone: (609) 720-4200 Website: www.tyco.com
Tyco International produces fire protection systems, operating 250 offices on 5
continents, with sales in North America, Europe, and the Asia/Pacific region.
Tyson Foods, Inc., 2210 West Oaklawn Drive, Springdale, AR 72764-6999
Phone: (501) 290-4000 Fax: (501) 290-4061 Website: www.tyson.com
Tyson operates production and distribution facilities in the US and 12 other countries,
participating in joint ventures in China and Mexico. Its products are sold in Canada,
Hong Kong, Japan, and in several other Asian countries and in the Caribbean.

UAL Corporation, 77 West Wacker Drive, Chicago, IL, 60601
Phone: (312) 997-8000 Website: www.ual.com
United Airlines serves 144 airports in 31 countries, with new cargo services to Japan
and other Asian destinations.
UBS Financial Services, 1285 Avenue of the Americas, New York, NY, 10019
Phone: (212) 713-2000 Fax: (212) 713-4889 Website: www.ubs.com
They offer a variety of banking, financial, and real estate services at 310 offices in the
US and Puerto Rico, the UK, Switzerland, Hong Kong, Singapore, and Japan.
Union Carbide Corporation, (subsidiary of the **Dow Chemical Company**), P.O. Box
4393, Houston, TX, 77210
Phone: (713) 978-2016 Fax: (713) 9787-2394 Website: www.unioncarbide.com
Union Carbide produces petrochemical products, operating in 14 countries around the
world with a new complex in Kuwait, and a joint venture in China.
Unisys Corporation, Unisys Way, Blue Bell, PA, 19424
Phone: (215) 986-4011 Fax: (215) 986-2312 Website: www.unisys.com
Unisys is one of the world's largest computer companies, producing computer systems,
software, and services to commercial and government clients. The company has clients
in 100 countries worldwide.
United Health Group, 9900 Bren Road East, Minnetonka, MN, 55343
Phone: (952) 936-1300 Fax: (952) 936-1819 Website: www.uhc.com
A managed care provider, operating in all 50 states and in Puerto Rico. It also has
operations in Germany, Hong Kong, and South Africa.
United Parcel Service, 55 Glenlake Parkway NE, Atlanta, GA, 30328

Phone: (770) 828-6000 Fax: (770) 828-6593 Website: www.ups.com
UPS is the world's #1 package delivery company, operating in more than 200 countries worldwide, and with hubs in North America, Germany, Hong Kong, and Singapore.
United Technologies, United Technologies Building, Hartford, CT, 06101
Phone: (860) 728-7000 Fax: (860) 728-7979 Website: www.utc.com
United Technologies is a conglomerate producing such diverse items as air-conditioning systems, elevators and escalators, aircraft engines and helicopters, with operations on all continents, and sales worldwide.
Universal Corporation, 1501 North Hamilton Street, Richmond, VA, 23230
Phone: (804) 359-9311 Fax: (804) 254-3584 Website: www.universalcorp.com
Universal buys and processes leaf tobacco, with operations in 33 countries and sales primarily in the US, Europe, and Latin America. It has a presence in Africa, Eastern Europe, and China.
USAA, 9800 Fredericksburg Road, San Antonio, TX, 78288
Phone: (210) 498-2211 Fax: (210) 498-9940 Website: www.usaa.com
USAA provides insurance and financial services worldwide, with regional offices in the US, UK, and Germany.
US Airways Inc., 111 West Rio Salado Parkway, Tempe, AZ, 85281
Phone: (480) 693-0800 Fax: (480) 693-5546 Website: www.usairways.com
USAir serves cities in the US, Canada, the Caribbean, France, Spain, Italy and Germany.
USG Corporation, 550 West Adams Street, Chicago, IL, 60661-3676
Phone: (312) 436-4000 Fax: (312) 436-4093 Website: www.usg.com
USG's wall and ceiling products are produced in 13 countries, including a joint venture in Saudi Arabia.
USX-Marathon Oil Corporation, 5555 San Felipe Road, Houston, TX, 77056
Phone: (713) 629-6600 Fax: (713) 296-2952 Website: www.marathon.com
Marathon conducts exploration and development activities in 15 countries and sells its petroleum products primarily in the US and Europe. It recently signed an agreement with the Russian government.

Verizon Communications Inc., 140 West Street, New York, NY, 10007
Phone: (212) 395-1000 Fax: (212) 571-1897 Website: www.verizon.com
As the # 2 telecommunications provider they provide land and wireless services to both global and domestic customers.
VF Corporation, 105 Corporate Center Blvd, Greensboro, NC, 27408
Phone: (336) 424-6000 Fax: (336) 424-7631 Website: www.vfc.com
V.F. manufactures apparel under a variety of brand names, and sells its products around the world.
VISA International, Inc, 900 Metro Center Blvd., Foster City, CA, 94404
Phone: (650) 432-3200 Fax: (650) 432-7436 Website: www.visa.com
VISA, the largest consumer payment system, operates in 247 countries worldwide.

Walt Disney Company, The, 500 South Buena Vista Street, Burbank, CA, 91521
Phone: (818) 560-1000 Fax: (818) 560-1930 Website: www.disney.com
Disney is the biggest entertainment company in the world, with theme parks, studios, retail stores, and other ventures in the US, Europe, and Japan.
Whirlpool Corporation, 2000 North M-63, Benton Harbor, MI, 49022-2692

Phone: (269) 923-5000 Fax: (269) 923-3722 Website: www.whirlpoolcorp.com
Whirlpool makes major household appliances in the US, South America (including Brazil), Mexico, France, Italy, Germany, Sweden, Slovakia, India, and China.
Wm. Wrigley Jr. Company, 410 North Michigan Avenue, Chicago, IL, 60611
Phone: (312) 644-2121 Fax: (312) 644-0097 Website: www.wrigley.com
Wrigley is the world's #1 maker of chewing gum, with operations in 29 countries, including factories in Hungary, Slovenia, the Czech Republic, and China. Its newest factory is under construction in Russia.
W.R. Grace & Co., 7500 Grace Drive, Columbia, MD, 21044-4098
Phone: (410) 531-4000 Fax: (410) 531-4367 Website: www.grace.com
Grace is the world's largest specialty chemicals company with operations around the world.

Xerox Corporation, 45 Glover Avenue, Norwalk, CT, 06856-4505
Phone: (203) 968-3000 Fax: (203) 968-3430 Website: www.xerox.com
Xerox operates offices, manufacturing plants, and other facilities and sells its products worldwide, and is currently forming a joint production venture with Japan and China.

Yellow Corporation, 10990 Roe Avenue, Overland Park, KS, 66211
Phone: (913) 696-6100 Fax: (913) 696-6116 Website: www.yellowcorp.com
Yellow Freight operates freight terminals and owns trucks, tractors, and trailers throughout North America.

Zenith Electronics, 2000 Millbrook Drive, Lincolnshire, IL, 60069
Phone: (847) 391-8183 Fax: (847) 391-7291 Website: www.zenith.com
Zenith has locations in the US, Canada, Mexico, and a purchasing office in Taiwan.

APPENDIX 5.
TRANSLATION COURSES AND PROGRAMS

Academic programs for those interested in translation and interpretation are in a state of flux. There is a growing recognition of the fact that the most critical need for the practicing translator is hands-on experience, although some of the policymakers in academia continue to cling to theory rather than practice. Programs are growing and expanding, to include many new areas. If interested in an academic program, contact one or more of the following schools and find out more about their latest offerings.

As with the Translation Agency listings in Appendix 4, detailed information in the following entries is the result of responses to an information questionnaire sent to the various schools. The quantity of such information is based on those responses and does not reflect any value judgment on the part of the editors.

A new development in American education is "distance learning," or learning at home through the Internet. This can become a real blessing for translators, many of whom are well past their school years. The translation program at New York University (see below) is in the process of setting up distance learning for translation. Check their website for details.

UNITED STATES

ARIZONA
Arizona State University, Languages and Literatures, P.O. Box 870202, Tempe, AZ 85287, Phone: (602) 496-0611 Fax: (480) 965-0135 Website: www.asu.edu
E-mail: maria.teresa.martinez@asu.edu
Contact: Maria Teresa Martinez
Spanish Translation Certificate Program, now in its seventeenth year. Covers literary, legal, medical, sci-tech, business and financial translation. Prerequisites include an introductory course in linguistics.

ARKANSAS
University of Arkansas, Department of English, 333 Kimpel Hall, Fayetteville, AR 72701, Phone: (479) 575-4301 Fax (479) 575-5919 Website: www.uark.edu
E-mail: mfa@uark.edu
Contact: Davis McCombs
Offers literary translation program (MFA).
This certificate program is for people bilingual in Spanish and English who wish to work in the courts as an Interpreter and Translator, or who desire to work as a State or Federally certified interpreter and translator in other areas of the public or private sector, or who want to sharpen their bilingual skills for translation and interpretation.

CALIFORNIA
Monterey Institute of International Studies, Graduate School of Translation &
Interpretation Studies, 460 Pierce St., Monterey, CA 93940
Phone: (831) 647-4170   Fax: (831) 647-3560   Website: www.miis.edu
E-mail: ddeterra@miis.edu
Contact: Diane de Terra
Now in its thirty-fourth year, the school offers an MA degree in Chinese, French, Ger-
man, Japanese, Korean, Spanish, Russian, and English Translation. All major techni-
cal areas of translation are taught, including computer-assisted translation, soft ware
localization, terminology, and the business of translation. The School also offers an
MA in Intepreting- Simultaneous, Consecutive, and Conference. Students must have
a BA with a 3.0 GPA and a TOEFL of 600+, as well as study abroad and GRE. The
Graduate School is an independent entitywithin the Monterey Institute. The School
also offers Certificate to students lacking a BA, but who demonstrates the necessary
level of language proficiency.

San Diego State University, Department of Spanish & Portuguese Languages &
Literature, 5402 College Ave., San Diego, CA 92182
Phone: (619) 594-6588   Fax: (619) 594-5293   Website: sdsu.edu
E-mail: cdegueld@mail.sdsu.edu
Contact: Christian DeGuelde
SDSU's Translationprogram has been in place eighteen years. The University offers
Certificates in Translation Studies and in Court Interpreting in Spanish-English. Trans-
lation covers all major technical areas; Interpreting is Legal only. Students must have
advanced Spanish grammar or equivalent courses, and must pass a proficiency exami-
nation in English. There are five courses in Translation and six in Court Interpreting,
including an internship, The University also provides training for State and Federal
accreditation examinations in Court Interpreting.

Stanford University, Stanford, CA 94305
Phone: (415)497-1068   Website: www.stanford.edu
Offers Certificate Program in Translation and Interpretation done in tandem with
Monterey Institute of International Studies.

University of California, Los Angeles, 10995 Le Conte Ave., Los Angeles, CA
90024   Website: www.ucla.edu
Offers Certificate in Interpretation and Translation in Spanish.

California State University, Long Beach, 1250 Bellflower Blvd, Long Beach, CA
90840   Phone: (916) 278-6011   Website: www.csulb.edu
Offers BA in Spanish translation.

California State University, Los Angeles, Certificate Program in Legal Interpretation and Translation: Spanish/English
Phone: 323-343-5964   Website: www.calstatela.edu
5151 State University Drive, Los Angeles, CA 90032-8619
California State University Sacramento, 6000 J St., Sacramento, CA 95819

Phone: (916) 278-6011 Website: www.csus.edu
Offers courses in translation and interpretation.

Fuller Theological Seminary, 135 N. Oakland Ave., Pasadena, CA   91182
Phone: (626) 584-5400 Website: www.fuller.edu
Offers graduate degrees in Bible Translation.

San Jose State University, Department of Foreign Languages, One Washington Sq.,
San Jose, CA 95192-0091, Phone: (408) 924-4602   Fax: (408) 924-4607
Website: www.sjsu.edu
E-mail: msigler@jsuvm.sjsu.edu
Contact: Dr. M. del Carmen Sigler, Chair
Although SJSU offers courses in Chinese, French, German, Greek, Hebrew, Italian,
Japanese, Latin, Portuguese, Russian and Spanish, its Translation offerings are limited
to one introductory course—"Translation: Theory and Practice"—in Spanish only. The
course has been offered for several years. It is considered an elective in the Bachelor's
Degree in Spanish program. The prerequisite for the course is the attainment of an
advanced level in the study of Spanish. The course deals with texts from most major
technical areas. SJSU plans to offer more courses in translation in the future, at least
one of which will be at the MA level.

CONNECTICUT
Wesleyan University, Middleton, CT 06457 Website: www.wesleyan.edu
Offers Interpreters for the Deaf Workshop

DISTRICT OF COLUMBIA
Gallaudet College, Department of ASL, Linguistics and Interpretation, 800 Florida
Ave., NE, Washington, DC 20002
Phone: (202) 651-5450   Fax: (202) 651-5741   Website: www.gallaudet.edu
E-mail: interpretation@gallaudet.edu
Contact: Valerie L. Dively
Only liberal-arts college exclusively for the deaf. Offers Master's degree in ASL.

Georgetown University, 1221 36th St. N.W., Washington, DC 20057
Website: www.georgetown.edu
E-mail: interp1@guvax.georgetown.edu
Offers Certificate of Proficiency as Conference Interpreter, and Certificate in Transla-
tion in French, Spanish, German, Italian, and Portuguese.

The American University, Department of Language & Foreign Studies, 4400 Mas-
sachusetts Ave., NW, Washington, DC 20016
Phone: (202) 885-2381   Fax: (202) 885-1076   Website: www.american.edu/lfs
E-mail: lfs@american.edu
Contact: Consuelo Galls
The American University's translation program has been operating for thirteen years.
It teaches French, Spanish, Russian and German translation, with an emphasis on
translation into English. Students are required to have completed the third-year level of

their language. Courses cover general translation, covering a variety of areas including business, literature, journalism, etc. Students are awarded a certificate on completion of the course. Study materials vary with the language. There is no interpreter training.

FLORIDA

Florida International University, Department of Modern Languages University Park Campus, Miami, FL 33199
Phone: (305) 348-2851   Fax: (305) 348-1085   Voice mail: (305) 348-2049
Website: www.fiu.edu
Contact: Dr. Leonel A. de la Cuesta, Director Translation-Interpretation Program
FIU's Translation-Interpretation Program has been in operation since 1980. It teaches Translation primarily in Spanish-English, with some French as well. The program awards Certificates in Translation Studies and Legal Translation. The University also offers Simultaneous and Consecutive (but not Conference) Interpreter training in English-Spanish and awards a Certificate in Court Interpreting. Students are required to have at least two years of college education and must be bilingual. Studies cover most major areas of technical translation (Legal, Medical, Business, Technological-Scientific, Literary, Journalism, Publishing, etc.).The University also provides support training for practicing translators and interpreters who want to strengthen their skills in the field.

Florida A&M University, Office of International Services and Summer Sessions, Translation and Critical Languages Center, 304 Perry Paige N., Tallahassee, FL 32307
Phone: (904) 561-2482   Website: www.famu.edu
Contact: Dr. Eva. C. Wanton, Associate Vice President for Academic Affairs.
Florida A&M's translation program has been operating for ten years, and offers a B.A. in Spanish and French and a minor in these degree programs. Instruction in German, Chinese, Japanese and other languages on request is also available. Prerequisites for the program include successful completion of a written entrance exam and an oral proficiency interview. The program teaches courses in Legal, Medical, Business, Scientific and Educational translation. Training materials include journals, newspapers, magazines and textbooks. Successful completion of the program requires 18 semester hours of translations and an internship at an overseas translation institute, as well as written and oral exit examinations.

Miami-Dade College/Inter-American Campus, 627 SW 27th Avenue, Room 1336, Miami FL 33135
Phone: (305) 237-6073   Website: www.mdc.edu
Contact: Humberto Cerna
Offers courses and concentration in Translation and Interpretation for Medical, Legal, and Business.

University of Florida, Translation Studies, 319 Grinter Hall, Gainesville, FL 32611
Phone: 352-392-0375 Ext. 809
Website: translationstudies.ufl.edu/program.shtml.
E-mail: elowe@latam.ufl.edu
Contact: Elizabeth Lowe
Offers Graduate and Undergraduate Certificates in Translation Studies.

GEORGIA
Georgia State University, Modern and Classical Languages, P.O. Box 3970, Atlanta, GA, 30302, Phone: 404-651-2747 or 404-651-2265 Fax: 404-651-1785
Website: www.gsu.edu/~wwwmcl/
E-mail: acash@gsu.edu
Contact: Dr. Annette G. Cash
The graduate level certificate programs in translation and interpretation were introduced in 1979 in the Department of Modern and Classical Languages. It provides professional training for bilingual students interested in a career in translation and/or interpretation. They have translation programs in French, German and Spanish. They are designed to develop advanced translation skills for students interested in acquiring a high level of proficiency in a specific language combination. The program provides professional training in medical and legal interpretation for students who wish to become interpreters. The program is currently offered in Spanish.

HAWAII
University of Hawaii at Manoa. Center for Interpretation and Translation Studies, 1859 East-West Rd, # 104, Honolulu, HI 96822
Phone: 808-956-6233 Fax: 808-956-2078 Website: http://cits.hawaii.edu/
E-mail: cits@hawaii.edu
Contact Person: David Ashworth, Director
The Center for Interpretation and Translation Studies (CITS) was established in 1988 at the University of Hawaii at Manoa within the College of Languages, Linguistics and Literature. The Center's primary goal is to provide, through theoretically-based academic programs, basic training in interpretation and non-fiction translation. The Center currently offers a Certificate Training program in the summer in translation and interpretation (SIIT) in English in combination with Japanese, Mandarin and Korean and will offer certificate programs for other languages when demand is sufficient and qualified instructors are available. Currently, CITS does not offer a degree at the graduate or undergraduate level, except as a Liberal Studies major. Additional objectives of the Center are the development of a research-based training methodology, a teacher-training program and interdisciplinary research through links with University-wide resources. CITS also serves the community by acting as a clearinghouse of information on professional resources and practices. It provides the community at large with a broad range of educational opportunities by sponsoring lectures, seminars and workshops.

IDAHO
College of Southern Idaho, PO Box 1238, Twin Falls, ID 83303 Phone: (208) 733-9554 Website: www.csi.edu
Offers courses with translation component.

IOWA
University of Iowa, 425 English Philosophy Bldg, Iowa City, IA 52242
Phone: (319) 335-0330 Fax: (319)5-2535
Website: http://illinois.edu
Contact: Daniel Weissbort,

Offers MFA in Comparative Literature with Translation Component.
Also: Graduate Level Apprenticeship. Contact: Gertrud G. Champe, Translation Labora-
tory, 123 N. Linn St., Iowa City, IA 52246 Also: BA, Major in Languages with Translation Component (French and Italian). Contact: Jacques Bourgeacq/Michel Laronde

ILLINOIS
University of Illinois at Urbana-Champaign, 707 S. Mathews St., Urbana, IL 61801,
Website: www.uiuc.edu
E-mail: emartin@uiuc.edu
Offers Courses in Russian and French literary translation.

Northern Illinois University, Department of Foreign Languages and Translation,
Watson Hall 111, De Kalb, IL 60115
Phone: (815) 753-1259   Website: www.forlangs.net
E-mail: annie@niu.edu
Contact: Annie Birberick, Chair
Offers programs of study in fifteen languages. Language majors may choose either a lan-
guage and literature emphasis or a business and translation emphasis for their program.

INDIANA
Indiana University, University Budget Office, Bryan Hall 115, Bloomington, IN
47405,   Phone: (812) 855-6818   Fax: (812) 855-8990
Website: www.indiana.edu/complit/trans.html
Contact: Mariam Ehteshamis
Indiana U. has been offering a literary translation program for about 20 years. The
school teaches about 26 languages, from Arabic to Zulu. Courses include the theory
and practice of literary translation, which have resulted in some highly-regarded
translations from Chinese, French, German, Greek, Italian, Japanese, Romanian, and
Spanish, among others.

KANSAS
Kansas State University, Department of Modern Languages, 104 Eisenhower Hall,
Manhattan, KS 66506-1003
Phone: (785) 532-1988   Fax: (785) 532-7004   Website: www.k-state.edu
E-mail: bradshaw@ksu.edu
Contact: Dr. Bradley A. Shaw, Associate Professor
Kansas State teaches Spanish, French, German, Japanese, Russian, Italian, Arabic and
Latin. Although there is no translation program, KSU offers an Introduction to Spanish
Translation course, designed for upper level undergraduates and graduate students. It
features bi-directional exercises, a variety of texts, and a discussion of professional issues.

Johnson County Community College, College Blvd. at Quivira Rd., Overland Pass,
KS 66210,   Website: www.jccc.net

MARYLAND
University of Maryland, French and Italian Deparment, 3106 Jimenez Hall, College
Park, MD 20742

Phone: (301) 405-4024 Fax: (301) 314-9928 Website: www.umd.edu
Offers translation courses in French and Italian. Subjects covered are literary, journalistic, commercial, and political. There are about four courses in French at the undergraduate level that deal with translation. Two of these focus on business French. There is also a French translation course at the graduate level. One undergraduate course in Italian deals with literary translation. Most other languages taught by the university offer courses in translation or with a translation component.

MASSACHUSETTS
Elms College, Chicopee, MA 01013 Website: www.elms.edu
Offers French and Spanish Translation courses.

University of Massachusetts Amherst, Translation Center, 442 Herter Hall, Amherst, MA 01003, Phone: (413) 545-2203 Fax: (413) 577-3400
Website: www.umass.edu/transcen
E-mail: gentzler@complit.umass.edu
Contact: Shawn Lindholm. Program director: Edwin Gentzler
The program is now in its twelfth year. Offers MA in Translation Studies. Also Court Interpretation Program. Program consists mainly of literary and cultural studies, but also of business and technical translation. Also teaches interpretation which leads to a certificate.

MICHIGAN
Marygrove College, 8425 West McNichols Rd., Detroit, MI 48221-2599
Phone: (313) 862-8000 ext. 374 Fax: (313) 864-6670 Website: www.marygrove.edu
Contact: Dr. Karen Davis
Marygrove's Translation Program has been in operation since 1974. It teaches Literary, Legal, Medical, Scientific and Commercial Translation in Arabic, French and Spanish. The program awards a Certificate of Achievement for the completion of three separate workshops. The College also offers training in consecutive interpretation in Arabic, French and Spanish. Students are required to have four semesters of college-level work in French or Spanish, and Arabic requires three semesters of college-level Arabic. The third workshop features an independent project chosen by the student, following guidelines set by the ATA and the MLA (Modern Language Association).

Western Michigan University, Kalamazoo, MI 49008
Website: www.wmich.edu
Offers technical translation courses.

MINNESOTA
St. Olaf College, 1520 St. Olaf Ave., Northfield, MN 55057
Website: www.stolaf.edu
Offers courses in Spanish and Russian translation.

NEBRASKA
University of Nebraska at Kearney, Dept. of Modern Languages, Thomas Hall 215, Kearney, NE 68849

Phone: (308) 865-8536   Fax: (308) 865-8806   Website: www.nebraska.edu
E-mail: gonzaleze1@unk.edu
Contact: Dr. Eduardo Gonzalez, Translation/ Interpretation Program
U-Nebraska at Kearney's Translation/Interpretation program has been in operation
for 21 years. Under the ægis of Modern Languages, the program offers both BAs and
certificates in French, German and Spanish Translation and Interpretation. Students are
required to demonstrate proficiency or successfully accomplish senior-level language
studies. Both literary and nonliterary translation are taught. Students who complete the
program are ready for graduate studies, and in some cases, professional employment
as translators and/or interpreters.

NEVADA
University of Nevada, Reno, NV 89557
Website: www.unr.edu
Offers Court Interpreter Seminar/Workshops and courses in Spanish Translation.

NEW JERSEY
Montclair State University, Department of Modern Languages and Literatures,
Dickson Hall, Upper Montclair, NJ 07043
Phone: (973) 655-4283 Website: http://chss2.montclair.edu/French/
E-mail: oppenheim@mail.montclair.edu
Contact: Dr. Lois Oppenheim
Montclair State's Translation program has been in operation for twenty-six years. It
concentrates in French, but the university also offers courses in German, Hebrew,
Arabic, and Russian. The University offers both Certificates and BAs. It teaches Sci-
entific, Economic, Legal, and Literary Translation. Specific areas vary from semester
to semester. There is also one course in Interpreting (Simultaneous, Consecutive and
Conference) for French-language students. Students must be at least juniors majoring
in their language. They are required to do an individual long translation in their senior
year. The program prepares students for career opportunities in the NY/NJ metropolitan
area, in industry and commerce, advertising and tourism, and governmental services.
Students are encouraged to double-major in a technical specialty.

Rutgers, the State University, Department of Spanish and Portuguese, 105 George
St., New Brunswick, NJ 08901
Phone: (732) 932-9412 ext. 25   Fax: (732) 932-9837   Website: www.rutgers.edu
E-mail: zatlin@rci.rutgers.edu
Contact: Phyllis Zatlin
Rutgers has been offering a Spanish translation program for 22 years. In 1987, an M.A.
option was added, along with a certificate in translation. Requirements include proficiency
at native or near-native level in Spanish and English. Areas covered are legal, technical,
literary, and other subjects. There is also simultaneous and consecutive interpreter training in Spanish. The program also offers an internship in translation and interpretation.

NEW YORK
Columbia University, Barnard College, 3009 Broadway, New York, NY 10027
Website: www.barnard.edu

Offers a B.A. in French with a concentration in Translation and Literature.

Binghamton University (SUNY), Translation Research and Instruction Program, PO Box 6000, Binghamton, NY 13902   Phone: (607) 777-6555   Fax: (607) 777-2280 Website: http://trip.binghamton.edu
E-mail: trip@binghamton.edu or rarrojo@binghamton.edu
Contact: Rosemary Arrojo
SUNY-Binghamton's Translation Research and Instruction Program is an autonomous graduate teaching unit, not affiliated with any department in the University. The program has been operating since January 1971. Languages offered are Arabic, Chinese, Spanish, French, German, Japanese, Korean, Portuguese, Italian, Russian and Modern Greek. The University offers Graduate Certificates incorporated into a Master's or Doctoral degree. Students must have high fluency in their source language and effective expression in their target language. Emphasis is on literary and scholarly translation, with generalist studies scheduled for January 1998. Management of terminology databases is also taught. Study materials include *Beyond the Western Tradition*. There is no Interpreter training. Computer-assisted translation is offered.

Brooklyn College, 2900 Bedford Ave., Brooklyn, NY 11210 www.brooklyn.edu Offers translation courses.

City University of New York, 33 W. 42nd St., New York, NY 10036
Phone: (212) 817-8480 Fax: (212) 642-2205
Website: www.cuny.edu
Contact: Rachel M. Brownstein
Offers MA in Liberal Studies: Specialization in translation, with an emphasis on business, legal, medical, and science/technology translation.

Fordham University, Fordham Rd., Bronx, NY 10458,   Website: www.fordham.edu Offers courses in translation through individual language departments.

Hofstra University, Hempstead, NY 11550,   Website: www.hofstra.edu
Offers literary translation courses in several languages and a "practical translation" course (French only).

New York University, School of Continuing Education & Professional Studies, Foreign Languages Translation Studies, 10 Astor Place. Suite 504E, New York, NY 10003 Phone: (212) 998-7028   Fax: (212) 995-4139   Website: www.nyu.edu
E-mail: milena.savova@nyu.edu
Contact: Milena Savova, Translation Studies Coordinator.
NYU's Translation program has been in operation for seventeen years. It offers translation certificates in English-Spanish, English-Portuguese, Spanish-English, French-English, Arabic-English, German-English on site, and English-Spanish on line, as well as English-Spanish court interpreting. The Arabic-English program a military document class unlike the other languages. The program emphasizes legal, commercial, medical, and technical translation with elective courses available in marketing, literary and terminology/database management, among others. Since it is a hands-on, intensive

translator and interpreter-training program, students translate "real-life" texts in the Translation program, and use language labs in the Court Interpreting program. In addition, a wide variety of internships are available. Students must pass an entrance exam to prove proficiency in both target and source languages. They must maintain a B or better average and complete the program within four years. NYU has recently added many online classes in their translation department.

State University of New York at Albany, 1400 Washington Ave., Albany, NY 12222
Website: www.albany.edu
Offers Post-Master's degree Certificate in Russian translation.

NORTH CAROLINA
University of North Carolina at Charlotte, Charlotte, NC 28223
Phone: (704) 687-4227   Website: www.uncc.edu
E-mail: msdoyle@e-mail.uncc.edu
Contact: Dr. Michael Scott Doyle
Offers a translation certificate program for undergraduates in French, Spanish and German. They also offer a graduate certificate in Translating and Translation Studies with a focus on English-Spanish.

Wake Forest University 1834 Wake Forest Road, Winston-Salem, NC 27106
Phone: (336) 758-5255
Website: www.wfu.edu
E-mail: furmano@wfu.edu
Offers graduate certificate in Spanish Translation/Localization.

NORTH DAKOTA
North Dakota State University, Fargo, ND 58105   Website: www.ndsu.nodak.edu
Offers translation courses in French and Spanish.

OHIO
Kent State University, Institute for Applied Linguistics, Kent, OH 44242
Phone: (330) 672-1814 Fax: (330) 673-0735   Website: http://appling.kent.edu/IAL-BSProgram.htm
E-mail: gkoby@kent.edu (for BS program)   or   bbauer@kent.edu (for MA program)
Contact: Geoffrey Koby
Offers M.A. in French, German and Spanish translation with an emphasis on computer-assisted translation and interpreting; literary and cultural translation; commercial, legal diplomatic, medical, technical and scientific. Also offers B.S. in French, German, Russian and Spanish translation.

Ohio State University, 1841 Millikin Rd., Columbus, OH 43210
Website: www.osu.edu
Offers BA in Russian translation.

Antioch College, Japan Program, Yellow Springs, OH 45387
Phone: (513) 767-7331   Fax: (513) 767-6469   Website: www.antioch-college.edu

Contact: Harold Wright, Professor of Japanese

Antioch offers courses in Japanese, Spanish, German, and French translation into English. Although there is no specific Translation program, the College does offer a workshop in poetry translation. Students are required to know the source and target languages in order to take this course.

Baldwin-Wallace College, Berea, OH 44017

Website: www.bw.edu

Offers translation courses in French, German, and Spanish.

Bowling Green State University, Bowling Green, OH 43403

Website: www.bgsu.edu

Offers translation courses.

Wright State University, Colonel Glenn Hwy, Dayton, OH 45435

Website: www.wright.edu

Offers translation courses.

OKLAHOMA

Tulsa Community College, International Language Center, 909 South Boston, MC-423, Tulsa, OK 74135

Phone: (918) 595-7851   Fax: (918) 595-7910   Website: www.tulsacc.edu

E-mail: tpena@tulsaacc.edu

Contact: Tina Pena

Tulsa Community College requires four semesters within the target language before accepting undergraduate students into its specialized translation program, which offers both Spanish and French. Students are introduced to the basic concepts and responsibilities related to translating. Instructor handouts and specialized documents provide practice with various types of materials. The result is an Associate degree. The college offers Spanish, French, Arabic, Chinese, Japanese, Greek, Hebrew, Italian, Latin and Russian.

PENNSYLVANIA

Carnegie-Mellon University, Department of Modern Languages, Baker Hall 160, Schenley Park, Pittsburgh, PA 15213-3890 Website: www.carnegiemellon.edu

Phone: (412) 268-2934   Fax: (412) 268-1328

E-mail: grtucker@andrew.cmu.edu

Contact: Professor G. Richard Tucker, Head, Department of Modern Languages

Carnegie-Mellon teaches French, German, Japanese, Russian, Spanish, Mandarin Chinese and Italian, but does not offer a specialized Translation program. Online courses in Spanish and French are also offered.

Mt. Aloysius College, 7373 Admiral Peary Highway, Cresson, PA 16630-1999 Website: www.mtaloy.edu

Offers an associate degree and B.A. Degree in Sign Language/Interpreter Education. The Sign Language/Interpreter Education Department at Mount Aloysius offers an Associate of Arts degree and a Bachelor of Arts degree intended to prepare students for entry-level positions primarily in educational settings.

Pennsylvania State University, 311 Burrowes Bldg, University Park, PA 16802
Phone: (814) 863-0589 Fax: (814) 863-8882 Website: www.psu.edu
Contact: Earl E. Fitz/Tom Beebee (Comparative Literature)
Offers PhD in Comparative Literature, Translation Option. Also: courses in French-American Business Translation; Commercial and Technical Translation; International Conference Terminology; and Russian Translation.

University of Pittsburgh, Language Learning Resource Center, Pittsburgh, PA 15260
Phone: (412) 624-5900 Fax: (412) 624-6793 Website: www.pitt.edu
E-mail: ptoth@pitt.edu or lctl@pitt.edu
Contact: Dr. Paul D. Toth
The University of Pittsburgh offers translation courses through each individual language department. There is also a certificate in American Sign Language program.

Immaculata University, Office #4, Faculty Center, Immaculata, PA 19345
Website: www.immaculata.edu
E-mail: kclark@immaculata.edu
Contact: Kathleen M. Clark
Offers an associate's degree in Professional Spanish and a B.A. program in International Business-French.

La Salle University, 1900 West Olney Avenue, Philadelphia, PA 19141
Phone: (215) 951-1209 Website: www.lasalle.edu
E-mail: gomez@lasalle.edu
La Salle offers graduate Certificate in Translation for Spanish-English through the department of Bilingual/Bicultural graduate studies. The curriculum for the CIT (Certificate in Translation) is designed to address three of the principal environments in which translations (English/Spanish-Spanish/English) are currently, and more intensely in the future, needed: that is, legal, medical and business environments. In addition, governing translation principles are also studied for application to language environments not covered by the program.

PUERTO RICO
Universidad de Puerto Rico, Translation Program, Rio Piedras, PR 00931
Phone: (787) 764-0000 ext. 2047 Fax: (787) 764-4065 Website: www.upr.edu
Contact: Yvette Torres
Offers M.A. in Translation and a Post-Graduate Certificate of Specialization in Translation

RHODE ISLAND
University of Rhode Island, Kingston, RI 02881
Website: www.uri.edu
Offers translation courses. Languages taught: Spanish, French, Hebrew, Modern Greek, Arabic, Chinese, Japanese, Portuguese, Russian, Italian, and German.
SOUTH CAROLINA
University of Charleston, 66 George St., Charleston, SC 29407
Phone: (803) 953-5718 Fax: (803) 953-6342 Website: www.cofc.edu

E-mail: benmaman@cofc.edu
Contact: Virginia Benmaman
Offers Certificate program in Legal Interpreting (Spanish) and Medical and Health Care Interpreting (Spanish).

Lander University, 320 Stanley Ave., Greenwood, SC 29649
Phone: (864) 388-8265   Fax: (864) 388-8090   Website: www.lander.edu
Contact: Warren Westcott
Offers translation courses in Spanish.

TEXAS
University of Texas at El Paso, El Paso, TX 79968
Website: www.utep.edu
Offers undergraduate certificate in Spanish-English Translation as a minor.

University of Texas at Arlington, Department of Modern Languages, Box 19557, 701 Planetarium Place (formerly 701 College Street), Arlington, TX 76019-0557
Website: www.uta.edu
E-mail: rosenboom@uta.edu
Contact: Becky Rosenboom
Offers courses in translation within individual language departments, and a certificate in Translation Studies for Spanish-English.

Texas Tech University, Lubbock, TX 79409
Website: www.ttu.edu
E-mail: cmll@ttu.edu
Offers French translation courses.

University of Texas at Austin, Spanish & Portuguese Department, Austin, TX 78712,
Phone: (512) 471-4936   Fax: (512) 471-8073   Website: www.utexas.edu
E-mail: fhensey@utexas.edu
Contact: Professor Fritz Hensey or Madeline Sutherland-Meier (Department Head)
Austin's Translation program started in Fall 1996. The University offers selected courses as part of an interdepartmental MA in Translation under the ægis of Foreign Language Education. Program emphasis is mostly on literary translation. There is also a general introductory course in Consecutive Spanish-English Interpreting.

UTAH
Brigham Young University, 3190 JFSB, Provo, UT 84602-6705
Phone: (801) 422-2837   Website: www.byu.edu
E-mail: cherilee_devore@byu.edu
Offers a BA in Spanish translation.

VIRGINIA
George Mason University, Fairfax, VA 22030
Phone: (703) 993-1220   Fax: (703) 993-1245   Website: www.gmu.edu
E-mail: dgerdes@gmu.edu

Contact: Dick Gerdes
Offers Graduate certificate program in translation. The certificate program in translation provides professional training for students who wish to acquire proficiency in a specific language combination, either English-French or English-Spanish.

WASHINGTON
Translation and Interpretation Institute at Bellevue Community College, World Language Program, Continuing Education, 3000 Landerholm Circle SE, Seattle, WA 98007, Phone: (206) 938-3600
Website: www.conted.bcc.ctc.edu
E-mail: rsiegent@bcc.ct.edu
Contact: Rene Siegenthaler
T&I Institute has been in operation since 1994, with Translation programs in various languages according to demand. The program awards a certificate, with college credit also available. The course covers basic Translation skills. Students must show a high proficiency in their working languages. T&I also awards a certificate in Simultaneous and Consecutive Interpreting in Spanish, French and Japanese. Courses at T&I include advanced workshops, training in ethics and business practices, and courses dealing with technology and terminology management.

University of Washington, 5001 25th Ave., NE, Seattle, WA 98195
Website: www.washington.edu
Offers translation courses.

WISCONSIN
NorthCentral Technical College, 1000 Schonfield Ave., Wausau, WI 54401
Website: www.ntc.edu
Offers Program for Interpreters.

University of Wisconsin-Milwaukee, PO Box 413, Milwaukee, WI 53201
Phone: (414) 964-6931   Fax: (414) 229-2939   Website: www.uwm.edu
E-mail: srascon@uwm.edu or kscholz@uwm.edu
Contact: Susan Rascon
MA in Foreign Languages & Literature – Translation Track and a graduate certificate program for Translation.
Offers translation of Spanish, French and German.

CANADA

ALBERTA
University of Alberta, Modern Languages & Cultural Studies, 200 Arts, Edmonton, AB T6G 2E6 Canada
Phone: (780) 492-1187   Fax: (780) 492-9106   Website: www.ualberta.ca
E-mail: amalena@ualberta.ca
Contact: Dr. Anne Malena
Offers M.A and PhD in Translation Studies. MLCS Certificate in Translation Studies:

Academic certificate in French, German and Spanish available as part of BA. Prepares students to further their education and training in translation and translation studies school and its program.

BRITISH COLUMBIA
Langara College, Department of Modern Languages, 100 West 49th Ave., Vancouver, BC V5Y 2Z6, Canada
Phone: (604) 323-5282   Fax: (604) 323-5555   Website: www.langara.ca
E-mail: dyada@langara.bc.ca
Contact: Dorothy Yada, Department Chair
Langara offers courses in French, Spanish, German, Japanese and Chinese, but does not have a Translation program.

NEW BRUNSWICK
Université de Moncton, Moncton, Nouveau Brunswick E1A 3E9, Canada
Phone: (506) 858-4214   Fax: (506) 858-4166   Website: www.umoncton.ca
E-mail: grognig@umoncton.ca
Offers B.A. in translation for English-French.

ONTARIO
Laurentian University, Department of French Studies and Translation, 935 Ramsey Lake Rd., Sudbury, Ontario P3E 2C6, Canada
Phone: (705) 675-1151   Fax: (705) 675-4885
Website: www.laurentian.ca/www.francais
E-mail: bdubeprevost@nickel.laurentian.ca
Contact: Ronald Henry, Chairman
The English-French translation program is 31 years old. Degree offered is Bachelor of Science in Languages (B.S.L.) Applicants must have solid background in English and French, and take a writing competence test in both languages. The program covers general, business-commercial, scientific, and technical translation. Simultaneous and consecutive interpretation are also taught.
University of Ottawa School of Translation and Interpretation, P.O. Box 540, Station A, Ottawa, Ontario KN16N5
Website: www.uottawa.ca
Contact: Dr. Annie Brisset
Offers B.A. in French-English and French-Spanish-English translation. It also has programs for M.A. in Translation and a PhD in Translation Studies.

QUÉBEC
Université Laval, 2289 Pavillon De Koninck, Cité Universitaire, Québec (Québec) G1K 7P4, Canada
Phone: (418) 656-2131 #e700   Fax: (418) 656-2622   Website: www.ulaval.ca
E-mail: alan.manning@lli.ulaval.ca
Contact: Dr. Alan Manning
Offers B.A., M.A. and graduate diploma in translation studies for French-English-Spanish. Covers literary, legal, medical, sci-tech, economic, sociological and administrative translation.

Université de Montreal, C.P. 6128, Succ. "Centre-Ville", Montreal QC H3C 317, Canada, Phone: (514) 343-6024 Fax: (514) 343-2284 Website: www.umontreal.ca
E-mail: gilles.belanger@umontreal.ca
Contact: Gilles Belanger
B.A. and M.A. in English-French translation. Areas covered are technical, commercial, legal, medical and literary.

APPENDIX 6.
TRANSLATOR ORGANIZATIONS

AMERICAN TRANSLATORS ASSOCIAION (ATA)

The ATA is the main organization of American translators.

ATA Chapters

Atlanta Association of Interpreters and Translators (AAIT)
info@aait.org   http://www.aait.org
Carolina Association of Translators and Interpreters (CATI)
catiadmin@catiweb.org   http://www.catiweb.org
Delaware Valley Translators Association (DVTA)
president@dtva.com   http://www.dvta.org
Michigan Translators/Interpreters Network (MiTiN)
info@mitin.org   http://www.mitinweb.org
Mid-America Chapter of ATA (MICATA)
micata@gmail.com   http://www.micata.org
Midwest Association of Translators and Interpreters (MATI)
MATIemail@gmail.com   http://www.matiata.org
National Capital Area Chapter of ATA (NCATA)
president@ncata.org   http://www.ncata.org
New York Circle of Translators (NYCT)
president@nyctranslators.org   http://www.nyctranslators.org
Northeast Ohio Translators Association (NOTA)
president@notatranslators.org   http://www.notatranslators.org
Northern California Translators Association (NCTA)
president@ncta.org   http://www.ncta.org
Northwest Translators and Interpreters Society (NOTIS)
info@notisnet.org   http://www.notisnet.org/
Upper Midwest Translators and Interpreters Association (UMTIA)
pres@umtia.org   http://www.umtia.org

ATA Affiliated Groups

Austin Area Translators and Interpreters Association (AATIA)
president@aatia.org   http://www.aatia.org/
El Paso Interpreters and Translators Association (EPITA)
bilingual.interpreter@yahoo.com   http://www.metroplexepita.org
Houston Interpreters and Translators Association (HITA)

president@hitagroup.org   http://www.hitagroup.org/
Iowa Interpreters and Translators Association (IITA)
info@iitanet.org   http://www.iitanet.org
Nebraska Association of Translators and Interpreters (NATI)
maria.natihq@gmail.com   www.natihq.org
Nevada Interpreters and Translators Association (NITA)
president@nitaonline.org   www.nitaonline.org
New Mexico Translators and Interpreters Association (NMTIA)
uweschroeter@comcast.net   http://www.cybermesa.com/~nmtia
Tennessee Association of Professional Interpreters and Translators (TAPIT)
http://www.tapit.org
Utah Translators and Interpreters Association (UTIA)
foliveira6@gmail.com   www.utianet.org

Other Groups

American Literary Translators Association (ALTA)
lindy.jolly@utdallas.org   http://www.literarytranslators.org
American Medical Writers Association (AMWA)
amwa@amwa.org   http://www.amwa.org
Arizona Court Interpreters Association (ACIA)
aciaboard@aciaonline.org   http://www.aciaonline.org
Arizonia Translators & Interpreters, Inc
info@atiinc.org   http://atiinc.org
Association of Language Companies (ALC)
info@alcus.org   http://www.alcus.org
Association of Translators and Interpreters in the San Diego Area (ATISDA)
abenzo@ucsd.edu   http://www.atisda.org
California Court Interpreters Association (CCIA)
ccia2006@aol.com   http://www.ccia.org/
Certification Commission for Healthcare Interpreters (CCHI)
info@healthcareinterpretercertification.org   www.healthcareinterpretercertification.org
Chicago Area Translators and Interpreters Association (CHICATA)
info@chicata.org   http://www.chicata.org
Colorado Translators Association (CTA)
president@cta-web.org   www.cta-web.org
Delaware Translators' Network (DTN)
matthew.f.schlecht@gmail.com   http://tech.groups.yahoo.com/group/delawaretranslators
Fédération Internationale des traducteurs/International Federation of Translators (FIT) (ATA is affiliated with FIT)
secretariat@fit-ift.org   http://www.fit-ift.org
International Medical Interpreters Association (IMIA)
imiaweb@gmail.com   http://www.imiaweb.org
Medical Interpreters Network of Georgia (MING)
michael@mingweb.org   http://www.mingweb.org

Metroplex Interpreters and Translators Association (MITA)
http://www.dfw-mita.com
National Association of Judiciary Interpreters and Translators (NAJIT)
headquarters@najit.org   http://www.najit.org
National Council on Interpreting in Health Care (NCIHC)
info@NCIHC.org   http://www.ncihc.org
New England Translators Association (NETA)
info@netaweb.org   http://www.netaweb.org
Society for Technical Communication (STC)
stc@stc.org   http://www.stc.org
Texas Association of Healthcare Interpreters and Translators (TAHIT)
tahit07@yahoo.com   http://www.tahit.us
Washington State Court Interpreters and Translators Society (WITS)
http://www.witsnet.org/

INTERNATIONAL FEDERATION OF TRANSLATORS (FIT)

FIT (Fédération Internationale des Traducteurs) is the worldwide federation of translator associations.

Member associations:

EUROPE

Austria
Österreichischer Übersetzer-und Dolmetscherverband "Universitas"
Gymnasiumstrasse 50, A-1190 Wien Phone: +43 1-368 60 60 Fax: +43 1-368 60 08
Site: www.universitas.org
Österreichischer Verband der Gerichtsdolmetscher Postfach 14, A-1016 Wien
Phone: +43 1 479 65 81 Fax: +43 1 478 37 23
Site: www.gerichtsdolmetscher.at
Übersetzergemeinschaft im Literaturhaus, Interessengemeinschaft von Übersetzern literarischer und wissenschaftlicher Werke Literaturhaus, Seidengasse 13, A-1070 Wien Phone: +43 1-526 20 44 18 Fax: +43 1-526 20 44 30
Site: www.translators.at

Belgium
Chambre belge des traducteurs, interprètes et philologues [Belgische Kamer van Vertalers, Tolken en Filologen] Secrétariat : rue Montoyer, 24, bte 12, B-1000 Bruxelles Phone: +32 2-513 09 15 Fax: +32 2-513 09 15
Site: www.translators.be

Croatia
Hrvatsko Društvo Znanstvenih i Tehnickih Prevoditelja (HDZTP) [Croatian Association of Scientific and Technical Translators]
Amruševa 19/II, 10000 Zagreb Phone: +385 1-49 22 730 Fax: +385 1-48 17 658

Cyprus
Pancyprian Union of Graduate Translators and Interpreters 51A Riga Fereou
Street, CY-3091 Limassol Phone: +357 5-35 90 51 Fax: +357 5-37 87 81

Czech Republic
Jednota tlumoĉníků a překladatelů (JTP) [Union des Interprètes et Traducteurs]
Senovážné námestí 23 CZ-110 00 Praha 1 Phone: +420 2-24 14 25 17 Fax: +420
2-24 14 23 12 Site: www.jtpunion.org

Denmark
**Forbundet Kommunikation og Sprog [The Union of Communication and Language
Professionals]** Skindergade 45-47, Postboks 2246, DK-1019 København K
Phone: +45-33 91 98 00 Fax: +45-33 91 68 18 Site: www.kommunikationogsprog.dk
**Dansk Translatørforbund [Danish Association of State-Authorized Translators
and Interpreters]** Nørre Farimagsgade 35, DK-1364 København K Site: www.dtfb.dk
Translatørforeningen-The Association of Danish Authorized Translators
Skindergade 45-47 3. Sal, DK-1159 København K Phone: +45-33 11 84 14 Fax: +45-
33 11 84 15 Site: www.translatorforeningen.dk

Finland
**Suomen kääntäjien ja tulkkien liitto (SKTL) [Finnish Association of Translators
and Interpreters]** Meritullinkatu 33 A, FI-00170 Helsinki
Phone: +358 9-44 59 27 Fax: +358 9-44 59 37 Site: www.sktl.net

France
Société française des traducteurs (SFT) a/s Certex 22, rue de la Pépinière, F-75008
Paris Phone: +33-01 42 93 99 96 Fax: +33-01 45 22 33 55 Site: www.sft.fr
**Union Nationale des Experts Traducteurs- Interprètes près les Cours d'Appel
(UNETICA)** att.: María Lebret-Sánchez 12, rue de Volembert, F-95100 Argenteuil
Phone: +33 1 39 80 97 66 Fax: +33 1 39 98 72 18 Site: www.unetica.fr

Germany
Bundesverband der Dolmetscher und ÜÜbersetzer e. V. (BDÜ) Bundesgeschäftsstelle,
Kurfürstendamn 170, D-10707 Berlin Phone: +49 30-88 71 28 30 Fax: +49 30-88 71
28 40 Site: www.bdue.de **FIT** Contact: Peter Krakenwitzer
Verband der ÜÜbersetzer und Dolmetscher Berlin e.V.(VÜD) Weydingerstraße 14-
16, Raum 316, 10178 Berlin Phone: +49 30 28096722 Fax: +49 30 28096723 Site:
www.vued.de **FIT** Contact: Natália Rózsa
Assoziierte Dolmetscher und Übersetzer in Norddeutschland e.V. (ADÜ)
Wendenstrasse 435, D-20537 Hamburg Phone: +49 40-219 10 01 Fax: +49 40-219
10 03 Site: www.adue-nord.de **FIT** Contact: Terence Oliver
ATICOM e.V., Fachverband der Berufsübersetzer und Berufsdolmetscher e.V.
Geschäftsstelle: Winzermarkstr. 89, D-45529 Hattingen Phone +49 23-24 59 35 99
Fax +49 23-24 68 10 03 Site: www.aticom.de **FIT** Contact: Reiner Heard

Greece
Panhellenic Association of Translators Komninon 8 Street, GR-54624 Thessaloniki

Phone: +30 2310 266 308 or +30 2310 268 542   Fax: +30 2310 266 010 Site: www.
pem.gr
Société hellénique des traducteurs de littérature (EEML) Tsakona 7, Paleo Psychiko,
GR-15452 Athens Phone: +30 1-671 74 66 Fax: +30 1-671 74 66

Ireland
Irish Translators' and Interpreters' Association Irish Writers' Centre, 19 Parnell
Square, Dublin 1 Phone: +353 1-872 13 02 Fax: +353 1-872 62 82
Site: www.translatorsassociation.ie   **FIT** Contact: Miriam Lee

Italy
Associazione Italiana Traduttori ed Interpreti (AITI) Viale delle Milizie 9, I-00192
Roma Phone: +39 347 24 04 45 31 Fax: +39 06 233 295 502 Site: www.aiti.org

Netherlands
Dutch Court Interpretes and Legal Translators Association Parijslaan 69, Nl-5627
TW Eindhoven Phone: +31 412 646 694 Fax: +31 412 646 694
Site: www.sigv-vereniging.nl
Nederlands Genootschap van Tolken en Vertalers (NGTV) Postbus 77, 2300 AB
Leiden Phone: 0031 71 524 9360 Fax: 0031 71 524 9360 Site: www.ngtv.nl

Norway
Norsk Oversetterforening (NO) Postboks 579, Sentrum, N-0105 Oslo 1
Phone: +47-22 47 80 90 Fax: +47-22 42 03 56 Site: www.oversetterforeninen.no
Norsk Faglitteraer Forfatter- og Oversetterforening Uranienborgvn 2, N-0258 Oslo
Phone: +47-22 12 11 40 Fax: +47-22 12 11 50 Site: www.nffo.no
Statsautoriserte Translatørers Forening (STF) Springarstien 17, N-4021 Stavanger
Phone: +47-51 54 21 90 Fax: +47-51 54 14 27 Site: www.statsaut-translator.no

Poland
Polish Society of Sworn and Specialised Translators P.O. Box 23, PL-00967 Warszawa
86 Phone: +48 22 839 4952 Fax: +48 22 839 4952 Site: www.tepis.org.pl

Russia
Union of Translators of Russia (UTR) 101B, b.1, Pr. Mira, RU-129085, Moscow
MIL Phone: 7-495-616-3980 Fax: 7-495-958-1076

Serbia
Association of Literary Translators of Serbia Francuska 7, 11000 Begrade
Phone: +381 011 626 081 Fax: +381 011 626 278

Slovakia
APTOS - Slovenská Spolo nost Prekladatel'ov Odbornej Literatury Laurinská 2,
SK-80508 Bratislava Phone/Fax: +421 7-54 43 12 94 Site: www.sspol.sk

Slovenia
Association of Scientific and Technical Translators of Slovenia (DZTPS)

Petkovskovo nabrezje 57, SLO-1000 Ljubljana Phone: +386 1-231 78 62   Fax: +386 1-232 01 31 Site: www.dztps.si

Spain
Asociación Colegial de Escritores de Cataluñña (ACEC) Carrer Canuda n° 6, 6è, 08002 Barcelona   Phone: +34 93 318 87 48   Fax: +34 93 302 78 18
Site: www.acec-web.org
Asociación Española de Traductores, Correctores e Intéérpretes (ASETRAD) Gran Vía, 71-2 planta, 28013 Madrid   Site: www.asetrad.org
Asociación Profesional de Traductores, Correctores e Intérpretes de Lengua Vasca [Euskal Itzultzaile, Zuzentzaile eta Interpretarien Elkartea (EIZIE)] Zemoria 25, E-20013 Donostia - San Sebastián   Phone: +34 943 277 111   Fax: +34 943 277 288
Site: www.eizie.org
Traductors i Interprets Associats Pro-Col.legi (TRIAC) Diputació 239, 1r 2a C, E-08007 Barcelona   Phone: +34 93-487 70 33   Site: www.traductors.com

Sweden
Federation of Authorized Translators in Sweden (FAT)
c/o Mr. Jan Runesten, Tegelbruksvägen 6, Se-17830 Ekero
Phone: +46 8 560 359 17
Site: www.eurofat.se   FIT Contact: Jan Runesten
Swedish Association of Professional Translators (SFÖÖ) Secretariat:Box 1091, SE-269 21 Båstad Phone: +46 4 31 755 00   Fax: +46 4 31 769 90 Site: www.sfoe.se
FIT Contact: Anne Verbeke

Switzerland
Association Suisse des Traducteurs, Terminologues et Interprètes (ASTTI) Secretariat: Postgasse 17, CH-3011 Bern
Phone: +41 31 313 88 10   Fax: +41 31 313 88 99   Site: www.astti.ch
FIT Contact: João Esteves Ferreira

Turkey
Çeviri Dernegi Association of Translators Büyükdere cad. 93 Kat 5, TR-34387 Mecidiyekoy þiþli, Istanbul   Phone: +90 0212 212 02 40   Fax: +90 0212 211 08 15
Site: www.ceviridernegi.org

United Kingdom
Cymdeithas Cyfieithwyr Cymru - Association of Welsh Translators and Interpreters Bryn Menai, Ffordd Caergybi, GB-Bangor, Gwynedd, LL57 2AJ
Phone: +44 1248 371 839 Fax: +44 1248 371 850
Site: ww.welshtranslator.org.uk
Institute of Translation and Interpreting Fortuna House, South Fifth Street, GB-Milton Keynes, MK9 2EU Phone: +44 1908 325 250 Fax: +44 1908 325 259
Site: www.iti.org.uk
The Translators' Association 84 Drayton Gardens London SW10 9SB
Phone: +44 171-373 66 42 Fax: +44 171-373 57 68 Site: www.societyofauthors.net

NORTH AMERICA

Canada
Canadian Translators, Terminologists and Interpreters Council (CTTIC) 1 Nicholas Street, Suite 1402, Ottawa (Ontario) K1N 7B7 Tel: +1 613-562 03 79 Fax: +1 613-241 40 98 Site: www.cttic.org
Literary Translators' Association of Canada (LTAC) SB 335 Concordia University, 1455, boul. de Maisonneuve ouest Montréal (Québec) H3G 1M8   Tel: +1 514-848 87 02 Fax: +1 514-848 45 14 Site: www.attlc-ltac.org

Cuba
Cuban Association of Translators and Interpreters Linea No. 507 esq.a D, Vedado, C. de La Habana, Cuba

Guatemala
Asociación Guatemalteca de Intérpretes y Tradutores (AGIT) Att: Alcira García-Vassaux 6a Avenida 14-21, Zona 9, Guatemala City, Guatemala Central America Tel: +502 2254-1114, +502 2289-5800 Fax: +502 2254-1114 Site: www.agitguatemala.org

Mexico
Organización Mexicana de Traductores Capítulo Occidente Av. Vallarta 1525-304, Col. Americana, Guadalajara, Jalisco 44100 Tél: (52-33) 3124 0236 Fax: (52-33) 3124 0237 Site: www.omt.org.mx

Panama
Asociación Panameña de Traductores e Intérpretes Apartado 6-9006, El Dorado, Republic of Panama

United States
American Translators' Association (ATA) 225 Reineckers Lane, Suite 590 Alexandria, VA 22314   Tel: +1 703-683 61 00   Fax: +1 703-683 61 22 Site: www.atanet.org
American Literary Translators Association (ALTA) The University of Texas at Dallas, Box 830 688 Mail Station MC35, Richardson, TX 75083-0688   Tel: +1 972-883 20 93   Fax: +1 972-883 63 03   Site: www.literarytranslators.org

SOUTH AMERICA

Argentina
Asociación Argentina de Traductores e Intérpretes Malabia 2379. 14th. Floor. Apt. "A", CP1425EZG. Buenos Aires. Argentina   Site: www.aati.org.ar
FIT Contact: María Cristina Pinto
Colegio de Traductores Públicos de la Ciudad de Buenos Aires (CTPBA)
Callao 289 - 4 Piso, 1022 Buenos Aires
Phone/Fax: +54 1-371 86 16 or: +54 1-372 79 61
Site: www.traductores.org.ar **FIT** Contact: Graciela Steinberg

Brazil
Sindicato Nacional dos Tradutores (SINTRA) Rua da Quitanda 194 / Salas 1206/1207, Centro - Rio de Janeiro - RJ CEP: 20.091-000 Tel: +55 21-22 53 16 16 Fax: +55 21-22 63 60 89 Site: www.sintra.ong.org

Chile
Colegio de Traductores e Intérpretes de Chile AG (COTICH) Luis Thayer Ojeda 95, Of. 207, Providencia, Santiago 9 Phone: +56 2-251 2887 Site: www.cotich.cl

Costa Rica
Asociación Costarricense de Traductores e Intérpretes Profesionales (ACOTIP) Apdo. 225-2050, San Pedro, San José

Peru
Asociación de Traductores Profesionales del Perú (ATPP) Casilla Postal 18-0251, Lima 18 Site: www.atpp.org.pe
Colegio de Traductores del Perú Boulevard Tarata 269, Of. 207, Miraflores, Lima 18 Phone: (51-1) 444-9084 Fax: (51-1) 444-9084 Site: www.colegiodetraductores.org.pe

Uruguay
Colegio de Traductores Públicos del Uruguay Colonia 892, Piso 6 esc. 604, 11.100 Montevideo Phone/Fax: +598 2-903 31 30 Site: www.colegiotraductores.org.uy

Venezuela
Colegio Nacional de Traductores e Intérpretes Apartado Postal 52108, Sabana Grande, Colinas de Bello Monte, VE-Caracas 1050A Site: www.conalti.org

AFRICA

Congo
Association de Traducteurs et Intérpretes Professionels du Congo (ATIPCO) Phone: 243 990111107, 243 815014540, 243 998003647

Egypt
Egyptian Translators Association (EGYTA) Cairo Phone: 202 26742627 Fax: 202 26742628

Ethiopia
National Association of Translators and Interpreters of Ethiopia (NATIE) P.O. Box 1542, Addis Ababa Phone: 251 111 220760

Morocco
École Supérieure ROI FAHD de Traduction Université Abdelmalek Essâdi, Route du Charf, B.P. 410, Tanger

South Africa
South African Translators' Institute (SATI) P.O. Box 1710 Rivona, 2128 Phone: +27 11-803 26 81 Fax: +27 11-803 26 81 Site: www.translators.org.za

ASIA

China
Science and Technology Translators' Association of the Chinese Academy of Sciences Bureau of International Cooperation, 52 Sanlihe Road, Beijing 100864 Tel: +86-10-821 33 44, poste 2422 Fax: +86-10-851 10 95
FIT Contact: Juliang Qiu Site: www.sttacas.org
Translators' Association of China Wai Wen Building, 24 Baiwanzhuang Street, Beijing 10037 Tel: +86-10-6899 5897 Fax: +86-10-6832 6681 **FIT** Contact: Youyi Huang Site: www.tac-online.org.cn

Hong Kong
Hong Kong Translation Society Ltd P.O. Box 20186 , Hennessy Road Post Office Tel: +852-816 82 18 Fax: +852-855 71 09 Site: www.hkts.org.hk

India
Indian Translators Association K-5/B, Lower Ground Floor, Kalkaji, New Delhi-110019 Phone: +91-11-26291676 Fax: +91-11-41675530 Site: www.itaindia.org

Indonesia
Association of Indonesian Translators Himpunan Penerjemah Indonesia C/o Pusat Penerjemahan FIB UI, Jalan Salemba Raya 4, Jakarta 10430 Tel: +62 21 319 021 12 Fax: +62 21 315 59 41 Site: www.wartahpi.org

Iran
Association of Iranian Translators and Interpreters P.O. Box 17665-315 Tehran, Iran

Iraq
Iraqi Translators' Association Al-Joboory sons Bldg, 2nd Floor, Opposite rear gate of Al-Mustansiriya University, Palestine Street, Bagdad Phone: 07902375609

Israel
Israel Translators' Association POB 16173, Tel Aviv 61161 Site: www.ita.org.il

Japan
Japan Society of Translators (JST) Surugadai-Yagi-Bldg. 4F, Kanda Ogawamachi 3-8-5, Chiyodaku Tokyo 101-0052 Phone/Fax: +81 3 5317 0578
Site: www.japan-s-translators.org

Jordan
Jordanian Translators' Association c/o Dr. Abdulla Shunnaq, P.O. Box 4990, Yarmouk University, 211 - 63 Irbid Fax: +962-2-727 78 00

Lebanon
Université de Balamand Deir El Balamand, El Koura, B.P. 100, Tripoli Phone: +961-6-83 02 50 Fax: +961-6-93 02 78 **FIT** Contact: Georges Nahas
Site: www.balamand.edu.lb
Ecole de Traducteurs et d'Interprétes de Beyrouth (ETIB) Rue de Damas, B.P. 17-5208, Mar Mikkael, Beyrouth 1104 2020 Phone: +961 1 421 000 ext. 5512
Site: www.etib.usj.edu.lb

South Korea
Korean Society of Translators (KST) 2F. Shinmunro Bldg, 238 Shinmunro 1-ga, Jongro-gu, Seoul 110-061 Tel: +82-2-725 0506 Fax: +82-2-725 1266
FIT Contact: Il-Jun Cho Site: www.kstinc.or.kr

Turkey
Çeviri Dernegi Translation Association Sehit muhtar cad. Tekyaz Apt. No: 2/2, Taksim-Istanbul Phone: 0212 250 85 78 Fax: 0212 253 98 52
Site: www.ceviridernegi.org

United Arab Emirates
Faculty of Foreign Language, Translation and Mass Communication Ajman University of Science and Technology, P.O. Box 346, Ajman Phone: +971-6-746 66 66 ext. 442 **FIT** Contact: Tarwat Al-Sakran Site: www.ajman.ac.ae

OCEANIA

Australia
Australian Institute of Interpreters and Translators (AUSIT) PO Box 1070, Blackburn North, VIC 3130 Phone/Fax: +61 3-98 77 43 69 Site: www.ausit.org

New Zealand
New Zealand Society of Translators and Interpreters (NZSTI) [Te Ropu Kaiwhakamaori a-waha, a-tuhi o Aotearoa] PO Box 109-677, Newmarket, Auckland Phone: +64 9 529 11 38 Fax: +64 9 529 11 38 Site: www.nzsti.org

APPENDIX 7.
TRANSLATOR ACCREDITATION

The American Translators Association (ATA) offers accreditation in 23 language pairs: from English into Dutch, Finnish, French, German, Hungarian, Italian, Japanese, Polish, Portuguese, Russian and Spanish, and from those languages (plus Arabic) into English. Once you have started to translate in any of these languages, I strongly urge you to look into ATA accreditation. While it is not a must, it is certainly prestigious and adds professional credibility to your work.

The ATA is the main organization of translators in the United States. During my twenty years of association with this organization, I have seen it double and triple its membership to some 6000 translators. Its annual conference and its local chapter meetings provide a wonderful opportunity for meeting colleagues and learning more about the world of translation. Its publications are very valuable tools for translators, and its monthly magazine, *The ATA Chronicle*, is a superb professional publication.

For more information about ATA accreditation, call or write to:

ATA Headquarters
225 Reinekers Lane, Suite 590
Alexandria, VA 22314
Phone 703/683-6100
Fax 703/683-6122
This information is also accessible at their website: www.atanet.org

APPENDIX 8.

PROFESSIONAL PERIODICALS FOR TRANSLATORS

For a field as rich and varied as translation, the number of professional periodicals for translators available is extremely sparse. The following is a list of such publications.

Available from the American Translators Association (ATA):
225 Reinekers Lane, Suite 590, Alexandria, VA 22314
Phone 703/683-6100; Fax 703/683-6122; E-mail: ata@atanet.org

ATA Chronicle
The best periodical publication for translators in the U.S. Monthly, with one issue for November-December.
ATA members - free Non-members: U.S. - $50; Canada and Mexico - $75; other - $95.
ATA Proceedings
A yearly publication containing papers presented at the annual ATA conference. A rich source of information in many fields of translation.
ATA members - free at the ATA Conference. Non-members: $50.
ATA Source
Newsletter of the literary division of the ATA. (25 Frederick St., Montclair, NJ 07042).
Sci-Tech Translation Journal
Publication of the Science and Technology Division of the ATA.
c/o A-B Typesetting, 806 Main St., Poughkeepsie, NY 12603.

From the ATA Chapters:
Gotham Translator
PO Box 6547, New York, NY 1-15—6547; Phone 212/912-9070
Published by the New York Circle of Translators.
Apuntes
j Leticia Molinero, 237 Lafayette St., #2W, New York, NY 10012;
E-mail: 1053.14462@compuserve.com
Published by the Spanish Group of the New York Circle of Translators.
CATI Quarterly
PO Box 482, Cary, NC 27512-0482; Phone 919/851-1901.
Published by the Carolina Association of Translators and Interpreters.
NCTA Translorial
PO Box 14015, Berkeley, CA 94712-5015; Phone510/845-8712.
Published by the Northern California Translators Association.
NOTIS Newsletter
PO Box 25301, Seattle, WA 98125-2201; Phone 206/382-5642
Published by the Northwest Translators and Interpreters Society.

Additional publications:

Translation Review
ALTA (American Literary Translators Association)
The University of Texas, PO Box 830688, Richardson, TX 75083.
Quarterly.

MT News International
AMTA (Association for Machine Translation in the Americas), 655 15th St., NW, Ste. 310, Washington, DC 20005.

Polyglot
Newsletter of CCIA (California Court Interpreters Association), 1722 J St., Ste. 20, Sacramento, CA 95814.

Babel
John Benjamins Publishing Company, PO Box 27519, Philadelphia, PA 19118-0519.
International journal of translation.

Language Today
Language Publications Limited, 128 Derby Rd., Long Eaton, Notting-ham NG10 4ER, UK.
Internet magazine accessible at logos.it/language_today
Also available in hardcopy print version.

Proteus
Quarterly newsletter of NAJIT (The National Association of Judiciary Interpreters and Translators), c/o D. Orrantia, John Jay College, 445 W. 59th St., New York, NY 10019.

Multilingual Communications and Computing
Multilingual Computing, Inc., 319 North First Ave., Sandpoint, ID 83864; Phone 208/263-8178.
A journal on the latest foreign language technology.

Target
International Journal of Translation Studies.
John Benjamins, PO Box 27519, Philadelphia, PA 19118-0519.

Language International
Magazine for language professionals.
John Benjamins, PO Box 27519, Philadelphia, PA 19118-0519.

Terminology
International Journal of Theoretical and Applied Issues in Specialized Communication.
John Benjamins, PO Box 27519, Philadelphia, PA 19118-0519.

BIBLIOGRAPHY

ATA Proceedings. Published annually by the American Translators Association, Alexandria, VA.

ATA Scholarly Monographs:

Bowen, David and Margareta Bowen, eds. **Interpreting: Yesterday, Today and Tomorrow**. Binghamton: SUNY, 1990.

Gaddis Rose, Marilyn, ed. **Translation Excellence.**

Hammond, Deanna L., ed. **Professional Issues in Translation and Interpretation,** 1994.

Krawutschke, Peter, ed. **Translator and Interpreter Training and Foreign Language Pedagogy.** Binghamton: SUNY, 1989.

Larson, Mildred, ed. **Translation: Theory and Practice, Tension and Interdependence.**

Vasconcellos, Muriel, ed. **Technology as Translation Strategy.** Philadelphia, PA: John Benjamins, 1995.

Baker, Mona. **In Other Words: A Coursebook in Translation.** New York, NY: Routledge, 1992.

Bassnett, Susan. **Translation Studies**. New York, NY: Routledge, 1991.

Bell, Roger T. **Translation and Translating: Theory and Practice**. Burnt Mill, Harlow: Longman, 1991.

Bierman, Bernard. **A Translator-Warrior Speaks: A Personal History of the ATA.** Nyack, NY: IRM Corp., 1987.

Biguenet, John and Rainer Schulte, eds. **The Craft of Translation**. Chicago: University of Chicago Press, 1989.

Child, Jack. **An Introduction to Spanish Translation.** Lanham, MD: University Press of America, 1992.

De Jongh, Elena M. **An Introduction to Court Interpreting: Theory and Practice.** Lanham, MD: University Press of America, 1992.

Delisle, Jean and Judith Woodsworth, eds. **Translators Through History.** Philadelphia, PA: John Benjamins, 1995.

Gambier, Yves, Daniel Gile and Christopher Taylor, eds. **Conference Interpreting: Current Trends in Research.** Amsterdam/Philadelphia: John Benjamins, 1997.

Gile, David. **Basic Concepts and Models for Interpreter and Translator Training**. Amsterdam: John Benjamins, 1995.

Glenn, John. **Glenn's Guide to Translation Agencies.** San Francisco, CA: John Glenn, 1997.

Gonzalez, Victoria Vasquez, and Holly Mikkelson. **Fundamentals of Court Interpretation: Theory, Policy and Practice.** Durham, NC: Carolina Academic Press, 1991.

Hammond, Deanna (ed.). **Professional Issues for Translators and Interpreters.** Philadelphia, PA: John Benjamins, 1995.

Lambert, Sylvie and Barbara Moser-Mercer. **Bridging the Gap (Empirical Research in Simultaneous Interpretation).** Philadelphia, PA: John Benjamins, 1994.

Larson, Mildred. **Meaning-Based Translation.** Lanham, MD: University Press of America, 1984.

Newmark, Peter. **Approaches to Translation.** Bristol, PA: Multilingual Matters Ltd., 1993.

Newmark, Peter. **Paragraphs on Translation.** Bristol, PA: Multilingual Matters Ltd., 1993.

Phillips, Michael, and Salli Raspberry. **Marketing Without Advertising.** Berkeley, CA: Nolo Press, 1990.

Rubinstein, Marv. **21st Century American English Compendium.** Rockville, MD: Schreiber Publishing, 2000

Samuelsson-Brown, Geoffrey. **A Practical Guide for Translators.** Bristol, PA: Multilingual Matters Ltd., 1993.

Seleskovitch, Danica. **Interpreting for International Confer ences.** Washington, DC: Pen and Booth, 1978.

Snell-Hornby, Mary. **Translation Studies: An Integrated Approach.** Amsterdam/ Philadelphia: John Benjamins, 1988.

Sofer, Morry. **Guide for Translators.** Rockville, MD: Schreiber Publishing, 1995.

Toury, Gideon. **Descriptive Translation Studies—and Beyond.** Philadelphia, PA: John Benjamins, 1995.

Whitmeyer, Claude, Salli Rassbery and Michael Phillips. **Running a One-Person Business.** Berkeley, CA: Ten Speed Press, 1989.

Wright, Sue Ellen and Leland Wright. **Scientific and Technical Translation.** Philadelphia: John Benjamins, 1993.

GLOSSARY FOR TRANSLATORS

Accreditation. A service provided by the ATA to confirm the com-petence of a translator.

A.I.D. Agency for International Development of the U.S. Government. Implements foreign aid programs, and sponsors the Peace Corps.

American Translators Association (ATA). The official organization of translators in the United States.

ANS. Advanced Network Services, which runs one of the large, high-speed networks on the Internet. Run By Merit, MCI and IBM.

Anti-Virus programs. Programs used to protect your computer and disks from destructive computer viruses.

Archie. A system for finding files anywhere on the Internet. It is both a program and a system of servers.

ARPAnet. The progenitor of the Internet, ARPAnet is a computer network originally developed by the U.S. Department of Defense to link research institutions.

ASCII. Pronounced askey, it stands for American Standard Code for Information Interchange. It is used to save text in order to covert it from one word processing program to another. The standard code contains 128 characters (96 of which are displayed in upper and lower case and 32 are non-displayed control characters). The extended character set contains 254 characters which include a number of foreign language, technical and graphics characters.

ATA. See American Translators Association.

Backup copy. A copy of a working file made either on the hard drive, on a separate disk, or on tape, in order to protect the user from losing data. One should have backup copies not only of working files, but also of one's software programs. Backup copies serve for both working and for archival purposes.

Binary system. A mathematical term referring to a system using only two digits, 0 and 1, instead of the decimal system of 10. This system is at the heart of the computing system used in word processing, in which code numbers are converted into characters. In other words, a computer doing word processing does not "think," but only responds to a mechanical "yes" and "no" process, or 1 and 0. For an attempt to make a computer "think," see **Neural network.**

Bit. Short for "binary digit," usually 8 bits make a byte, that stands for one character in computers, bit is the smallest unit of measure for computer data.

BITFTP. FTP-by-mail server. See **FTP.**

BITNET. An IBM mainframe network connected to the Internet.

bps. Bits per second. A measurement used to describe how fast data is transmitted. Usually used to describe modem speed.

Broadband network. A network that can handle many separate signals at the same time. Broadband networks use different channels to transfer different forms of information, such as data, voice and video.

Browser. The software tool to access the World Wide Web. Some of the better known are Firefox, Chrome, Safari, and Internet Explorer.

Buffer. A holding area for data in a computing system. Information sent to a printer is held in a buffer.

Bulletin board. Electronic message system for reading and posting messages. It lets users read other people's messages and post new ones.

Byte. The amount of memory space needed to store one character, which is normally 8 bits. The size of the computer's memory is measure in kilobytes, where 1 kilobyte (K) = 1,024 bytes.

C.A.T. or CAT. Computer-assisted translation.

CD-ROM. Compact Disk-Read Only Memory. A high capacity disk for storing such information as entire dictionaries and encyclopedias.

Cello. A program for accessing the World Wide Web, created originally by the law school at Cornell.

com. In an Internet address it stand for "company," showing that the address is handled by a company rather than a university or a government agency.

Certificatiom. The vouching for the completeness and accuracy of a translation by a second translator.

Chip. A single silicon chip contains an integrated circuit consisting of many miniature transistors and other circuit elements, used in computers.

CompuServe. An online service which includes such items of interest to translators as the Foreign Language Forum, or FLEFO.

Computer language. A computer programming term referring to a system of instructions used in operating computer software. Also called programming language. See **Natural language.**

Computational linguistics. The use of computers in the study of human language, and the study of how to make computers understand information expressed in human languages.

Conference interpretatiom. Interpreting with the aid of earphones at a conference at the same time the speaker of the original language speaks.

Consecutive interpretatiom. Interpreting each time the speaker of the source language stops speaking.

Copy. A term used in editing and in journalism, referring to raw text being worked on.

CPU. Central Processing Unit. The part of the computer where arithmetic and logical operations are performed and instructions are decoded and executed. The CPU controls the operation of the computer. A micro-processor is an integrated circuit that contains a complete CPU on a single chip.

Cultural adaptation. Adapting a translation to the cultural environment of the target language.

DARPA. Defense Advanced Research Projects Agency, which operated the ARPAnet, the forerunner of the Internet.

Domain. The system of naming Internet sites, which most users prefer over numerical Internet addresses.

DOS. Disk Operating System, or a program that makes a word-processor work.

Dot matrix printer. A computer printer using tiny pins for impact printing. The larger the number of pins the clearer the image. Dot matrix printers have been largely replaced by inkjet and laserjet printers.

Downloading. Transferring data from one source into your computer or disk, as in the case of downloading fonts, or downloading data from E-mail or from a modem transmission.

DRAM. Dynamic Random Access Memory (see RAM). This is a RAM chip that represents memory states using capacitors that store electrical charges.

EDI. Electronic Data Interchange, is the latest U.S. Government system of doing business by supplying RFQs over the net. If you want to do translation work, and it's worth your while to invest about $1,000 up front, get EDI on your computer and you'll be able to follow the bids. Not recommended for little-volume use.

Email (electronic mail).

Escort interpreter. A language expert who accompanies foreign visitors to the U.S. as their interpreter.

FAQ. Frequently asked questions. This designation appears in newsgroups, to facilitate answering the most commonly asked questions by visitors.

Fax. Short for facsimile. A device for transmitting printed text over the phone line from one fax machine to another.

Fax Modem. Modems that allow the sending and receiving of faxes in addition to ordinary computer data.

FDD. Floppy Disk Drive, into which you insert a disk in your computer, as opposed to a hard drive, which is attached internally or externally to your computer.

FIDONET. A worldwide network of bulletin board systems (BBS).

FIT. International Federation of Translators. (*Fédération Internationale des Traducteurs*)

Font. A set of characters (letters, numbers, punctuation etc.) which has a defined typeface, style, and size.

Freelancer. Someone who works independently as a translator. Also called Independent Contractor, or Subcontractor.

FTP. File transfer protocol. This is the name of a program that uses the protocol to transfer files all over the Internet.

Gateway. A computer used to connect one network with another.

Gigabyte (GB). Approximately one billion bytes, the size of a memory on a current PC.

Globalization. The combined process of Internationalization and localization.

Gopher. An Internet system for finding information by using menus. Largely supplanted by the World Wide Web.

HTML. HyperText Markup Language. Used in writing pages for the World Wide Web. It lets the text include codes that define fonts, layout, embedded graphics, and hypertext links.

HTTP. HyperText Transfer Protocol. This is the method for transfer World Wide Websites over the net.

Human translation. Or HT, is a term used in computer programming to distinguish between MT, or Machine Translation, and the usual process.

Hypermedia. Same as hypertext, used in the regard to visuals and sound in addition to text.

Hypertext. A system of writing and displaying text that enables the text to be linked in multiple ways, available at several levels of detail, and containing links to related documents.

Hypertext link. A connection between two documents that enables a reader to move from one document to another by clicking on a highlighted text. This is one of the key features of the Web.

IBM PC. Or its compatible, are computers widely used by translators.

IBM-compatible. A reference to computers that use the same operating systems and software as the IBM PC.

IFB. Invitation for Bid. A U.S. Government request for products or services.

Inkjet printer. A printer that uses ink to print. Not as advanced as a laser printer.

Internationalization. The process of programming software so that it can be localized in other languages and cultures.

Internet. A collection of individual computer networks, both in the U.S. and around the world, forming a huge international network, and which can be used for sending electronic mail, files, graphic data, even sound, around the world.

IOMEGA. An external drive with high capacity disks used to store a great number of files and/or operate as an external hard drive with your PC. Small, compact, and very useful for translators.

IP. Internet Protocol. A system that enables information to be transferred from one network to another.

IRC. Internet Relay Chat. A system that enables Internet users to talk to each other in real time (rather than by sending messages).

IT. Information Technology. Essentially, all aspects of data processing.

JPRS. Joint Publications Research Service. A U.S. Government agency which has historically provided a large volume of translation to freelancers.

Kermit. File transfer protocol used by modems.

LAN. Local Area Network, or a system of interconnected computers, which share programs and often share a powerful storage system called a server.

Laptop computer. Portable computer, also known as **Notebook.**

Laser printer. A high resolution printer that works basically as a fast copier. This is currently the state-of-the-art printer, preferred by most clients.

Link. See **Hypertext link.**

LISA. Localisation Industry Standards Association. An organization that seeks to establish universal standards for localization.

Localization. The process of translation, usually of software, which includes modification and adaptation of text in a way that meets the needs of a local market, usually in other countries.

Machine translation. Or MT, refers to translation by computer.

Megabyte. Amount of computer memory, about one million bytes (MB).

Microprocessor. An integrated circuit containing the entire CPU of a computer, all on one chip, so that only the memory and the input-output devices need to be added.

Microsoft Localized Software. The international division of Microsoft has most of the English-language Microsoft products localized into most of the major languages of the world.

Microsoft Word. Word processing program produced by Microsoft, Inc. It is used with Windows, and is considered the leader in the field.

Modem. The MODulator/DEModulator is a devise for transmitting electronic text (computer files) over the phone line from one computer to another.

Monitor. The components of a computer which displays the data on a screen.

Mosaic. A Windows-based browser for finding documents and Websites.

MT. See Machine Translation.

Natural language. A term used to differentiate between a natural language such as English or French and computer programming lang-uages.

Neural network. A computer program that imitates nerve cells in the human brain. This is an attempt to have a computer act like a person, making choices and decisions out of a range of possibilities. Here may lie the beginning of a translating computer, although there is quite a long way to go.

Newsgroup. An online bulletin board system devoted to a particular topic.

NIH. National Institutes of Health. A U.S. Government entity which performs a great deal of medical translations.

OCR. Optical Character Reader. A card used in a scanner to transfer text from a page into a word processing program.

On-line. A program or device that is connected directly to a computer and is available while using a program application.

Operating system. Software program for running a computer. All other programs depend on the operating system to function. The most common operating system used to be DOS (Disk Operating System). The favorite today is Windows.

Optical Character Scanner. See OCR.

Page. A document available on the World Wide Web (also known as a website). Information on the web is organized into one or more pages.

Parallel port. A port that enables a high flow of information along parallel lines from say, a computer to a printer.

PC. Personal computer. The term usually applies to IBM or IBM-compatible computers.

PKZIP. File compression program which creates a ZIP file that greatly reduces the space on the disk occupied by that file. To restore the file to its original condition, one uses PKUNZIP. This is a shareware program available in various programs.

Platform. A piece of equipment (or software) used as a base on which to build something else. For example, a mainframe computer can serve as a platform for a large accounting system.

PPP. Point-to-Point Protocol. See **Protocol.**

Processor. See **Microprocessor.**

Programming language. See **Computer language.**

Protocol. A system of regulating data transmission between computers. It determines how the two systems will establish communications, what codes will be used, and so on. PPP is an example of a "communications protocol."

Quality Control. Or QC, is that part of the translation process prior to submitting a finished translation product to the client. It entails proofreading, checking for omissions or other errors, and making sure that all the specifications have been met.

RAM. Random Access Memory. This describes the operating capacity of the computer.

Resolution. The minimum size of a dot that can be produced by a scanner or a printer. The higher the resolution, the sharper the image. Resolution is defined by dpi (dots per inch). A resolution over 300 dpi is considered high.

RFP. Request for Proposal. A competitive bid put out by the U.S. Government, which entails writing a technical and a business proposal for a multi-year contract.

RFQ. Request for Quote. A non-competitive request by the U.S. Government for products or services, including translation. Usually for less than $5,000.

ROM. Acronym for Read Only Memory. A ROM contains computer instructions that do not need to be changed, such as permanent parts of an operating system. No data can be stored on ROM.

Scanner. An electronic device for copying text or graphics from a page to a computer disk. Text is scanned by an OCR, or Optical Character Reader, and can be manipulated like a normal word-processing file. Graphics are scanned by a graphic scanning device.

Server. A remote computer that handles requests for data, electronic mail, file transfers, etc. Also called "host."

Sight translation. Or interpretation, this term refers to translating a document orally or in writing without prior preparation, usually during a conference.

Sign language. A system of gestures for communication with the deaf or hearing impaired.

Simultaneous interpretation. Interpreting at the same time the speaker of the source language speaks.

Source language. The language one translates from.

Speed. See Translation Speed.

Spell checker. A function in word-processing programs which checks the spelling of words and offers correct alternatives. Now available in some foreign language word-processing packages as well.

Spreadsheet. A computer program representing an open-ended table with rows and columns, that can be used for databases. Lotus 1-2-3 has ruled the field for a long time,and now Microsoft's Excel is a leader. Spreadsheets are extremely popular in the business world, but can be used by anyone to keep track of things.

Subcontractor. Either a translation company subcontracting with another company for translation services, or a freelancer subcontracting with a translation company or any other entity.

Surge protector. This box with sockets for the electric plugs of your computer system is a must for protecting your system against electric surges.

Target language. The language one translates into.

Telex. Teletypewriter Exchange. An international system similar to the telephone system, but linking typewriters. TELEX messages can be sent and received by computer using carriers such as MCI Mail.

Telephone interpreting. Providing interpretation services over the phone.

Translation Bureau. Same as translation company.

Translation Agency. Same as translation company.

Translation Company. A company which provides translation services, and subcontracts with freelancers.

Translation Memory. Software that stores sentences and other parts of translation to be used in a future project. It also stores terminology and creates glossaries. Used mainly in large repetitive translation projects.

Translation speed. One of the key elements in translation is speed, since many assignments are time-critical. Translation speed is a function of experience in a given language and subject.

Unicode. A system in word processing for encoding all the letters of all the languages of the world. Used by Microsoft for its foreign language word processing software.

Upload. To send data from your computer to another computer.

URL. Uniform Resource Locator. The address for a resource or site on the World Wide Web, and the convention Web browsers use for locating files and other remote services.

Verbatim translation. Complete translation of every word of the original text.

VGA. Visual Graphics Array. Used in reference to color monitors.

Virus. A man-made disruptive set of commands, produced by less than mentally stable computer buffs around the world, and transmitted through file transmittal systems. They usually attack your computer's operating system and can cause havoc. A good anti-virus program, such as Norton's, is a must for translators.

Voice-over. Taping a translated text for audio or video media.

WAIS. Wide Area Information Servers. A system for searching docu-ments containing information one is looking for.

Word count. The method of arriving at a total of words in a given text for the purpose of determining the cost of the translation.

INDEX